PROGRAM OPTIMIZATION

PROGRAM OPTIMIZATION

Infotech State of the Art Report

Published by Infotech International Limited,
Nicholson House, Maidenhead, Berkshire,
England

UDC 681.3
Dewey 658.505
ISBN 8553-9300-9

CONTENTS

Foreword 1

Program Optimization: Analysis

INTRODUCTION

The nature of program optimization 7

The need for optimization 9

Introduction 9

Optimization versus better hardware 9

Optimization versus efficient programming techniques 12

Conclusion 13

Motives for improving program performance 15

Introduction 15

Avoiding system upgrade 15

Reducing operating costs 16

Improving turnaround times 17

Constraints in program optimization 19

Introduction 19

Economic constraints 19

Program tuning versus system tuning 20

Limitations of optimizing compilers 20

PROGRAM DEVELOPMENT

Introduction 25

Trade-offs in programming 25

Programming methodology 27

Programming languages and optimization 31

Introduction 31

Language design for efficient programs 33

Language design for easier optimization 36

Conclusion 44

Structured programming 47

Introduction 47

Structured programming and efficiency 51

Optimizing structured programs 52

Conclusion 59

Program transformation
Introduction 61
Transformation techniques 61
Applications of transformation 63
Transformation as an optimizing technique 64
65

TRANSLATION
Introduction
The role of translation in optimization 69
Language processing 69
Empirical studies of programs 70
73

Compilation and interpretation 75
Introduction 75
Relative merits of compilation and interpretation 76
Combining compilation and interpretation 80

Optimizing compiler techniques 85
Introduction 85
Machine-dependent optimizations 86
Architecture-dependent optimizations 87
Architecture-independent optimizations 92

Selective optimization 99
Introduction 99
Programmer-supplied feedback 100
Automated feedback 105

Conclusion 113
The need for compiler optimization 113
Optimization as an aid to clearer programming 114
Limitations in compiler optimization 114

EXECUTION
Program monitoring 119
Introduction 119
Techniques of program monitoring 119
Choice of programs to monitor 123
Program tuning 126

Machine architecture 129
Introduction 129
High-level language architectures 130
Microprogramming 132

Virtual storage systems 139
Introduction 139
Special considerations for VS 140

Invited papers

OPTIMIZING INPUT/OUTPUT 147
G G Brown

THROW-AWAY COMPILING: A MIDDLE PATH BETWEEN INTERPRETATION AND COMPILATION 153
P J Brown

TRANSFORMING CLEAR PROGRAMS TO EFFICIENT ONES: A PROGRAM DEVELOPMENT METHOD 161
R M Burstall and J Darlington

COMPUTER SYSTEM DESIGN FOR RUN-TIME EFFICIENCY 171
P C Capon

ADAPTIVE CODE OPTIMIZATION 185
G Hansen and W A Wulf

PROGRAM OPTIMIZATION IN A SERVICE BUREAU ENVIRONMENT 209
A Jones

LIVE PROGRAM TUNING: A PRACTICAL METHODOLOGY 217
D Lankey

HIGH LEVEL PROGRAMMING: LANGUAGES AND OPTIMIZATION 235
J G Laski

INSTRUCTION SET ENHANCEMENT 253
W D Manville

BEHAVIOURAL ASPECTS OF PROGRAM OPTIMIZATION 267
P R Newsted

MACHINE EFFICIENCY VERSUS PROGRAMMING EFFICIENCY 279
J Palme

SYSTEM PERFORMANCE OPTIMIZATION IN A VIRTUAL STORAGE ENVIRONMENT 291
M Patel

EXPERIENCE IN PROGRAM AND SYSTEM OPTIMIZATION 313
I Ramage

A SURVEY OF COMPILER OPTIMIZATION TECHNIQUES 327
P B Schneck

FUTURE DEVELOPMENTS IN PROGRAM PERFORMANCE OPTIMIZATION 345
P B Schneck

PROGRAM BEHAVIOUR AND ITS IMPROVEMENT 357
J R Spirn

INTER-RELATIONSHIPS BETWEEN OPTIMIZATION AND STRUCTURED PROGRAMMING 369
M V Zelkowitz

Bibliography and Contributors' References

AN ANNOTATED BIBLIOGRAPHY OF SELECTED PAPERS ON PROGRAM OPTIMIZATION 383
F E Allen

CONTRIBUTORS' REFERENCES 409

Indexes

CUMULATIVE SUBJECT INDEX 425
CONTRIBUTOR INDEX 443
SUBJECT INDEX 447

FOREWORD

The need for program optimization is in many respects an indication of fundamental limitations in current commercially available computer technology. Specifically, these limitations are most evident in the following aspects of computing:

- *Programming methodology*

  Paradoxically, the underlying fault in current programming methods seems to be that concern with run-time efficiency is often allowed to intrude too early, thus obscuring the search for the best program; in the words of Donald Knuth (310), "premature optimization is the root of all evil". This premature concern with efficiency is partly a legacy from the days when such concerns were made necessary by the limited capacity, in memory and instructions, of the early machines. Because of these machine constraints, good programming was regarded as the art of producing programs with the minimum of instructions, regardless of their comprehensibility (308).

- *Programming languages*

  Two fundamental limitations can be identified in almost all widely-used programming languages in terms of their potential for translation into efficient object code.

  The first is the survival of language constructs that permit arbitrary flow of control around the program. The advantage of the more restricted structured programming control constructs in this context, quite apart from their easier comprehension, is that they permit efficient code to be produced by straightforward translation without the time-consuming analysis that is necessary in current optimizing compilers.

  The second weakness of current programming languages is that they provide no means for a programmer-compiler dialogue about the most efficient translation of a given piece of source text for a particular context. Moreover, compilers do not make any provision for supplying the information, in the form of program profiles, on which the programmer could base the judgements implied by such a dialogue or which could be used as automatic feedback to the compiler itself.

- *Machine design*

  In terms of the hardware on which programs are run, most widely-used machines are notoriously unsympathetic both to high-level languages and to well-structured programs. This unsuitability is hardly surprising since, with the exception of a few manufacturers, most machines have not been designed with the primary aim of giving effective support to the particular high-level languages or applications they will be used for.

For scientific applications, the most significant example of this unsuitability is probably the inordinate overhead of procedure calls on many machines. For commercial applications, there is another (and probably more significant) source of inefficiency. In such applications, a significant amount of machine time is spent in moving data around. The instruction set of most machines does not permit this operation, and the associated editing and validation procedures, to be performed as efficiently as its importance demands.

Clearly, these various limitations are to some extent inter-dependent. For example, the acceptance of structured programming methods has been greatly hindered by the inefficient machine implementation of procedure calls and by the patent unsuitability of the obsolescent languages in widespread use. Moreover, these limitations have a tendency to be self-perpetuating. For example, thought is sometimes given to devising efficient architectural features to support the FORTRAN arithmetic IF statement, which was in fact incorporated into FORTRAN simply as a result of a peculiarity in the order code of the IBM 704. This machine had a conditional branch of exactly that form and so the arithmetic IF was chosen as the standard conditional statement for FORTRAN I. The logical IF statement, usually regarded as the more natural and comprehensible form of conditional, was not added until much later.

Though these limitations need to be recognized as the underlying reasons for sub-optimal programs, it would be naive to argue that optimization is unnecessary because ultimately avoidable. Instead, the implications of these limitations need to be considered when thinking how run-time efficiency can be improved. For example, it is clear that the currently standard techniques of compiler optimization cannot be regarded as the sole method of achieving more efficient software. Not only is it necessary to consider other ways in which a given source text can be translated into more efficient object code, it is also important that the other stages of a program's life-cycle be taken into account. In particular, accurate profiles of a program's run-time behaviour, derived either by compiler-inserted instrumentation or by external monitoring, can be invaluable as feedback both to the program development stage and to the translation stage. The information thus provided can enable the improvement effort to be concentrated where the maximum benefit can be derived.

This idea of selective optimization applies both at the intra-program and inter-program level. That is, most attention (whether by recoding the source text or by means of more sophisticated optimizing techniques during translation) should be devoted to those portions of a program's code that account for most of its execution time and to those programs that account for most of an installation's prime-shift execution time.

D Bates: editor.

EDITORIAL CONVENTIONS

The following editorial conventions concerning the Analysis should be noted.

1 Material in *Courier italic* is attributable to the editor.

2 Other material is attributable to the person whose name precedes it. It should be noted that the opinions expressed do not necessarily reflect the views of any organization with which the contributors are associated.

3 Consecutive passages in the Analysis imply no chronological sequence whatsoever; passages are juxtaposed entirely at the editor's discretion. However, any given extract always represents consecutive speech, except where four stops separate text. These stops indicate that separate extracts from the same contributor have been juxtaposed by the editor.

4 Numbers in bold and enclosed in brackets refer to items catalogued in the Bibliography and References section.

5 The quotations used in the Analysis derive from the following sources:

(a) a discussion session at the Infotech State of the Art Conference on Program Performance Optimization;

(b) an invited paper;

(c) other external sources – an explicit bibliographic reference for each external source is given following the name(s) of the author(s) concerned.

The affiliation of any person quoted in the Analysis is given in the contributor index.

COPYRIGHT

PROGRAM OPTIMIZATION

ANALYSIS

Introduction

THE NATURE OF PROGRAM OPTIMIZATION

THE NEED FOR PROGRAM OPTIMIZATION

- Introduction
- Optimization versus better hardware
- Optimization versus efficient techniques
- Conclusion

MOTIVES FOR IMPROVING PROGRAM PERFORMANCE

- Introduction
- Avoiding system upgrade
- Reducing operating costs
- Improving turnaround times

CONSTRAINTS IN PROGRAM OPTIMIZATION

- Introduction
- Economic constraints
- Program tuning versus system tuning
- Limitations of optimizing compilers

THE NATURE OF PROGRAM OPTIMIZATION

For any given problem that is to be solved by means of a computer, an infinite number of different solutions can be envisaged, each with totally different characteristics. The possible characteristics of these solutions would include such factors as robustness, development time, accuracy, extensibility, speed of execution, and many more. The concern here is with those characteristics that can be loosely termed as 'efficiency'.

Program efficiency is not easy to define adequately but it will include such aspects as

- *execution speed*
- *memory requirement*
- *use of I/O devices.*

Clearly, the best solution in any particular situation will involve a specific trade-off not only between efficiency and the other characterizing features of programs but also between the various aspects of efficiency.

This Report is concerned with how reasonably efficient programs can be achieved, given the various trade-offs outlined above. In particular, the discussion will be concerned with the relevance of the following stages in a program's life-cycle to the achievement of efficiency:

- *program development, including design and coding*
- *translation into machine-executable form*
- *execution.*

It is a major thesis that these three stages cannot be viewed in isolation. Rather, the achievement of efficiency is thought of as an iterative process in which information from later stages, perhaps from different projects, is used as feedback to the earlier stages. For example, the translation of a source program into efficient machine code is much easier if its eventual run-time pattern of behaviour can be taken into account; monitoring a program's execution can provide information that can be used to indicate where the original program needs reprogramming; and so on.

THE NEED FOR OPTIMIZATION

INTRODUCTION

Two common objections are often raised against the idea of program optimization.

The first is that, since the cost/performance of hardware is improving so rapidly relative to the cost of producing software, it makes more sense to ignore expensive optimization techniques and to rely instead on faster, cheaper machines.

The second argument is that optimization is in any case unnecessary because it merely remedies defects in programs that should have been better written in the first place.

OPTIMIZATION VERSUS BETTER HARDWARE

The argument that better machine performance obviates the need for efficient programs has been used both to dismiss the importance of language design for efficient object code and to deny the need for optimizing compilers.

HOARE (309): There is an argument, which is all too prevalent among enthusiastic language designers, that efficiency of object code is no longer important; that the speed and capacity of computers is increasing and their price is coming down; and that the programming language designer might as well take advantage of this. This is an argument that would be quite acceptable if used to justify an efficiency loss of ten or twenty percent, or even thirty and forty percent. But all too frequently it is used to justify an efficiency loss of a factor of two, or ten, or even more; and worse, the overhead is not only in time taken but in space occupied by the running program. In no other engineering discipline would such avoidable overhead be tolerated, and it should not be in programming language design, for the following reasons:

- The magnitude of the tasks we wish computers to perform is growing faster than the cost-effectiveness of the hardware.

- However cheap and fast a computer is, it will be cheaper and faster to use it more efficiently.

- In the future we must hope that hardware designers will pay increasing attention to reliability rather than to speed and cost.

- The speed, cost, and reliability of peripheral equipment are not improving at the same rate as those of processors.

- If anyone is to be allowed to introduce inefficiency it should be the user programmer, not the language designer. The user programmer can take advantage of this freedom to write better-structured and clearer programs, and should not have to expend extra effort to obscure the structure and write less clear programs just to regain the efficiency that has been so arrogantly pre-empted by the language designer.

CAPON: The increasing cost of software production is resulting in decreased use of coding at assembly language level and an increased dependence on high-level languages, not just for user programs but also for system software. The decreasing cost of hardware makes it feasible to continue to reduce the relative cost of running high-level language programs by providing more suitable architectural facilities. The areas in which there is greatest scope for significant architectural improvements are operand accessing and procedure entry. When the correct architectural features are available, much of the present program optimization effort will become the past necessity of the 1970s.

In the context of optimizing compilers, this argument illustrates the differing viewpoints of the manufacturer and the user.

OUTRED (302): It seems to me that with processor costs dropping all the time, concern with the efficient use of the hardware is becoming more and more irrelevant. For example, one can get a PDP-11 for $8500 but one cannot hire a programmer for four months for that money. Surely what we should be concentrating on now is how to utilize programming ability and stop worrying about the efficient use of hardware.

WULF (302): I know that is an official Burroughs' position, and it is one with which in some sense I have a lot of sympathy. On the other hand, if that argument is taken too far, I think it becomes a red herring.

Let me draw an analogy. I live in an organization housed in a building. Although our department is charged overhead for the use of that space, it is money we never see; it is put into our budget and taken right out again before we see it.

So in some sense that space is free. That does not mean that we do not have any office-space problems. In fact, the only violent arguments that we ever have in the department have to do with the allocation of office space. The reason for this is not because office space is expensive but because at any instant there is a finite amount of it; and exactly the same argument holds for processors and memories. I really do not care if the computer is free. If I have only one and it has 32 billion bytes of memory and someone else is using the whole machine then I cannot; if he runs five times longer than he should then I am held off of it five times longer than I should be. So, rather than cost, it is the finiteness of the machine at any instant in time that forces one to be concerned about efficiency.

OUTRED (302): Every year, so I am told, the cost/performance ratio of a machine increases by a factor of about two. I have a choice. If I am designing a machine and writing software for it, I can in two years provide you with some hardware and a compiler that works; alternatively, I can produce the sort of complicated optimizing system that you are suggesting and that will take four years. Which of those two do you prefer?

WULF (302): I do not want either one of those. If your system, because it does not optimize, runs ALGOL five times slower than someone else's, and they both cost the same amount and are both available, then I will buy the other person's.

OUTRED (302): The two systems would not be available in the same time scale. The optimizing system takes much longer, at the moment, to produce. If you can find a good way of producing an optimizing system in the same time as a simple minded system then I might start agreeing with you.

WULF (302): The Adaptive FORTRAN system (page 185), which is comparable to FORTRAN H quality, took one man nine months to write. If what you are telling me is that a bunch of manufacturers have managed to screw up what they have done, that is an obvious fact. There seems to be an opinion that somehow optimization is a very expensive business. It is not.

It is not how much you optimize that takes compile time, it is how dumb you are when you write the compiler; and exactly the same holds true for the actual writing of programs themselves. Given an arbitrarily dumb programmer, he will take arbitrarily long to do a job. If you have a bad programmer and a bad compiler, the execution time increases exponentially.

The role of machine design for better run-time performance of high-level language programs is discussed in detail separately in a later section (page 129).

OPTIMIZATION VERSUS EFFICIENT CODING TECHNIQUES

Efficient object code can result either from translating a given source program with a highly-optimizing translator or by so coding the source program that efficient code is produced by standard translation techniques. Though this Report is primarily concerned with the first aspect, the second must be constantly borne in mind. Indeed, it is one of the bounding limitations of current optimizing compilers that no amount of compile-time optimization can produce from a hopelessly inappropriate algorithm object code that could compare with the code produced from the best-known algorithm.

What is not so clear, however, is whether, given a reasonable algorithm for a given problem, the programmer should be expected to indulge in the very low-level optimizations that an optimizing compiler can perform.

ZELKOWITZ: In discussing optimization techniques, it is important to realize that most global flow analysis algorithms modify source language constructs, that is, program variables are merely moved around. Thus a truly careful programmer could hand-code routines that come close to optimized code. The question that must be answered then is why have it?

Optimization does save program execution time. While a programmer could hand-optimize the code, a compiler can generally do a better job at less cost. Although an expert programmer may do as well as an optimizer, in the vast majority of cases the optimizer will do better. Since computer costs are decreasing while programming costs are increasing, it is better to improve a program mechanically than manually.

There are also some cases where a programmer cannot optimize by hand. For example, the expression A(I,J) involves a calculation of the form (Address-of-A + I*N + J). This gets more complex with more dimensions. A global optimizer generally has access to these subscript calculations – expressions that are not available at the source language level.

Since an optimizer does save execution time, a programmer can make use of it to make a program more understandable. Redundant calculations can be added to a program to improve the documentation and readability with the programmer knowing that the optimizer will remove those calculations.

CONCLUSION

Though it can be argued, with some justification, that program optimization should not be necessary since the required efficiency could be achieved by sensible algorithms written in sensible languages and running on sensible machines, such arguments have little appeal to the average user. Given the limitations of current machines and languages and the chronic shortage of good programmers, it seems that optimizing compilers and system tuning exercises will remain a necessity for some considerable time.

MOTIVES FOR IMPROVING PROGRAM PERFORMANCE

INTRODUCTION

There are a variety of reasons why a performance improvement exercise may be carried out and the major motives are examined below. It should be noted that such an exercise is generally just one of the possible solutions to the problem of an overloaded system.

G G BROWN (317): Most computer systems that have been operational for more than one year will have become "fully loaded" according to well-known laws of utilization. At this time the managers of the system have three choices of action:

1 Limit the load to that currently being processed.

2 Acquire more powerful hardware in the form of a major upgrade.

3 Undertake an optimization project to reduce the effect of the existing load and thus create spare capacity.

AVOIDING SYSTEM UPGRADE

The most pressing reason for wanting to improve the performance of the major programs in an installation is to avoid the expense of buying more powerful hardware.

MUNRO: Most installations have a continuously increasing work load. The reason for that is not always that more processing is being done, but simply because of changing requirements. When a new requirement emerges, that requirement has to be accommodated; but the code for the superseded requirement does not always get removed. For example, if at the beginning of the year the government decides that it is going to alter the tax scheme, then the payroll program will have to be altered to accommodate the new rules but sometimes people do not remove the coding associated with the old tax scheme. So the load can build up even though no more productive work is being done. In addition, many organizations are still in the process of adapting their business to a computer, so they can expect an increasing work load from new applications as well. So, given a load that is continually increasing, we either have to go on buying bigger and bigger computers, or get more out of the one we have. So one of the aims of performance improvement might be to make the existing machine work better, which in this context means faster.

G G BROWN (317): Just as Parkinson's Law will quickly load a brand new system, so can the old one, when there is no hope of a replacement, be squeezed and squeezed. The salesman will tend to refer to this as "10% of 10% of 10%". In fact, the improvement to be had from optimization is often greater than 10%. The key is measurement. Without measurement one can be led to a benchmark on the new system and shown it all being done so much faster without knowing whether or not the same results could be achieved for far less cost on existing equipment.

Just in case your system is measured by someone who is not entirely disinterested in the outcome, the right question to ask is not "when will it run out of steam?" but "which component will run out of steam first?", "who is the major user of that component?", and "can the use by that user be reduced?".

REDUCING OPERATING COSTS

MUNRO: A second aim of optimization would be to reduce the operating costs associated with a computer. One might, for example, find oneself faced with a directive from above that the computer costs are going to be reduced by 10%. In such a situation, one has to find a way of reducing the hardware costs so that one's own salary, or job itself, is not placed in jeopardy.

By improving program performance, substantial savings can be made if the previous expense included such items as bought-out time, machine overtime rentals, or personnel overtime.

IMPROVING TURNAROUND TIME

Improving the performance of certain application programs not only relieves the burden on the machine; it can also add to the profitability of the organization.

MUNRO: One of the commonest reasons for optimizing is to improve turnaround times. Turnaround time is tremendously important for some applications, much more important than throughput. It is sometimes the most important goal in many installations. For example, practically every commercial installation sends out bills for the services and products that the organization has supplied. In many industries, customers pay on receipt of the invoice, or at least they pay with some constant delay after they receive the bill. It might be 10 days after receiving the bill or it might be 30 but we can see that our payments are received a certain time after we have sent out the bills. Therefore, if we can get the bills out one day sooner, we will get our money in one day sooner, which makes a very big difference. For example, if the computer is being rented for, say £15 000 a month and if a day's invoices will bring in approximately £600 a day, the net cost of the computer will be doubled if the invoices go out a day late.

Though turnaround time can thus be very critical for invoices, it is much more so for the basic operations on which the organization depends. In almost every distribution organization, an incoming order arrives and finds its way into the computer somehow, via a display screen or via a punched card, etc. In due course out comes a picking slip, which goes to someone in the warehouse, who goes travelling round the warehouse bins, pulls out the items, packs them, and ships it off to the customer.

It is obviously pretty catastrophic if, at half-past eight in the morning, when all the pickers show up, there are no picking lists for them. I think that those examples serve to illustrate just how crucial turnaround time can be for certain programs.

There are sometimes complaints about programmers who use certain dodges to ensure that their programs are run as rapidly as they can be; that is, they will affect other programs very adversely in their own selfish interests. In some circumstances that is completely justified. It is difficult to imagine, for example, that a file back-up should have equal priority to the program that produces these picking slips, because a file back-up can be done at any time of day. So there are cases where it would be well justified for one program to degrade the performance of other programs, simply in order to get quite a small improvement in its own turnaround.

The ways in which the required improvement can be achieved are discussed in later sections.

CONSTRAINTS IN PROGRAM OPTIMIZATION

INTRODUCTION

In considering the potential benefits of any procedure, the bounding limitations need to be borne in mind. In the case of program performance improvement, these limitations are of two kinds:

- *global limitations of the whole principle of improvement*
- *local limitations that apply to specific types of optimization.*

ECONOMIC CONSTRAINTS

Clearly, the cost of achieving a given improvement has to be considered when deciding whether to implement it. Frequently, the source of some inefficiency will be well known and the savings that could be expected from removing it will be fairly predictable. However, if the cost of making the improvement is not significantly less than the cost of the inefficiency, it is invariably better to live with the inefficiency. This principle is admirably illustrated by the compiler tuning exercise described by Darden and Heller (301). *Though it was clear that further improvements could still be achieved, the benefits of these improvements were thought not to justify further effort (see page 125).*

One of the objectives that can be raised against optimizing compilers is that they can expend a lot of effort in optimizing code that will rarely be executed. An approach to optimization that avoids this problem is discussed later (page 99).

PROGRAM TUNING VERSUS SYSTEM TUNING

Another constraint to improving the performance of an individual program is the performance of the whole system. It is quite possible that any improvement that is achieved for that one program will have to be paid for in the decreased performance of other programs.

PATEL: Unless you reduce the total kilobyte-seconds for a particular program, when you improve it, the system performance will be degraded. For example, suppose you make your program run twice as fast but, in the process of doing so, it takes up $2\frac{1}{2}$ times the amount of store required. That improved program, which takes only half the time, will degrade system performance; although it takes less time to execute, you have fewer overall resources left for executing other programs. As a result, the system throughput will actually do down. Unless the total kilobyte-seconds of the improved program is reduced, the system throughput will be worse.

I know examples of compilers where the primary objective for the improvement was the elapsed time. As a result of the changes that were made, the amount of store required was greater than that compensated by the reduction in the existence time, and as a result the system throughput was reduced.

To compare the relative performance of two equivalent pieces of programs, you need to compare the kilobyte-seconds for each of the programs, and not either the kilobytes or the seconds alone, or some other function.

Of course, in particular circumstances, the degrading of total system performance may be a valid sacrifice, if the particular program is very critical.

LIMITATIONS OF OPTIMIZING COMPILERS

The local limitations that were referred to earlier are almost all connected with the translation stage. An obvious example, discussed in detail in a later section, is that poor algorithm design is a fundamentally bounding limitation to optimization during translation.

Other limitations of optimizing compilers are discussed in the section concerned with the translation stage (page 114).

Program development

INTRODUCTION

- Trade-offs in programming
- Programming methodology

PROGRAMMING LANGUAGES AND OPTIMIZATION

- Introduction
- Language design for efficient programs
- Language design for easier optimization
- Conclusion

STRUCTURED PROGRAMMING

- Introduction
- Structured programming and efficiency
- Optimizing structured programs
- Conclusion

PROGRAM TRANSFORMATION

- Introduction
- Transformation techniques
- Applications of transformation
- Transformation as an optimizing technique

INTRODUCTION

This section examines the importance of the development stage in a program's life-cycle in terms of its potential for improving performance.

TRADE-OFFS IN PROGRAMMING

One of the major problems in discussing the performance of programs is that priorities and acceptable levels of performance vary so much according to circumstances. For example, the performance of typical 'quick and dirty' compilers in a teaching environment, where the priority is usually for very fast compilation at the expense of execution efficiency, would be completely inadequate for production environments, where programs are supposed to be run many times between recompilations. Similarly, the arduousness of assembly language programming would scarcely be worthwhile for one-off programs, but may be justified in exceptionally time-critical applications.

Therefore in program development, as at all other stages in a program's life-cycle, various trade-offs need to be recognized. Laski (page 235) lists the following factors:

1. *ease of program conception, maintenance, and modification*
2. *program security*
3. *compiler speed*
4. *compiler size*
5. *compiled code security and accuracy*
6. *compiled code speed*
7. *compiled code size.*

Many of these trade-offs centre round the single question of programming cost.

PALME: The actual time to write a computer program usually represents only a small fraction of the programming cost. The costly and time-consuming parts are debugging and maintenance. Making the software safe, reliable and dependable is costly, but in most cases necessary, since the losses caused by unreliable software are often even larger.

Since errors will always occur with large computer applications — machine errors, human operator errors and software errors — good software products are expected to protect against disasters which these errors may cause. Such products are called fail-soft, and all except very small computers contain at least some fail-soft capabilities. For example, an error in a user application program should not destroy the operating system in the computer. Getting fail-soft capabilities contributes significantly to the programming cost.

Maintenance of a software product does not only include correction of errors, but also development of extended capabilities and program changes. In many cases, the total programming effort spent on such development is much larger than that of the initial development. If the initial design of the software is such that the new capabilities are difficult to accommodate, maintenance becomes especially difficult and costly.

To some extent, programming costs can be reduced by good programming techniques, well-trained software development personnel, etc. In addition, there is a trade-off between four cost factors:

1 buying or developing general-purpose software (compilers, software analysis tools, application packages, etc)

2 hardware costs during the development of programs

3 hardware costs during the production runs

4 personnel costs for program development, maintenance and use.

The balance between these cost factors depends on the application.

If the cost of production runs is high compared to the development cost, then it might be worthwhile to spend more money on the other three cost factors. One might then choose to use an expensive, highly optimizing compiler. Such a compiler may be more expensive to buy or develop; it will use more hardware resources during program development and it will also often increase the personnel costs for program debugging, since highly optimizing compilers tend to be less reliable than other compilers. Another solution is to use a programming language which closely mirrors the architecture of the machine – assembler language or a machine-oriented language of the PL/360 kind. Such languages yield more hardware-efficient object programs, but are less secure and therefore cause higher debugging cost. However, the use of such machine-close languages may very often not give as hardware-efficient object programs as people tend to believe.

By using more advanced program development tools, personnel costs are saved at the expense of hardware costs and general-purpose software costs. This will often give a net saving, since the cost of developing general-purpose software can be shared between many users.

In many applications, the hardware cost for production runs is actually a small part of the total cost, and it may be profitable to use more advanced program development tools even if these give higher hardware costs during production. The more advanced programming tools may for example give increased reliability and reduce the time to develop and modify the software. Low reliability can be very costly, and having to wait a long time before software can be modified can also be very costly.

PROGRAMMING METHODOLOGY

To a large extent, the cost factors involved in program development are matters of programming methodology. Two of the most important aspects of programming methodology, the role of programming languages and structured programming, are examined separately later in this section.

At a more basic level, there are the important questions of how to organize the programming effort, what standards to enforce, which techniques to adopt and which to dismiss, etc. Many of these questions are discussed, in the context of the behavioural aspects of programming, by Newsted (page 267), who assesses the significance both of traditional programming tools such as flowcharts and of many newer ideas such as 'egoless programming'. Above all Newsted argues that better software performance will require a more professional attitude on the part of programmers.

NEWSTED: Brown (127) cautions programmers and analysts to be 'lookers' and not 'blunderers'. His five rules of thumb are undoubtedly true with their strong appeal to one's sense of the "right way to do things given human frailties". He suggests that we:

1 keep putting ourselves in the shoes of others such as the user, the manager, the manual reader, and the person who takes over the project when we get promoted;

2 document everything, continually assuming we are going to have an attack of amnesia next week;

3 verify and test and repeat this every time the smallest detail is changed;

4 plan for a changing environment;

5 imagine everything in terms of what happens when it goes wrong.

Rogo (128) details the need for functional specifications for any proposed program or system. This is very much like a turn-key system for software. Users are queried in detail as to what they need and how their desired system should *function* irrespective of how it is coded. Crucial interests of the users include report formats and frequencies, types of runs (in non-jargon terms), input descriptions, and descriptions of the clerical tasks the system can perform. When such specifications are detailed (that is, documented) before programming commences, negotiation and discussion can take place and a desired system as well as one that is possible (given software and hardware) can result. Functional specifications can eliminate most of the "that's great, but what I really wanted is" requests by getting them out in the open to begin with.

Attractive as functional specifications are, they do not get to the actual programming – though following them makes it safe to proceed with coding. What guidelines are to be offered in the actual writing of statements? One can depend on amusing and often helpful proverbs (129,130). Detailed – if not experimentally supported – books on 'style' can be consulted (for example (131)). There is much in such a book of style to lead to professionalism:

- a prologue definition of a program and its variables
- logical indenting (especially with **ifs**)
- use of blank lines and carefully set-off comments
- mnemonic names and labels
- standard abbreviations and punctuation
- generality
- use of pre-programmed modules
- non-repetitious calculation of constants
- optimized ordering of arithmetic operators
- non-mixing of data modes or types
- efficient looping (where as much is outside the loop as possible)
- few **gotos**, and the only those that jump short distances
- minimal subscript usage
- a full knowledge of all language and system features

And the list can go on.

Care must be taken in following this lore and style when confronted with the need for hard efficiency. Knuth (132) correctly points out that the hard optimization of code has been overstressed. He notes that

> "most of the running time in non-I/O bound programs is concentrated in about 3% of the source text. We often see a short inner loop whose speed governs the overall program speed to a remarkable degree; speeding up the inner loop by 10% speeds up everything by almost 10%. And if the inner loop has 10 instructions, a moment's thought will usually cut it to 9 or fewer."

Thus Knuth is suggesting that too much tinkering under the guise of achieving hard efficiency should not be done because tightening in all but small sections of code will lead to a less transparent program that is difficult to read and hard to debug.

The individual subsections that follow discuss the following factors of program development:

1 *the significance of programming languages for optimization, especially with reference to the possibility of expressing optimizations at the source level (page 31);*

2 *the relevance of structured programming to program efficiency and optimization (page 47);*

3 *the possibility of a program transformation system, as an indication of future trends in programming methodology and optimization (page 61).*

The relationship between inherently efficient programming techniques and compile-time improvement of sub-optimal techniques is discussed in an earlier section (page 12).

PROGRAMMING LANGUAGES AND OPTIMIZATION

INTRODUCTION

To a large extent, advances in optimization, both at the development stage and during translation, are determined by developments in language design. Even with the most primitive languages, some degree of optimization was possible.

SCHNECK: The first programming languages were one-to-one assembly codes, transliterated into machine language. The purpose of assembly code was to permit use of mnemonic names in place of absolute machine locations. Strange as it may seem, optimization was required even at that level of language availability. The IBM 650, a popular drum-oriented system, was extremely sensitive to the placement of instructions and data on its storage drum. Revolving at 12 500 revolutions per minute, a single revolution required 4.8 milliseconds. If instructions were carefully placed, no time delay was incurred; in the worst case, a full 4.8 milliseconds would be wasted waiting for the appearance of the next instruction on the drum. When storage assignments were performed by hand, placement of instructions was taken into account. When an assembler took over the task of performing the storage assignments, it was necessary to account for the drum rotation in order to produce a program that would run in a reasonable time. This was one of the earliest machine-dependent optimizations.

The creation of the FORTRAN language and compiler introduced another degree of freedom in the process of creating a machine language program from a source program. At the assembly language level the preparation of a machine language program is merely *transliteration*; apart from storage allocation, few choices are left to the assembler. The *translation* process from FORTRAN to machine language takes place at a much higher level. The compiler determines how effectively various features of the target machine will be utilized:

- Does the compiler generate 'accumulator' instructions for a multiple-register machine?

- Does the compiler utilize the special loop increment/test instructions found on the target machine?

- Does the compiler perform instruction scheduling for a machine with autonomous execution units?

- Does the compiler utilize indirect addressing?

The list could be extended significantly and would still merely scratch the surface of the range of implementations available to the compiler writer. Despite the great number of questions which might be asked concerning the operation of a compiler for FORTRAN (or ALGOL, PL/1, or COBOL), the output of such a compiler is fairly predictable. The language has left the generation of machine instructions to the compiler, but not the approach or choice of algorithm.

Very high-level languages such as SETL (279) introduce another degree of freedom into the compilation process. The compiler will be charged with deciding *how* to accomplish a program's objective, and then producing machine language instructions to carry out the objective. The very high-level languages will not require that the programmer pay attention to details which are not relevant to the solution of his problem. Instead, the programmer must carefully control the use of data structures and type of variables or he will inadvertently prevent the compiler from being able to perform the reduction from worst-case to best-case coding necessary for efficiency.

A simple example suffices to illustrate these ideas. To obtain the smallest value of a set, the FORTRAN programmer must create a loop and search on an element-by-element basis for the minimum value. Not only is the programmer forced to indicate explicitly the search process, but he must also specify an order for carrying out the search. The programmer may not have any knowledge of interest in the storage of the elements of the set, and the entire process is best left in the care of the high-level language compiler. In circumstances where the extreme elements of sets are repeatedly referenced, the compiler may choose to maintain, for example, the maximum, minimum and cardinality of sets as attributes which are easily obtained when required.

In his introduction to SETL, Schwartz states:

> "It is this fundamental difficulty with which the language designer struggles, attempting to invent dictional patterns which are highly expressive and yet can be compiled into reasonably efficient running code... Improved optimization techniques therefore form an essential part of an overall attack on the problems of programming."

The major factors in language design for program efficiency and optimization potential are examined below. Language design in general is discussed in detail in the State of the Art Report High-level Languages (311) *and* Commercial Language Systems (304) *and in* (309).

LANGUAGE DESIGN FOR EFFICIENT PROGRAMS

It is a widely-held view that the older lower-level languages are more efficient in terms of machine resources than more modern high-level languages. Though this may be true in certain respects, it is certainly not universally so.

PALME: There are several reasons why assembly language programs sometimes do not turn out to be as efficient as people tend to believe.

Every large software product has to contain a lot of internal checking. When a program is executed, then there is usually at least two levels of checking. One level is the checking done by the module 'programming language system' on the module 'applications program'. And the second level is the checking done by the module 'supervisory system' on the module 'programming language system'. In large systems, these three main modules are divided into submodules with further checking in-between them.

If a large application package is written entirely in assembly language, then much of this necessary internal checking goes into the run-time code. The different modules of the large application will thus contain a lot of code, often as much as 50%, just to check that other modules are not misusing it. This checking code is executed at run time, requiring both memory and CPU time.

If a good high-level language is used instead, a language that allows the compiler to do this checking, then a lot of this internal checking can be moved from run time to compile time, thus giving more efficient object programs.

There are other related reasons why assembly language programs sometimes tend to be less efficient. For example, since assembly language is tedious to write, programmers in assembly language tend to write their programs as interpreters, which interpret commands stored in tables, text strings or other data structures. This may be a good way of structuring the programs, but such interpreters can be very inefficient in terms of CPU time in comparison with the code derived from a high-level language.

In any case, the efficiency of object programs seems to be more a function of the programmer than of the programming language and the variations between individual programmers are so great as to overshadow the differences between languages (312).

As discussed earlier (page 26), efficiency at the expense of reliability is a very questionable goal, as illustrated by some of the insecure features of FORTRAN.

PALME: Software should be secure by definition. By this I mean that the software should be defined in such a way that, when you use it, nothing can happen which does not follow from the definition of the software. This point is best illustrated by counter-examples, and FORTRAN is a good choice since FORTRAN is such a very insecure language. The following are some examples of what can happen in FORTRAN:

- If there is a lack of correspondence between two subroutines, then funny things can happen, usually with little or unhelpful, diagnosis. Examples are non-similar COMMON statements, and the lack of correspondence between actual and formal subroutine parameters. Consider for example why the following piece of program will often output 2 instead of 1:

```
SUBROUTINE SUB(I)
...
I = I + 1
RETURN
END

CALL SUB (1)
J = 1
WRITE (6) J
```

- If your program depends on the fact that certain compilers initialize all un-initialized data to zero, or that certain compilers keep local data in subroutines between different calls to these subroutines, then you are in for a surprise when you change to a new version of the compiler or the operating system.

- FORTRAN has few data structures except dimensioned variables, and FORTRAN programmers are therefore encouraged to use dimensioned variables. These are however very insecure. The array bounds are easy to exceed, and there is no checking against using the wrong index in the wrong array.

Please note that these examples do not primarily indicate faults in bad FORTRAN implementations. They indicate faults in the FORTRAN programming language itself. A good compiler can seldom improve very much on a bad language.

A way to protect against insecure programming languages (like FORTRAN or PL/1) is to develop special check-out compilers. This is however not usually a good solution, since it is difficult with an insecure programming language to get adequate compatibility between the check-out and the optimizing compilers. Also, the cost of developing two compilers reduces the choice of manufacturer.

A good programming language should therefore be secure in its own definition. Examples of such languages are SIMULA and SNOBOL. SIMULA and SNOBOL do not need any check-out compilers, since every compiler is by definition also a full verifier that programs are within the language.

The importance of security in programming languages is discussed in more detail in the State of the Art Reports Commercial Language Systems (304) *and* Computer Systems Reliability (313) *and in Palme's paper (page 279).*

LANGUAGE DESIGN FOR EASIER OPTIMIZATION

Given an arbitrary piece of machine code, it is not always possible, or at least economically justifiable, to perform certain optimizations. However, these optimizations would be relatively straightforward with some knowledge of the source constructs from which the machine code was derived.

LASKI: Consider the two following sequences of machine code:

```
--- LD  E ;  JFLS  L1 ;  DO  C1 ;  JUMP L2 ;          (1)
    L1:DO  C2;  L2: ---

--- L1:LD  E ;  JFLS   L2 ;  DO C ;  JUMP L1 ;        (2)
    L2: ---
```

Without a full flow analysis of the surrounding program to ensure that there are no other occurrences of jumps to L1 or L2, which is expensive to perform, especially if we bear in mind that the LD and DO macros may stand for arbitrarily long sequences of code, we can make no assumptions about the machine state when we arrive at L1 and L2.

Thus we can take no advantage of any knowledge we might have that some fast register has the same value, since it had been loaded thence, as some word of store or that the value that should be in some word of store is presently in some fast register and has not yet been stored where it should be. We must therefore, to account for possible flow-paths, perform the delayed stores before any jump and, after any label, make no assumptions that the value of any word of store is already in some fast register.

However, from the source **if** *e* **then** c_1 **else** c_2 and **while** *e* **do** *c*, we know without further analysis that there is no non-local flow to the labels our translator will generate. More, from what we know of the state of the registers and stores before the code sequence we can deduce directly and simply what we may assume within any part of it and at the start of whatever follows it....

Suppose one knows that, in every case, the body of some loop is to be repeated at least once. Rather than code 2, one would wish to achieve:

```
--- L1:DO C ;  LD E ;  JTRU L1 ; ---                        (3)
```

One could write: *c* ; **while** *e* **do** *c*, but some analysis would be needed to recognize that the command preceding the loop is the same as that that forms its body and most compilers would not take the trouble and would generate:

```
--- DO C ;  L1:LD E ;  JFLS L2 ;  DO C ;                    (4)
    JUMP L1;  L2: ---
```

However, if the source construct: **repeat** *c* **while** *e* is available code 3 will be achieved without any analysis.

Unless the average number of times the loop body is expected to be repeated is less than one, a better translation than 2 of **while** *e* **do** *c* is:

```
--- JUMP L1 ;  L2:DO C ;  L1:LD E ;  JTRU L2: ---           (5)
```

... No modern programming language would repeat FORTRAN's treatment of its DO-loop, which translates not to 5 but to 3, assuming that in every instance of every loop, its body is to be executed at least once. In the context of arrays, which was what FORTRAN was designed for, this assumption is valid; it only begins to fail when we use FORTRAN to process possibly empty lists. This should serve as a warning to language designers today not to assume that their language will necessarily always be used for the kinds of programs they expect and, more importantly, for language choosers to be aware of the language designer's assumptions and their consequences.

The ideas that Laski is presenting have obvious implications for the relationship between structured programming and optimization, which is discussed in detail separately (page 47). They are also relevant to the concept of providing feedback to the compiler to help it decide on optimal code in particular cases, since the information on which such decisions can be made is often known, or at least knowable, by the programmer. Compiler feedback is discussed separately elsewhere (page 99).

Perhaps the most significant aspect of the foregoing discussion is the idea that optimizations should be expressible in the source language and not applied as post hoc modifications to the generated machine code.

KNUTH (310): For 15 years or so I have been trying to think of how to write a compiler that really produces top quality code. For example, most of the MIX programs in my books are considerably more efficient than any of today's most visionary compiling schemes would be able to produce. I've tried to study the various techniques that a hand-coder like myself uses, and to fit them into some systematic and automatic system. A few years ago, several students and I looked at a typical sample of FORTRAN programs (041), and we all tried hard to see how a machine could produce code that would compete with our best hand-optimized object programs. We found ourselves always running up against the same problem: the compiler needs to be in a dialogue with the programmer; it needs to know properties of the data, and whether certain cases can arise, etc. And we couldn't think of a good language in which to have such a dialogue.

For some reason we all (especially me) had a mental block about optimization, namely that we always regarded it as a behind-the-scenes activity, to be done in the machine language, which the programmer isn't supposed to know. This veil was first lifted from my eyes when I ran across a remark by Hoare (309) that, ideally, a language should be designed so that an optimizing compiler can describe its optimizations in the *source* language.

HOARE (309): There is a widespread myth that a language designer can afford to ignore machine efficiency, because it can be regained when required by the use of a sophisticated optimizing compiler. This is false: there is nothing that the good engineer can afford to ignore. The only language that has been optimized with general success is FORTRAN, which was very specifically designed for that very purpose. But even in FORTRAN, optimization has grave disadvantages:

- An optimizing compiler is usually large, slow, unreliable, and late.

- Even with a reliable compiler, there is no guarantee that an optimized program will have the same results as a normally compiled one.

- A small change to an optimized program may switch off optimization with an unpredictable and unacceptable loss of efficiency.

- The most subtle danger is that optimization tends to remove from the programmer his fundamental control over and responsibility for the quality of his programs.

The solution to these problems is to produce a language for which a simple straightforward "non-pessimizing" compiler will produce straightforward object programs of acceptable compactness and efficiency: similar to those produced by a resolutely non-clever (but also non-stupid) machine code programmer. Make sure that the language is sufficiently expressive to enable most other optimizations to be made in the language itself; and finally, make the language so simple, clear, regular, and free from side-effects that a general machine-independent optimizer can simply translate an inefficient program into a more efficient one with guaranteed identical effects, and expressed in the same source language. The fact that the user can inspect the results of optimization in his own language mitigates many of the defects listed above.

In order for some optimizations to be thus expressible in the source language, languages would need new constructs for expressing them.

LASKI: Adding a new high-level construct to a programming language may have one of two entirely distinct effects; it cannot have both and it is always perfectly clear which of the two is the case.

The first kind of construct (of which allowing the size of vectors to be decided at run time rather than compile time will serve an as example) increases the run-time space overhead of representation and the time and space overhead of subroutine calls in order to buy increased flexibility. Optimization, in this case, comes from allowing the programmer to specify no more expensive a flexibility than he in fact requires and to enable that expensive overhead to be confined to that subpart of the running program within which it is necessarily required.

The second kind of construct (of which allowing conditional expressions as well as conditional commands will serve as an example) always has beneficial effects both on the source program, and on the practical achievement of optimal code. Its only harmful effect is to require a very slight increase in basic compiler size, say 30-100 words per construct, and a proportionally smaller decrease of compiler speed; this latter effect is almost certainly more than compensated for by the fact that a given algorithm can be expressed by a more concise source program which, more importantly, can be more easily conceived, understood and maintained by programmers to whom the construct is a familiar part of their language and thought.

The effect of these second kind of constructs is to enable a translator to achieve optimal code with less analytic effort. In practice, this means either that better code will be produced for the same amount of optimizing analysis or that similar code will be generated by a compiler which does less and costs less; this disjunction expresses two points on a continuum on which the compiler designer will make his choice.

The only *good* reason not to include such constructs in a modern programming language is when it is to be compiled in a machine with a small store whose designers have made it technically impossible to add to; the reader will notice that management ignorance of the advantages of buying more store at today's prices for a machine that is to be used for compiling is not included in this good reason. An *acceptable* reason is that language and compiler designers do not yet know what constructs will enable certain cases to be dealt with. The *usual* (and *bad*) reason for excluding such constructs from the majority of languages used at the majority of installations is the ignorance, timidity and conservatism of elderly obsolescent programmers; amongst these I include beginner programmers who have been taught obsolescent ideas on the job, in programming schools, and a substantial proportion of universities.

Laski illustrates the use and implication of new language constructs of this type in the context of indicating common subexpressions. As Knuth points out (310)*, removing common subexpressions from the source text can impair the readability and comprehensibility of the program. Though such practices are very often necessary in order to achieve reasonable efficiency, the same effect could be achieved at the source level without the associated obscurity.*

LASKI: We would like the source $a[3 \times i + 1] := b[3 \times i + 1] + c[3 \times i + 1]$ to generate:

```
LOAD      2  I
MULTI     2  3
ADDI      2  1
LOADIND   1  B,2
ADDIND    1  C,2
STOREIND  1  A,2
```
(8)

and not recalculate the value of the index on each of the three occasions it is required.

If the source construct :

$a[x] := b[x] + c[x]$ **where** $x = 3 \times i + 1$; (9)

is available, code 8 can be achieved without any analysis.

Code 9 has precisely the same meaning as:

begin let $x = 3 \times i + 1$; $a[x] := b[x] + c[x]$ **end** ; (10)

so that, as far as program structure is concerned, we do not need the **where** construct. Comparison of the texts 9 and 10 illustrates the pragmatic value of allowing synonymous structures to be available in a single language. In fact, pragmatically, we might well restrict **where**-declared locals to be constant so that they cannot appear on the left hand of an assignment, etc, unlike **let**-declared locals. Such considerations are, of course, logically subsequent to those we are mainly concerned with in this paper; from this it does not follow, of course, they they are any the less important for the design of an efficient system for the programmer.

Our final point in these examples is a little difficult to make since we do not have familiar syntax to do so, and necessarily so because it is precisely to observe that we may not necessarily have syntax available to express what we may conceive of as expressible and to examine the consequence of this fact.

In 9 we did not avoid reduplicating the largest possible subphrase, but only the largest possible expression subphrase within it. In a clumsy syntax we wrote an analogue of:

$$a \ \mathbf{sub} \ x := b \ \mathbf{sub} \ x + c \ \mathbf{sub} \ x \ \mathbf{where} \ x = 3 \times i + 1 \quad (11)$$

rather than the shorter:

$$a \ x := b \ x + c \ x \ \mathbf{where} \ x = \mathbf{sub}(3 \times i + 1). \quad (12)$$

Even with a suitable syntax, this latter form does not, in fact, make it easier to reach the optimal code of our imaginary target machine. Suppose, however, that this had a special register SB, such that if a word were a vector descriptor, any operation whose effective address was that word would, in fact, work on the element by using the contents of SB as a subscript selector – this could be useful if, in the style of the Burroughs machines this involved hardware bounds-checking, etc.

Then, from the source texts 9 or 10, a simple-minded compiler might only generate:

```
LOAD 2   I ;  MULTI 2 3 ;  ADDI 2 1 ;
LOAD SB  2 ;  LOAD  B ;
LOAD SB  2 ;  ADD   C ;
LOAD SB  2 ;  STORE A ;                     (13)
```

rather than the optimal:

```
LOAD SB  I ; MULTI SB 3 ; ADDI SB 1 ;
LOAD  B    ; ADD   C    ; STORE A   ;
```
(14)

which will be generated without optimizing analysis from the source text 11 (assuming programming syntax allows the programmer to give any common subphrase and not just those given phrases that are also expressions). This example illustrates a number of very important principles of language design, compiler design and machine design which, if ignored, will inhibit efficient computing. Consequent upon our experience of language and thinking, our programming languages do not necessarily allow the expression, and hence hide from us, unfamiliar yet meaningful structures; putting in syntax to allow us to be aware of them, as the source text 11 illustrates, seems, within our traditional ways of thinking, inherently clumsy, unless and until we have absorbed them into our intellectual tools; moreover, as code 8 illustrates, our existing machines, whose design assumes that they are not part of our language and our thought, cannot take advantage of their use, whereas they suggest new and useful machine designs, as shown by the code in 13 and 14.

The question is whether or not they should be included in the programmer's language; if they are, learning to use them is a burden which may or may not reward the programmer; if they are not, certain optimizations may be missed.

We take the view that the programmer should be made aware of them by providing them in the language that provides him with his tools of thought but not necessarily in that part of it which his compiler accepts. This implies, if we want to reach optimal code, that the compiler requires to retain common subphrase optimization, etc. If a program involves these optimizing phases, it is vital to discover why and take note of what and why as input to language and machine design.

Further discussion of this topic can be found in Laski's paper (page 235) and in the section dealing with compilation (page 99), in the context of pragmats, *programmer-supplied directives to the compiler.*

Related to this idea of source-level optimization is the idea of a separate preprocessor for optimization.

SCHNECK: Current program optimizers are usually found as part of language translators. An independent optimizer, used as a separate program to improve source programs, has recently been implemented (277). This use of an optimizer permits a significant simplification of the programming/debugging task while also providing efficient programs. The optimizer is able to perform its restructuring on the source program level. This has three major effects:

1 The programmer is able to see the restructured program. Debugging is simplified because the restructured program represents the program in actual use and all changes made by the compiler are in evidence.

2 The programmer need not spend time searching out and performing optimizations. Programs may be written in a form close to the problem statement which is easily maintained, and the optimizer will be used to create efficient versions. Changes or additions may be applied directly to the optimized program.

3 The benefits of sophisticated program optimization techniques are available even for machines which have no optimizing compiler.

An external optimizer may also be used in an inverse mode. The goal of such a 'semantic preprocessor' (278) is increased language capability and its corresponding increase in programmer productivity, without a decrease in performance. A frequent effect of increased language capability is a decrease in program efficiency. A semantic preprocessor based on program optimization techniques permits introduction of extensive language facilities without penalty.

CONCLUSION

The idea that optimizations can be expressed given suitable constructs in high-level language terms, leads further to the idea that programs can be written in clear but possibly inefficient terms and then transformed into efficient programs with the help of information provided by the programmer. This concept is discussed elsewhere in the context of program development methods (page 61).

STRUCTURED PROGRAMMING

INTRODUCTION

The most significant development in programming in the last few years has been the growing interest in structured programming. Though there is little agreement about precisely what structured programming is, a common theme in most expositions is a greater concern with program correctness and clarity.

NEWSTED: In addition to the assortment of published and underground wisdom that exists about optimizing programming, there has been one specific thrust (which is still without much experimental validation) that, if nothing else, is proving a rallying point for those concerned with the behavioural aspects of programming. This is structured programming. Structured programming is as much an attitude as it is a series of techniques. Top-down programming, logical code blocks, gotoless code, and modularity are all part of it, but it is more than this. Structured programming is a realization of the limited information-processing capabilities of human programmers. Wirth's definition (123) sums it up quite well. To him, structured programming is

> "the expression of a conviction that the programmer's knowledge must not consist of a bag of tricks and trade secrets, but of a general intellectual ability to tackle problems systematically, and that particular techniques should be replaced (or augmented) by a method. At its heart lies an attitude rather than a recipe: the admission of the limitations of our minds."

Specifically, one's mind cannot be expected to understand

ridiculously tight or 'tricky' code. This view is strongly reinforced by Knuth's comments on the usefulness of the **goto** statement (132). Though **gotos** are viewed as harmful, most programmers still feel the need for a statement that in fact 'goes to' without saying **goto**. Short jumps with **gotos** are acceptable; branching over many statements is not, because easily grasped abstractions are not possible. All levels of a program (with or without **gotos**) should be easily 'chunked' or abstracted into one basic concept or function. 'Chunked programming' is really what is meant by structured programming – it is not simply **goto**less coding.

Elimination of **gotos** can lead to better and more easily understood abstractions or program chunks. Though such code may be harder to write, it should certainly be within the grasp of the real professionals envisioned by Kraft and Weinberg (124).

Structured programming, because it seems to relegate program efficiency to a secondary position, thus seems to run counter to program optimization.

WIRTH (308): In the first decade of computers, say up to the early sixties, computers were quite limited in their power. The task of the programmer was to formulate algorithms in the specific order codes of these machines so that they were utilized as effectively as possible. Primarily because of their limitations, this task was achieved by collecting sets of clever techniques and startling tricks, and by finding applications for them as frequently as possible. Examples of such techniques were the programmed self-modification of parts of the program, such as, for instance, the conversion of conditional jumps into dummy instructions and vice versa, or the sharing of store for functionally independent, but never simultaneously used auxiliary variables.

Tricks were necessary at this time, simply because machines were built with limitations imposed by a technology in its early development stage, and because even problems that would be termed 'simple' nowadays could not be handled in a straightforward way. It was the programmers' very task to push computers to their limits by whatever means available. We should recall that the absence of index registers (and indirect addressing), for example, made automatic code modification a simple necessity.

The essence of programming was understood to be the *optimization of the efficiency* of particular machines executing particular algorithms.

BURNS: It is gratifying to observe that certain practices that were born of necessity in the confined spaces of first generation computers have fallen into disrepute and are nowadays rarely encountered. They do however serve to illustrate the sort of habits that lead to inefficiency. For example, because instruction space was at such a premium it was quite normal to create a subroutine from any arbitrary sequence of instructions longer than the subroutine call mechanism. Similarly, it was common to merge paths of programs together merely so that they might share a few instructions regardless of any logical justification. These and many similar 'techniques' were essential to the evolution of that popular (but now hopefully extinct) species — the convoluted monolith.

It may be argued that such programs are in fact efficient and that structure merely increases overhead. This was probably true when programs rarely exceeded 1000 instructions, but now, when 50 000 instruction programs are commonplace, it is beyond the wit of man to comprehend their totality without the assistance of some visible structure. Hence, there must be a limit to achievable efficiency for a program of given size and complexity. If complexity can be reduced, the way to improve efficiency may be more readily apparent.

However, it should not be thought that the champions of structured programming dismiss program efficiency as irrelevant. Rather, they are campaigning for languages and methods in which efficiency and clarity are not irreconcilable.

HOARE (309): There is an argument, which is all too prevalent among enthusiastic language designers, that efficiency of object code is no longer important; that the speed and capacity of computers is increasing and their price is coming down; and that the programming language designer might as well take advantage of this. This is an argument that would be quite acceptable if used to justify an efficiency loss of ten or twenty percent, or even thirty and forty percent. But all too frequently it is used to justify an efficiency loss of a factor of two, or ten, or even more; and worse, the overhead is not only in time taken but in space occupied by the running program. In no other engineering discipline would such avoidable overhead be tolerated, and it should not be in programming language design, for the following reasons:

- The magnitude of the tasks we wish computers to perform is growing faster than the cost-effectiveness of the hardware.
- However cheap and fast a computer is, it will be cheaper and faster to use it more efficiently.
- In the future we must hope that hardware designers will pay increasing attention to reliability rather than to speed and cost.
- The speed, cost, and reliability of peripheral equipment are not improving at the same rate as those of processors.
- If anyone is to be allowed to introduce inefficiency it should be the user programmer, not the language designer. The user programmer can take advantage of this freedom to write better-structured and clearer programs, and should not have to expend extra effort to obscure the structure and write less clear programs just to regain the efficiency that has been so arrogantly preempted by the language designer.

KNUTH (310): The conventional wisdom shared by many of today's software engineers calls for ignoring efficiency in the small; but I believe this is simply an overreaction to the abuses they see being practiced by penny-wise-and-pound-foolish programmers, who can't debug or maintain their 'optimized' programs. In established engineering disciplines a 12% improvement, easily obtained, is never considered marginal; and I believe the same viewpoint should prevail in software engineering. Of course I wouldn't bother making such optimizations on a one-shot job, but when it's a question of preparing quality programs, I don't want to restrict myself to tools that deny me such efficiencies.

There is no doubt that the grail of efficiency leads to abuse.

> Programmers waste enormous amounts of time thinking about, or worrying about, the speed of non-critical parts of their programs, and these attempts at efficiency actually have a strong negative impact when debugging and maintenance are considered. We *should* forget about small efficiencies, say about 97% of the time: premature optimization is the root of all evil.
>
> Yet we should not pass up our opportunities in that critical 3%. A good programmer will not be lulled into complacency by such reasoning, he will be wise to look carefully at the critical code; but only *after* that code has been identified. It is often a mistake to make a priori judgement about what parts of a program are really critical, since the universal experience of programmers who have been using measurement tools has been that their intuitive guesses fail. After working with such tools for seven years, I've become convinced that all compilers written from now on should be designed to provide all programmers with feedback indicating what parts of their programs are costing the most; indeed, this feedback should be supplied automatically unless it has been specifically turned off.

The principles and techniques of feedback systems, both programmer-controlled and automatic, are discussed separately elsewhere *(page 99).*

STRUCTURED PROGRAMMING AND EFFICIENCY

One of the most often expressed reservations about structured programming is its supposed inefficiency. Even when this criticism is not based on the over-narrow view of efficiency discussed above, the cause of the inefficiency is very often the result of other factors, such as poor compiler design.

KNUTH (310): Sooner or later, people are going to find that their beautifully structured programs are running at only half the speed – or worse – of the dirty old programs they used to write, and they will mistakenly blame the structure instead of recognizing what is probably the real culprit – the system overhead caused by typical compiler implementation of Boolean variables and procedure calls.

There is very little hard evidence either way since few organizations could afford to experiment by coding the same problem in two different ways, even if they could ensure that all the other variables in such an experiment were comparable. However, for certain applications, and given an adequate compiler, programs written in structured languages do not appear to be any less efficient than FORTRAN, which has survived so long partly because of its allegedly greater efficiency.

ZELKOWITZ: One large numerical analysis program, involving sparse matrix calculations and written in FORTRAN, was recoded into SIMPL for the UNIVAC 1108 computer. The UNIVAC FORTRAN compiler has a relatively sophisticated statement optimizer, but performs no global flow analysis. SIMPL for the 1108 is a straightforward compiler with no global optimizer, but good peephole optimization. In spite of that, the SIMPL program ran in 10% less time. Since every effort was made to preserve the original FORTRAN algorithms in the SIMPL program (although some changes had to be made because of the necessity of eliminating the **goto** of FORTRAN), this seems to indicate the efficiency of such a structured programming language.

OPTIMIZING STRUCTURED PROGRAMS

There is also little evidence on how far well-structured programs are easier to optimize than programs with arbitrary flow of control. What evidence there is seems in fact to indicate that structured programming is not conducive to optimization.

ZELKOWITZ: In one study (113), an optimizer was written for a language called SIMPL-XI (114), which generated code for a PDP-11 computer. This language is a variant of the SIMPL language developed at the University of Maryland (115). This language implemented only the **procedure**, **if**, **while**, and **case** constructs. Running the optimizer on several programs showed that the optimizer performed very poorly.

There is, however, strong reason to suppose that the failure of the optimizer to improve the code was attributable to other factors.

ZELKOWITZ: Firstly, optimization was on a procedure-by-procedure basis. However, the top-down design strategy employed in the programs being tested meant that many different procedures were written. Since this optimizer did not optimize any global variables across a procedure call (since any procedure could modify any global variable), not much code was available for optimization.

One major source for optimization is in register allocation. In the SIMPL compiler, a straightforward register allocation strategy was added to the code generator. A round-robin allocation strategy was used to allocate one of the four available registers each time one was needed. Within any block of code, the compiler kept track of which variables still had their current value in one of the registers. If any of these variables were used again within that block, no LOAD instruction need be generated. Upon reaching the end of any block, such as the end of a **while** loop, all registers were assumed to have no values in them. This was due to the fact that the block of code that set the registers (body of the **while** loop) may not have been executed if the expression in the **while** statement was false. This simple strategy saved about 10% of the generated code over the previous version of the compiler, which used only a single register for its calculations. This register allocator, which certainly did not do a global flow analysis of the program and hence was not optimal, did a creditable job and was used for each program whether optimized or not. Thus, register allocation was always optimized and did not count in calculating the effectiveness of the optimizer.

SIMPL also had extensive peephole optimization algorithms built into the code generator. The consequence was that these also did not show up in calculating the effectiveness of the optimizer.

Another possible cause for the poor results was that SIMPL implemented only one-dimensional arrays. As Knuth seemed to indicate (116), much of the available optimization is achieved by optimization of subscript calculations. This optimization is only minimally available for one-dimensional array references. And as Knuth so aptly states, with more complex data structures in future languages, there should be less emphasis on array calculations and hence less possible optimization possibilities.

A final possibility is that most of the test programs were

relatively short. This fact enables a programmer to spot common subexpressions before they appeared in the code. Moreover, SIMPL was being used as a systems programming language, and some other results seem to indicate that optimization does not work as well on such programs as they do on numerical calculations, such as in a typical FORTRAN program.

Furthermore, as mentioned earlier by Zelkowitz, SIMPL programs seem, even without optimization, to be quite efficient in comparison with equivalent FORTRAN programs.

There seems little doubt that optimization should be easier to apply to a structured program than to an unstructured one, provided the optimization is applied at the most appropriate stage.

SCHNECK: I don't think program analysis is a trivial task, even with structured code. The elimination of the direct backward branch with a **goto** makes life a lot simpler, but it does not completely eliminate the problems. Even with structured programming the control structures are still obscure.

LASKI: Given a genuine structured programming language in which one can express cleanly that which one intends, the process of compilation can be divided into two phases - analysis and synthesis; and in between there is what is popularly known as the parse tree. The effect of interval analysis, or any of these other techniques on final code, is to recreate from that final code the parse tree that should have been there in the first place. Given that parse tree, one has the global structure of the program. Given a language in which the structure of the program comes out in that parse tree, which is not, of course, the case for FORTRAN, and only too rarely the case for ALGOL, one can gain an awful lot.

Given a language (and my favourite example is BCPL, because that is the one I know) in which one has the forms of expression that enable one to speak of the structures that one wants, global, architecture-independent optimization can best take place not on the final synthesized linear target code, but on the tree itself. The problem of finding the innermost loops and finding the most frequently occurring paths can all be done on the tree.

ZELKOWITZ: The foregoing discussion seems to indicate two basic conclusions:

1 Structured programming, without an optimizer, can often lead to programs that are more efficient than correspondingly unstructured ones.

2 Current optimization techniques are generally inadequate to improve structured programs to any great extent.

This second point deserves further consideration. Most global flow analysis algorithms work 'inside out' This is done by constructing the program graph from the internal parsed form of the program. The fact that this is the usual technique is not surprising, since most experience with optimization has derived from the FORTRAN language. FORTRAN has no real structure, so any loop or conditional structure has to be built by the programmer out of the more primitive FORTRAN statements. This meant that the optimizer had to build up this same structure by analysing across several statements. Most optimizers today utilize this strategy. That is, the parser knows the control structure of a program, yet throws it away when the internal parsed form of the program is created. The optimizer then has to recreate the structure to optimize the program.

When looked at from that point of view, a great duplication of effort becomes apparent. If a program uses only **if**, **while**, or the block as the basic control structures, then a single pass through the program is sufficient to produce the flow graph of a program. All loops that are dynamically nested within a given loop during program execution will also be syntactically nested. This knowledge can be utilized by an optimizer, which would be more efficient than present-day techniques.

The capability that Zelkowitz is discussing has in fact been known for many years.

ZELKOWITZ: An early FORTRAN optimizer by Gear (119) was one of the first to exploit this fact. This compiler was a three-pass compiler with optimization being performed during the second pass. Only explicit DO-blocks were optimized; loops created by IF statements and GOTOs were ignored.

At the heart of the optimization algorithm was the concept of a change vector. This vector contained the names of all variables altered within a loop. There was always such a vector that described the variables of the program during the entire compilation process.

During the first pass, as a DO-loop was encountered, the current vector was saved (in a stack), and a new vector, to contain the name of variables altered in the DO-block, was initialized to empty. Each assignment statement added a variable to this vector. Upon exit from the block at the end of the DO-loop, this vector was added to the parsed program. This vector was also merged with the previously saved vector, which described the enclosing block, since all variables altered within the inner loop are also altered within the enclosing loop. This first pass had the effect of placing in the parsed program at the end of a DO-loop the names of all variables altered within that loop.

The second pass was a backward pass through the program to perform the optimization. Upon entry to a loop (backwards), the vector describing the changed variables was obtained. Any expression that contained variables not in this vector was a loop-invariant calculation. A temporary was allocated and the expression moved to a holding location. When the DO statement was processed, all of these moved expressions were added to the enclosing loop.

For example, the code:

```
          DO 10 I = 1,10
     10   A(I) = B*C
```

would result in B*C being replaced by a temporary. The program would be restructured as follows:

```
          T1 = B*C
          DO 10 I = 1,10
     10   A(I) = T1
```

An efficient register allocation strategy would keep T1 in a register, and since it is never used outside of this loop, would never store its value into memory. This means that even though a new temporary variable was created, no additional storage space or instructions would have to be generated.

The third pass was a straightforward code generation pass.

This shows that with a rather simple scheme, a global flow analysis routine can be written that works very well for well-structured programs.

This technique has also been used more recently in an extended form, in the SIMPL-X1 compiler, which Zelkowitz mentioned earlier.

ZELKOWITZ: Since SIMPL has only the **if**, **case**, and **while** constructs, an extension to the above technique for FORTRAN allows for efficient global flow analysis.

The algorithm used for this optimizer was based upon a recursive descent scheme (120). As with the Gear FORTRAN optimizer, three passes were needed. The first two passes were executed sequentially one block at a time, while the third-pass code generator generated code after all optimization had been completed.

In the first pass, every time a block was encountered (**while** statement, **then** part of an **if** statement, **else** part of an **if** statement, or one of the blocks in a **case** statement), the optimizer called itself recursively to first optimize the inner block. Upon entry, it created a change vector similar to the Gear FORTRAN optimizer. When it reached the end of the block, it immediately scanned the block backwards removing invariant expressions and common subexpressions. After reaching the beginning of the block, the change vector was added to the vector of the outer block and the invariant expressions were added to this outer block for further optimization. The optimizer then continued with the statement following the inner block.

In this case, since SIMPL has no **goto** statement, this algorithm is equivalent to the global flow analysis algorithms mentioned for FORTRAN optimizers. In this case, however, it is not necessary to implement routines to compute the loop structure of the program. This loop structure is apparent by the recursive nature of the nested control structures. This algorithm is both efficient and easy to program.

In order to bypass some of the problems that were encountered by the above project, a new project is underway to improve the optimizer (121). In this case, Hecht is creating a call graph to indicate which procedures call which procedures. If the optimizer then proceeds by optimizing those procedures that call no others, it is not necessary to assume that a procedure can modify any global variable. This method will allow for optimizing most global variables across procedure calls.

It seems clear that the full benefit of structured programming in terms of program efficiency and optimization potential will be realized only through the use of compilers purpose-built for structured programming.

ZELKOWITZ: The efficiency of such optimizers is leading to the development of new techniques that are tailored to structured programs and to structured programming languages. Rosen (122) has defined a technique that assumes that a program is decomposable into a set of one-in, one-out control structures. That is, his technique assumes that any program may be decomposed into structures of the form

$$C(S_1, \ldots, S_K)$$

where the S_1 through S_K are other structures. (Note that this includes the one-in, one-out structures mentioned previously.) His algorithm computes usage information for each variable within each internal block and then passes it out to the enclosing block. Not only does he keep track of variables that are modified, but he also keeps track of which variables are 'live', that is, will be used again before being modified. This helps in allocating registers and in determing whether a calculation need be performed at all. The basic recursive descent nature of this process makes it quite efficient – more so than with classical flow analysis procedures. When random jumps (that is, **goto**s) are taken into account, his mechanism still works; however, it becomes progressively less efficient, becoming similar to previously used techniques. However, for a structured programming language, or a well-structured program in any language, the technique is quite practical.

The implications of optimization for language design are discussed

in detail elsewhere (page 31).

CONCLUSION

Given suitable languages for structured programming and adequate compilers for them, structured programming should provide scope for more effective optimization techniques.

ZELKOWITZ: As Knuth has stated (116), current optimization techniques already come reasonably close to optimal program execution – for a given algorithm – while his experience has shown that modifying the algorithm can improve the program more than optimization. This suggests that optimizers will not get much better than the best ones of today without some major breakthroughs in optimization technology. Better execution characteristics will depend upon more efficient program algorithms.

Structured programming, however, is one technique that can improve the execution characteristics of a program. The disciplined approach forces the programmer to think more about a program than would otherwise be the case. The few examples that do exist seem to indicate that 'restricting' oneself to structured programming does not lead to inefficient programs and, in fact, the exact opposite may be the case.

Another point is that structured programs allow for efficient optimization possibilities. Only two passes through a program are needed to discover the block structure and eliminate common subexpressions and loop-invariant calculations. This would add minimal time onto the normal compilation time. Optimizers would be cheaper to use and easier to implement. As a corollary to this, with standard optimization being cheaper, more exotic schemes can be tried to get still better code than is now possible.

In any case, both optimization and structured programming do not seem to be going at cross purposes. Although the available data is not conclusive, it does indicate that one need not sacrifice one for the other. In fact, structured programming can be seen as an enhancement to existing optimization possibilities.

PROGRAM TRANSFORMATION

INTRODUCTION

One of the basic ideas of structured programming is the greater emphasis on clarity in programming. In the past, clarity has often been sacrificed to efficiency. For example, it used to be common practice to recommend to would-be programmers that the essence of their new art was to code an algorithm as efficiently as possible. To this end, techniques such as the avoidance of common subexpressions, self-modifying code, and arbitrarily chosen subroutines were advocated. Such practices led almost inevitably to obscure programs that were very difficult, especially for other people, to modify.

To some extent, the availability of optimizing compilers reduces the necessity for such obscure programming techniques; the programmer can leave common subexpressions or even loop-invariant code in his program if it helps to make the logic easier to understand because he knows the optimizer will recast the program to make it more efficient.

A development of this idea is that the whole program should be written with clarity and correctness as the main concern and transformations specified that could help the system to make the algorithm more efficient without endangering its correctness.

KNUTH (310): Once we have a suitable language, we will be able to have what seems to be emerging as the programming system of the future: an interactive *program-manipulation system*, analogous to the many symbol-manipulation systems which are presently undergoing extensive development and experimentation. We are gradually learning about program transformations, which are more complicated than formula manipulations but really not very different....

Darlington and Burstall (020) describe a system which removes some recursions from a LISP-like language (curiously, without introducing any **gotos**), and which also does some conversion of data structures (from sets to lists or bit strings) and some restructuring of a program by combining similar loops. I later discovered that program manipulation is just part of a much more ambitious project undertaken by Cheatham and Wegbreit (314); another paper about source-code optimizations has also recently appeared (050). Since LISP programs are easily manipulated as LISP data objects, there has also been a rather extensive development of similar ideas in this domain, notably by Warren Teitelman (315,316). The time is clearly ripe for program-manipulation systems, and a great deal of further work suggests itself.

The programmer using such a system will write his beautifully-structured, but possibly inefficient, program; then he will interactively specify transformations that make it efficient. Such a system will be much more powerful and reliable than a completely automatic one. We can also imagine the system manipulating measurement statistics concerning how much of the total running time is spent in each statement, since the programmer will want to know which parts of his program deserve to be optimized, and how much effect an optimization will really have. The original program should be retained along with the transformation specifications, so that it can be properly understood and maintained as time passes. This idea certainly isn't my own; it is so exciting I hope that *everyone* soon becomes aware of its possibilities.

BURSTALL and DARLINGTON: Our work is based on the idea that much of the difficulty in writing and modifying programs derives from the attempt to make them efficient, not just by good low-level coding but by the very structure of the algorithm chosen. It suggests an approach to programming in which an initial program is written with all the emphasis on clarity and this is then transformed systematically into one of acceptable efficiency. Such a policy requires the use of programming languages of a much simpler structure than current widely-used programming languages, in order to make such transformations practicable. We are encouraged that a number of people are taking this general view and hope that it will ultimately lead to cheaper and more reliable programming methods.

TRANSFORMATION TECHNIQUES

BURSTALL and DARLINGTON: The transformation rules that are needed are:

1 *definition*: add a definition defining some new function symbol;

2 *instantiation*: substitute some expression for a variable;

3 *unfolding*: replace some call to a function by its definition;

4 *abstraction*: factoring out some common subexpression and introducing **where**;

5 *folding*: replace some instance of the definition of a function by a call to it;

We may add an extra rule, not needed in our example (page 164):

4a *use of rewrite lemmas*: use some known facts such as the associativity or commutativity of multiplication to rewrite some subexpression.

Folding is the key transformation since it can introduce new recursive calls. It is the goal of the whole process and to avoid combinatorially explosive search we use lemmas or abstraction only when they enable us to achieve a fold. In fact they can economically be combined with the search for a fold.

The rules are used in the order given above. They involve human help in

1 providing definitions;
2 suggesting suitable instantiations;
3 supplying useful lemmas like the associativity of multiplication.

The use of these techniques is illustrated by Burstall and Darlington

in their paper (page 161) by means of some simple examples.

APPLICATIONS OF TRANSFORMATION

BURSTALL and DARLINGTON: An optimizing compiler accepts an algorithm (presumably a sensible one) represented as a program in a high-level language and converts it into good machine code, making computational economies and using machine resources to advantage. But where does this sensible algorithm come from? It is probably rather a complex entity quite difficult to reason about. We take the point of view that it may often be seen as an optimized version of a much simpler algorithm, but optimized in a more radical sense involving major changes in the loop/recursion structure.

Some common situations like this would be:

1. two loops (or recursions) in sequence which have essentially the same control (for example, they both count from 1 up to n) and whose bodies may be combined to yield a single loop;

2. two loops (or recursions) in which the first creates a data structure which the second takes to pieces, where it may again be possible to combine these with elimination of the intermediate data structure;

3. generate-and-test programs where the testing may be 'promoted' into the generation process, and where earlier testing will often avoid unnecessary generation;

4. converting a recursive program to an iterative one.

Examples would be

- in searches where a single successful test may terminate the whole generation process;

- generation of 'all x such that P' and each x is generated from a 'father' $f(x)$ such that x only has P if its father has P, in which case if an element does not have P we do not need to generate its sons.

It turns out that a considerable number of algorithms which we have examined can be derived, using just our transformations, from much simpler algorithms. When inventing algorithms ourselves we may often think in a similar way, considering some naive algorithm and then using some programming tricks from our repertoire to transform it into a more sensible one.

We do not see how to carry out such transformations entirely automatically; even though our folding, abstraction and unfolding rules can be automated, it is still necessary to supply the machine with new definitions, with possible instantiations and sometimes with useful lemmas. However we have been able to program a semi-automatic system which does all the laborious work of the transformations, given the user assistance in the form just mentioned. The system performs satisfactorily on the Fibonacci problem and on other more complex examples.

TRANSFORMATION AS AN OPTIMIZING TECHNIQUE

Though the transformation technique described by Burstall and Darlington seems a very promising idea, it is as yet still a long way from being of practical benefit.

BURSTALL and DARLINGTON: The properties of our transformation technique are as follows:

1 It preserves correctness so that if we start off with a correct program we will obtain a new one which is also correct.

2 It does not necessarily preserve termination; the new program may fail to terminate on data for which the original program does terminate. This means we need either a separate correctness proof or else some restrictions on folding to ensure preservation of termination.

3 It does not guarantee an improvement; however one may see informally that if the **where**-abstraction and rewrite lemmas lead to faster computation then the overall transformation

including folding will do so.

4 The transformation system is not uni-directional and there is usually more than one possible next move in the transformation process; however rather severely restrained strategies seem to lead to good results.

Given this lack of theoretical reassurance the reader will hardly be convinced that the method is interesting by the two small examples given here. If we have awakened his curiosity he may care to look at the rather more impressive examples in (217). He will also find there further discussion of the properties of the method and strategies for applying it. The revised version describes our computer implementation of the method which demands from the user only a set of equations, any auxiliary equations he wishes, guidance on instantiation and any rewrite lemmas which he may consider useful. This is an experimental implementation and we do not consider our method a practical optimizing tool.

Translation

INTRODUCTION
- The role of translation in optimization
- Language processing
- Empirical studies of programs

COMPILATION AND INTERPRETATION
- Introduction
- Relative merits of compilation and interpretation
- Combining compilation and interpretation

OPTIMIZING COMPILER TECHNIQUES
- Introduction
- Machine-dependent optimizations
- Architecture-dependent optimizations
- Architecture-independent optimizations

SELECTIVE OPTIMIZATION
- Introduction
- Programmer-supplied feedback
- Automated feedback

CONCLUSION
- The need for compiler optimization
- Optimization as an aid to clearer programming
- Limitations in compiler optimization

INTRODUCTION

THE ROLE OF TRANSLATION IN OPTIMIZATION

In the narrow view, program optimization is thought of as belonging almost exclusively to the translation phase in a program's life-cycle. More particularly, optimization is seen as a set of techniques for converting a given source text into faster, more compact machine code than would otherwise be achieved. Optimization of this kind is normally provided as a compile-time option, either by a special optimizing compiler, or more frequently, by a switch-selected optimization pass in a single compiler.

If this narrow kind of optimization is regarded as the only avenue of program improvement (that is, if the program development and program execution phases are ignored), many opportunities for significant improvement will be missed. Furthermore, even at the translation phase, there is much more to optimization than merely applying the standard techniques used in optimizing compilers. Other important issues, examined in more detail later in this section, include such issues as the different trade-offs of compilation and interpretation, the use of mixed compilation/interpretation methods, the possibility of taking account of a program's run-time behaviour during its translation, etc.

Two topics warrant a brief preliminary treatment, since they underlie much of the discussion later in this section.

First, some understanding is required, at least in general terms, of the translatory process by which a source program in a high-level language is converted into an equivalent machine code program.

Secondly, many of the most important developments in program optimization stem from the results of empirical studies of typical programs, and some of these results are summarized later.

LANGUAGE PROCESSING

The translation of a high-level source program into executable machine code involves several component processes. These are shown schematically in Figure 1, which is adapted from (300).

It should be noted that the diagram is necessarily stylized and, in practice, many of the processes that are shown separately are merged together. In addition, the two optimization stages shown in the diagram are not of course essential parts of the translation process; they are included in order to show at what stage such optimizations are typically performed.

The tasks that are performed at each of the various stages are summarized very briefly below:

1 *Lexical analysis is the process of scanning the source text and tendering it in a form more suitable for the later phases. The precise nature of what is done at this stage is to some extent language-dependent. In some languages, certain elements can be recognized by purely lexical rules and hence some of the phase recognition can be performed during lexical analysis; for example, statements in BASIC can be uniquely identified by the first three letters. In other languages, more complex rules, involving contextual information, are required and these normally involve syntactic analysis; for example, in FORTRAN, DO 17 I = 1 could be the start of a DO statement but could be an assignment statement.*

   Another task commonly performed during lexical analysis is the removal of redundant blanks from the source text.

   Although lexical analysis is a fairly straightforward process (possibly occupying, for example, less than 10% of a compiler's total code) it can account for as much as 50% of compilation time. (However, it should be noted that these figures are by no means

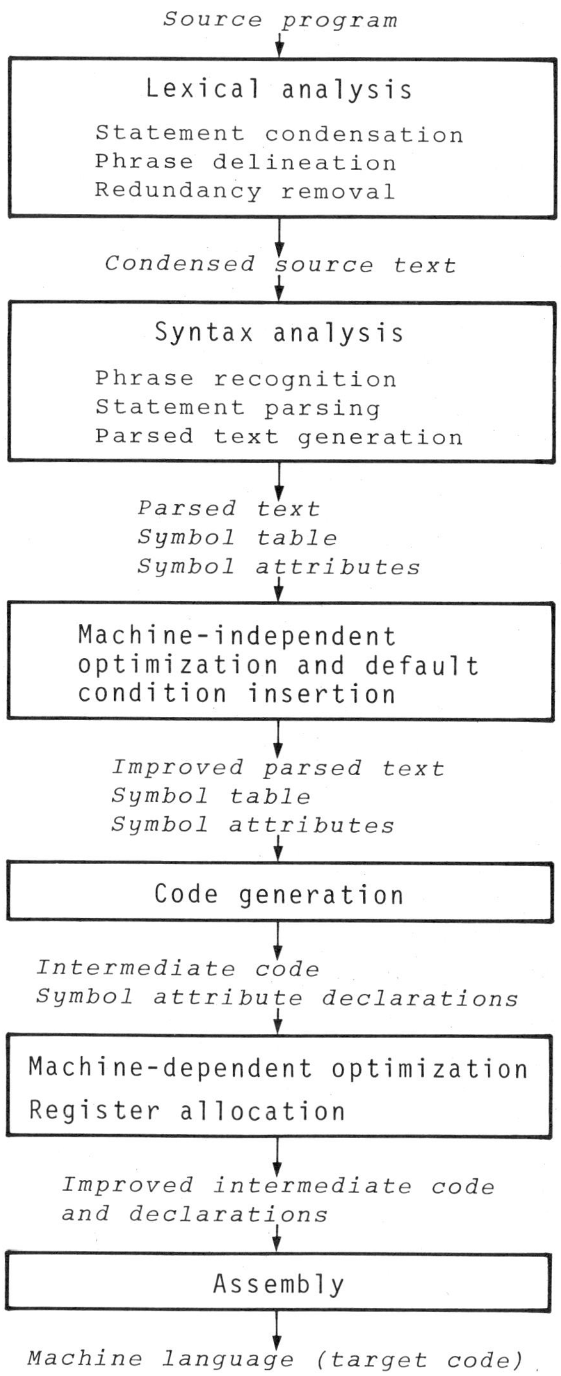

Figure 1: Steps in the translation of a high-level language into machine code

universal. Not only are such factors implementation-dependent, they are also liable to wide fluctuations as a result of modifications to other parts of the compiler. For example, Darden and Heller (301) report how a compiler was modified to decrease the time spent on code generation from 69% of the total right down to 4.2%. As a result of this change, other parts of the compiler that had before been responsible for a negligible proportion of the compilation time began to assume more significance. Lexical analysis, for example, had been responsible for only about 6% of the original compiler's time but after several other parts of the compiler had been improved, its proportion rose to 45% and so it became itself a candidate for the next phase of optimization.)

2 *Syntactic analysis* is the task of transforming the condensed source text produced by the lexical analyser into a form (the parsed text) from which code can be generated by a later process. The parsed text can be conveniently represented as a tree structure, though in practice linearized forms (for example, reverse Polish strings) are frequently used.

3 After syntactic analysis, some *machine-independent optimization* can be performed. The techniques used and the effects of this optimization are discussed in detail later.

4 Code generation is the stage where the actual translation is performed, the parsed text produced by the syntax analyser being converted into machine code. Though this translation is the prime function of a compiler, it normally occupies only a small proportion of a modern compiler's time (often as little as 10%); even with extensive optimization on features built in, translation does not take as long, for example, as lexical analysis.

5 The code produced by the code generator can, as implied above, be improved by applying *machine-dependent optimization* to exploit special features of the target machine. Details of these optimization techniques are given later.

6 The improved code can then be finally *assembled* into executable machine code.

EMPIRICAL STUDIES OF PROGRAMS

Several studies have been published to show what actual programs are really like. The most influential of these, by Knuth (041)*, was a survey of almost 500 FORTRAN programs, by both professional programmers and students. The results have very important implications for compiler designers, especially in terms of the cost/benefits of various optimization strategies. Knuth's findings are summarized below:*

1. *Less than 4% of the code accounted for over 50% of the execution time in typical programs.*

2. *About half of the statements were assignment statements. When measured dynamically (that is, as a proportion of the number of statements executed rather than the number of statements in the program text), the proportion of assignment statements was even higher, about two-thirds of the statements executed being assignments.*

3. *About two-thirds of these assignment statements are of the simplest type, replacements of the form A = B (where B is a simple variable or constant). A high proportion of the remaining assignments involved simple modifications (that is involving a single operator) to the same variable, such as A = A + 1.*

These results suggest that

- *compiler writers would be well advised to base their compiling strategies on the assumption that compilers spend most of their time doing extremely simple things;*

- *if the compiler does not take into account the frequency with which various parts of the program are executed, it will spend most of its time and effort on code whose improvement will be insignificant in terms of the total run time.*

Some current work based on these ideas is discussed in more detail later in this section.

COMPILATION AND INTERPRETATION

INTRODUCTION

There are two basic approaches to the translation of high-level source languages into executable machine code: compilation and interpretation.

With compilation, the whole source program is first translated, by a process similar to that described earlier (p 70), into machine code. This object code can be loaded into the computer and executed each time the program is required again.

With interpretation, the two activities of translation and execution alternate continuously; each statement of the program is translated and then immediately executed. This is normally achieved by a two-part process; the statement is recognized and then a call is made to the subroutine that corresponds to that statement type. Each subroutine is a set of compiled object code that will perform the action associated with a particular statement in the language.

Despite the obvious differences between compilation and interpretation, the two translation techniques are by no means mutually exclusive.

BROADBENT (302): At their extreme positions, the two techniques are readily distinguishable. Compilation involves the production of a sequence of macros and subroutines in the machine code of the computer on which execution is to occur; interpretation proceeds by a program examining each statement of the source text and performing there and then the operations required. However, most interpretive systems involve a translation from the source text into an intermediate code (the object or target code) which is then subject to interpretation. Also, you might argue that many of the functions required in a secure implementation of, say, FORTRAN, like array bound checking, are basically interpretive functions rather than compile and execute functions, even if they happen to be implemented actually by means of macros in the object code, or perhaps subroutine calls in the object code.

In addition, certain language features cannot be compiled but must be interpreted. For example, the use of variable FORMAT statements in FORTRAN, where the details are unknown at compilation time, requires that part of the compiler is incorporated into the object code to interpret the associated input/output statements. Similarly, languages, such as ALGOL, that require dynamic storage allocation need a certain amount of run-time interpretation.

RELATIVE MERITS OF COMPILATION AND INTERPRETATION

There are advantages and disadvantages associated with both techniques and, as with all trade-offs, the choice of which technique to use for a specific application depends on particular circumstances.

BROWN (P J): The relative merits of compilation and interpretation can be summarized as follows:

1 When a program is run, compiled code runs faster than interpreted code. The relative speed varies enormously, but a factor of ten would be typical.

2 Interpretation needs less storage than compilation, even allowing for the fact that the interpreter must be present at run time. Interpretation is particularly good when extensive error checking and good diagnostics are required.

3 For some languages (for example PAL), operations such as type checking cannot be performed until run time. For languages with these features, it is impossible to compile code in advance so (total or partial) interpretation is vital. In general, these languages are rare; they probably have less than 1% of the market.

BROADBENT (302): The advantages for interpretation include:

1 *Easier alteration to a running program.* This can be either at the statement level or at the procedure level. Because of the retention of a fair amount of source program oriented information in the code string generated by a preprocessor in an interpretive system, there is sufficient information around for one to be able to type in a new statement, or procedure, and have it incorporated in place of some existing code. The rebinding can be carried out when the procedure is first activated.

2 *Reduction in object code size.* The principal situation in which there is scope for reduction in object code size is when the types in the language are not known at run time and you have to include code in line with the object program to do type checking. If these type checking operations are done interpretively, they become part of the interpreter and therefore are not duplicated throughout the various points in the object program at which type checking is thought to be necessary.

3 *Greater diagnostic capability.* The object code string for an interpretive system is much closer to the source program than is the case with compiled code and so much of the information needed for diagnostics is more easily obtainable.

4 *Easier object program portability.* I am not saying that interpretation enables you to cart your source program round from one installation to another with no problems. What you have to do is to write a minimal interpreter on the next installation, in the programming language that is available on that installation, and then your object program, not your source program, is transportable.

5 *Simplification of the translator.* Because much is done at run time that is normally done at compile time, for example type checking, the translator itself is greatly reduced in size.

BROWN (P J): In deciding whether to compile or to interpret, the software designer has to trade optimization of speed against optimization of storage. Sometimes the decision is an easy one: for a BASIC system designed for short student programs on a very small machine, interpretation is clearly the answer; for COBOL or FORTRAN systems that run on a large machine, compilation is obviously preferable. At other times, the decision is a difficult one. If one is designing a BASIC system to run in 16-32K words of storage on a machine with slow backing storage, or even with no backing storage at all, does one compile or interpret? One section of the potential user market wants fast execution while another wants to be able to run long programs. Neither compilation nor interpretation will satisfy both sets of users.

Moreover, the relative merits have tended to change with technological advances.

ROSIN (302): In the early and middle 1950s, on anything but the very largest machines, many programs were processed through interpretation, not through direct execution on machines. This was not simply a vogue; the machines generally were not well designed for the kinds of applications that were emerging. Most of the small and medium machines, for example, did not have floating point facilities.

Another problem with those early machines was that storage was very expensive. Typically, there would be at least two levels of storage; there would be a relatively small amount of relatively expensive, relatively fast storage, 1000 words or 2000 words perhaps, and then there would be a much larger, much slower, much less expensive, backing storage. One way to use such a storage system is to roll things in and out of the small storage. Another way to use it, which turned out to be eminently reasonable for a large number of applications, is to write a program in the small, fast storage that simulates a hopefully reasonable, application-oriented system and then write a program in the language of that system that resides on the backing storage, an interpreter. The discrepancy in size and, in particular, cost of storage, is what tended to lead people in that direction. Indeed, if you look at one of the most popular and heavily used interpreters of that era, the Bell interpretive system on the IBM 650, you find that lack of storage was their primary motivation for construction of an interpreter.

In the mid-1960s, the justification for the use of interpretation changed considerably. People came to feel that compilation was the only way to go....

However, in the mid-1960s, interpreters were still used rather heavily. They were used to simulate machines. IBM used them to simulate System/360s, for example. Other computer manufacturers did the same sort of thing. It is safe to say that in the installation of an IBM 360/30 or 360/40, all the programs were run interpretively. Interpreters were really the only way to run programs in such small and perhaps medium systems. Also, the entire IBM System/370 product line is microprogrammed, if I understand correctly.

We have a dictum that tells us this trend may continue. If one wants to build a small, cheap, slow machine, one has a problem. You cannot go to the chip manufacturer or the memory manufacturer to buy small, cheap, slow components; such components do not exist. Try, for example, to buy 10-microsecond core. It would perhaps not be a bad replacement for disk if it were cheap enough. But you cannot find it; it does not exist. Clearly, the idea of anybody putting together a chip in which the gate times are slower than 50 nanoseconds is incredible; as a matter of fact, 50 nanoseconds is the upper bound of respectability, any kind of respectability. So, if you want to build a small, cheap, slow machine, you have to buy a small number of relatively expensive (although the cost is going down), fast chips, and write programs on these to simulate your small, cheap, slow machine. This is the only choice you have.

So, we find again that interpretation, the simulation of one machine on another, and in some cases the simulation of desk calculators, is indeed running rampant. Interpreters are here to stay.

Various developments are now tending to bring interpretation into increased favour:

1 *Microprogramming makes practical the idea of fast interpreters implemented directly in the firmware. Early machines of this type were designed to interpret a single language, some by hard-wired techniques, others by microprogrammed interpreters. More*

recently, machines have been implemented that will directly interpret several high-level languages. This approach is typified by the pioneering Burroughs B1700. The influence of microprogramming on language processing is discussed in detail in the State of the Art Report Microprogramming and Systems Architecture (302).

2 *The increasing use of multiprogramming systems for the on-line development and testing of programs places much greater emphasis on extensive error reporting. Interpretation, with its much greater diagnostic capability, is well suited to an interactive mode of programming.*

Moreover, there is now a much greater appreciation of how compilation and interpretation can be effectively combined to get some of the best of both worlds.

COMBINING COMPILATION AND INTERPRETATION

In view of the fact that a small part of a typical program is responsible for most of the execution time, it seems possible, and attractive, to combine interpretation and compilation for the same program. If the part of the program that is responsible for most of the run time is compiled and the rest interpreted, little would be lost in terms of execution time and all the advantages of interpretation would still be obtained. In practice, however, the cost of developing both a compiler and an interpreter has tended to outweigh the potential advantages. In addition, there is a considerable problem of ensuring that the compiler and the interpreter remain compatible as modifications are made to one or the other.

A technique has been developed recently that avoids the disadvantages traditionally associated with combining compilation and interpretation. It is based partly on the idea of dynamic compiling.

BROWN (P J): The source program is first translated into an intermediate form as for interpretation. This intermediate form is divided into units that are natural for the language concerned. The unit might be a single statement or a basic block.

At run time, the intermediate form is not interpreted, but is taken one unit at a time, compiled into machine code, and then immediately executed. Thus instead of an interpreter there is a *code-generator* present at run-time. For example, consider the following BASIC program:

```
 10  LET X = 3
 20  GOTO 100
 30  ...
  .
  .
  .
100  LET Y = X + 1
```

If this program is divided into units of statements, the run-time sequence of events would be as follows. Statement 10 is compiled (from its intermediate form) and immediately executed; statement 20 is then compiled and executed; then statement 100 is compiled and executed.

On its own, dynamic compilation, far from achieving the best of both worlds, combines the worst of both. It is even slower than ordinary interpretation and will also require more storage. However, if the idea is extended a little, the disadvantages no longer apply.

BROWN (P J): Assume that there is a fixed area of storage available. Then at run time, this storage will contain:

1 the source program in its intermediate form,
2 the code-generator
3 an unused area, which we will call *workspace*

The technique of *throw-away compiling* uses this workspace. The source program is dynamically compiled, as described above, but the compiled code for each unit is kept in the workspace and cross-referenced with the source. If a unit is executed a second time, and its compiled code is still in the workspace there is no need to re-compile it. Instead the previously compiled code will be re-executed. If, at any stage, the workspace becomes full up some or all of the compiled code must be *thrown away*, and if this is ever needed again it must be re-compiled. We will use the term *throw-away algorithm* to denote the algorithm that manages the workspace.

With throw-away compiling, if there is enough room to compile all the units of the program that are executed on a given run (not necessarily the whole program), then nothing will ever be compiled more than once and the program will run almost as fast as an ordinary compiled program would. If, on the other hand, there is insufficient workspace to compile everything (and thus an ordinary compiler would be useless, unless there was some overlaying capability) the program will still run but will run more slowly. In the extreme case, where there is almost no workspace, it will run as slowly as ordinary interpretation. Thus the merit of throw-away compiling is that it adapts itself to make use of whatever workspace is available and thus optimizes program performance.

It is perhaps in the area of error diagnosis that the chief advantage of throw-away compiling lies.

BROWN (P J): It is an increasing opinion that implementations of programming languages should check for all possible run-time errors, including such things as out-of-bound subscripts, variables used but not set, underflow and overflow, dangling references, stack overflow, etc. Moreover, error detection must be supported by good facilities for reporting errors in meaningful terms, pinpointing where they occur in the source program, and possibly recovering from them. Thus, a good error diagnosis system consists of error detection, error reporting, and possibly error recovery. All three are difficult to achieve.

It is often said that interpreters are better at error diagnosis than compilers. This is not completely true. The real problem is that compilers do not generate code that performs good error diagnosis because this makes programs much bigger, with the result that some may be too big to run. With throw-away compiling there are no limits on the size of compiled code and so this problem is removed (though programs with full checking will, of course, run slower than those without).

The easing of the problem of error diagnosis is one of the greatest benefits of throw-away compiling.

The performance of the system can be illustrated by the results of an initial project, where the technique was used for a BASIC compiler.

BROWN (P J): It appears that, if enough workspace is available to compile the whole program without any throwing away, then throw-away compilation runs at the same speed as traditional compilation and running. (Throw-away compiling gains by not compiling units that are never executed on a given run, but loses through the need for extra housekeeping.) Figure 1 shows how the performance of throw-away compiling deteriorates as the size of workspace is reduced to various fractions of that needed for dynamic compilation of every used unit of the program.

Percentage of necessary workspace available	*Total run time*
100	100
80	177
60	282
40	369
20	496

Figure 1: Degradation of performance as a result of reduced workspace

Thus, even when only one-fifth of the necessary workspace is available, the average program only runs about five times slower than a totally pre-compiled one. One would expect the performance of an interpreter to be worse than this. However, it must be re-emphasized that the figures quoted are approximate ones, subject to experimental error.

The techniques and advantages of throw-away compiling are discussed in more detail by Brown (page 153), who here summarizes its potential.

BROWN (P J): Clearly, throw-away compiling is not the answer for all compilers on all machines. However, when there are severe absolute constraints on program size, throw-away compiling can adapt itself both to run programs that are bigger than a compiler could deal with and to run most programs much faster than an interpreter would. It should be ideal for small time-sharing systems and, increasingly more important, simple microprocessor systems. Moreover, by improving the economics of error diagnosis, it helps make software more reliable.

Another project that combines an interpreter and a compiler is the

Adaptive FORTRAN system developed by Hansen and Wulf, but the most significant characteristic of their system is the feedback of run-time performance data into the compiler. Their system is discussed in detail elsewhere (page 99).

OPTIMIZING COMPILER TECHNIQUES

INTRODUCTION

The standard techniques that are used in most optimizing compilers have been well-known for many years, and some of them were incorporated into the first FORTRAN compiler over 20 years ago.

SCHNECK: Optimization has been around since the very first compilers were produced. For example, in the FORTRAN I compiler produced by IBM some 25% of the code was devoted solely to optimization. The reason for such a high percentage was simply that, in those days, there were plenty of people around who said that it was impossible to write a compiler that would translate high-level language statements or (to use the words of IBM publicity at that time) mathematical formulae into machine language, with anything nearly resembling the efficiency that could be obtained by a hand coder or assembly language programmer....

At that time most programming was done in machine language and a compiler which offered convenience at the expense of machine time would not have been acceptable. The following quotation from the IBM specification reveals that the convenience of the new language was believed insufficient to cause its widespread acceptance.

> "... FORTRAN may apply complex, lengthy techniques in coding a problem which the human coder would have neither the time nor inclination to derive or apply. Thus, in many cases, FORTRAN may actually produce a better program than the normal human coder would be apt to produce." ...

The FORTRAN team consisted of 13 people and claimed to have produced this compiler in six months. We have gone backwards a lot since then, because I am sure that they could not do that today. Of those 13, there were three people who essentially did nothing but work on optimization and, as I said earlier, 25% of the compiler was devoted to optimization.

These techniques are summarized here and discussed in more detail by Schneck (page 327) and in several specialized books and articles, notably (004).

There are several ways of classifying these optimizing techniques but Schneck's classification will be used here:

1 *machine-dependent techniques*
2 *architecture-dependent techniques*
3 *architecture-independent techniques*

MACHINE-DEPENDENT OPTIMIZATIONS

Machine-dependent optimizations are those that exploit some characteristic of the instruction set of a particular machine in such a way that the time or space occupied by the program can be reduced. Such optimizations tend to be very local, usually confined to short sections of the object code. Precisely because they are machine-dependent, there is comparatively little to say about such techniques. A few typical instances are discussed here to illustrate the general nature of such optimizations.

SCHNECK: The FORTRAN I compiler was originally written for the IBM 704 machine, which was a single-instruction machine with many peculiarities (some of which still exist on the IBM 360), such as the differences between floating-point and fixed-point instruction sets, and the way in which registers were used. A series of multiplications could not be performed on that machine without intervening instructions to move the answer back into the multiplier register. An algorithm was devised by Sheridan (223) to handle this sort of moving around. The algorithm also went further; in fact, it looked to see whether or not a sequence of multiplications coexisted with a sequence of divisions.

If so, it permuted the input so that division followed multiplication as often as possible. It turned out that these two processes were inverse not only in the mathematical sense, but also in their handling of registers; so that if a multiply preceded a divide and was followed by a multiply, no extra instructions were necessary.

That was perhaps the very first and lowest-level machine dependent optimization first applied in a compiler. Some years later, McKeeman (224) pointed out that optimizations of that sort could be handled in a way which made them a little less integral to the compiler code proper, but rather enabled them to be accomplished by a two-stage process. The first process compiled code for a conceptualized machine, which in fact may not exist at all. The second stage of processing took that conceptual code and tailored it for a specific machine. It did so by sliding a window past the stream of code which was generated, looking for specific pattern matches. If a known pattern of code was found, then a substitution was made, and the optimized code was output in place of the initially generated code. McKeeman called this 'peephole analysis', that is, he viewed the window as a little peephole, with a very local view, ignoring the wider context.

For example, in a simple compiler very many superfluous STORE instructions are generated. If the item being stored is also the subject of a LOAD in the very next instruction, then it is clear, if there is no label on the load instruction, that the LOAD need not be generated. A global analysis may be necessary to determine that the STORE need not be generated either, but McKeeman's method was able at least to get rid of the LOAD instruction.

ARCHITECTURE-DEPENDENT OPTIMIZATIONS

The architecture-dependent optimizations also rely for their effectiveness on exploiting the characteristics of the underlying hardware, but in a much more general way than the machine-dependent ones. The features that they depend on are higher-level considerations of the general architecture of the machine and so are common to large classes of different computers.

Schneck distinguishes three examples of such general features:

1. *machines with n accumulators;*
2. *machines that can execute independent instructions in parallel;*
3. *machines that can operate on multiple data streams with a single instruction.*

The *n*-accumulator machine

The first class of architecture-dependent optimizations relate to machines with multiple accumulators (or, more accurately, multiple registers, since there is often only a single adder).

SCHNECK: Straightforward code generation of expressions involving non-commutative operations poses a special difficulty for a one-accumulator computer. In an expression such as $(a+b)/(c-d)$, the denominator should be computed first so that it is available for division when the numerator is computed and is in the accumulator. Anderson (226) discusses a technique which implements this procedure and does away with the need for storing and recovering the values of many subexpressions. This is accomplished by looking ahead and delaying code generation for the left side expression of a non-commutative operator until code generation for the right side occurs. On a multi-accumulator machine the technique is also valuable because it decreases the number of registers required to evaluate an expression.

Nakata (227) has extended the procedure to handle n accumulators. The procedure is enhanced by the fact that some heuristic observations are included to make the output similar to ordinary coding practices. The programming problem of using a minimum number of accumulators is equivalent to a graph-theoretic tree transformation proposed by Redziejowski (228). An algorithm for performing the tree transformation is proposed, proved, and shown to be equivalent to that of Nakata. An investigation into the properties of tree-structure representations of arithmetic expressions by Schneider (229) yields the number of registers required. In particular, for k nested parenthetical subexpressions with n operator precedence levels, $(k+1)\ n+1$ registers are required.

Finkelstein (230) describes a technique, aptly named 'deferred store', which eliminates much unnecessary storing and loading of partial results within loops on multiple-register machines ('register' is used here to indicate either an accumulator or index register). When an assignment statement is executed, the accumulator is not actually stored in the result variable. Instead, other registers are used in place of those containing data for deferred stores. If a result variable is to be modified before the deferred store has been performed, the value of the variable is in place and need not be fetched. The following example indicates a common situation where the deferred store saves a significant amount of time:

$$\sum_{i=1}^{n} a_i$$

```
      DO 1  I = 1,N
    1 SUM = SUM + A(I)
```

A special case of the n-accumulator machine is one where the accumulator is the top element of a push-down stack. The Burroughs 5000 and English Electric KDF9 are examples of such a machine. Randell and Russell (231) describe a one-pass procedure for translation of arithmetic expressions into Reverse Polish form suitable for a stack machine. An interesting point is their architecture-independent optimization of calculating a constant during compilation when both operands are constants.

Parallel instructions

The second class of architecture-dependent optimizations are those related to machines, such as the CDC 6600, that can execute several instructions in parallel. This capability is sometimes referred to as 'micro-parallelism'. Such machines are in effect sequential but the several units that comprise the machine can operate independently and simultaneously on the stream of data as it arrives.

SCHNECK: The CDC 6600 computer was the first commercially available machine able to overlap the execution of several instructions. This class of computer, capable of parallel instruction execution, has independent functional units which are able to operate simultaneously. The programmer (or compiler) need not be explicitly aware of the parallel execution capability. It will be used when possible. However, if the instructions are ordered to maximize parallel execution, a performance advantage of up to a factor of three can be obtained. Allard, Wolf and Zemlin (232) describe the parallel capabilities of the 6600 and briefly mention the speed advantage gained by reordering instructions. Thorlin (233) describes the technique used in CDC FORTRAN, based on a PERT-like analysis of dependency and timing for ordering 6600 instructions. The independent functional units of the machine are kept busy by placing unrelated instructions together and by sequencing the longest activities first. A similar instruction scheduling technique was implemented by Blum *et al* (234) in the IBM FORTRAN-H compiler. A dependency array is constructed which defines the area within which each instruction may be moved. A weight is assigned to each instruction by adding a base weight (a function of the instruction time) and the weight of every instruction which is dependent on it. Instructions are then ordered by decreasing weight.

The improvement attainable by instruction reordering is limited by a parallelism inherent in the original instruction sequence. Stone (235) summarized techniques which may be used to translate arithmetic expressions to achieve a high degree of inherent parallelism. The process corresponds to a tree structure with minimal height. This is the opposite result from that of the previous section where minimizing the number of registers increased the tree height. Figure 1 (page 333) shows two different trees for evaluating the expression

A*B*C*D*E*F*G*H.

The first tree employs only one register for evaluating the expression, while the second results in the minimum evaluation time on a machine with at least four simultaneous multipliers. Because of the effects of data store/load instructions, this tree may not result in minimum time on machines with fewer multipliers. Figure 2 (page 333) shows two different sets of instructions for evaluating the expression corresponding to the two trees, and resulting in serial and parallel execution.

The general problem of minimizing the tree height of a set of expressions has been examined by Han (236). He describes a procedure for determining the minimum tree height of an expression. This can be used by a compiler as a measure of the degree of parallelism that can be obtained in a program. A method for attaining the maximum amount of parallel execution on a machine with a fixed number of processing units is given by Ramamoorthy and Gonzalez (237). They present a method for ordering subexpressions which indicates those expressions to be delayed in the event that not enough processing units are available to perform all computations in parallel.

Multiple data streams

The final class of architecture-dependent optimizations relate to machines that can perform the same operation on several data items. Such machines as ILLIAC IV, the CDC STAR (String and Array processor), and the Texas Instruments ASC (Advanced Scientific Computer) can be included in this category.

SCHNECK: The STAR is a pipeline computer, processing operands sequentially but with a high degree of overlap. The ILLIAC is a parallel computer, processing up to 64 operands simultaneously. The instruction sets of the two machines bear remarkable similarity, and high-level language programs must be designed from the same viewpoint for either machine....

The deliveries of commercial vector processor computers in 1974, the Texas Instruments ASC and the CDC STAR, have resulted in intense interest in the practical use and effectiveness of these systems. Research is continuing into the development of techniques to detect and generate vector operations from standard FORTRAN code. The ASC compiler implements these techniques and is able to discover virtually all code which may be processed by vector instructions. The compiler must consider not only the vector architecture, but also the fact that 1, 2, or 4 processors (pipelines) may be available on a system.... As things stand today, this is quite difficult, and in terms of execution time of the optimizer or the compiler, it takes a considerable amount of time. In fact, the Texas Instruments ASC machine often takes 20 minutes to compile a several-thousand-line FORTRAN program, whereas the 360, which it replaced, took about a minute for that same program.

The development of parallel architectures is examined in detail in the State of the Art Report Multiprocessor Systems (305).

ARCHITECTURE-INDEPENDENT OPTIMIZATION

In many respects the most interesting, and also the most powerful, class of optimizations are the architecture-independent kind. These are global in nature and are based on an analysis of the program structure. One of the purposes of this analysis is to derive information about the flow of control within the program. To this end the program is divided into blocks and probabilities are attached to the various interconnections to indicate the relative frequencies of execution.

This information has been derived by a variety of techniques:

1 *In the earliest FORTRAN optimizing compilers, simulation, based on a random number generator and programmer-supplied estimates (in FREQUENCY statements), was used. However, this was extremely time-consuming, often requiring about 15 minutes even though the compilation itself took only 2 or 3 minutes.*

2 *Matrix methods were used later but proved impractical as programs tended to grow in size and complexity.*

3 *Current analyses are based on the method of 'interval analysis' a graph-theoretic technique developed by Cocke and Allen* (005, 006,007,009,010,019).

Further details can be found in the papers of Schneck (page 327) and Hansen and Wulf (page 185).

The actual optimizing techniques are mainly concerned with reducing the number of times certain constructs need to be processed, typically by removing them altogether or by moving them to lower-frequency sections of the program.

LOVEMAN and FANEUF (306): With the available information, a number of program optimizations are performed. We present them here in a logical order, not necessarily the most efficient processing order:

- *Linearize array references*: Multi-dimensional arrays are replaced by appropriately sized vectors and the addressing calculation is made explicit. For example, assuming row-wise storage, if *A* is declared to be a $5 \times 4 \times 3$ array, *A* will be replaced by a vector *A'* of 60 elements and each reference to *A* of the form *A*(*I*,*J*,*K*) will be replaced by *A'*((*I*-1)*12 + (*J*-1)*3 + *K*), or A'(12**I* + 3**J* + *K* - 15). In making the addressing calculations explicit, they are exposed for later optimizations.

- *Constant propagation and computation*: For any assignment of a constant to a scalar variable *X*, all uses of this generation of *X* can be replaced by the constant. If the scalar *X* is a local variable and the assignment is not needed for a merge pseudo-generation, the assignment statement may be deleted. If all references to the scalar *X* are deleted, its definition may be removed from the symbol table. Some constant computation was performed when expressions were placed into canonical form. Constant computation is again performed during constant propagation whenever a variable use is replaced by a constant. Note that if this reduces the right hand side of an assignment to a constant, another constant propagation is necessary. It appears that constant propagation is a recursive process; in fact if the program is searched for assignments in block order we almost never produce a requirement for a new constant propagation where the assignment is 'upstream' of where we now are. The occasional exception is stacked for processing when the primary scan is complete. It is important to note that, in a cross compiler, constant computation must be done using target machine arithmetic and not using host machine arithmetic.

- *Dead code elimination*: As a result of constant propagation some assignment statements and data declarations may be eliminated. It may be that after constant computation some DO-loops can be determined as having exactly one iteration. In this case, the extraneous loop structure is eliminated (and also, perhaps, the loop variable). In some IF statements, the value of the predicate will now be TRUE or FALSE. This allows pruning of unreachable portions of the program. Since these transformations destroy the collected global information, they are all done together and the global information is recomputed.

- *Scalar propagation*: Assignments of the form $X \leftarrow Y$ for which only one generation of Y exists in the program can be eliminated and all uses of that generation of X can be replaced by Y.

- *Invariant code motion*: Computations which are invariant within a loop are moved to a point immediately between the loop entry. Loops are processed in lexical order and nests of loops are processed inside out: in other words in the lexical order of their end statements. A computation represented canonically as (op, X, Y) is loop-invariant if the generators of X and Y are not within the loop. This test is simple because of the block order: find the block number i of the first block in the loop, the block number j of the last block in the loop, and the block number k of the block containing the generation of A. The generation of X is not within the loop if $k < i$ or $k > j$.

- *Strength reduction*: Computations of the form $I * L$ where I is the loop variable and L is loop invariant are candidates for strength reduction. The assignment $t \leftarrow I_{init} * L$, where I_{init} is the value I takes on the first iteration of the loop, is placed before the loop, the use of $I * L$ is replaced by t, and the assignment $t \leftarrow t + L$ is inserted at the end of the loop.

- *Test replacement*: After strength reduction, if the loop variable has no explicit uses within the loop, replace the loop variable in the loop statement with the most frequently used variable generated by strength reduction. Incorporate its initial, increment, and final values into the loop statement.

- *Folding*: If for a generation $X \leftarrow$ *expression* there is only one use of X, and if the variables of *expression* do not have generations before the use of X, the generation can be deleted and the use of X replaced by the expression. This is done only within a flow block since testing the conditions globally is difficult and the payoff, globally, is low.

- *Common subexpression elimination*: The program is scanned in block order, and statements are scanned bottom up looking for candidate computations. A candidate computation is an operation with at least one scalar operand *X*. Given a candidate, the set of uses of the generator of the variable *X* is searched to find a set of possible common subexpressions; these are computations containing a use of the generator of the variable *X*, and with the same operator as the candidate computation. The set of possible common subexpressions is pruned by comparing the second operations with the second operand of the candidate computation. We have now found a set of common subexpressions. All of these are eliminated in favour of the generated variable *t* and the computation *t* ← *cse*, where *cse* is the candidate computation, is placed in an appropriate place. This assignment is placed in a block which is dominated by the generators of every variable in the *cse*, and which dominates every occurrence of the *cse*. There must be at least one such block, there may be several. The computation is put in the latest one (in block order) which is of lowest frequency (as measured by depth of loop nesting). The operations for which common subexpressions are compute are the common arithmetic, relational and logical ones, as well as functions (such as trigonometric) about which the system has knowledge. Since division is expensive, it is represented in the canonical form as a unary inversion operator. Thus common subexpression elimination will transform " ...*A/D* ... *B/D*..." into "*t* ← 1/*D* ...*A*t* ... *B*t* ...". The requirement for identical match is relaxed for the operations + and *. In these cases partial matches are allowed also. The search for a partial match is aided by the canonical form requirement that scalar appearances are ordered. Careful sign conventions in the canonical form allows *cse* to recognize, for example, that " ... *A-B* ... *B-A* ..." can be written "*t* ← *A-B* ... *t* ... -*t* ...". Because the check for identity occurs first, it is necessary to check generated statements for *cse* also. Consider the example:

$\ldots\ A + B + C\ \ldots$

$\ldots\ A + B + C\ \ldots$

$\ldots\ A + B + D\ \ldots$

$\ldots\ A + B + D\ \ldots$

$t_1 \leftarrow A + B + C$

$t_2 \leftarrow A + B + D$

$\ldots\ t_1\ \ldots$

$\ldots\ t_1\ \ldots$

$\ldots\ t_2\ \ldots$

$\ldots\ t_2\ \ldots$

$t_3 \leftarrow A + B$

$t_1 \leftarrow t_3 + C$

$t_2 \leftarrow t_3 + D$

$\ldots\ t_1\ \ldots$

$\ldots\ t_1\ \ldots$

$\ldots\ t_2\ \ldots$

$\ldots\ t_2\ \ldots$

The second transformation would not occur unless the generated statements were also processed.

Schneck illustrates the four commonest techniques by the simple program in Figure 1.

When such examples are seen in isolation the typical reaction is to wonder how the programmer could be so stupid in the first place. However, examples are invariably misleading in this way; they have to be simple so as not to obscure the principle. In practice, redundant code is rarely so obvious to the human reader. Such code in the program is very often left over after a previous modification, typically for debugging purposes, possibly by a different programmer.

Sample program:

```
      A=B+C
      Y=Y+1
      Z=C
      Q=(Z+B)*SIN(.7854)
      DO 1 I=1,100
1     P(I)=P(I)*(A+B)
```

Optimized program:

```
      A=B+C
      (1)
      (2)
      Q=A*.7071   (3) (4)
      T00001=A+B   (5)
      DO 1 I=1,100
1     P(I)=P(I)*T00001
```

1 *Elimination of dead variable*
2 *Elimination of dead variable, caused by* 3
3 *Common subexpression elimination*
4 *Constant propagation*
5 *Code motion*

Figure 1: Architecture-independent optimizations

SCHNECK: Dead variable elimination may seem a rather trivial optimization, but it can have a major impact. Very often one computes some value during testing of the program, to make sure that the program is running correctly or to track down where it has gone wrong. At the conclusion of debugging, the WRITE statement is removed, because it is no longer needed and it was cluttering up the output. However, the computation can get forgotten. Very often, the final computation is trivial, but the computations which support that, for instance earlier computations of any of the variables involved, may be quite lengthy and cumbersome. So dead variable analysis can remove quite a bit of code.

SELECTIVE OPTIMIZATION

INTRODUCTION

The observation that about 5% of a source program is responsible for most of the execution time implies that optimizing only that portion will be only slightly less effective (and far cheaper in terms of compilation time) than applying the same optimizations to the whole program. If the compiler could recognize these critical portions of the source text, it could apply its optimization effort where it would have most effect. The time saved by not optimizing the whole program could be spent instead in applying more optimization to less code.

LASKI: There seems a general concensus among leading computing scientists that it would be worth doing [*sacrificing compiled code speed and size*] to discover the most frequently executed part of a program in order that it can receive concentrated attention both by the programmer on the local polishing of the source program and by the compiler's applying locally additional expensive, elaborate optimizing techniques which it would not be economic to apply to the whole program. The experimental FORTRAN system of Wulf and Hansen, in which the frequency with which regions of the program are entered at run time is monitored and triggers their partial recompilation with more sophisticated optimizing already beats both WATFOR and optimizing FORTRAN H by the measure of compile + execution costs. Although blue-sky, this is certainly not beyond the horizon.

The problem is, of course, that it is not possible with current techniques for the compiler to know which portions of a program warrant the most optimization effort.

There are basically two ways in which this information could be provided to the compiler:

1 by directives from the programmer

2 by automatic analysis during the compilation phase.

These two approaches are examined in more detail below.

PROGRAMMER-SUPPLIED FEEDBACK

In many instances, the programmer knows where most of the execution time will be concentrated when he submits his program for compilation. The information he has will not always be complete though sometimes (when for example, he is recompiling an existing program after a modification) he could give quite detailed indications of the run-time characteristics.

Currently, detailed information about the relative frequencies of various program parts is difficult to come by. Some of the methods for obtaining such information are discussed in the next section (page 119). In his classic study of program behaviour Knuth (041) *argued strongly that "all software systems should provide frequency counts to all programmers".*

Given this kind of information, the programmer would need some means of supplying it to the compiler.

LASKI: It is worth having constructs in one's language that only enable the programmer to direct the translator as to the context within which it should choose what the code it generates should aim to achieve, provided that using such constructs does not get in the way of the programmer's apprehension of the source text.

In the instance of loop frequency, one might expect while *e* do *c* to translate to

```
        JUMP L1
L2:     DO C
L1:     LD E
        JTRU L2
```

If one had good reason to wish

```
L1:  LD E
     JFLS L2
     DO C
     JUMP L1
L2:  ...
```

to be generated, one would write

while, rarely, *e* **do** *c*

Rarely is an example of what has been called a *pragmat*. It may well recall to old hands the FREQUENCY statement of early FORTRAN.

SCHNECK: The original FORTRAN compiler (243) contained an optimizer which gathered information on the source program's structure as described below. The source program was analysed and broken down into a set of basic blocks, and a table listing the predecessors of each basic block was created. This table was then used in a Monte Carlo simulation, to find the relative frequency of execution of each basic block. A random number generator, augmented by programmer estimates supplied in FREQUENCY statements, was used to traverse paths in the program flow graphs, and a count was kept for each basic block.... According to John Cocke, the FREQUENCY statement was removed from the language, without any user reaction, after it was discovered to have been incorrectly implemented, causing frequencies to be assigned inversely.

LASKI: We said above that the kind of target code to aim at was knowable by the programmer. Before the program runs he will, sometimes, be certain, and correctly so, that the conditions hold water which **rarely** will yield what is, for a certain loop in a certain context, better code, or equally certain that they do not. More often he will be doubtful, and rightly so.

It is for this practical situation that the run-time monitor comes into its own. We envisage some such sequence of events as the following.

Initially, the programmer should include **rarely** in those loops where it needs little thought to be certain of the worth of doing so, allowing himself to think a little more deeply about those parts of the program that he suspects to be executed most frequently.

After the program has been run often enough for the monitor's report of execution patterns to be accepted as valid, he will know where he can usefully think deeply about his program; he may, as a result, add or delete **rarely** from loops, and, most probably, will remain doubtful about certain loops. These he can qualify by writing **possibly rarely**. A second stage of monitoring takes over to report the average number of repetitions of the body each time the loop is encountered, and, in due course, the programmer knows enough to be able to delete **possibly**, since he knows whether or not **rarely** should be deleted. If he can use the qualifier **possibly** with or without the pragmat **rarely**, the translator can, during this second bout of monitoring, take account of what the programmer regards as more probable.

SCHNECK: Knuth addressed the concept of an iterative system in his ACM Turing Lecture (281):

> "All that we have been giving programmers is an optimizing compiler, which mysteriously does something to the programs it translates but which never explains what it does. Fortunately we are now finally seeing the appearance of systems which give the user credit for some intelligence; they automatically provide instrumentation of programs and appropriate feedback about the real costs. These experimental systems have been a huge success, because they produce measurable improvements, and especially because they are fun to use, so I am confident that it is only a matter of time before the use of such systems is standard operating procedure."

We suggest that this will be carried further. Future programming systems will carry on a dialogue with the user. Additional information will be requested to enable the system to choose a problem-solving strategy from among the many which may be possible. In order to accomplish this, a true dialogue will be necessary, not merely a sequence of batch job submissions. The compiler will request information which is required (for example, for determination of correctness), or which is desirable (for example, for choosing an optimization strategy). The questions will not be 'standard', or prepared as in today's programmed instruction material, they will relate directly to the program in development. By supplying the requested information, the programmer will aid in obtaining major performance increases.

Will it work? Today's interactive compilers which operate in a timesharing mode are already performing some of these activities. They are concerned solely with creating a program, and therefore check for syntactic and logical errors. By offering immediate feedback, it becomes attractive for the programmer to examine and measure the effect of alternative problem formulations. This sort of system offers the opportunity for immense productivity increases – the programmer can offer guidance to the compiler on the job of performance optimization – the computer will act as an agent of the programmer and carry out the optimization.

Increased computational capabilities coupled with inexpensive conversational terminals will encourage a programmer/computer dialogue as a means of program development and optimization. The effectiveness of the programmer and computer in this symbiotic relationship will far surpass that of the isolated batch-oriented programmer.

The benefits of a feedback system do not seem to be in doubt. What is not clear, however, is how far the system should be automated.

LASKI: In the system I outlined above, the responsibility for deciding what optimal code the compiler should aim for is left entirely to the programmer; all that is automated is the provision of the evidence on which he acts. The question arises at once as to whether or not more should be automated. In part, the answer to this question depends on an economic judgement of the relative cost-effectiveness of programming talent against machine costs, tempered by a judgement of the relative value of a programmer's unreliable intuition against a machine's exhaustive reliability....

Wulf has expressed the extreme view that everything should be automated and pragmats not used. He gave as his reasons not only that optimizing analysis was reliable whereas not all programmers were, but also that use of pragmats obscured the ease of apprehension of the algorithm from the program text. A similar argument made him wish to call a halt to a proliferation of the kind of programming language constructs that I have advocated, admitting these only if they simplified the expression of algorithms and not for the fact that they enabled simple compilers to generate optimal code.

These arguments are cogent and cannot be ignored. They are not completely persuasive to me for two equally cogent contrary arguments. The first, for which **rarely** serves as an example, is that, in some situations not only can the programmer be better informed than some mechanical system, but also, if he makes an incorrect decision, the consequences will only be non-optimal code and not an invalid program. If an incorrect use of a pragmat may lead to an insecure program, that pragmat should only be used where it can be established to be correct and we fully accept that an automated system is the only method of doing so in which we may have complete confidence. However, we claim that, where potential optimizations have contrary effects on independent desiderata, only non-local considerations can mediate and these are available solely to the programmer.

The second argument in favour of leaving to the programmer an involvement in achieving optimal code, even where this is possible automatically, is psychological, since it will engage him more with the program, which helps its maintenance. Moreover, if the system gives him adequate feedback to feel proud of his successes and aware of his misjudgements, he will educate himself as a programmer.

Curiously, as a programmer develops, there is both more and less reason to automate more: more reason since the simpler optimizations no longer challenge and engage him, less reason, since doing so distracts his attention less from considering deeper possibilities. Finally, invention of high-level expressive constructs and discovery of optimizations from study of machine code are activities that reinforce one another and together add to the power of the programmer's conceptual apparatus.

AUTOMATED FEEDBACK

As Laski points out above, the opposite view to his is represented in the approach adopted by Hansen and Wulf in their adaptive FORTRAN system.

HANSEN and WULF: Knuth and others have suggested that statistics should be collected during program execution which can then be used by the user and/or compiler on subsequent compilations to optimize the program's performance.... The feedback approach has much to recommend it; in fact, its only drawback may be that (we claim) it is not really necessary to have the human in the loop.

In our paper (page 185), we present the design of a system which dynamically and automatically detects and optimizes those portions of a program which are most frequently executed. Successively sophisticated optimizations are applied to sections of the program during execution, and in proportion to their contribution to total execution time. Thus the quality of the code in these sections dynamically adapts, and the amount of optimization effort is proportional to the need for it.

We make two strong claims for this scheme. First, that the total cost of compiling and running a program is reduced significantly when compared to any fixed optimization strategy (or set of them) And, second, that the scheme suggests an obvious implementation methodology which has significant merit in its own right.

To demonstrate the validity of their dynamic optimization technique, Hansen and Wulf compared the performance of their system against various FORTRAN compilers, each with totally different characteristics.

The three main compilers against which the comparisons were made were:

WATFIV, which compiles very quickly but produces very inefficient object code. This is typical of the 'quick and dirty', 'student-crunching' approach that is used for situations where there will be a high rate of failed compilations and where most programs are run only once or twice after compilation.

- *FORTRAN-G, which is slower in compilation than WATFIV but produces better object code.*

- *FORTRAN-H, which applies various optimizations, is therefore slow to compile, but produces the best object code of the three systems under discussion.*

The existence of three such disparate compilers is in itself an indication of the problem of finding a compilation strategy where the optimization effort is proportional to the need for it.

HANSEN and WULF: There are a number of practical problems in making these comparisons. First, not many computers have all three compilers available. Second, the differences in characteristics of various computers (for example, speed, word size, and instruction set) must be taken into account. Finally, the differences between the compilers themselves, for example, the parsing and code generation techniques employed, the type of machine language generated, and the run-time support package must be taken into account.

The ideal situation would be to have all the compiler systems run on the same machine and to use the same compiling techniques, optimizers, machine language generators, and run-time support package. The construction of these compiler systems was considered to be too large an undertaking. Therefore, a more expedient approach was taken in which the Adaptive FORTRAN system (AF) was transformed to resemble each of the other three compilers. It was easy to make the necessary changes because of the way AF was constructed. The main discrepancy between the transformed systems and the actual compilers lies not in the type of code produced, but in the way it is produced. Each transformed system uses the Adaptive FORTRAN compiler to translate FORTRAN source text into quads. After loading the quads, but before starting execution, the quads are translated to the machine language form that most resembles the code produced by the compiler being emulated. We feel this discrepancy in no way alters the validity of the test results, since the use of a consistent approach does not bias the results.

The internal structure of the system is described in detail in Hansen and Wulf's paper (page 185).

The optimizations applied by the Adaptive FORTRAN system are the standard ones

HANSEN and WULF: Adaptive FORTRAN uses four machine-independent optimizations: constant folding, non-homogeneous fusion, common subexpression elimination, and code motion, and a host of machine-dependent optimizations. There are a number of reasons why these optimizations were selected over other possibilities. First, these optimizations are among the most commonly used. Second, they allow us to construct systems similar in characteristics to existing compilers against which it is possible to compare the Adaptive FORTRAN system. Third, to show the flexibility of the system, we wanted to include optimizations that applied both to basic blocks and segments. Finally, we wanted to include enough optimizations to prove the technique was not only feasible, but that the system could perform at least as well as current compiler systems.

In order to compare the performance of the AF system with the other three compilers, it was used on a number of different test programs, carefully selected to avoid biasing the results. As Hansen and Wulf point out in their paper, it would be fairly easy to devise a test program that would show any one of the systems in the best or worst light. The selection criteria for the test programs are discussed by Hansen and Wulf in their paper. A common characteristic of all the test programs was that they have a control parameter that determined the execution time by controlling the number of times the critical portion of the program was executed; for example, the control parameter might determine the number of elements to be processed or the accuracy to which results were to be obtained.

Figure 1, adapted from (303)*, shows the predicted performance of the various compilers. Lines AFW, AFG, and AFH represent the simulated versions of WATFIV, FORTRAN-G, and FORTRAN-H respectively. It should be noted that the relative positions of the various cross-over points are arbitrary and will depend on the characteristics of individual programs.*

HANSEN and WULF: AFW, AFG and AFH differ only in the amount of compile-time optimization they apply to a program, and thus in the efficiency of the machine language they produce. At the start of execution, the AFH curve lies above the AFG curve which in

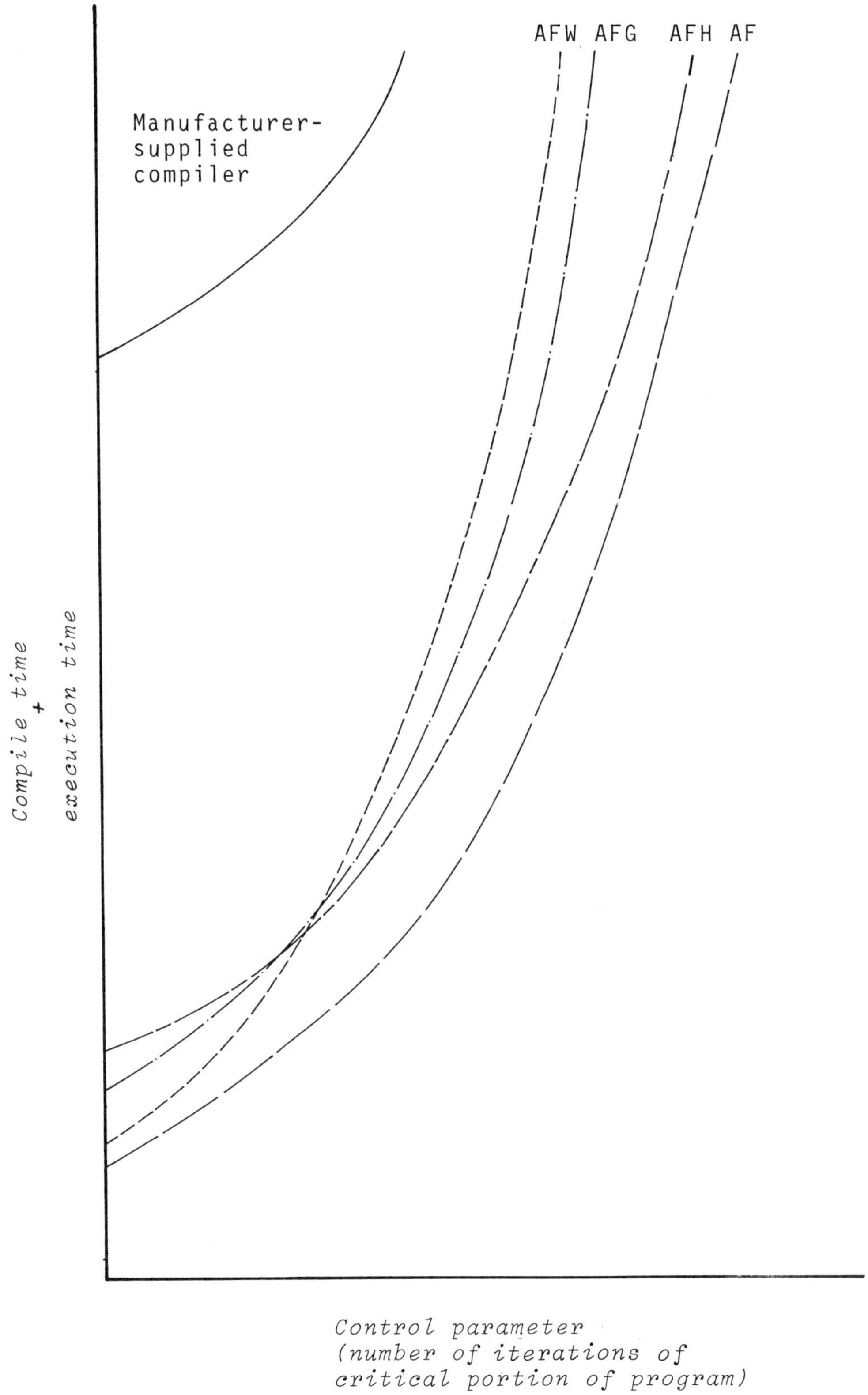

Figure 1: Comparison of adaptive FORTRAN with other compilers

turn lies above the AFW curve. Because of the relative efficiency of the code, the AFW curve eventually will cross the other two, and the AFG curve will cross the AFH curve. These cross-over points occur when the difference in compilation time equals the difference in execution time. It is expected then that if a program is run long enough, the AFW curve will lie above the AFG curve which in turn will lie above the AFH curve. If, however, the additional optimization (code motion) performed by AFH has no effect, that is, does not remove any invariant quads from any loop, then the effort is wasted and the AFG curve will lie below the AFH curve.

By checking the figures for each test program (Figures 4 to 7, page 205), it is seen that the curves do indeed follow this behaviour pattern. Only for one test program does the AFG curve lie below the AFH curve. The reason is exactly that given above, viz: code motion has no effect. An examination of the optimization results showed that the loops did not contain any invariant quads.

As for the AF curve, it is expected to lie initially below all the other curves since it performs no initial optimizations. This is indeed the case. If a program is run long enough, the AF curve will asymptotically become parallel to the AFH curve because the executable code becomes identical to that produced by AFH. There are indications that it approaches the AFH curve from above if the time required for the program to be optimized exceeds the compile-time optimization time for AFH; otherwise, it approaches it from below.

Details of actual test programs and their associated performance graphs are given by Hansen and Wulf (page 205).

The results raise several interesting questions. First, there is probably significant scope for improving the system. For example, the optimization possibilities have by no means been exhausted. Several other techniques, such as strength reduction, opening subroutines, etc, could be added.

Secondly, the performance graphs relate to a single execution. It is only when the optimization overhead can be spread over several executions that the full benefits of such optimizations can be realized.

On the other hand, there are possible reservations about the general applicability of the concept. For example, the demonstrated benefits may be language-dependent.

HANSEN and WULF: FORTRAN-IV was selected as the source language for this system because:

1 it is one of the most widely used programming languages and hence it is a rich source of example programs and comparisons with existing systems;

2 it contains enough interesting constructs to give credibility to the validation results;

3 many of the compile-time optimization algorithms currently in use were developed for FORTRAN compilers; they are well understood and are easily adapted for use at run time.

LASKI: Personally, I am of the opinion that, for a less archaic language than FORTRAN for which known and not excessively expensive techniques can produce near optimal code from well-expressed source programs, the results of focusing programmer attention will have a better pay-off than mechanical optimizing techniques, however crafty.

Moreover, the principle of the system may not be applicable to commercial programming. In the first place, the strategy is based on the assumption that

1 the eventual run-time behaviour of the program depends only on the values of the various control parameters, which merely determine the number of times the central code in the program is executed;

2 the compilation-time behaviour will be typical of actual program executions.

Though these assumptions clearly hold for the scientific applications associated with FORTRAN programs, many commercial programs behave very differently, depending, for example, on whether the data presented to them is good or bad. In programs of this type, it is the distribution of various kinds of data, rather than the values, that determine which parts of the program will be most frequently executed.

Moreover, optimization is generally very different in the commercial environment.

McMANUS: It should be pointed out that optimization means rather different things to the commercial and to the scientific user. For the scientific user, all the classical optimization techniques seem to pay off: moving expressions out of loops, evaluating sub-expressions once only, optimizing subscript references, strength reduction, and so on. In some extreme cases that we have measured, we have seen the execution time of a scientific program reduced from 1500 seconds before optimization to 300 seconds after optimization. That may be an extreme case, but it shows the improvement that those scientifically oriented techniques can bring. The improvement for commercial programs is relatively small from these techniques. Much more significant is a highly tuned implementation of input/output, efficient storage management, carefully honed subroutine code design, and efficient treatment of special cases of decimal arithmetic expressions.

Despite these reservations, the idea of adaptive optimization is an intuitively attractive one and could be a major step forward in the neat future.

HANSEN and WULF: The test results indicate that AF does not outperform all the other systems across the entire spectrum of run times, but that for a particular program there is a given range in which one compiler system is better than any of the others. However, AF is better than any other single compiler system over the spectrum. Thus, we conclude that it is better to build one compiler system to cover the run-time spectrum than three separate specialized compiler systems, each designed for a different range of the spectrum....

We feel that we have demonstrated a worthwhile alternative to compiler design that should be considered seriously. The approach makes more sense, from an implementation viewpoint, than building many special-purpose compilers. The system can be built in an incremental fashion because of its modularity. Each step consists of programming and debugging an optimizer module and then adding it to the system. The final product is an adaptive compiler that does not require much more effort to build than a full optimizing compiler. AF was built in this manner: in 3 man-months we had programmed the compiler and interpreter, and had programs running. Then each optimizer was programmed in ½ to 1 man-month, debugged and added to the system. In less than a man-year, the system was completed.

CONCLUSION

THE NEED FOR COMPILER OPTIMIZATION

It often seems that optimizing compilers merely apply crude first aid to programs that could have been better written initially. However, even leaving aside those cases (such as register allocation and efficient subscript handling) that the programmer has no way of optimizing in his source language, there are many counter-arguments to such a view of optimization.

Especially in view of the trend for a greater involvement of non-specialist and users in programming, the insistence that programmers should always write efficient programs is very much a counsel of perfection.

MOREL: What is the main goal of an optimizer: to enable a bad programmer to get good programs, or to enable a good programmer writing in a high-level language, to get optimal code? You cannot do both, in my opinion.

SCHNECK: I do not see any *a priori* reason why both cannot be done; but I think the more important goal is to permit the bad programmer to produce decent code, simply because there are more bad programmers around than good; and they are more of a drain in terms of capital resources.

Except for the academic community, which is interested in optimization of performance as a mountain climber is in climbing Everest, simply because it is there, most of us are interested in it because it lets us do things we could otherwise not afford to do. My one criterion for optimization is total system cost;

and I weight that by the number of poor programmers against the number of good programmers, and I say that it is more important to be able to produce decent code with a poor programmer – and that poor programmer eventually turns out to be the user.

OPTIMIZATION AS AN AID TO CLEAR PROGRAMMING

Moreover, the coding of programs in such a way as to render compile-time optimization unnecessary can lead to very obscure programs. This style of programming, much advocated in early programming manuals, is less frequently heard now that obscure and unmaintainable programs have been recognized as a greater evil. This trade-off between programmer efficiency and program efficiency is further discussed in the section dealing with program development *(page 23)**.*

LIMITATIONS IN COMPILER OPTIMIZATION

There is obviously a limit to how far a compiler, however sophisticated, can eliminate the effects of bad programming.

SCHNECK: We have been concerned here with the very narrow view of program performance as meaning simply the run-time efficiency of a given set of code. Other speakers have been more concerned with the overall systems design and analysis of a function that has to be obtained or a problem that has to be solved. What we are concerned with now is the fact that once those choices are made, we want to examine them as efficiently as possible. Clearly, if it was not necessary to compute this function at all, because, for example, it was previously obtained, then while the optimized solution is faster than the original, it is not the best possible one. So that is a constraint one has to keep in mind.

A specific instance of this problem is the ignorance on the part of programmers about algorithms.

SCHNECK: I think that perhaps one of the major causes of poor performance is the use of poor algorithms or problem solution techniques. This is a problem that is not easily measured, because we can have a system that performs very well in terms of its use of resources, but it is just chewing up time doing nothing. For example, I would often give a programming class the task of writing a program to solve the following:

sum the numbers between 1 and 1000

and anyone who did it would fail!

Schneck's point, though jocular, does illustrate an important principle, that many programmers are unaware of what should be well-known problem-solving techniques, often readily available in such books as those by Knuth (307) *or in the algorithms supplement of the technical journals. This point is discussed by Newsted (page 267) in the context of a professional approach to programming. However, many of the limitations are specific to current approaches.*

CHEATHAM (320): An objective review of program optimization technology has revealed a number of problems whose solutions are both essential (if new methods of organizing program development are to be successful) and relatively accessible today.

1 Structured programming techniques emphasize modular program construction and well-defined layers of representation in order to minimize the cost of producing correct, reliable software. Often, however, the structure introduced for clarity inhibits direct translation of an abstract algorithm to an efficient machine language form. The trend toward structured programming increases the need for tools to merge isolated modules and to eliminate inefficient layers of structure in a cost effective way. If efficiency remains the price for clarity and maintainability, the new disciplines will not be fully accepted.

2 Development of programs by stepwise refinement should be synonymous with program optimization. Program improvement aids should not be limited to the translation of source to machine code; they should be employed at each step from an abstract level of representation to a more concrete level.

3 Optimizers are too often expensive, weakly governable engines

whose workings are not easily grasped by users and whose effects are only indirectly observable through changes in the run-time behaviour of compiled programs. While it should not be necessary to understand a tool in order to use it, the tool should nevertheless be precisely controllable and readily adaptable to accomplish special tasks. Its effects should be expressed in terms the programmer can appreciate, preferably a modified or augmented copy of his program. Where the user must take control of operator definitions and data representations at the hardware level, he should be able to do so without completely suspending optimization.

4 It is now time for the results of research in the field of verification and automatic programming to begin affecting the design of practical tools. Current optimizers make too little use of knowledge deducible from programs or from measurements of their behaviour, and are inflexible about accepting help in the form of assertions about the programs or their data. Too often the lack of a complete or efficient algorithm for a particular problem has inhibited the use of sound heuristics in critical regions.

A development and optimization methodology that incorporates many of these ideas is described by Burstall and Darlington (page 161) and discussed in the section concerned with program development (page 61).

Execution

PROGRAM MONITORING
Introduction
Techniques of program monitoring
Choice of programs to monitor
Program tuning

MACHINE ARCHITECTURE
Introduction
High-level language architectures
Microprogramming

VIRTUAL STORAGE SYSTEMS
Introduction
Special considerations for VS

PROGRAM MONITORING

INTRODUCTION

Throughout this Analysis, great emphasis has been laid on the importance of an accurate knowledge of the run-time behaviour of programs. This information has many users such as

- *as feedback to the compilation system, either automatically or via the programmer, to indicate where the best pay-off for optimizing techniques can be expected;*

- *as an indication to the programmer of the sections of program that could profitably be recoded;*

- *as a means of educating programmers about the precise effects of their programming techniques and their programming language.*

This subsection will summarize some of the techniques and implications of run-time program monitoring. Further details can be found in the State of the Art Reports Computer Systems Measurement (317) *and* System Tuning (318).

TECHNIQUES OF PROGRAM MONITORING

There are several ways that a program's performance can be monitored, such as

- *external monitors, either hardware or software*

- *self-measurement, by instrumentation routines explicitly placed by the programmer in his program*

- *by compiler-inserted measurement routines.*

BROWN (G G): There is a significant difference between the sort of analyser that inserts counters at various stages throughout the program, thus often significantly altering its run-time characteristics, both in terms of core taken up and in time used, and the monitor that sits outside the program and takes either a regular look or an occasional look at it. My main objection to building performance measurement tools into programming languages is that they would be rather too subjective. What I think is required in most cases is an easy way to relate the measurement that you take outside the program to the source code. In most cases, a simple procedure map is sufficient, giving statement numbers and core locations.

The most difficult situation that I come across, and come across quite frequently, is where all the time is being spent in a compiler-supplied subroutine; but that has never been discovered because the part of the user's written code responsible for calling that subroutine has always been the next highest peak. It does not matter how small that peak is in itself, if it has been responsible for invoking the large peak.

SCHNECK: I should like to take an opposite view to that. I think that performance monitoring is important in a programming language. As a specific example, users sometimes complain that a measuring tool is not producing proper results because it indicates certain numbers of overlays occurring in programs which they think have no overlays. When they know that one of the operating system components that they are calling contains multiplicities of overlays, they can then attempt to do something about it. When I look at external measurements of a program and see that perhaps the program has performed 10 000 I/O transfers, I have some information. Let us say those are physical blocks. If I find out that I have 10 000 WRITE statements or READ statements in the program, that is one thing; if I have 100 READ or WRITE statements in the program, that is something else. I would certainly tend to increase the block size on the assumption, in the latter case, that they could not possibly be getting any significant degree of overlap if each WRITE statement were spawning 100 physical blocks. So the correlation, or lack of correlation, between internal measurements as the program thinks it is generating them, and external measurements as the operating system sees the requirements placed upon it, I think is an important one. Therefore, I would require facilities in a programming language.

I think that the deficiency has made it necessary for people to build preprocessors and systems that insert monitoring statements. I think also that our naivety as programmers has led us into putting in counters all over the place, when such counters are in fact required only at certain branch points within the program. By judicious positioning of counters one need not in fact radically alter the behaviour of the programs. I think that built-in language features are useful, if the counters are put in where they belong, and that can be done from the programming language system.

CAPON: I think that some of the measurements will have to come from outside the program, rather than the program just looking at itself. Perhaps what the programming language needs is some facility to kick the outside world, as it were, to say "You ought to be measuring something about me at this stage", so that the program can induce the system to measure the paging activity or the store map over a particular area of the program. With MU5, the way that we put this sort of facilitity in the programming language is actually to enable the programming language to make a procedure call to prod the system; and this sets the external monitoring process on its way.

PATEL: I think we have to recognize that there is a certain proportion of system resources that one ought to be justifiably prepared to pay in order just to make sure that one is not wasting a lot more. I would qualify 'a certain proportion' as being not more than 2%. I think that it is perfectly justifiable to spend 2% of each of the system resources that one has in order to monitor sufficient information to be able to make gains of 50% to 100%, which is quite possible. Most people do not even notice it is there. So 2% of all our system resources can be used with discretion to measure a lot of information, or obtain instrumentation on a lot of different parts of the system, purely by such devices as counters. Counters are a very useful mechanism to indicate how often a certain activity performs. The frequency of that activity is a very direct indication of where there may be a great mismatch. One of the things that we have done on the 2900 is to put in hundreds of counters all over the place, to examine the frequency with which the system procedures are being called upon. The overall cost of that is no more than 2% in each of the system resources required; and a procedure call, as Peter Capon just mentioned, triggers the operating system not only to collect the information but to put it in a job journal, which when printed later gives the particular user the information about his job.

SAMET: How does that 2% compare with the degree of distortion produced in a system by having a software monitor?

BROWN (G G): It depends on what you consider to be the software monitor, and whether you take into account the analysis function, because that has to be carried out as well at some stage.

SAMET: I was thinking rather more in terms of the actual monitor that is collecting the data, the analysis being performed later on.

BROWN (G G): They are not all like that, though; there are a number of IBM-supplied analysers that actually sit in core and do the analysis at the same time that the work is being done. The sampling monitors are much more often of this type than the event-driven ones, because they cannot do it otherwise. Much more interpretation has to be done at execution time by the sampling monitor. But the actual data gathering function, from a CPU point of view, is of the order of 2% to 3%.

I think that the most serious problem with monitoring arises when you affect some of the other resources that, in particular installations, might be critical. An example is where one takes up 12K of core, which is not very much unless core is your tightest resource. Another example is the recording device. If you are short of tape drives, for example, and you take up one to record your output, then you will significantly alter the work pattern while you gather your data, and therefore perhaps invalidate the interpretation entirely.

SAMET: This would seem to be a problem more with monitors that look at the system than at an individual program.

BROWN (G G): Yes, because the ones that look at an individual program tend to be far simpler. I should like to comment on what Dr Patel said earlier about counters, because I think that is a fairly easy trap to fall into. Time is the important thing: it does not really matter how often you do something, as long as it does not take very long. In my experience, time is the most critical thing in measuring anything.

PATEL: You are right, what matters is, of course, time. Counters do not give you exact information as to how much time you have spent, but they do give you a simple indication of where to look.

McDOWELL: Driving most operating systems is like driving a car with an opaque windscreen. With a queueing theory model of a system, like Dr Patel's, it is easy to make all systems look alike to the human driver. The best control could be achieved by displays showing resource usage in real time and queueing and service times. Why can't the industry adopt a standard which insists on these things being displayed and recorded in standard form on any large computer.

BROWN (G G): Tom Bell, who chaired the SHARE computer measurement and evaluation project for some time, said that asking the manufacturer to do it was like setting the fox to watch the chickens. I don't think one can expect much from them.

The incorporation by manufacturers of effective system instrumentation facilities into their machines is discussed in detail in the State of the Art Report Computer Systems Measurement (317).

CHOICE OF PROGRAMS TO MONITOR

Clearly, all programs do not justify the same attention to their run-time performance.

LANKEY: A typical data processing installation will process several dozen application systems comprising hundreds of programs. The optimization of a few programs, each requiring skilled analysis to measure and diagnose inefficiencies therefore demands that the programs are selected carefully.

The criteria for the selection process will, of course, partly depend on the precise objectives of the program performance study. Typical objectives are:

1 the reduction of particular program/suite elapsed run times to meet external deadlines;

2 improvements in overall installation performance from the optimization of major programs;

3 increasing the awareness and skills of programmers so that overall program performance is improved steadily.

In case 1, the choice of programs to be investigated is usually trivial and a representative selection can easily be specified.

The general requirement of case 2 requires more consideration however, since the interaction between programs in a multi-programming environment becomes an important parameter. The criteria in this case cannot be simply defined but will probably include:

- programs whose aggregated run times are long (either from periodic long runs or frequent shorter runs);
- time-critical programs which require priority facilities which downgrade overall site performance;
- unsociable programs which degrade overall site performance by virtue of their excessive resource demands (for example, by requiring 5 of the 6 available magnetic-tape decks);
- general-purpose software which is incorporated in many programs so that the benefits of selective optimization effort can easily be shared.

MUNRO: We want to reduce the running time of programs in general, and specifically of the programs which consume the bulk of time in the critical part of the day. Often, there is little to be gained from speeding up a program which runs for three hours every night, if the night shift is always going to be in anyway and there are no other night runs. It will be much more vital to speed up a program which is running in the middle of the day, even if it is running for only half an hour, or perhaps even less.

KOLENCE (317): The way to approach the problem is to find out where you most need to improve performance, that is, to discover what the biggest cause of lost capacity or lost performance is. You do this by using the data from your accounting routines to sort your production programs in order of the average elapsed time they use; you then simply focus on the top ten of these problem programs, and continuously work away at each until, finally, it drops out of the top ten and another one pops up.

The procedure recommended by Kolence, whereby effort is concentrated on the programs that matter most is exactly analogous to the principle of devoting the most optimizing effort to the critical portions of individual programs, as discussed in the subsection Selective Optimization *(page 99).*

An example of this approach is given by Darden and Heller (301)*, who successively tuned the four most time-consuming phases of a compiler. They thereby increased its speed from 740 lines per minute to 8000. The table below shows the proportion of total compilation time required for each of the phases at each stage in the exercise:*

	Compile speed (lines/minute)	*Code generation*	*Input/ output*	*Syntax phase*	*Lexical phase*	*Table look-up*	*Utilities*	*Semantics*	*Memory management*
Original compiler	740	69.0	13.8	6.4	6.2	2.1	0.9	0.7	0.6
After optimizing code generator	2300	4.2	42.7	19.9	19.3	6.5	2.8	2.2	1.9
After optimizing input/output	3800	7.1	4.7	33.1	32.2	10.9	4.7	3.7	3.3
After optimizing syntax phase	5300	9.9	6.6	6.6	45.0	15.2	6.6	5.2	4.6
After optimizing lexical phase	8000	15.2	10.1	10.1	16.6	22.9	10.1	8.0	7.0

The improvements were achieved by using better algorithms and by rewriting critical sections in assembly language. However, only 5% of the final program was in assembly language.

This project illustrates several principles that are as applicable to the tuning of individual programs as to the tuning of portions of code within a program:

1 *As tuning proceeds, components that originally seemed negligible become critical and therefore potential candidates for tuning.*

2 *There is a limit to how far such iterative improvements should proceed. Each stage of optimization has to be economically justifiable; there is little point in squeezing out the last source of inefficiency if the cost of doing so is greater than the expected pay-off. In the case of the compiler under discussion, the next candidate for tuning would be the table look-up routines, which initially accounted for less than 1% of the time but now were responsible for almost a quarter of compilation time. However, the compiler was now working 10 times faster than the original system and compilation was therefore no longer such a critical factor in the computer centre (less than 5% of the total time). Table look-up was hence occupying about 15 minutes a day and this was not thought to warrant further tuning. However, if compilation activity had later increased, the decision could easily be changed.*

PROGRAM TUNING

Having discovered, by monitoring, where the bottlenecks in a program are, then the next step is to decide what to do about them.

LANKEY: The actual recommendations for optimization must take into account:

- the availability of resources to change the program, recognizing the costs and benefits of each improvement;
- any constraints imposed on the program by the computer system, for example, main store size limits, disk file space limits;

- any side-effects of improvements which will mean changes to other programs or systems, for example, as a result of changing file designs.

What should be done in any particular context will clearly depend on the nature of the bottleneck, whether, for example, the problem concerns CPU usage or I/O.

G Brown discusses techniques of improving the I/O performance of programs (page 147) and Lankey describes several case studies in program tuning (page 217).

MACHINE ARCHITECTURE

INTRODUCTION

An obvious factor in the run-time performance of any program is the performance of the machine on which it is run. Until recently, machine architectures have generally been notoriously unsuited to the high-level language programs they execute. In fact, the necessity for conventional program optimization techniques stems partly from this unsuitability.

CAPON: Attempts to implement high-level languages efficiently on processors architecturally unsympathetic to the task has resulted in elaborate optimizing compilers. The most obvious example on many conventional machines is the attempt to make optimal use of a set of registers for a language, such as ALGOL or FORTRAN, which contains no inherent concept of registers. A more extreme example is found in attempts to convert FORTRAN code comprising scalar or element-by-element array operations into code which can be effectively exploited by processors such as the CDC STAR and ILLIAC IV. Here very elaborate compilers are only partially successful in converting to an instruction set unsympathetic to the source language and unsuited to many problems.

These types of optimization have resulted in the investment of considerable effort in large and often difficult-to-maintain compilers at a time when all software costs are increasing. A more effective approach is to make use of relatively decreasing hardware costs to build computers more suited to executing programs written in typical high-level languages. This immediately reduces the size and cost of compilers, and also the total system software, while at the same time providing efficient run-time execution.

HIGH-LEVEL LANGUAGE ARCHITECTURES

An example of the approach suggested by Capon is the MU5, the experimental processor developed at Manchester University.

CAPON: In the MU5 processor, considerable attention has been paid to the requirements of high-level languages. The processor has been designed to deal efficiently with those constructs which occur most often in such languages. One example of this is the way in which frequently used scalar operands such as counters and modifiers reside automatically in associatively addressed fast buffer registers rather than being optimized into conventional registers. Another example is the way in which a series of functions and operands is streamed into the main arithmetic unit. In the resulting processor the gains from elaborate compiler optimizations are very small compared with those on conventional machines. The hardware itself effectively optimizes the behaviour of the program.

The architecture of the MU5 is described in detail by Capon (page 171). Two examples are given here for illustration.

The first example concerns storage allocation and operand accessing.

CAPON: The space required for the local variables associated with a procedure or subroutine must be allocated dynamically at run-time in many languages. Dynamic allocation has the advantage that only storage actively used is allocated, so the scheme is economical in store used. The loading of programs is simplified since store references do not need to be modified at load time, and mixed language programming is facilitated since problems of store allocation and parameter passing largely disappear.

In most conventional computer systems, dynamic storage allocation is more expensive than static allocation. This is because the instructions required for the modified store access needed to fetch a variable are either longer, or take longer to execute than those for an unmodified access. In MU5, dynamic variables of the current procedure are accessed using the contents of the NB base register to the offset within the instruction.

The simplest way for a compiler to process expressions with scalar operands is to generate zero-address or stacking code. It is much easier to generate code for a zero-address computer with a stack of effective infinite depth than for a machine with only a limited stack or with multiple accumulators for partial results.

In MU5, a single address form, in which the accumulator holds the result so far, is used. Operations are between a single operand and this accumulator, and partial results are held in the stack. There is little extra complication in generating the single address form, and greater program efficiency can be achieved this way. This is because less instructions are needed for the single address version, so more concise code can be obtained, and also because less moving of operands between the accumulator and the stack, which is outside the arithmetic unit in MU5, is required.

Frequently used scalar variables and stacked partial results do not return to the store between instructions. Instead, they are automatically held in associative buffer registers close to the arithmetic unit. This achieves performance similar to that with conventional registers but without the usual overhead of optimizing operands into specific registers.

The second example concerns procedure calls, which have often been mentioned, in the context of structured programming, as causes of considerable inefficiency.

CAPON: The advantages of writing well-structured programs in which reasonable use is made of procedures with parameters are well understood. Unfortunately the cost of procedure entry and exit on many machines discourages the use of procedures when run-time efficiency is important. It is therefore vital to the efficient execution of well-constructed programs that a powerful procedure calling mechanism is available.... In MU5, only seven 16-bit instructions are required.... The equivalent for the ICL 1900 Series is sixteen 24-bit instructions while the PDP-11 takes ten 32-bit instructions. In those systems where dynamic interpretive parameter matching is used, several hundred instructions may be required, so an unacceptable inefficiency is imposed.

The approach that is embodied in the MU5 design has not yet been widely adopted in the industry except for a few manufacturers, such as Burroughs and, more recently, ICL with their 2900 series.

MICROPROGRAMMING

One way of improving the efficiency of a particular program, or set of programs, would be to adapt the instruction set of the machine to make it more suitable for the tasks being performed.

MANVILLE: To modify the instruction set of a computer which used special-purpose hard-wired logic is so formidable a task that few would consider it a practicable proposition.

However, many computers are microprogrammed, that is, the instruction set that the programmer is presented with is interpreted by a lower-level microprogram which generates the control signals in the processor. This general-purpose instruction set is usually a small subset of the operations which would be performed on the same hardware and will not be ideal for any particular application. Thus, a possible way of improving the performance of particular programs or sets of programs on a microprogrammed computer is to add to, or modify, the microprogram to interpret additional, or alternative, instructions. When the microprogram store is writable, the proposition is more attractive than when special read-only memories have to be produced. It also permits dynamic changes to the microprogram to support different programs at different times....

Consider, as an example, a program which frequently searches an ordered array by means of the 'binary chop' technique. Expressed in Coral 66, the main loop of this procedure could be:

```
for i := (bottom + top)/2 while i ≠ bottom
do if a [i] > value then top := i
   else if a [i] < value then bottom := i
   else goto found;
```

The code generated by the single-pass Coral compiler on the GEC 4080 is such that an average of 13½ instructions are obeyed each time round the loop. The best that could be achieved by writing the loop in machine code, or by using a perfect optimizing compiler, would be an average of 8½ instructions each time. Thus, the greatest reduction in execution time possible by the use of conventional techniques would be about 40%.

If there was a single machine instruction to perform this operation, considerably greater reductions would be possible. It would be feasible to implement such an instruction on the microprogrammed 4080 and I estimate that it could execute about 8 times faster than the Coral version or 5 times faster than the optimum machine code program.

There are several ways in which instruction set enhancement can be envisaged. Four such possibilities are:

1 *special instructions suitable for a particular programming language*

2 *special instructions suitable for a particular application area*

3 *special instructions to support operating system functions*

4 *special instructions suitable for undivided programs.*

MANVILLE: The most effective way of enhancing the instruction set of a computer depends on the application for which it is being used.

For example, if most programming is done in a particular high-level language, provision of special instructions to perform the primitive operations and to operate on the data types of that language could produce worthwhile improvements. This would be especially true for languages like APL which operate on whole arrays at once.

Alternatively, if most of the work done is scientific calculations, then provision of additional instructions to perform trigonometric functions, logarithms and square roots could produce beneficial effects.

In many systems, total throughput could be improved considerably by providing additional instructions to support the most common operations of the operating system. Thus, on a multiprogramming system in which processes typically only run for a short time it would be beneficial to provide support for the operations required in process change. For example, the designers of the GEC 4080 realized that this could be particularly useful for real-time applications and implemented process scheduling, inter-process message handling and other operating system functions in microprogram, with the result that process change takes about 10% of the time needed on computers where software is used.

In systems where one program runs for long periods of time (for example, a weather forecasting program, or a sorting program), then it is appropriate to consider support for that particular program, provided that the program is limited by processor or store speed and not by the speed of some peripheral device. The parts of the program which account for most time can be determined and special instructions implemented to perform the required function, as in the binary chop example considered above....

The four types of support can well exist in parallel. A particular program could benefit from special instructions suited to the language in which it is written, others which support the application area and some which are used to speed up sections of this particular program. The throughput of the system in which it runs could be improved by support for its operating system.

The two prime benefits that could be expected from a special-purpose instruction set are

1 reduced execution time
2 reduced storage requirement.

Execution time can be reduced in several ways.

MANVILLE: Consider the sequence of operations performed for a typical instruction (for example, add from store to an index register):

1 Fetch program counter
2 Increment program counter

3 Decode instruction
4 Fetch data from store
5 Gate operands to adder
6 Perform addition
7 Gate result to index register
8 If interrupts have occurred deal with them, otherwise go to 1.

Firstly, by using a special instruction in place of a sequence, the time spent on fetching and decoding instructions is reduced. Stages (1) to (3) and (8) may be regarded as a necessary overhead for each obeyed instruction. By replacing a sequence of n instructions by a single one, the time spent on these stages should be reduced by a factor of about n.

A second way in which time can be saved by the use of special instructions is by the elimination of unnecessary operations from the processing parts (4) to (7) of the instruction previously used. For example, it may be unnecessary to gate a result from a processor register to an index register at the end of one step and then to retrieve it at the beginning of the next.

A general-purpose instruction set often restricts the full range of operations that the underlying hardware is capable of. By implementing a special instruction it may be possible to use a method which could not be done easily with the regular instruction set even though the processor could do it simply. For example, implementing arithmetic of a different precision from normal is likely to need strings of instructions for each operation, especially for dealing with signs and carries. A special instruction may be able to use 'hidden' registers and facilities not available directly to the programmer and thus reduce considerably the processing time required.

Finally, it may be possible to perform some operations in parallel which had been constrained by the nature of the regular instruction set to be done sequentially.

The extent to which these gains can contribute to a real gain in speed of the program will depend on what the limiting factor in the computer is. Where the store is slow and the processor could work faster than it can be supplied with instructions and data, the elimination of instruction fetches will have a direct result and the other gains will not contribute much. If, at the other extreme, the processor is continually busy and never has to wait for instructions or data from store, the savings in stages (2) and (3) and those due to the elimination of redundant operations and the use of parallelism will have the most effect.

Reductions in the storage requirement of a program is not only beneficial in itself; it can also bring further improvements in execution speed.

MANVILLE: The amount of store required for the program will be reduced and in cases where this reduction is significant, it can also have an effect on the performance of the program. On a paged system, the program would probably occupy fewer pages and therefore the overhead of dealing with page faults would be reduced. If a slave, or cache, store is in use, there is a greater probability of finding the desired instruction in the slave.

The major problem with instruction set enhancement is that the technique is not available to most users and is in any case beyond the capabilities of most users' staff.

WHITE: I should think that very few users would dare to dabble in microprogramming because of problems of support and other allied problems.

MANVILLE: On currently available computers it is not an easy task to extend the instruction set. An increasing number of machines have writable microprogram stores but they have not generally been designed with user extensions in mind. To enable instructions to be added to a basic set, there should be sufficient free space in the microprogram store, or else it should be possible to add extra store to that required for the basic set. Also, there must be some unassigned operation codes which can be used for the new instructions.

The task of writing the microprogram is not an easy one for most machines, particularly those in which the microprogram is at a very low level. Micro-instruction sets vary from those which resemble the instruction sets of small computers, with operation and address fields which are transformed by decoding logic into the control signals required, to those in which a wide word is used and very little decoding need be done to produce the control signals. The latter are most often used for the faster machines and when microprogramming them it is very necessary to know in detail about the operation of the processor hardware, its timing constraints, and which operations can be carried out in parallel.

Most manufacturers are reluctant to support user microprogramming and will not provide the details of the micro-instruction set and processor hardware which are required. Some manufacturers would even withdraw normal engineering support if the user were to modify the microprogram. The tools available for the development of microprograms are often primitive and are not often available to the user.

A problem which must be faced when considering the use of microprograms supplied by users is that, on currently available computers, the microprogrammer can usually bypass protection systems. Thereby, whether accidentally or maliciously, he can interfere with the operation of the system as a whole or with other user's programs or data in a multiprogramming machine. Protection may be enforced at the microprogram level either by building it into the underlying hardware and disallowing certain operations when the machine is in non-privileged mode, or by restricting the set of micro-instructions that a user can cause to be executed.

BACHTIN: I think that it is the trend nowadays for a user not to need an awareness of what is going on in the computer; that is, he should be able to state his problem in his own terms. Isn't this business of microprogramming apt, once more, to force the user to know the intimate details of the computer itself?

MANVILLE: I would not advocate that every programmer should learn about microprogramming; it is still a very specialized job. To a large extent, the responsibility should still lie with the people who already know about such things in great detail.

The feasibility of user microprogramming, and many other aspects of microprogrammed support for high-level languages, is discussed in detail in the State of the Art Report Microprogramming and Systems Architecture (302).

PROGRAM PERFORMANCE IN VIRTUAL STORAGE SYSTEMS

INTRODUCTION

Virtual storage systems present many special problems in program performance. A detailed description of the characteristics of such systems would clearly be out of place here but it is worth noting that such systems work at all because programs have a typical run-time pattern.

SPIRN: In a paged virtual memory system, programs run with only some fraction of their total set of pages in memory at any given time. If an instruction or data item in some page not in main storage is referenced, the missing page must be fetched from an external memory device, typically a drum. Since current such devices are perhaps 10000 times slower than main memory, it is essential that missing page references (known as page faults) be rare. Page fault rates exceeding one in about every five thousand references lead to intolerable drum fetching overhead. Yet typical programs can achieve better than this rate with many pages missing. The (intuitively reasonable) conclusion is: in the vicinity of any given time instant, a program uses only part of its total set of pages. Others are not referenced at all about this time. This is called the principle of locality. Note that this is an empirical, not a formal effect; it is certainly possible to succeed in writing a program that uses all of its pages in any reasonably short time interval. Locality is a consequence of the way people tend to consider a complex problem part by part.

For efficient virtual memory operation, the set of pages in use at a given time must be loaded into main memory. For convenience, we refer to this set as the locality set, or simply as 'the locality'. Successful paging algorithms attempt to estimate each program's locality set, and to retain it in memory. When a page must be removed from main memory, the one selected is one that is supposed to be no longer in the locality. In general, we can only estimate a locality with some error, since we cannot know exactly what a program will do next (without actually executing it). The effectiveness of various paging algorithms generally depends on the accuracy of their locality estimators.

For example, two commonly used paging algorithms are Least-Recently-Used (LRU) and First-In-First-Out (FIFO). When a page is to be displaced from main memory, LRU chooses the page referenced least recently by the program, whereas FIFO chooses the page first fetched into memory. It seems reasonable (and there is some statistical basis) to assume that the page not used for the longest time is least likely to be used again in the near future. Much less reasonable is the supposition that a page is no longer in the locality set simply because it was fetched a long time ago. The page may in fact have been heavily referenced in the near past. Consequently, we expect that LRU leads to a lower fault rate than FIFO, as has been shown by experiment (148,149).

It is possible to be more specific about the nature of the locality phenomenon. In order to define it formally, we must propose one or more mathematical models for it. Such models may be used as program behaviour models to drive analyses or simulations of memory management systems. Once we understand the properties of locality, we may attempt to improve a program's behaviour by increasing its degree of locality. Specifically, if a program's locality sets are made smaller, and if it changes locality sets less frequently, it will exhibit improved virtual memory performance.

SPECIAL CONSIDERATIONS FOR VS

All users of virtual storage storage systems are probably familiar with the standard list of "do and don't" recommendations for programming in such an environment, covering such matters as accessing array elements in their storage order (FORTRAN stores arrays by column, PL/1 by row), storing data used concurrently as close together as possible, and so on. These recommendations serve to indicate that special care has to be taken in virtual storage environments. Unsuitable coding techniques can lead to horrendously inefficient programs and systems.

A particular aspect of this problem is that experienced programmers, when they first come into contact with a virtual storage system, have to 'unlearn' many of the techniques they have previously thought of as efficient.

MUNRO: Pageable operating systems differ in some of their characteristics quite spectacularly from operating systems which are not paged. For example, almost every commercial suite of programs has, somewhere or other, a table look-up routine, which looks up prices or some such information. If those tables reach any size, as they frequently do, then the table look-up routine is the first place to go when one is trying to optimize the program, because if one does an instruction map of the program, that is, an execution time by location map, there is generally a gigantic spike in the region of the table look-up routine. So with a non-pageable operating system, we always think in terms of a binary search of the table; it is easy to do and very fast. As soon as we have changed the search algorithm in this way, the spike will go out of the execution time map of the program, the program will run spectacularly faster, and it will co-exist much better with other programs.

However, all that changes if the operating system supports paging, because it is a characteristic of a binary search that it will dash across half the table for any given search. So if there was any possibility of the table being paged out, every search is going to bring back half of it. In general, that means that the entire table will become permanently resident in core, in real memory; and if the table is a substantial size, as it can easily be with a VS machine, that can be extremely anti-social. So one needs a different approach to looking up large tables in VS systems. I am not sure that there is a single best answer, as there clearly was in non-VS systems. The most popular approach that I have seen so far is to sift out the 'hot' items, about 5%, from the table as the program executes, and put them into a separate table, which is very easy to do. By one's choice of relative sizes for the two tables, one can arrange for any required number of look-ups to be found in the hot table.

Another possibility, quite the reverse of the recommended solution in a non-VS environment, is to make a serial search of the table. With a table sorted according to the frequency with which the individual items are accessed, a serial search may be very effective, if the number of active items is very small in relation to the whole.

RAMAGE: With the advent of virtual systems came a whole new 'code of good programming'. Many of the earlier points applicable to non-VS systems remain valid but there are also a few new ones to add to the list. The new system overheads introduced by virtual storage include:

1 *Dynamic address translation*: Dynamic address translation is a remarkably small overhead because of the efficient hardware implementation, in particular the Look Aside Buffer, which resolves the translation in a very high percentage of cases.

2 *Paging*: The overhead incurred by paging depends partly on the programmer to keep it at a minimum and partly on the scheduling, being careful not to over-commit the machine. In non-VS environments, the program needed to have enough main storage to accommodate the maximum required but in VS environments it needs only enough main storage to accommodate the working set of the program.

The working set is a somewhat nebulous quantity, but for our purposes, we will define it as the amount of main storage required to run the program with a paging rate of not more than 3 per second.

The programmer must make efforts to keep his working set to a minimum. Some of the things he can do are as follows:

- Avoid having too many I/O buffers or there is a good chance of their being paged out before they are used.

- Organize the program so that the program's usual path is sequential and if certain subroutines are used in only two or three places, repeat the coding in-line.

- Error or other exception routines should be kept out of the main line through the program with other little used subroutines and page-aligned at the end of the program.

- Associated routines should be grouped together on the same page.

- Overlays should, in general, be removed, although in one or two programs in our installation it was found that the un-overlayed versions actually took longer to run. This was because the very efficient overlay structure that had been generated was in fact reducing the paging in comparison with that of the unoverlayed version. This was certainly found to be the exception rather than the rule.

In general, one should aim to reduce paging wherever possible using whatever techniques may happen to be appropriate.

3 *CCW translation*: CCW translation is a very considerable overhead on I/O operations. This is one area where the VS implementation could be said to be done on the cheap. The channels have not been modified for VS operation and are therefore unable to deal with virtual addresses in CCWs, therefore the supervisor must convert these to a series of real CCWs in work space before starting the I/O operation. On average, this involves the execution of some 1500 extra instructions per data transfer over a non-VS system. Because of this, it is imperative to keep I/O down to a minimum.

Similar considerations apply to sorting in a virtual storage environment, where the classic binary sort methods can cause excessive paging activity. A better method is described here by Guertin who is talking in the context of a paging system model with the following characteristics:

- *demand paging system*
- *2048-word page size*
- *16 pages of swappable physical memory (that is, 32768 words)*
- *1-microsecond memory cycle time and average instruction time*
- *virtual memory on a drum with an average page transfer time of 30 milliseconds.*

GUERTIN (319): There are a variety of in-core sort techniques available, and most perform poorly in a paging environment. Binary sort methods yield minimum numbers of comparisons for n sort elements (the minimum number of comparisons is slightly more than $n\log_2 n$. Such sorts reference the elements in an order that is sufficiently random to cause significant paging for large n. Assume, for example, a 32768 word array to be sorted by a FORTRAN program in the model system. We would have at least a 17-page working set including the sort program and, since this exceeds the swappable physical memory, we have a self-paging situation. Now let us assume we can have a logical work space of 64K (including the 32K array) and we make use of it in the following manner:

1 Sort the first 16K words of the array using a binary sort. The working set would only be 8 pages of data and no paging would occur.

2 Sort the second 16K words of the array in the same manner. One page swap would be needed at some point and then no further paging would occur.

3 Merge the two 16K sorted sections into a separate 32K word area by running linearly through the two 16K sections comparing and moving elements in the process. This would require only about 16 page swaps with a working set that stays at 4 pages (a page from each 16K section, a page in the merge section, and the instructions).

A little arithmetic on the minimum number of comparisons needed to sort by the above sort-merge, as opposed to just sorting the entire 32K array, shows that the two methods take the same number of comparisons!

• Sort-merge	$16K \times \log_2 16K$ =	229 376	first section
	$16K \times \log_2 16K$ =	229 376	second section
		32 768	merge process
	Total:	491 520	
• Sort only	$32K \times \log_2 32K$ =	491 520	

Of course, we should move the merged result back on top of the original array to complete the process, but that would take only about 16 page swaps to accomplish. So the conclusion is that sort-merge (in core) yields a smaller working set and therefore is more efficient in a paging environment, even though it requires a very large virtual memory space.

A four-way sort-merge would be even more effective because the working set would be kept small during the critical sort phase. Each 8K section is binary sorted, then pairs of 8K sections are merged into the 16K sections, then the 16K sections are merged back into the original area to produce the final result.

There is one other important item concerning sorts and swaps. Typically, when two items are to be interchanged, a temporary area is used to hold one item during the interchange. For example, to interchange A and B, a sequence such as the following is usually coded:

```
TEMP = A
A = B
B = TEMP
```

If the computer supports an 'exclusive injunction' function (XOR), done in-line as a single instruction, not as a subroutine, then the temporary can be eliminated by XORing A with B three times to accomplish the interchange. That is

```
A = XOR(B,A)
B = XOR(A,B)
A = XOR(B,A)
```

B XOR A replaces A; A XOR B replaces B, and then B XOR A replaces A. By eliminating the temporary area, we eliminate an unnecessary page reference and reduce the working set.

The important point to remember is that one unnecessary page swap is equivalent to 30 000 or more instructions! The smaller the working set, the faster your program will run in a paging environment.

Detailed discussion of the operation of virtual storage systems can be found in the State of the Art Report Virtual Storage (319) ***and in***

the papers of Spirn (page 357) and Patel (page 291).

INVITED PAPERS

OPTIMIZING INPUT/OUTPUT

G G Brown

Brown's Operating System Services

G G BROWN is a software specialist, particularly in the IBM 360/370 field. He established his own consultancy - Brown's Operating System Services - in 1969. As well as being the current chairman of the BCS specialist group on the measurement of computer performance, and a member of the SHARE CME project, he is an honorary consultant to University College, London University. He is a fellow of the British Computer Society. Software produced by him includes the BOSS Instruction Execution Analyser, used by about twenty companies in the UK and abroad, and the Activity Analyser, an advanced software monitor for OS and VSI systems, used by several discriminating installations. The BOSS teleprocessing monitor, THIRST, currently controls about 1000 visual display units.

INTRODUCTION

With large sophisticated systems one of the major problems of optimizing input/output is the detection of the bottlenecks. This paper describes a system measurement tool called the Activity Analyser that is used to monitor IBM 360s and 370s running under OS.

THE ACTIVITY ANALYSER

While it can be used to advantage in benchmark situations, the Activity Analyser was intended to be used mainly to assess running systems where it is necessary to keep the overheads of performance monitoring to a minimum. To this end, the analysis function is carried out in a two-stage process. In view of the multiplicity of activities to be monitored on large-scale systems, an event-oriented technique was chosen in preference to a sampling technique.

Structure of the Activity Analyser

Before delving into too much detail let us take a look at the major components of the Analyser. The heart of the tool is a modification that is made to the supervisor of the Operating System. This modification is responsible for recording in a convenient form all the significant events that take place in the system. We shall refer to this component as the data generator.

In order to collect the event data for subsequent analysis, a data gathering program is run for the period under review. It donates buffers to the data generator and, as these become full, writes them to an external medium, either disk (if the period to be monitored is fairly short) or tape.

The data thus collected is processed at some convenient time by the Analyser proper to provide summary reports for the period under review and summary files to be processed by ancillary programs. The latter produce reports on seek movements and on job-step activity in various levels of detail.

Events monitored

Let us now return to consider the types of event that must be recorded in order to be able to reconstruct the activity of the system. The events can be divided into three main categories: task events, I/O events and other events.

From task events we are able to keep track of the task in control of the CPU at any given time; provision is made in the Analyser for monitoring two CPUs to cater for the multiprocessing variant of the IBM 360/65. By noting the state of a task as it loses control of the CPU we are able to classify its inactive periods into Waiting or Interrupted. At the macro-level, job-step start and stop times (provided by links between the standard accounting routine and the data generator) allow the association of partition activity with a particular job-step.

In the recording of I/O events, something of a compromise is made. Ideally one would record all the stages from the request for a logical record through to the physical operations. This data generator only records the start of a physical I/O operation and its finish, as usually indicated by an I/O interrupt. On the 360 under OS, seeks on direct-access devices are easily distinguished from other operations, thus allowing seeking to be treated as a separate activity. I/O operations are linked to logical file names to make the reports on I/O activity more meaningful.

The other types of event recorded relate mainly to requests for supervisory services such as loading a program or opening a data set. While provision is not made by the data generator to keep track of main storage requests, there is a facility to record the core used by a program if other means of calculating it are available.

The timing of events is achieved through the use of the timer maintained by the supervisor. Events are timed explicitly or implicitly with a timer value in 1200ths of a second. The accuracy of this will depend on that of the hardware timer which, for 360s, is normally one power-cycle time (i e 1/50th second in the UK). 370s and 360s with high-resolution timers can maintain time-of-day values with much greater accuracy.

The volumes of items to be processed is a fairly important factor both at the data capture stage and at the analysis stage. A moderately active 360/65 can generate about one million event items per hour. It is perhaps worth bearing in mind the magnitude of these rates when considering the overhead of extensions to supervisory functions such as interrupt handling. At a rate of 5 million interrupts per day, and assuming an average instruction time of 2 microseconds, an extra 360 instructions represents one hour's CPU time.

Operation of the Activity Analyser

The Analyser itself operates like a simple simulator. Control blocks are built to represent the various entities in the system such as devices, channels, partitions and data sets. Activities are 'started' and 'stopped' as directed by the event items. As mentioned earlier, a program at any point in time is considered to be active (i e using the CPU), interrupted by a higher priority program, or waiting, either for an event or to regain control of the CPU after waiting for an event. Combined with the four I/O states (no I/O, reading or writing, seeking, and reading or writing and seeking) this gives 12 I/O-CPU states. Another set of wait states is maintained with respect to the incidence of the I/O within the wait period; these are called pre-I/O, between-I/O, post-I/O and I/O-completed waits. The pre-I/O and between-I/O waiting times are indicative of the time spent queueing for I/O, while the I/O-completed wait time will approximate to the time waiting to regain control of the CPU after a wait (often called ready time). A low post-I/O wait time compared with I/O-completed wait time will indicate the program is issuing sufficient I/O requests for there to be some in the queue at the completion of others. Similar states are maintained with respect to the I/O on a given data set to arrive at indications of the queueing time and wait time for particular data sets.

Measurement reports

The summaries produced by the Analyser for the overall period include a report for each partition or region of the system indicating the amount of time spent in each of the I/O-CPU states, together with the use made of each channel and of the major system data sets. In addition to these, utilization reports are produced for each channel and device and for the total activity on each of the major system data sets. The other summaries deal with the use of supervisory services and with the frequency of access to the various program modules in the system libraries.

Much of the output from the Analyser is presented in a pictorial form. The Kivigraph program will print Kivigraphs for the total period monitored and for intervals within the period. The values to be displayed can be selected by the user as they can with the activity profiles. The seek pattern reports enable a rapid appreciation of the arm-movement on a particular disk volume.

ASSESSING THE ACTIVITY

As a measure of 'work done', a value called total activity is used. The total activity is the sum of the active time, the time for which each channel was used, and the time spent seeking on each direct-access device. This can be arrived at for the total system, for each partition, or for a job-step. The use made of slow-speed devices such as card-readers and line-printers is ignored in computing this value. In attempting to determine how well the system is performing, we ought to have some prior notion of the values for total activity that we might expect from our system. For example, on a system with one CPU and three channels all used to 65% capacity and allowing 20% of the total activity to be the seeking component, we would expect the total activity of the whole system to be 325% of the time monitored. Working back from this point, if we allow 25 out of the 325% to be devoted to spooling and similar activities, we have 300% to distribute among the worker partitions. Multiprogramming seems to be the way to do things now so let us postulate a system with four worker partitions; we would then expect each partition's total activity to be about 75% of the time monitored.

As targets, those suggested above do not seem to be too ambitious; it would be interesting to know how many installations operate at or above this level of activity. It is perhaps worth restating the total activity as the time that would be taken by the system if there were no gaps between any of the operations and only one operation were carried out at a time.

In the area of attempting to improve the performance of the system, the Analyser helps by providing data on both the performance of the system as a whole and on the performance of individual jobs. The key to system tuning is a knowledge, in as much detail as possible, of the system and its applications. On small systems it is possible to acquire this without the aid of a performance monitor; on large systems running upward of 2000 steps a day it is a well-nigh impossible task. With the details of the 50 most active (in terms of total activity) steps that it is possible to get from such an analysis as this, there is a chance of making some impact on the throughput of the system without too much effort. Blocking, buffering, and data set positioning are the areas most likely to give most return. After the first 50 have been dealt with, the main requirement then is to have faith in the belief that there are real savings to be made from improving on a step that lasts 30 seconds.

CONCLUSION

The Activity Analyser has now been in use for over five years. While the original development took place in Canada at Ontario Hydro, all subsequent development (which is by now the larger part) has been carried out in England, mainly at Unilever Computer Services Ltd. Not the least of the benefits it brings to its users is the encouragement to understand their performance in greater depth with the consequent realization that considerable untapped power is available on their existing system. Somebody put it very succinctly – "to measure is to improve".

THROW-AWAY COMPILING: A MIDDLE PATH BETWEEN INTERPRETATION AND COMPILATION

P J Brown

Computing Laboratory
University of Kent at Canterbury

P J BROWN is a Reader in Computer Science at the University of Kent at Canterbury. Previously he worked at IBM on a PL/1 compiler, at Cambridge University on a doctoral thesis, and at the University of North Carolina on an ALGOL 60 compiler, under the direction of Peter Naur. Some of the work described here was done at the University of Colorado on a visiting appointment. As well as compilers, Dr Brown is interested in macro processors and in software portability; he is the author of a book on these subjects.

THROW-AWAY COMPILING: A MIDDLE PATH BETWEEN INTERPRETATION AND COMPILATION

DESCRIPTION OF THE TECHNIQUE

There are two approaches to implementing a high-level language on a machine: *compiling* the language into the order code of the machine or *interpreting* the language. Usually interpretation is not applied to the original source language, but instead the source is translated into an *intermediate form,* which is a more concise and more easily manipulated version of the original source. Popular intermediate forms are Reverse Polish strings, triples, quadruples, and trees.

Relative merits of compiling and interpreting

The relative merits of compilation and interpretation are well-known. They can be summarized as follows.

1 When a program is run, compiled code runs faster than interpreted code. The relative speed varies enormously, but a factor of ten would be typical.

2 Interpretation needs less storage than compilation, even allowing for the fact that the interpreter must be present at run time. Interpretation is particularly good when extensive error checking and good diagnostics are required.

3 For some languages (for example PAL), operations such as type checking cannot be performed until run time. For languages with these features, it is impossible to compile code in advance so (total or partial) interpretation is vital. In general, these languages are rare - they probably have less than 1% of the market - and we will ignore them in this discussion.

Thus, in deciding whether to compile or to interpret, the software designer has to trade optimization of speed against optimization of storage. Sometimes the decision is an easy one: for a BASIC system designed for short student programs on a very small machine, interpretation is clearly the answer; for COBOL or FORTRAN systems that run on a large machine, compilation is obviously preferable. At other times, the decision is a difficult one. If one is designing a BASIC system to run in 16-32K words of storage on a machine with slow backing storage, or even with no backing storage at all, does one compile or interpret? One section of the potential user market wants fast execution while another wants to be able to run long programs. Neither compilation nor interpretation will satisfy both sets of users. We will now introduce a technique that will.

Dynamic compiling

The technique of *dynamic compiling* works as follows.

The source program is first translated into an intermediate form as for interpretation. This intermediate form is divided into units that are natural for the language concerned. The unit might be a single statement or a basic block.

At run time, the intermediate form is not interpreted, but is taken one unit at a time, compiled into machine code, and then immediately executed. Thus instead of an interpreter there is a *code-generator* present at run-time. For example, consider the following BASIC program:

```
 10   LET X = 3
 20   GOTO 100
 30   ...
  .
  .
  .
100   LET Y = X + 1
```

If this program is divided into units of statements, the run-time sequence of events would be as follows. Statement 10 is compiled (from its intermediate form) and immediately executed; statement 20 is then compiled and executed; then statement 100 is compiled and executed.

At first sight, dynamic compilation appears to be a really stupid idea. Compared with ordinary interpretation, it will be slower and will require more storage (since the code-generator will be bigger than an interpreter). However, we will now introduce a second facility, which transforms the economics of dynamic compiling.

Throw-away compiling

Assume that there is a fixed area of storage available. Then at run time, this storage will contain:

1 the source program in its intermediate form,

2 the code-generator

3 an unused area, which we will call *workspace*

The technique of *throw-away compiling* uses this workspace. The source program is dynamically compiled, as described above, but the compiled code for each unit is kept in the workspace and cross-referenced with the source. If a unit is executed a second time, and its compiled code is still in the workspace there is no need to re-compile it. Instead the previously compiled code will be re-executed. If, at any stage, the workspace becomes full up some or all of the compiled code must be *thrown away*, and if this is ever needed again it must be re-compiled. We will use the term *throw-away algorithm* to denote the algorithm that manages the workspace.

With throw-away compiling, if there is enough room to compile all the units of the program that are executed on a given run (not necessarily the whole program), then nothing will ever be compiled more than once and the program will run almost as fast as an ordinary compiled program would. If, on the other hand, there is insufficient workspace to compile everything (and thus an ordinary compiler would be useless, unless there was some overlaying capability) the program will still run but will run more slowly. In the extreme case, where there is almost no workspace, it will run as slowly as ordinary interpretation. Thus the merit of throw-away compiling is that it adapts itself to make use of whatever workspace is available and thus optimizes program performance.

Further technical details

An important design question is how the throw-away algorithm is to work. (A similar question arises with page-turning algorithms, though here the constraints are quite different). We will discuss this question in detail later, and simply observe at this stage that the simpler the algorithm the better. In some programming languages, workspace might also be needed for such things as stacks and dynamic arrays. In this case, they would share the workspace with dynamically compiled code and where necessary the latter would be thrown away to make room for the former.

On machines with fast backing storage such as fixed-head discs, hardware or software paging or segmentation schemes are an alternative to throw-away compiling. For example, GIER ALGOL (186), the LISP system of Bobrow and Murphy (187), and STAB-1 (188) all have schemes for swapping in sections of compiled code from disc. The relative merits of these schemes compared with throw-away compiling depend on whether the overheads of swapping from backing storage are greater than the overheads in computer time of re-compiling.

Similar considerations apply on machines with hardware virtual storage systems, where it may be advisable, though not necessary, to restrict jobs to a relatively small fixed amount of workspace.

A second important question concerns the boundary between compiled units. If two successive units are compiled and then re-executed, control should ideally flow direct from the first to the second; the alternative, to be avoided if possible, is, after executing the first unit, to call a *control program*, which tests whether the second unit has been compiled, and if so finds where it is and then jumps to it. Usually this ideal of avoiding calls to a control program can be achieved; we will give more details later.

Error checking

It is an increasing opinion that implementations of programming languages should check for all possible run-time errors, including such things as out-of-bound subscripts variables used but not set, underflow and overflow, dangling references, stack overflow, etc. Moreover, error detection must be supported by good facilities for reporting errors in meaningful terms, pinpointing where they occur in the source program, and possibly recovering from them. Thus, a good error diagnosis system consists of error detection, error reporting, and possibly error recovery. All three are difficult to achieve.

It is often said that interpreters are better at error diagnosis than compilers. This is not completely true. The real problem is that compilers do not generate code that performs good error diagnosis because this makes programs much bigger, with the result that some may be too big to run. With throw-away compiling there are no limits on the size of compiled code and so this problem is removed (though programs with full checking will, of course, run slower than those without).

The easing of the problem of error diagnosis is one of the greatest benefits of throw-away compiling.

Relative size of code

Many different figures have been quoted in the literature for the size of compiled code compared with the size of an equivalent intermediate form (for example, Reverse Polish notation) that can be interpreted. With throw-away compiling, there is even more merit in keeping the intermediate form concise than with interpreting. This is because the average unit may be executed several times for each time it is compiled, so the overheads of decoding the intermediate form are proportionately less.

A factor that has a huge effect on relative size is error diagnosis. Without complete diagnosis, compiled code might be twice as big as the intermediate form; with diagnosis, it might be three to ten times as big, depending on how much the hardware helps.

When making a comparison of size, however, it may be necessary to add the size of the run-time system, which, for throw-away compiling, includes the code-generator. We say may because it depends on circumstances: in a time-sharing environment, one run time system might be shared between ten users so one should count one-tenth of it against each user; some computers have systems software locked in (for example, to read-only memory), irrespective of whether it is used, so it makes no difference how much of it is employed at run time. Whatever the situation, however, it is best to make the code-generator small and simple - hence dumb. Throw-away compiling is not suitable for producing highly optimized code.

APPLICATION OF THROW-AWAY COMPILING

So far we have described throw-away compiling in general terms. Now, we describe the results of practical projects to apply the technique to real languages. The purpose of this practical work is to answer the following questions:

1 Does the technique really work, or are there some terrible unforseen practical snags?

2 What is the performance of throw-away compiling?

3 What is the best throw-away algorithm?

4 Can calls of a control program be avoided?

At the time of writing, one project, a BASIC compiler, is complete and others are in progress. The answer to question 1 is that the technique really works, at least for the languages and machines so far examined. The only possible difficulty is on machines that regard a data area as something radically different from an area of executable code; throw-away compiling involves frequent switches from compile mode (where the compiled program is the output data) to execute mode, and, for good performance, the operating system must allow this change to be simple and fast.

The BASIC project

Further details of the BASIC compiler are given elsewhere (189), and we will here state the main points that have emerged from the project. The most valuable information is the performance measures. The figures that were produced, although subject to a number of caveats, do indicate that throw-away compiling meets its design aims. Firstly, it appears that, if enough workspace is available to compile the whole program without any throwing away, then throw-away compilation runs at the same speed as traditional compilation and running. (Throw-away compiling gains by not compiling units that are never executed on a given run, but loses through the need for extra housekeeping.) Figure 1 shows how the performance of throw-away compiling deteriorates as the size of workspace is reduced to various fractions of that needed for dynamic compilation of every used unit of the program.

Percentage of necessary workspace available	*Total run time*
100	100
80	177
60	282
40	369
20	496

Figure 1: Degradation of performance as a result of reduced workspace

Thus, even when only one-fifth of the necessary workspace is available, the average program only runs about five times slower than a totally pre-compiled one. One would expect the performance of an interpreter to be worse than this. However, it must be re-emphasized that the figures quoted are approximate ones, subject to experimental error.

The BASIC compiler also provides some information for questions 3 and 4. Its throw-away algorithm is the simplest possible one: workspace is filled sequentially and if it becomes full, everything is thrown away. This strategy has two great advantages:

1 Since everything is cancelled at one go, it can be guaranteed that when a statement is cancelled all references to it go at the same time. Hence there is no need for housekeeping, no problem of 'dangling references', and it is quite safe for one dynamically compiled statement to jump directly to another without passing through a control program.

2 Since storage is allocated contiguously, control can flow from a statement to its successor without any jump in between.

Because of these two advantages, it is possible to compile code that runs without any calls to a control program, except for subroutine and function calls and returns. The main tactic used in accomplishing this is, after the first use of any call to the control program to get a particular statement, to overwrite the call with a direct jump to the compiled form of the statement. Concrete examples of this are given in (189).

Further projects

Evidence from other projects confirms that the simplest throw-away algorithm appears to be the best and that, with this strategy, it is possible to reduce calls to a control program to a negligible overhead. There may be some languages or some machines where this is not so, or some brilliant throw-away algorithm waiting to be discovered, but they have not been found yet.

RELATION TO OTHER WORK

We will conclude this paper by relating the work described above to other techniques with similar aims. We have already mentioned one such technique: the software segmentation used in the GIER ALGOL compiler and its successors.

Three comparable techniques

There are three other techniques especially relevant. Like the GIER ALGOL technique, none of them is wholely 'worse' or 'better' than throw-away compiling, each shines in its particular environment. We will describe the three techniques in increasing order of adaptability.

1 *Threaded code* (190,191) is a half-way stage between compiling and interpreting. It is simple and performs very well on certain machines, such as the PDP-11. It is a fixed point on the spectrum between pure compilation and pure interpretation, whereas throw-away compiling adapts to vary along this spectrum according to the storage available.

2 A *mixed-code approach* (192, 198, 194) is an actual mixture of compiling and interpreting. It relies on the fact that a small part of most programs accounts for most of the execution time. If these parts can be identified and compiled, and the rest of the program interpreted, then speed can be combined with conciseness. Indeed, the proportion of compilation can be varied to suit particular requirements, though this proportion does need to be fixed in advance. A possible disadvantage of the mixed-code approach is that it is necessary to write both an interpreter and a compiler, make them compatible, and, hardest of all, keep them compatible throughout their life.

3 *Adaptive code generation* is described by Hansen and Wulf in this volume. This is attacking only part of our problem, since it is concerned only with speed, but attacks this problem much more deeply, since it deals not only with interpretation and compilation but with various levels of optimization as well.

Throw-away compiling actually evolved from a project for an adaptable mixed-code approach. It is very easy for a throw-away compiler to provide a facility whereby the user can say that certain parts of a program are to be pre-compiled. In this case the code-generator can be called before a run starts to compile the necessary parts and thus 'lock them in' to the workspace. (Similarly certain paging systems allow users to lock into core parts of their program.) Preliminary tests indicate that this facility is not valuable when applied on top of throw-away compiling; the best speed improvement was only 15%, and the average was under 10%.

CONCLUSION

Clearly, throw-away compiling is not the answer for all compilers on all machines. However, when there are severe absolute constraints on program size, throw-away compiling can adapt itself both to run programs that are bigger than a compiler could deal with and to run most programs much faster than an interpreter would. It should be ideal for small time-sharing systems and, increasingly more important, simple microprocessor systems. Moreover, by improving the economics of error diagnosis, it helps make software more reliable.

TRANSFORMING CLEAR PROGRAMS TO EFFICIENT ONES: A PROGRAM DEVELOPMENT METHOD

R M Burstall and J Darlington

Department of Artificial Intelligence
University of Edinburgh

ACKNOWLEDGEMENT

Our work was funded by the Science Research Council. We are indebted to Bob Boyer, J Moore, Z Manna and R Waldinger for stimulating ideas and to the members of IFIP Working Group 2.3 for discussion and encouragement. We are grateful to Eleanor Kerse for typing this paper.

R M BURSTALL originally worked in Operational Research, but soon became absorbed in computing with a particular interest in Artificial Intelligence. He worked for two years as a Research Fellow at Birmingham University on heuristic problem solving. He moved to Edinburgh in 1964, and is now Reader in the Department of Artificial Intelligence. His work has been mainly on the theory of computation and its applications, particularly on methods of proving properties of programs. He now runs a small research group, supported by the Science Research Council.

J DARLINGTON worked briefly with ICL before going to the London School of Economics in 1966 to study computational methods. He came to Edinburgh in 1969 to work for a PhD under Dr Burstall, obtaining his doctorate in 1972. Since then, he has been a member of Dr Burstall's research group. His main area of interest is the theory of computation, particularly techniques for transforming and improving programs.

TRANSFORMING CLEAR PROGRAMS TO EFFICIENT ONES: A PROGRAM DEVELOPMENT METHOD

INTRODUCTION

We have been studying transformations which would enable us to write clear but extremely inefficient programs and transform them into sensible ones. This paper gives a brief account of our work, which has been reported in more technical detail elsewhere. The source language and the target language for our transformations are identical, a high-level language of great simplicity chosen because programs in it are easy to manipulate and to reason about. This is the language of recursion equations. For example, here is the Fibonacci function as Fibonacci might have written it:

```
Fib(0)   <= 1                     (1)
Fib(1)   <= 1                     (2)
Fib(n+2) <= Fib(n+1)+Fib(n)       (3)
```

This is a program in our recursion equation language, and we have an interpreter for this language. To evaluate, say, *Fib*(4) we simplify a term using any equation whose left hand side 'matches' that term. Thus:

```
Fib(4) <= Fib(3)+Fib(2)                        binding n to 2 in equation 3
       <= (Fib(2)+Fib(1))+Fib(2)               binding n to 1 in equation 3
       <= ((Fib(1)+Fib(0))+Fib(1))+Fib(2)      binding n to 0 in equation 3
       <= ((1+Fib(0))+Fib(1))+Fib(2)
          ...
          ...
          ...
       <= 3+2
       <= 5
```

Our interpreter does not do all this rewriting in a literal sense, but the computation sequence is equivalent to the above, as indeed it would be in a more conventional language where the same program might be written:

```
procedure Fib(m);
    if m=0 then result:=1;
    if m=1 then result:=1
           else result:=Fib(m-1)+Fib(m-2)
    end;
```

Now this is a neat definition but a silly program, because to evaluate *Fib*(*n*) it takes time proportional to 2^n, whereas we can clearly do it in time proportional to *n* by evaluating *Fib*(0), *Fib*(1), *Fib*(2), *Fib*(3),... in sequence and remembering the last but one in order to work out the next.

Here is how we can transform the silly Fibonacci program into a sensible one. We will write

```
...u..u... where u=....
```

to mean 'evaluate *u* first and then use this value in the expression to the left of **where** whenever *u* appears'; (for example, *x*+*x***x* **where** *x*=*y*/(*y*+1) means 'evaluate *y*/*y*+1 and then evaluate *x*+*x***x* using that value for *x*').

Recall the definition:

```
Fib(0)   <= 1                        (1)
Fib(1)   <= 1                        (2)
Fib(n+2) <= Fib(n+1)+Fib(n)          (3)
```

Now let us define *g* as a pair of Fibonacci numbers:

```
g(n) <= <Fib(n+1),Fib(n)>            (4)
```

To get a nice definition for *g* let us look at its value for 0 and *n*+1:

```
g(0)   <= <Fib(0+1),Fib(0)>                   by instantiating n in (3)
       <= <1,1>                               using (1) and (2)
g(n+1) <= <Fib(n+1+1),Fib(n+1)>               by instantiating n in (4)
       <= <Fib(n+1)+Fib(n),Fib(n+1)>          using (3)
       <= <u+v,u> where <u,v>=<Fib(n+1),Fib(n)>  rewriting to introduce
                                              where and so abstract the
                                              common subexpression
                                              Fib(n+1)
       <= <u+v,u) where <u,v>=g(n)            using (4) backwards
```

But we can easily rewrite (3) to use *g*

```
Fib(n+2) <= u+v where <u,v>=<Fib(n+1),Fib(n)>
         <= where <u,v>=g(n)
```

We now have the recursive program

```
Fib(0)   <= 1
Fib(1)   <= 1
Fib(n+2) <= u+v where <u,v>=g(n)
g(0)     <= <1,1>
g(n+1)   <= <u+v,u> where <u,v>=g(n)
```

If this is evaluated for, say, *Fib*(5), it calls *g*(3), which calls *g*(2), which calls *g*(1), which calls *g*(0), and the results are combined to give *Fib*(5). So *Fib*(*n*) now just takes time proportional to *n*.

We should now take stock of the transformation rules which are needed. They are:

1 *definition*: add a definition defining some new function symbol (for example, definition of *g* above);

2 *instantiation*: substitute some expression for a variable (for example, getting expressions for $g(0)$ and for $g(n+1)$ above);

3 *unfolding*: replace some call to a function by its definition (for example, using the definition of $f(n+2)$ above);

4 *abstraction*: factoring out some common subexpression and introducing **where**, as above;

5 *folding*: replace some instance of the definition of a function by a call to it, (for example, using the definition of $g(n)$ *backwards* above).

We may add an extra rule, not needed in our example above:

4a *use of rewrite lemmas*: use some known facts such as the associativity or commutativity of multiplication to rewrite some subexpression.

Folding is the key transformation since it can introduce new recursive calls. It is the goal of the whole process and to avoid combinatorially explosive search we use lemmas or abstraction only when they enable us to achieve a fold. In fact they can economically be combined with the search for a fold.

The rules are used in the order given above. They involve human help in

1 providing definitions, like g above;

2 suggesting suitable instantiations, often obvious ones like 0 and $n+1$ for a non-negative integer variable as above;

3 supplying useful lemmas like the associativity of multiplication.

DISCUSSION

What is the interest of such program transformation? An optimizing compiler accepts an algorithm (presumably a sensible one) represented as a program in a high-level language and converts it into good machine code, making computational economies and using machine resources to advantage. But where does this sensible algorithm come from? It is probably rather a complex entity quite difficult to reason about. We take the point of view that it may often be seen as an optimized version of a much simpler algorithm, but optimized in a more radical sense involving major changes in the loop/recursion structure.

Some common situations like this would be:

1 two loops (or recursions) in sequence which have essentially the same control (for example, they both count from 1 up to n) and whose bodies may be combined to yield a single loop;

2 two loops (or recursions) in which the first creates a data structure which the second takes to pieces, where it may again be possible to combine these with elimination of the intermediate data structure;

3 generate-and-test programs where the testing may be 'promoted' into the generation process, and where earlier testing will often avoid unnecessary generation;

4 converting a recursive program to an iterative one.

Examples would be

- in searches where a single successful test may terminate the whole generation process;
- generation of 'all x such that P' and each x is generated from a 'father' $f(x)$ such that x only has P if its father has P, in which case if an element does not have P we do not need to generate its sons.

It turns out that a considerable number of algorithms which we have examined can be derived, using just our transformations, from much simpler algorithms. When inventing algorithms ourselves we may often think in a similar way, considering some naive algorithm and then using some programming tricks from our repertoire to transform it into a more sensible one.

We do not see how to carry out such transformations entirely automatically; even though our folding, abstraction and unfolding rules can be automated, it is still necessary to supply the machine with new definitions, with possible instantiations and sometimes with useful lemmas. However we have been able to program a semi-automatic system which does all the laborious work of the transformations, given the user assistance in the form just mentioned. The system performs satisfactorily on the Fibonacci problem and on other more complex examples

ANOTHER EXAMPLE

We can extend the equational programming language to handle programs about sets. We need the constant θ, the empty set $\{x\}$, the singleton set whose only member is x, and $X \cup Y$, the union of equations we also allow them on the left. For example we could compute the Cartesian product of S and T (set of all pairs with first in S and second in T) by

```
pairs(θ,T)          <= θ
pairs(S,θ)          <= θ
pairs({s},{t})      <= {<s,t>}
pairs(S1 ∪ S2,T)    <= pairs(S1,T) ∪ pairs(S2,T)
pairs(S,T1 ∪ T2)    <= pairs(S,T1) ∪ pairs(S,T2)
```

Notice that in cases like *pairs*(θ,θ) or *pairs*$(\{1\},\{2,3\})$ more than one equation will apply and we must ensure (for example, by proving it) that the result is the same whichever equation is used. To ensure termination the interpreter must bind $S1$ and $S2$ to sets which are smaller than $S1 \cup S2$ and have no elements in common.

A function to select all elements having property p would be

```
selectp(θ)          <= θ
selectp({s})        <= {s} if p(s)
```

```
                      <= θ if not p(s)
     selectp(S1 ∪ S2) <= selectp(S1) ∪ selectp(S2)
```

Now we can consider how these interact. Suppose for example we have a set of men and a set of women and wish to discover all the compatible pairs. We need a function *pairsp*

```
     pairsp(S,T) <= selectp(pairs(S,T))
```

Unfortunately this produces a big intermediate set of pairs before doing any selection. Let us transform it as we transformed the Fibonacci example.

```
pairsp(θ,T)        <= selectp(pairs(θ,T))                        (instantiate)
                   <= selectp(θ)                                 (unfold)
                   <= θ                                          (unfold)
pairsp(S,θ)        <= θ                                          (similarly)
pairsp({s},{t})    <= selectp(pairs({s},{t}))                    (instantiation)
                   <= selectp({<s,t>})                           (unfold)
                   <= {<s,t>} if p(<s,t>)                        (unfold)
                   <= θ       if not p(<s,t>)                    (unfold)
pairsp(S1 ∪ S2,T)  <= selectp(pairs(S1 ∪ S2,T))                  (unfold)
                   <= selectp(pairs(S1,T) ∪ pairs(S2,T))         (unfold)
                   <= selectp(pairs(S1,T)) ∪ selectp(pairs(S2,T)) (unfold)
                   <= pairsp(S1,T) ∪ pairs(S2,T)                 (fold)
pairsp(S,T1 ∪ T2)  <= pairsp(S,T1) ∪ pairsp(S,T2)                (similarly)
```

We now have a direct recursive definition of *pairsp* which avoids computing a large intermediate set of pairs. We have converted a simple generate-and-test algorithm to one which tests while generating.

DISCUSSION OF TRANSFORMATION AS AN OPTIMIZING TECHNIQUE

Let us now be more explicit about the properties of out transformation technique:

1 It preserves correctness so that if we start off with a correct program we will obtain a new one which is also correct.

2 It does not necessarily preserve termination; the new program may fail to terminate on data for which the original program does terminate. This means we need either a separate correctness proof or else some restrictions on folding to ensure preservation of termination.

3 It does not guarantee an improvement; however one may see informally that if the **where**-abstraction and rewrite lemmas lead to faster computation then the overall transformation including folding will do so.

4 The transformation system is not uni-directional and there is usually more than one possible next move in the transformation process; however rather severely restrained strategies seem to lead to good results.

Given this lack of theoretical reassurance the reader will hardly be convinced that the method is interesting by the two small examples given here. If we have awakened his curiosity he may care to look at the rather more impressive examples in (217).

He will also find there further discussion of the properties of the method and strategies for applying it. The revised version describes out computer implementation of the method which demands from the user only a set of equations, any auxiliary equations he wishes, guidance on instantiation and any rewrite lemmas which he may consider useful. This is an experimental implementation and we do not consider our method a practical optimizing tool.

TRANSFORMATIONS AND PROGRAM SYNTHESIS

One would like to start program development from a specification, preferably a mathematically precise one.

Our initial programs, written for lucidity without regard for efficiency, can be taken as such.a specification. At about the same time (1973-1974) as we were developing our transformation method other workers were considering 'program synthesis' (218) or 'formal derivation of programs' (219). The distinction between optimization and synthesis blurs once one considers very lucid programs as specifications. We have since followed up this idea (220) using our transformation system to convert such a specification into an acceptable program.

John Darlington is currently working on a systematic synthesis of six well-known sorting algorithms using these transformations. One can define the 'sort' of an array as that permutation of it which has elements in ascending order. This clear but inefficient definition would, if executed, lead to generating all permutations and testing each for ascending order. Nevertheless, one can transform it into an efficient set of recursion equations corresponding to one of the known sorting algorithms. Three different permutation algorithms each lead to two sorting algorithms, giving six in all.

But where does the permutation generator come from? We can specify a permutation as any sequence of the original indices such that each occurs exactly once. Again, this suggests generating all sequences and testing each for non-repetition and exhaustiveness. But this silly algorithm can be systematically transformed into any of the three permutation algorithms and thence into any of the six sorts. At the moment this work is in handwritten form and the sequences of transformations have not been checked by machine. We hope to check and publish them quite soon.

The virtue of such a style of program development is that one could split the development into

1 a mathematical specification, and a few pithy mathematical facts which make the algorithm possible

2 a lot of tedious symbol manipulation.

The former would be supplied by the user after a deep study of the problem, the latter could be performed accurately by the machine. The result would be a program guaranteed to conform to the specification.

CONCLUSIONS

Our work is based on the idea that much of the difficulty in writing and modifying programs derives from the attempt to make them efficient, not just by good low-level coding but by the very structure of the algorithm chosen. It suggests an approach to programming in which an initial program is written with all the emphasis on clarity and this is then transformed systematically into one of acceptable efficiency. Such a policy requires the use of programming languages of a much simpler structure than current widely-used programming languages, in order to make such transformations practicable. We are encouraged that a number of people are taking this general view and hope that it will ultimately lead to cheaper and more reliable programming methods.

COMPUTER SYSTEM DESIGN FOR RUN-TIME EFFICIENCY

P C Capon

Department of Computer Science
University of Manchester

P C CAPON is a Senior Lecturer in Computer Science at Manchester University. He graduated with first class honours in Mathematics from Southampton University in 1965, and obtained the Diploma in Computer Science at Cambridge University a year later. Since joining the Computer Science Department at Manchester in 1967, his main research interest has been compiling systems. He is now responsible for the compiling system and compilers on MU5, the research computer developed at Manchester. He has published a number of papers on this subject. He was awarded the degree of PhD in 1970.

COMPUTER SYSTEM DESIGN FOR RUN-TIME EFFICIENCY

INTRODUCTION

In the optimization of the run-time performance of a program, three major areas can be considered:

1 *Improvement of the method or algorithm used in the program*

This is substantially the responsibility of the user. The only way in which the computer system is likely to help him is in monitoring the performance of the program in such a way that the area where improvement is needed is apparent. Even then some types of gross error in method will not be demonstrated directly by system performance.

2 *Improvement of the means of expressing the program*

The varying high-level programming languages each introduce different areas of inefficiency when the program is run. Improved language design may reduce some of that inefficiency which is independent of the computer being used. At present this problem is sometimes partly overcome by use of global compiler optimization techniques.

3 *Improvement of program performance*

Given an effective algorithm coded in a suitable language inefficiences result from the translation to machine instructions. This may be because the compiler produces ineffective code, or because the machine architecture is not sufficiently suited to the original language, or both.

Attempts to implement high-level languages efficiently on processors architecturally unsympathetic to the task has resulted in elaborate optimizing compilers. The most obvious example on many conventional machines is the attempt to make optimal use of a set of registers for a language, such as ALGOL or FORTRAN, which contains no inherent concept of registers. A more extreme example is found in attempts to convert FORTRAN code comprising scalar or element-by-element array operations into code which can be effectively exploited by processors such as the CDC Star-100 and Illiac IV. Here very elaborate compilers are only partially successful in converting to an instruction set unsympathetic to the source language and unsuited to many problems.

These types of optimization have resulted in the investment of considerable effort in large and often difficult-to-maintain compilers at a time when all software costs are increasing. A more effective approach is to make use of relatively decreasing hardware costs to build computers more suited to executing programs written in typical high-level languages. This immediately reduces the size and cost of compilers, and also the total system software, while at the same time providing efficient run-time execution.

In this paper we consider, with examples, some of the architectural requirements for better run-time performance and the extent to which the MU5 processor (173,174), developed at Manchester University, meets these requirements.

THE MU5 COMPUTER SYSTEM

In the MU5 processor, considerable attention has been paid to the requirements of high-level languages. The processor has been designed to deal efficiently with those constructs which occur most often in such languages. One example of this is the way in which frequently used scalar operands such as counters and modifiers reside automatically in associatively addressed fast buffer registers rather than being optimized into conventional registers. Another example is the way in which a series of functions and operands is streamed into the main arithmetic unit. In the resulting processor the gains from elaborate compiler optimizations are very small compared with those on conventional machines. The hardware itself effectively optimizes the behaviour of the program. Before giving examples of the object code compiled for some typical constructs, the MU5 order code is outlined.

MU5 has two major groups of instructions: computational and organizational. The computational set are single address instructions of the form:

F N

where F specifies the central register (cr) and the function (f) required. N specifies the operand. Instructions are basically 16 bits long but certain operand types cause this to be extended up to 80 bits.

There is a single central register for each type of arithmetic. Instead of a multiple register architecture, the machine uses fast associative buffer stores to hold partial results and frequently used operands. The arithmetic registers are:

X 32-bit fixed-point arithmetic
ACC 32 and 64-bit floating-point arithmetic
B 32-bit fixed-point subscript calculations

The instruction set comprises a conventional set of orders, uniform across these registers, but includes reverse subtract and divide rather than load negative or store negative.

The registers associated with operand accessing are:

NB a modifier register which usually points to the start of the scalar variables of the current procedure.

XNB a modifier register used for accessing non-local variables.

SF a stack front register used in conjunction with the facility to stack and recover operands, and in procedure entry.

DR a descriptor register which can hold the descriptor of a data structure and which is used when accesing a vector element

XDR a second descriptor register

The operand specification N consists of operand type and some bits specifying the operand itself. The more important operands are:

1 Literals which follow immediately with the instructions and may be between 6 and 64 bits.

2 Variables of the current procedure or routine. These are accessed relative to the NB register. The first 64 such variables in each procedure only require a 16-bit instruction. Variables of procedures other than the current one may also be accessed but the XNB register must first be set to the start of the variables for that procedure.

3 Vector elements or other elements contained within data structures. The subscript or modifier is computed in the B register. Use of the S[B] operand type causes the specified variable S to be treated as a 64-bit descriptor variable. This descriptor is loaded into the D register. The vector origin, in the descriptor, is combined with the subscript from B and the resulting location accessed.

4 Stack operands, used for partial arithmetic results and in the procedure calling mechanism, and implemented by use of the SF register.

The organizational orders include conditional and unconditional relative control transfers, NB and SF manipulation orders, orders used in procedure entry and exit and a set of orders for Boolean arithmetic.

Scalar Operands and Simple Arithmetic

The space required for the local variables associated with a procedure or subroutine must be allocated dynamically at run time in many languages. Dynamic allocation has the advantage that only storage actively used is allocated, so the scheme is economical in store used. The loading of programs is simplified since store references do not need to be modified at load time, and mixed language programming is facilitated since problems of store allocation and parameter passing largely disappear.

In most conventional computer systems, dynamic storage allocation is more expensive than static allocation. This is because the instructions required for the modified store access needed to fetch a variable are either longer, or take longer to execute than those for an unmodified access. In MU5, dynamic variables of the current procedure are accessed using the contents of the NB base register to the offset within the instruction.

The simplest way for a compiler to process expressions with scalar operands is to generate zero-address or stacking code. It is much easier to generate code for a zero-address computer with a stack of effective infinite depth than for a machine with only a limited stack or with multiple accumulators for partial results.

In MU5, a single address form, in which the accumulator holds the result so far, is used. Operations are between a single operand and this accumulator, and partial results are held in the stack. There is little extra complication in generating the single address form, and greater program efficiency can be achieved this way. This is because less instructions are needed for the single address version, so more concise code can be obtained, and also because less moving of operands between the accumulator and the stack, which is outside the arithmetic unit in MU5, is required.

Frequently used scalar variables and stacked partial results do not return to the store between instructions. Instead, they are automatically held in associative buffer registers close to the arithmetic unit. This achieves performance similar to that with conventional registers but without the usual overhead of optimizing operands into specific registers.

Consider

$$i := 1$$

where i is integer. The corresponding MU5 instructions are:

```
X =  1    :: integer accumulator X = 1
X => i    :: X stored in local variable accessed relative to NB.
```

This is two 16-bit instructions. For speed and convenience the literal 1 is embedded in the instruction.

The assignment:

$$e := a \times b - c \times d$$

requires the temporary storage of the partial result $a \times b$. The stack is used for this in MU5:

```
X =  a
X ×  b
X *= c        :: stack a × b and load c
X ×  d
X ⊖ STACK     :: subtract X from stacked quantity with result in X
X => e
```

This gives a total of six 16-bit instructions where, for example, ICL 1900 code requires nine 24-bit instructions and DEC PDP11 requires five 32-bit and two 16-bit instructions. In MU5, the code required for real operands is similar but using the accumulator register ACC:

```
ACC =  a
ACC ×  b
ACC *= c
ACC ×  d
ACC ⊖ STACK
ACC => e
```

whereas in both the 1900 and PDP11 the instruction sequences for real arithmetic differ considerably from those for integers but are equally long.

Procedure calling

The advantages of writing well-structured programs in which reasonable use is made of procedures with parameters are well understood. Unfortunately the cost of procedure entry and exit on many machines discourages the use of procedures when run-time efficiency is important. It is therefore vital to the efficient execution of well constructed programs that a powerful procedure calling mechanism is available. In MU5, the layout of store before entry to a procedure P and after a call P(A,10) is shown in Figures 1 and 2.

Hence a return link must be created, the parameters stacked, NB and register SF updated and the procedure entered. On exit, NB and the stack front SF are reset and the LINK used for a return address. In MU5 only seven 16-bit instructions are

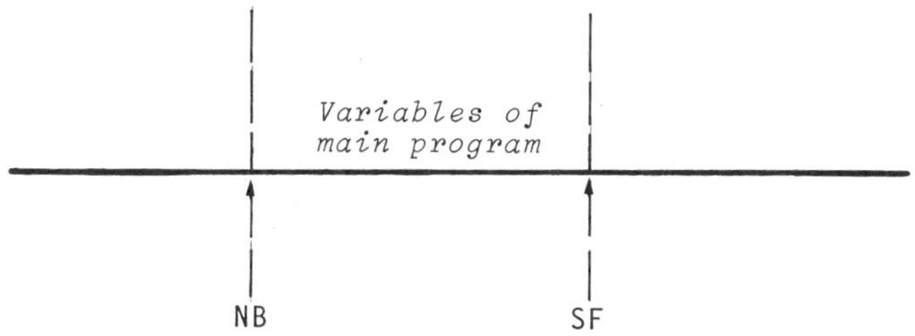

Figure 1: Layout of store before entry to procedure P

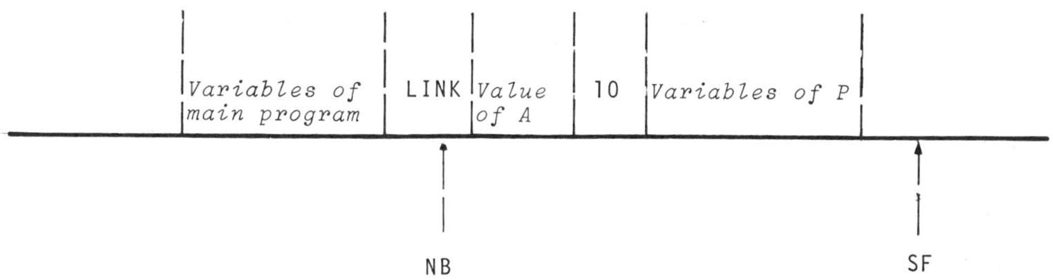

Figure 2: Layout of store after call P(A,10)

required for this series of actions:

```
       ⎧   STACK LINK L
       ⎪   STACK A
CALL   ⎨   STACK 10
       ⎪   JUMP P
       ⎩ L:
         P: NB = SF - number of parameters
            SF + number of variables
            ....
            RETURN              :: automatically resets NB and SF
```

The equivalent for the ICL 1900 Series is sixteen 24-bit instructions while the PDP11 takes ten 32-bit instructions. In those systems where dynamic interpretive parameter matching is used, several hundred instructions may be required so an unacceptable inefficiency is imposed.

Array operations

The instructions and operand forms available for vector operations are now examined in more detail. Data structures, and fields within such structures, are described using vector descriptors of the form:

TYPE	BOUND	ORIGIN

The type bits include the size of each element of the vector which may be between 1 and 64 bits. The bound field contains the number of elements in the vector, while the origin field comprises the address of the start of the vector. The instructions required to access element i of a vector a are:

```
B = i          :: Load the B (modifier) register with the subscript i
ACC = a[B]     :: Load the accumulator with Bth element of a
```

The instruction ACC = a[B] first loads the descriptor a into the DR (descriptor) register. B is scaled according to element size, added to the origin of DR and the required element is then accessed. Simultaneously a check is made that B is in the range $0 \leq B < \text{bound}$ in DR and an interrupt occurs if this check fails. On conventional machines, even omitting the bound check, several orders are used to access an array element. This is the principal reason that many compilers attempt to optimize subscript calculations. The descriptor a may describe a vector of descriptors so that the sequence

```
B = i
DR = a[B]
B = j
ACC = DR[B]
```

accesses an element $a[i,j]$ of a two-dimensional array using an addressing vector technique. Use of a multiplication technique with the subscript arithmetic taking place in B has the advantage that the subscript calculation is independent of operations queued for the main accumulator. Then $a[i,j]$ becomes:

```
B = i
B * n
B + j
ACC = a[B]
```

A further, but more expensive, hardware technique, which is convenient for arrays with dynamic lower bounds, or cross sections of arrays, uses a dope vector containing three 32-bit elements for each dimension, namely a lower bound which is subtracted from the subscript, an upper bound against which the subscript value is checked and a stride by which the subscript is multiplied. The hardware instructions SUB1 and SUB2 use the dope vector for such subscript calculations. Thus $a[i,j]$ with bound checking, becomes:

```
B = i
SUB1 a¹       :: process first subscript using dope vector a¹
```

```
        B = j
        SUB2           :: process next subscript
        B = DO         :: move composite subscript to B
        ACC = a[B]     :: access element
```

A simple example of the use of vector accessing orders is the scalar product loop:

```
        for i := 1 step 1 until n do
                sum := sum + x[i] × y[i] ;
```

which becomes:

```
        B = 1
LOOP:   B => i
        ACC = x[B]
        ACC × y[B]
        ACC + sum
        ACC => sum
        B CINC n        :: compare B with n and increment
        IF /=, ->LOOP
```

This assumes that the compiler optimizes out three unnecessary B = *i* orders but that it does not optimize to the extent of moving B => *i* to outside the loop. Hence the loop comprises seven 16-bit instructions.

The performance of this loop in the MU5 processor will now be considered in detail. In order to do this, some of the hardware features of MU5 are now described.

Hardware Organization

The distinction in the order code between directly addressed (primary) operands (that is, literals, variables, stack operands) and indirectly addressed (secondary) operands (that is, data structure elements) is reflected in the hardware by the provision of separate Primary and Secondary Operand Units, as shown in Figure 3. The Primary Operand Unit (PROP), together with the Instruction Buffer Unit (IBU) and B-Arithmetic Unit (B-ARITH) constitute the primary pipeline of the processor whilst the Secondary Operand Unit (SEOP) and the Accumulator Unit (ACC) constitute the secondary pipeline. During array processing activity, the secondary pipeline is responsible for accessing and processing the array elements, whilst the primary pipeline is responsible for supplying descriptors and modifiers to the secondary pipeline at a sufficiently high rate for the latter to be kept almost permanently busy.

Instructions enter the primary pipeline in groups of eight supplied to the instruction buffer unit from the store via the Store Access Control Unit (SAC). The IBU performs two main functions. Firstly, it pre-fetches the groups of instructions from store and passes on individual instructions to PROP in their correct program sequence. Although the store can supply instructions at a sufficiently high rate to match the rate at which they are executed, the random store access time is much longer than the instruction execution time and hence instructions must be requested far in advance of their being obeyed. Secondly, the IBU predicts the result of an impending control transfer instruction in order to make the correct early call, even if the required instructions are not in sequential addresses. The effect of the instruction buffer unit on a loop of instructions such as the scalar product loop is that on the second

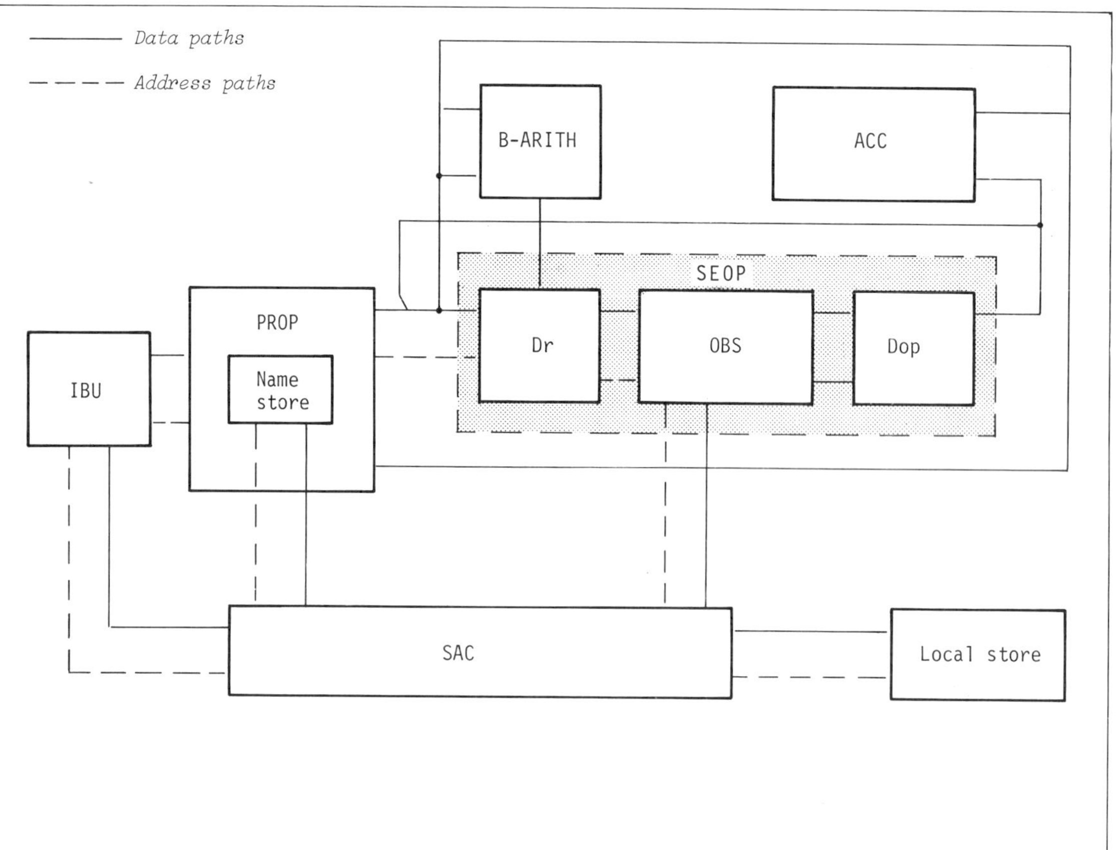

Figure 3: The MU5 central processor

and subsequent iterations round the loop execution of instructions is never held up while instructions are fetched from store.

PROP is concerned with accessing the operand specified directly by the instruction and routing the instruction, together with its operand, to the appropriate following sub-unit for execution or further processing. Instructions altering the contents of the base or control registers (in PROP) or the B register, normally use primary operands and can be executed directly, whereas instructions involving data structure elements must be sent to the secondary pipeline. Frequently used scalar operands, such as i,n and the descriptors x and y are held within the PROP Name Store, a buffer store made up of 32 associative registers containing addresses of scalar names in current use with conventional registers containing the corresponding values. Thus the variables which control the operation of the scalar product or a similar loop have neither to be fetched from store each time they are used nor optimized into registers by the compiler.

The PROP pipeline is split up into five independent stages, each of which carries out part of the instruction processing. The first stage receives instructions from the instruction buffer unit and carries out the decoding and interpretation of the instruction required to deal with multi-length orders and to select the appropriate base register to which the name part of the instruction is added in the second stage. The resulting address is presented in the third stage as an input to the associative field of the Name Store. If the address is identical to an address in one of the associative registers, an equivalence occurs and the value of the operand is read out of the conventional field of the store in the fourth stage. If the required address is not in the associative store, an access is made to the main store and the value obtained, together with the address, is written into an 'empty' line of the Name Store. Any subsequent access for the same operand does not then require an access to the main store. In the final stage of the PROP pipeline the operand is assembled in its correct format ready to be sent to the appropriate following sub-unit.

The B arithmetic unit carries out logical and signed arithmetic functions between an incoming operand and the contents of the 32-bit B-Register. Most functions are completed in 45 nanoseconds, the main exceptions being multiply and shift which take a variable time according to the value of the operands involved. The principal use of the B register is as the modifier in a data structure access. When an instruction is sent from PROP to SEOP as a result of a modified data structure operand specification, a modifier request is sent, in parallel, to the B arithmetic unit. No function is executed as a result of this request, but the value in the B register is sent, via a dedicated highway, to SEOP. The provision of the B arithmetic unit means that subscript calculations are usually independent of the main calculation and do not impede the stream of operations through the main arithmetic unit.

As illustrated in Figure 1, the secondary operand unit is divided into three major sections. The first and last sections (Dr and Dop) constitute the Descriptor System. Dr generates operand addresses, whilst Dop selects the operand (1 - 64 bits) from the appropriate part of the store word received as a result of the corresponding store access. Interposed between Dr and Dop is the Operand Buffering System (OBS) which, although serving the same end as the Name Store in PROP, that is, overcoming the speed limitation of the main store, acts in a different manner since data structure elements, unlike names, are often accessed sequentially from a large group.

When an instruction is sent to SEOP as a result of a data structure operand specification, the descriptor is first loaded into the Descriptor Register (DR) in the Dr sub-unit. The type and size bits are decoded and the appropriate action needed to generate the operand address is initiated when the modifier arrives from the B arithmetic unit. The modifier is shifted according to the element size, and added to the 32-bit Origin Address. This address is sent to OBS together with the function bits and various control bits, and Dr proceeds to check the range of the modifier against the Bound field of the descriptor.

In OBS, the address is presented to the associative field of an 8-line buffer Store. Whether equivalence occurs in this store or not, the function is entered into a 6-entry queue. If non-equivalence occurs and store request is made and an operand is eventually returned to a line allocated in the buffer. The instruction rate through the queue is such that an operand from store is normally returned at about the time that the corresponding function has reached the end of the queue and is ready to be sent to Dop.

Since OBS contains eight buffer registers it frequently contains the operand requested by Dr. The probability of this increases when data structure elements are accessed sequentially, and several are contained in one 128-bit buffer register. The present OBS hardware does not prefetch operands beyond a 128-bit boundary but the principle can be extended to predictive early fetching of sequentially accessed operands. This would speed up the passage of functions through OBS.

Dop contains facilities which permit operands down to the single-bit size to be selected from or written into any position in the 64-bit word received from OBS. For store orders a 64-bit word is received from OBS, modified, and returned to OBS. For any computational or organisational order, Dop sends the function and operand to the appropriate sub-unit for execution.

In the case of orders using the main Accumulator Unit, which has 64-bit floating-point and 32-bit fixed-point arithmetic facilities, all orders (including those using primary operands directly) pass through SEOP in order to maintain the correct sequencing of instructions. OBS contains additional buffers to hold these operands - an 8-line Literal Store and a 24-line Name Store. The Name Store is similar to the one in PROP, but the hardware distinguishes between names used as descriptors or modifiers and those used as operands in the Accumulator Unit. This means that in the scalar product loop, for example, the running total is held in a buffer which is only a few pipeline stages away from the Accumulator Unit.

Figure 4 is a schematic timing diagram for the scalar product loop, showing two typical cycles of the loop.

It is assumed that at least one cycle has preceded those shown so that the variables *i* and *n* and descriptors *x* and *y* are all in the name store, and that the jump trace in the IBU correctly predicts the control transfer. The diagram shows the overlapping sequence of instructions through the five stages of PROP:

- decode(D)
- addition of name to base(+)
- association for name store(A)
- read operand(R)
- align operand(S)

and onto the highway(H) to the correct unit for execution. For B instructions the operation takes place immediately. For secondary operands the function and operand pass through Dr and the OBS buffer association(OA). If the operand is not already in the buffer (this is assumed for simplicity in the timing diagram) it arrives back at time OB whereupon the order continues through Dop to the Acc input buffer(Ab), and execution of the accumulator order.

The most important feature of this diagram is that the accumulator unit is busy for most of the time. The execution of the statements controlling the loop in the primary pipeline does not slow down the accumulator operations. Hence optimization of these orders has no material effect on the overall performance of the loop. In fact the diagram shows the present MU5 hardware executing the loop at about 1 μs per cycle.

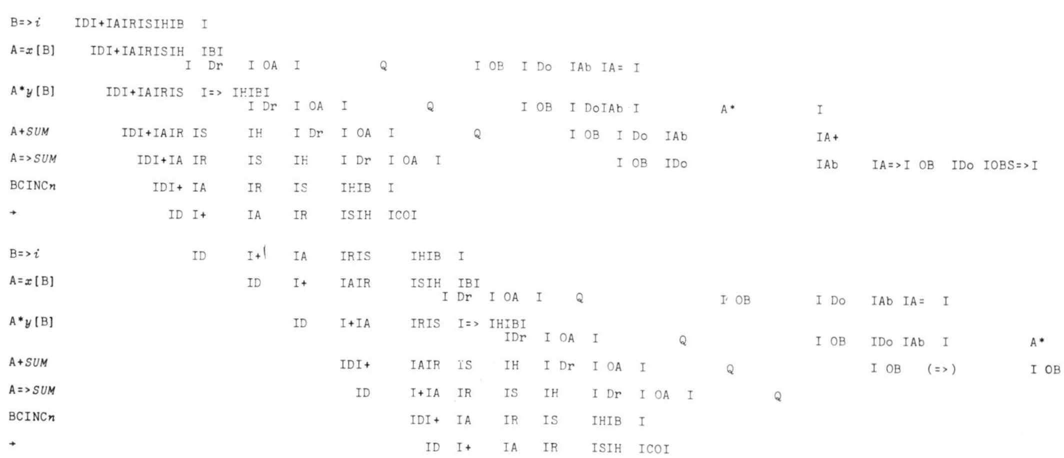

Figure 4: Scalar product loop timing diagram

String and vector operations

Consider finally the types of editing and field manipulation which are often required in data processing languages such as COBOL or PL/1. In many systems, time-consuming subroutines are required for this manipulation. In MU5, a rudimentary set of hardware orders utilizing the same basic mechanisms as the array accessing facilities has been provided. This set could be expanded in future systems. These special purpose orders are called store-to-store orders. These fall into two classes: string-string and byte-string. The string-string orders operate on two fields, or strings, each described by a descriptor. The descriptor of the destination string is held in the DR register while that for the source string is held in a second descriptor register, XDR. As the operation of the instruction proceeds the descriptor in DR and XDR move along the strings. No visible register is used by the strings themselves. The operand of the order is an 8-bit mask which determines which bits within each byte are to be operated on, and an 8-bit filler used as described below. The operation of the instructions is entirely controlled by the secondary operand unit and thus takes place in the secondary pipeline without intervention from the primary pipeline. Examples of the orders are:

SMVB: Move one byte from source to destination string, or filler byte if the source is exhausted.

SMVF: Move whole source string to destination string followed by filler bytes if source is shorter than destination.

SCMP: Compare source and destination strings byte by byte ending when inequality is found, or the destination string is exhausted.

SLGC: Logically combine source and destination strings into destination. The form of combination, for example, logical OR, is selected by additional bits in the operand.

Consider the use of these orders in the implementation of the MOVE verb in COBOL. Suppose that two fields *C* and *D* are specified:

```
02  C  PIC X(7)
02  D  PIC X(7)
```

In MU5, descriptors would be created at compile time for *C* and *D*, each describing a 7-byte field starting at the required byte address. The COBOL sentence:

```
MOVE C TO D
```

would then become in MU5 instructions:

```
XDR = C   ::  set source descriptor for C
DR = D    ::  set destination descriptor for D
SMVF      ::  move the field described by XDR to that
              described by DR.
```

If *D* is specified as:

```
02  D  PIC X(9)
```

then the final two bytes of *D* must be spaces. The filler option of SMVF allows this to be carried out automatically. The sequence becomes:

```
XDR = C
DR = D
SMVF ''space''
```

If the source field is too long, then the SMVF order terminates when the receiving field is full, and an optional interrupt enables this condition to be monitored if required.

It is possible to use the techniques applied in the store-to-store orders for an implementation of vector operations for scientific languages. Thus a vector add of the form:

$$F := F + E$$

which in present MU5 instructions is the loop:

```
       B = 1
LOOP:  ACC = F[B]
       ACC + E[B]
       ACC => F[B]
       B CINC n
       IF <, -> LOOP
```

(that is, five 16-bit instructions obeyed *n* times within the loop) would become:

```
DR = F
XDR = E
vector add
```

(that is, three instructions obeyed once).

With the present MU5 hardware, there would be little speed advantage in this approach since the accumulator speed limits the overall performance. Financial constraints prevented any significant improvement in accumulator performance. However provision of additional accumulator capability and greater throughput in the secondary pipeline would allow the hardware instruction to perform significantly better.

CONCLUSION

The increasing cost of software production is resulting in decreased use of coding at assembly language level and an increased dependence on high-level languages, not just for user programs but also for system software. The decreasing cost of hardware makes it feasible to continue to reduce the relative cost of running high-level language programs by providing more suitable architectural facilities. The areas in which there is greatest scope for significant architectural improvements are operand accessing and procedure entry. When the correct architectural features are available, much of the present program optimization effort will become the past necessity of the 1970s.

ADAPTIVE CODE OPTIMIZATION

G J Hansen

Department of Computer and Information Sciences
University of Florida

W A Wulf

Department of Computer Science
Carnegie-Mellon University

G J HANSEN received the BS Degree in Physics and the MS Degree in Engineering from the Case Institute of Technology, Cleveland, Ohio, in 1962 and 1964, respectively; and the PhD Degree in computer science from Carnegie-Mellon University, Pittsburgh, Pennsylvania, in 1974. In 1962, he received the Dayton C Miller prize for the best senior thesis in Physics. From 1968 to 1969, he was an Instructor at the University of Houston, Texas. From 1969 to 1971, he was an Instructor and Assistant Director of the Computing Center at Vanderbilt University, Nashville, Tennessee. Currently Dr Hansen is an Assistant Professor of Computer and Information Sciences at the University of Florida. He has written ALGOL 60 compilers for the UNIVAC 1107, SCC 650 and the XDS Sigma 7 computers; and the simulation language SOL for the CDC 621 and XDS Sigma 7 computers. His areas of research include programming languages, particularly the areas of compiler theory and code optimization, software portability and microprogramming.

W A WULF is currently Professor of Computer Science at Carnegie-Mellon University. He received his doctorate in Computer Science from the University of Virginia where he was also an instructor of Computer Science and Applied Mathematics. Dr Wulf also holds a masters degree in Electrical Engineering and a batchelor's in Engineering Physics from the University of Illinois. Dr Wulf's primary research interest is in the design and implementation of computer software (especially operating systems and compilers), languages suitable for software implementation, and hardware architecture for the efficient execution of these software systems. Related research interests include protection structures, programming methodology, and compiler optimization. He has directed the construction of several large software systems and is currently directing the construction of C.mmp, a 16-processor multiprocessor computer system, and its associated software. He is a member of IEEE, and the Association for Computing Machinery. He is also chairman of the IFIP Working Group on Machine-Oriented Higher-Level Programming Languages, a member of the SIGPLAN executive committee, and an editor of the IEEE Transactions on Software Engineering.

ADAPTIVE CODE OPTIMIZATION

SUMMARY

This paper reports on a compiler system for the FORTRAN IV language that performs, during program execution, code optimizations based on the dynamic behaviour of the program as opposed to current approaches that employ a fixed code generation strategy, that is, one in which a predetermined set of code optimizations are applied at compile time to an entire program. The system was implemented and tested with programs having different behavioural characteristics. The test programs were also run under variants of the system which approximate the behaviour of WATFIV, FORTRAN-IV G, and FORTRAN-IV H compilers. The results show that adaptive FORTRAN performs as well or better than any of the variant systems at each specific test point, and significantly better than any one of them across the entire range of test points.

INTRODUCTION

This paper investigates the feasibility of exploiting an empirical observation that only a small portion of a program generally is responsible for the bulk of its execution time. Knuth (195), for example, studied a large collection of FORTRAN programs and found that 4% of the program accounts for more than 50% of the execution time. In a study of a smaller sample, Darden and Heller (196) found approximately 3% of the program accounting for 60% of the execution time.

A particular consequence of these observations is that it is highly desirable to optimize the code produced for the crucial 3-5% of the program, but relatively far less important to optimize the remainder. Current compilers, being unable to determine which is the relevant portion of the program, apply a uniform optimization strategy to the entire program - thus potentially wasting compile-time effort. Two responses to this situation are common:

1 to build a spectrum of compilers. For example, on the IBM 360-370 series at least three FORTRAN compilers are available (WATFIV, FORTRAN IV-G, and FORTRAN IV-H). WATFIV compiles very rapidly, but produces rather poor object code, and thus is the compiler of choice for short-execution jobs such as student programs. FORTRAN IV-G is slower, but produces better code, and FORTRAN IV-H is the slowest but produces the best object code.

NOTE: This work was supported by the Advanced Research Projects Agency of the office of the Secretary of defense (F44620-73-C-0074) and is monitored by the Air Force Office of Scientific Research.

2 to generate feedback to the user and/or compiler. Knuth and others have suggested that statistics should be collected during program execution which can then be used by the user and/or compiler on subsequent compilations to optimize the program's performance.

The spectrum-of-compilers approach responds to the gross classification of a program into short/medium/long executions, but has several disadvantages; for example, it implies building and maintaining three compilers and it is unable to respond to dynamic behaviour - such as an error early in the execution of what was thought to be a production run. The problems of maintaining complete compatibility between three compilers is well-known and may not be resolvable in practice. The feedback approach has much to recommend it; in fact, its only drawback may be that (we claim) it is not really necessary to have the human in the loop.

In the remainder of the paper, we present the design of a system which dynamically and automatically detects and optimizes those portions of a program which are most frequently executed. Successively sophisticated optimizations are applied to sections of the program during execution, and in proportion to their contribution to total execution time. Thus the quality of the code in these sections dynamically adapts, and the amount of optimization effort is proportional to the need for it.

We make two strong claims for this scheme. First, that the total cost of compiling and running a program is reduced significantly when compared to any fixed optimization strategy (or set of them). And, second, that the scheme suggests an obvious implementation methodology which has significant merit in its own right. To support these claims a demonstration FORTRAN-IV system has been built. Example performance measures are presented later.

ADAPTIVE COMPILER SYSTEMS

In this section, we will look at the problems associated with constructing an adaptive compiler and present a solution that can be realistically implemented. The basic issues that we will address are:

1 what information must be collected during the translation and loader phases to facilitate run-time optimization;

2 the characteristics of the code the translator must produce for the optimizers;

3 methods for grouping the code into blocks to facilitate its processing by the optimizers;

4 attributes of code blocks that can be metered to determine which blocks to optimize;

5 methods for determining which optimizations to apply to the code blocks and when;

6 control of the running program so optimization can be intermixed with execution.

Three of the issues, viz: determining which code blocks to optimize, when, and how much, form the basis for any dynamic optimization strategy. The approach used is heuristic, based on the notion that one optimization at a time should be applied to a code block, and on the assumption that the execution time per code block is proportional to the frequency with which it is executed. Such an assumption allows a frequency count to be used as a metric for controlling the adaption process. To control the execution and invoke an optimization strategy requires a supervisor. We will describe the operational characteristics for such a supervisor.

The primary goal in the design of an adaptive complier system is to minimize the total cost of running a program. This goal has direct implications with respect to the design of the translator and the dynamic optimization strategy.

The design of the translator can proceed along the lines currently employed in the construction of any translator, but it must be as efficient as possible. This means that

1 it should expend a minimum of effort in translating the source code and, in particular, should not perform any optimizations that can be done more effectively and efficiently at run-time;

2 it should employ the best translating algorithms available;

3 it should itself be optimized;

4 it should be one-pass* and compile directly to core.

Minimizing total cost also requires the optimization algorithms to be efficient, and the overhead incurred by deciding when to perform what optimization on which sections of code to be small compared to the expected payoff. There are four basic design decisions that must be made; they are a consequence of both the fact that optimization is to be performed at run time and the nature of the optimizers:

1 An internal representation of the source code that can be efficiently manipulated by the optimizers must be selected. This internal form cannot be machine language because at this level too much information that will be needed by the optimizers has been lost, and it should not be the source code because the source code does not explicitly indicate the structure of the program and takes too much time to scan. Possible internal forms include: Polish notation, quadruples, triples, indirect triples, or trees (cf. (197). The translator can produce the internal form as object code, for it is amenable to being executed (interpreted).

2 The internal form (which we will assume is an *n*-tuple that denotes an 'instruction') must be grouped according to the program's structure into aggregates so that the optimizations which require global flow information can be applied. It is a characteristic of the classical optimizations that we will employ that they operate on two kinds of aggregates: a group of sequential instructions terminated by an unconditional branch (a *basic block*) and a group of basic blocks which form a loop-like structure (a *segment*). Initially, as the internal form is being generated, it is partitioned by the translator into basic blocks. As the program executes, optimizations are performed on those basic blocks executed most frequently. In order for additional optimizations to be performed, the segment containing an optimized basic block must be formed. The process of combining basic blocks or segments into a (larger) segment we call *fusion*.

---

* *A second pass over the object code is needed to complete the translation process, e g allocate data storage, patch addresses, patch forward references, relocate the object code, etc. This second pass of the compilation process is handled by a program which, due to its similarity to others of the same name, we shall call a 'loader'.*

3 A dynamic optimization strategy must be proposed, that is, a scheme for determining which basic blocks or segments to optimize, which optimizations to apply, and when to perform the optimizations. Even though there is more information available at run time than at compile time to aid in making these decisions, it is not complete (we cannot predict a program's future behaviour with absolute accuracy). A reasonable approach is to assume that future behaviour of a program will be similar to past behaviour, for it is better to base the decision-making on this information than none at all. Such an assumption is not uncommon; it is often made in other areas of computer science (for example, paging algorithms and schedulers). As is the case with the other areas, such decisions are susceptible to anomalies. For example, it is possible to waste optimization effort if the program terminated soon after the effort was expended, or the program is phased and after the optimization of a phase it is only executed a few times more and then never executed again. By selecting a strategy that causes optimization of basic blocks or segments to be gradual, the amount of effort wasted can be kept tolerably small.

4 Some means of controlling the execution of a program so it can be adapted must be determined. Basic blocks and segments are the discrete units of execution. A logical point at which to interrupt a program's execution for adaption is when control passes between two basic blocks or segments, since program status is well defined at such points and the amount of state information required to record this status is small. When execution is interrupted, data which aids in the decisions made by the dynamic optimization strategy is collected, and it is decided whether to invoke the dynamic optimization strategy and perform optimizations. Our approach is to centralize these functions and control of execution in a supervisor known as the *segment driver*.

The structure of an adaptive compiler system is now apparent. Source code is translated by a fast and efficient translator into an internal form that is grouped into basic blocks. Execution of the program is controlled by a segment driver and optimization by a dynamic optimization strategy. Various optimizations are applied to basic blocks and/or segments as execution proceeds and the performance of the program warrents. A new optimization, fusion, is necessary for grouping basic blocks into segments. In the following sections, we will define more precisely the concepts of basic block, segment, fusion, and segment driver, and propose a dynamic optimization strategy.

Basic blocks and segments*

When performing code optimizations, it is advantageous to partition the program according to its flow of control into basic blocks. A basic block is a linear sequence of instructions with the first instruction being the single entry point. The block is terminated by one or more branch instructions, the last of which is unconditional while the others (if any) are conditional. All code between the first instruction and the branches is executed in sequence.

A program's flow of control may be represented by a directed *control flow graph* in which a node represents a basic block and an edge represents a flow path. Those

---

* *In this section, some of the definitions follow the terminology introduced by Allen* (198,199) *(viz: basic block and directed control flow graph) and Lowery and Medlock* (200) *(viz: predominance), while others pertaining to directed graphs can be found in any introductory textbook on graph theory (cf* (201)*) (viz: immediate successor or predecessor, subgraph, path and strongly connected region).*

basic blocks that branch to a given block are its *immediate predecessors*. Likewise, those blocks branched to by a given basic block are its *immediate successors*. A basic block may have more than one immediate predecessor or successor, including itself. Program entry blocks have no predecessors, and program terminating blocks have no successors. A basic block B_1 *predominates* a block B_2 if every path along a sequence of successors from a program entry block to B_2 always passes through B_1.

The basic block is the smallest program unit commonly considered for optimization. However, there is a limit to the amount of optimization that can be performed on a basic block, and in order to perform additional optimization it is necessary to consider the more global context. Since it is desirable to optimize those basic blocks executed repetitively, some loop-like structure must be imposed on the flow graph. Two loop-like constructs have been described in the literature: the strongly connected region (198) and the interval (199, 202). A strongly connected region is a subgraph of the flow graph in which there is a path leading from any block in the region to every other block. The region may have several entry points. An *interval* is the maximal single entry subgraph of the flow graph in which all closed paths contain the entry block.

We introduce another similar, but not equivalent, concept called a *segment*. With respect to a given strongly connected region (loop) in the directed control graph, a segment is the minimal directed subgraph with the following properties:

1 The segment contains all the basic blocks in the loop.

2 There is a single *entry block*. This entry block may have one or more immediate predecessors of which at least one is not contained in the segment. Those immediate predecessors of the entry block that are predominated by it are contained in the segment.

3 Except for the entry block, all immediate predecessors of each basic block in the segment are contained in the segment.

4 The segment (A_i) and another segment A_j are either *disjoint*, that is, they have no basic blocks in common and therefore are parallel structures, or one is embedded inside the other. If $A_i \cap A_j = A_j$, then A_j is *embedded* inside A_i and A_i is said to *cover* segment A_j.

Thus, if a loop has a single entry block, it is identical to a segment whose segment entry block is the same as the loop entry block. If the loop has multiple entry points, the segment is the loop extended to include the minimum number of basic blocks satisfying properties 2, 3 and 4. Property 4 defines a properly nested set of segments, and allows the optimizations to be ordered in the manner suggested by Allen (198).

Unlike a strongly connected region, there is not necessarily a path leading from any block in a segment to any other block because of the requirement that a segment have a single entry point. A segment always contains a strongly connected region, but the single entry point for the segment may not necessarily be contained in the region. Consider example (d) in Figure 1 in which segment 2' contains the strongly connected region {4,5,6} which has two entry points (blocks 4 and 5), and the entry point of the segment (block 2) is not contained in the region. Like a segment, an interval contains a single entry point, but it does not necessarily contain a closed path, and the intervals of a graph are disjoint. In example (b) in Figure 1, the intervals are {1} and {2, 3}.

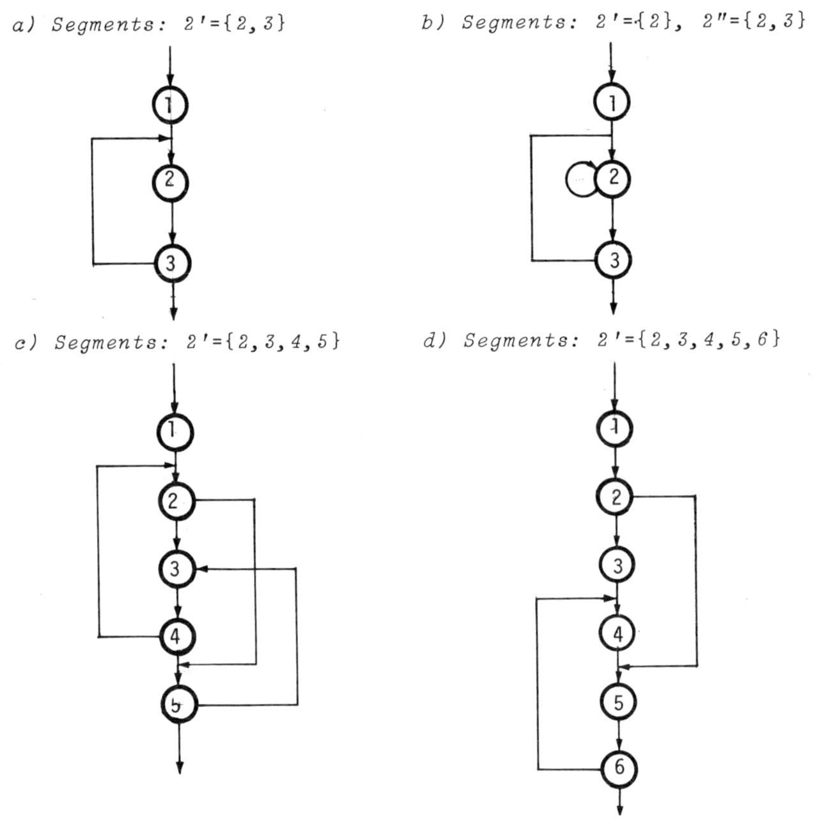

Figure 1: Examples of segments

Fusion

When a segment is formed via fusion, what optimizations are applicable to it depend on how embedded segments are treated, that is, whether or not the new segment is considered to be a homogeneous structure with respect to future optimizations. Define the *optimization state* of a basic block/segment to be the result of the application of an optimization. As optimizations are performed on a basic block/segment, they will advance through different optimization states. One basic block/segment is said to have a higher optimization state than another if more optimizations have been applied to it. If we employ *homogeneous fusion*, then the optimization state of a segment is uniform, that is, the maximum optimization state of its constituents, and the result is a *homogeneous segment*. If the segment contains no embedded segments, then its optimization state is the maximum optimization state of its basic blocks; otherwise it is the maximum optimization state of the segments it covers. In order to advance the segment to its optimization state, it may be necessary to perform one or more optimizations on its embedded basic blocks/segments. For future optimizations, the covering segment could be considered a basic unit. But this has a distinct disadvantage if at the time of fusion the embedded basic blocks/segments have not attained the highest optimization state, for the effect of additional optimizations on these embedded units will never be realized. Alternatively, if the identity of the embedded basic blocks/segments is retained, further optimization could be applied to them before being applied to the covering segment. The only constraint is that all units attain the same optimization state.

If on the other hand we employ *non-homogeneous fusion,* a segment and its embedded basic blocks/segments are allowed to exist at different optimization states. This approach is more restrictive in the sense that the optimizations that are applicable to a segment and the segments it covers depend on the current optimization state of each. There are a number of ways in which optimizations can take place. One method is to let the covering segment control when the embedded segments get optimized further; other approaches are to let each segment be optimized separately at its own rate, or to freeze the optimization state of each embedded segment at the time of fusion and let future optimizations be applied only to the covering segment.

The result of fusion is a segment that is formed by combining each of the segment's basic blocks, and is considered a basic unit with respect to execution (that is, transfer of control between basic blocks within the segment are not processed by the supervisor).

Incremental dynamic optimization

The incremental dynamic optimization scheme is based on the assumption that the total execution time for a basic block/segment is proportional to the frequency with which it is executed. This assumption allows a frequency count to be used as a metric for deciding not only which basic block/segment to optimize, but when to apply optimization. Each time the basic block or segment is executed, this count is incremented*. When it exceeds a predetermined threshold, the basic block or segment is advanced to the next representation by the application of the next optimization. Therefore, optimization is applied incrementally, that is one optimization at a time to one basic block/segment at a time. Fusion is automatically handled by this scheme as just one of the possible optimizations.

Define the *optimization count* for an optimization to represent the number of times a basic block or segment is to be executed in its current representation before applying the optimization (this is the threshold alluded to above). The optimization count associated with a basic block or segment must have the properties that it is proportional to the basic block/segment's execution time, and it determines the proper time at which to optimize the basic block/segment. Therefore, an optimization count will not be the same for each basic block/segment. Instead, it will be some function of the basic block/segment's characteristics, such as the length of the basic block/segment measured in some appropriate units, the basic block/segment's level of nesting in a loop structure, or the amount of effort required to apply the next optimization.

The segment driver

Optimization and execution of a program are under the control of the segment driver. Execution of a program proceeds one basic block or segment at a time. At the start of execution, the segment driver is called with a parameter indicating which basic block or segment to execute; before executing it, however, the segment driver decides whether or not to optimize. If optimization is to be performed, it decides which basic blocks/segments to optimize and how much, and calls the appropriate optimizers. Then it executes the basic block/segment. If the executable code is interpretive, a subroutine call is made on the interpreter; otherwise a subroutine call is made on the machine language representation of the basic block or segment.

---

* *In practice, the count is decremented until it becomes negative.*

During the execution of the code, there may be a call on a subprogram; these calls may be nested. To execute the subprogram, the segment driver is called recursively. Execution of the subprogram proceeds as just described, but any calls on the interpreter must be recursive, for the interpreter may have made the subprogram call.

Execution of the basic block or segment is terminated by a branch instruction to another basic block or segment. If the branch occurs in a basic block or is external to a segment, control is returned to the segment driver by a subroutine return which passes back the destination of the branch instruction. Branches internal to a segment are performed directly, while a return from a subprogram causes an exit from the segment driver.

This entire process, depicted in Figure 2, is repeated until an instruction that terminates the program is executed.

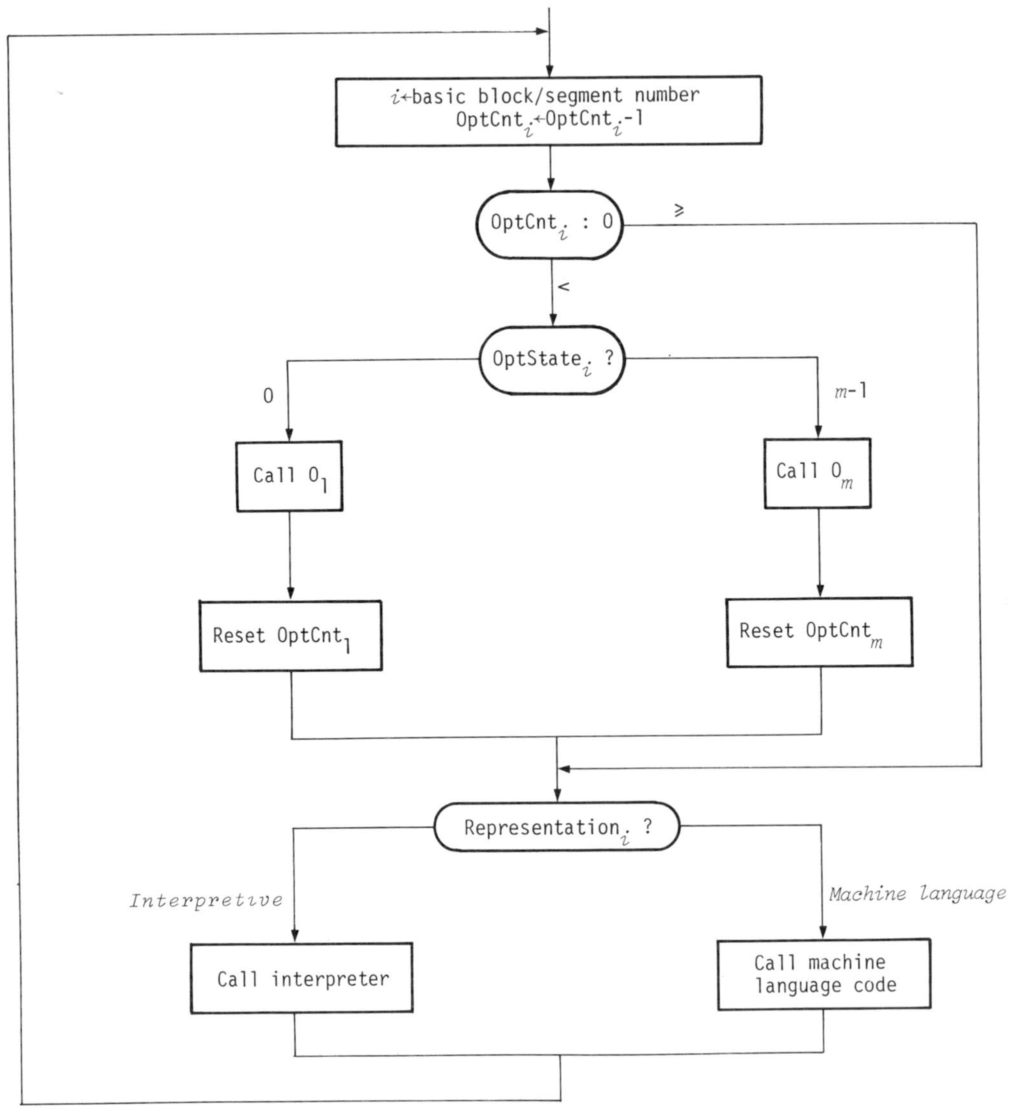

Figure 2: Execution cycle of segment driver

THE DEMONSTRATION SYSTEM

In order to demonstrate the validity of the dynamic optimization scheme, a demonstration system was built and its performance measured. FORTRAN-IV was selected as the source language for this system because:

1 it is one of the most widely used programming languages and hence is a rich source of example programs and comparisons with existing systems;

2 it contains enough interesting constructs to give credibility to the validation results;

3 many of the compile-time optimization algorithms currently in use were developed for FORTRAN compilers; they are well understood and are easily adapted for use at run time.

It is not necessary to adhere strictly to the formal definition of FORTRAN-IV or to implement the entire language in order to demonstrate that our technique is workable and valid. We assume the reader is familiar with FORTRAN-IV. Instead of describing the complete subset, we therefore list all the features in FORTRAN-IV that were altered, extended or deleted. The following extensions and alterations were made:

1 an arbitrary number of dimensions for arrays were allowed;

2 multiple assignment statements were allowed;

3 real as well as integer control variables could be used in DO statements;

4 parameters could be used as initial, incrementation, and terminal values in DO statements;

5 negative increments could be used in DO statements;

6 the use of expressions in output lists was permitted;

7 automatic real-to-integer conversion was performed for subscripts, in relational expressions, and in DO statements;

8 exclusive OR and equivalence were included as logical operators.

The following features were deleted:

1 the use of embedded blanks in identifiers;

2 the use of double precision and complex arithmetic as types;

3 usage of the computed GO TO statement;

4 usage of the PAUSE statement;

5 usage of auxiliary and unformatted I/O statements;

6 the use of the DO-implied specification in I/O lists;

7 usage of the DATA statement;

8 usage of the EQUIVALENCE specification statement;

9 the use of statement functions;

10 the requirement that symbolic names which identify statement types or operators may not be reserved words;

11 the ability to compile program units separately

These modifications were made because they simplified the experiments without affecting their results.

The process of running a FORTRAN program is broken down into three major phases:

1 the compilation of FORTRAN source code to relocatable quadruples*, or 'quads' for short;

2 the loading of the relocatable quads to absolute quads

3 the execution of the program.

Execution of the program is controlled by a supervisor known as the segment driver and is performed by either an interpreter (which interprets the quads), or the machine language equivalent of the quads, called as a subroutine.

The structure of the system is shown in Figure 3.

The bulk of the system was written in BLISS-10 (203), a systems programming language for the DEC PDP-10. Those portions of the system written in machine language were the segment driver (hand-optimized to minimize overhead) and the run-time FORTRAN support package (the mathematical routines, I/O package, etc) borrowed from the PDP-10 FORTRAN system with slight modifications.

The entire system is loaded at once into approximately 50K 36-bit words. This is not necessary; the three phases could be overlaid (and would be in a production-quality system). Again, this does not affect the validity of the results.

The compilation phase

The first phase in running a FORTRAN program is the translation of the FORTRAN source text into the internal form manipulated by the optimizers, viz, quads. The compiler is one-pass and compiles relocateable quads directly to core. It occupies approximately 9K of core and compiles at the rate of nearly 9000 cards per minute.

A secondary function of the compiler is to partition the program into basic blocks. Code is compiled into a basic block until the occurrence of one of several conditions in the source text, at which time the basic block is terminated and another one started. The conditions are:

1 a labelled statement (except a FORMAT statement);

---

* *Also known as three-address code. A quadruple consists of an operation, two operands, and a result temporary.*

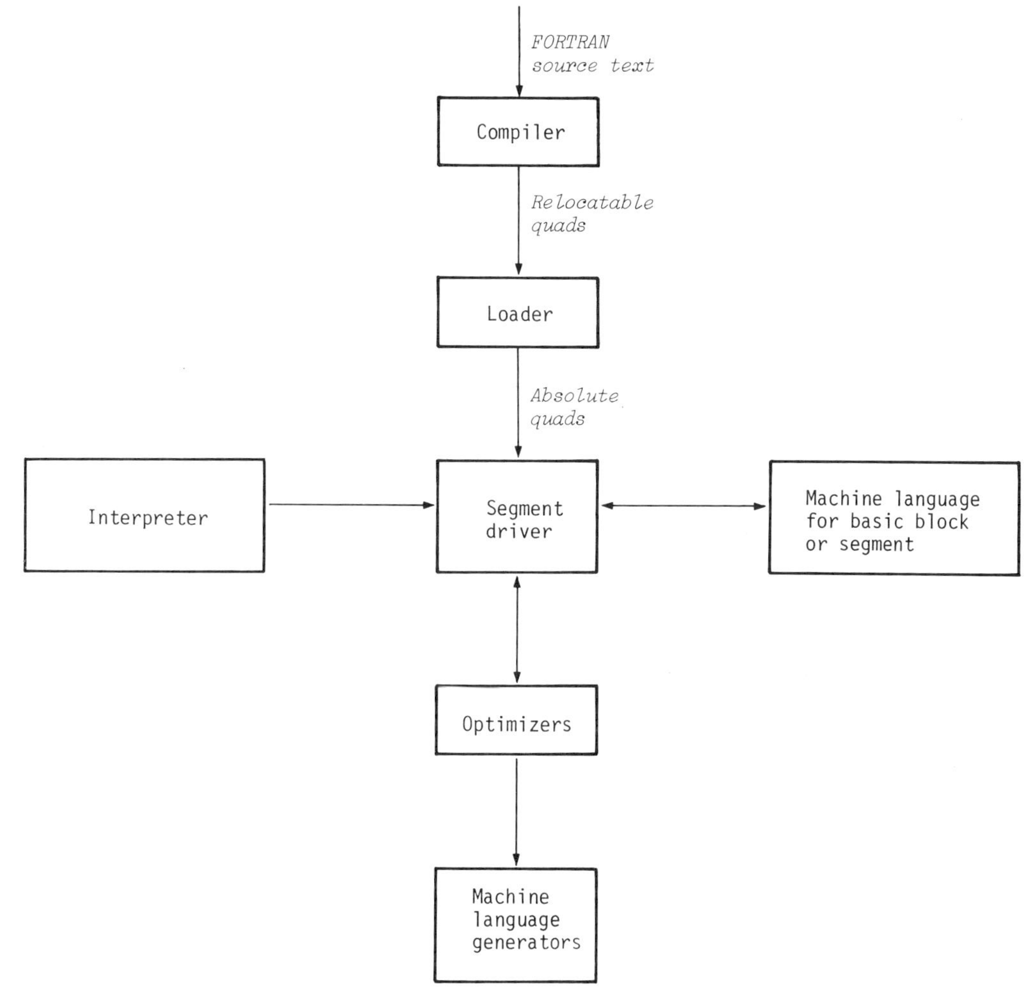

Figure 3: Structural organization of the Adaptive FORTRAN system

2 a subroutine or function call (except for a library function or output subroutine call, since they produce no side effects, that is, they do not change the value of a variable);

3 a 'call exit' (eg, STOP, RETURN) or END statement;

4 a consecutive sequence of conditional transfer operations terminated by an unconditional transfer, for example, an arithmetic IF, or a logical IF of the form:

a) IF () GO TO *k*

b) IF () STOP

c) IF () RETURN

5 a GO TO statement;

6 a READ statement.

During compilation, each result generated in a basic block is associated with a unique temporary location. This is to facilitate the translation of quads to machine language and the optimization of the basic block.

The loading phase

After all program units have been compiled, the relocatable quads are immediately loaded by a loader if the program contains no errors. The loader occupies less than 0.5K of core. The primary function of the loader is to load the quads into absolute core locations; this requires changing relative locations to absolute and 'back patching' address fields.

The second function of the loader is to build the *segment table*, which is crucial for the adaptive process. Each entry in this table contains all the information about a basic block that is needed by the optimizers. A single entry in the table consists of the following information fields:

QUADREP: The address of the basic block's first quad.

CURREP: The absolute address of the current representation of the basic block. When the block is executed, this address determines how it is executed. The initial value is the address of the quad interpreter; when the basic block's quads are translated to machine language, the value is the starting address of the machine language.

SEGNO: The segment number to which the basic block belongs when the basic block is fused into a segment.

OPTCNT: The basic block/segment's optimization count. This field is decremented by the segment driver each time the basic block/segment is executed by the segment driver. When it goes negative, the basic block/segment is optimized according to the OPTSTATE field.

OPTSTATE: The optimization state of the basic block/segment. This field determines which optimization is to be performed next when the OPTCNT field goes negative.

PREDPT: A pointer to the first item in the linked list of immediate predecessors for the basic block. This list contains the block number of all basic blocks that are immediate predecessors of the block in increasing order.

LASTPRED: A pointer to the last item in the basic block's immediate predecessor list.

AENTRY: The address of the alternative entry point to the segment's entry block. The segment's invariant quads are affixed to the start of the segment's entry block. When the segment is translated to machine language, the CURREP field points to the first machine language instruction of the segment's entry block, that is, to the invariant code. But the invariant code need only be executed once, hence any internal branch to the segment's entry block need only go to the alternative entry point.

The execution phase

Execution of the program is controlled by the segment driver. The main loop of the segment driver consists of two machine language instructions; one decrements the OPTCNT field for the basic block/segment being executed and tests if the count has gone negative; the other calls the interpreter or machine language segment as a subroutine. If the optimization count goes negative, the basic block/segment is optimized according to the OPTSTATE field before being executed. Execution of the basic block/segment is terminated by a branch instruction. The branch behaves as a subroutine return so control is returned to the segment driver, which executes the next basic block/segment specified by the branch. Thus the overhead incurred as two machine language instructions in the segment driver plus the number of instructions to effect the branch.

The optimizations

Adaptive FORTRAN uses four machine-independent optimizations: constant folding, non-homogeneous fusion, common subexpression elimination, and code motion, and a host of machine-dependent optimizations. There are a number of reasons why these optimizations were selected over other possibilities. First, these optimizations are among the most commonly used. Second, they allow us to construct systems similar in characteristics to existing compilers against which it is possible to compare the Adaptive FORTRAN system. Third, to show the flexibility of the system, we wanted to include optimizations that applied both to basic blocks and segments. Finally, we wanted to include enough optimizations to prove the technique was not only feasible, but that the system could perform at least as well as current compiler systems.

There are two machine language generators which apply various machine-dependent optimizations. The first is the dumb code generator, which performs straight-forward translation of quads to machine language. It is used when individual basic blocks are being optimized. The second machine language generator is the fair code generator, which is considerably more sophisticated. It utilizes information gathered from the translation of previous quads and in certain cases combines consecutive quads in order to generate more efficient machine language. It is used to generate machine language for optimized segments.

Optimization is either at the basic block level (fusion and/or the dumb code generator), or the segment level (common subexpression elimination or code motion in combination with the fair code generator). Regardless of which is used, the net effect is the creation of machine language from the basic block/segment's quads.

The optimization states and their associated optimization counts

The optimization states for the system on whose performance we shall report in the next section were as follows:

0: Translate the interpretive code for the basic block to 'dumb' machine language

1: Perform a non-homogeneous fusion of the basic block into a segment. Basic blocks in interpretive code are translated to 'dumb' machine language; blocks in machine language are moved as is with their branches retranslated.

2: Perform code motion on the segment. Before the optimization is performed, the common subexpression elimination (CSE) algorithm is performed on all basic blocks in the segment. After the optimization, the quads of each basic block are translated to 'fair' machine language.

Note that CSE is not a separate optimization, but is combined with code motion (CM). The reason was that the time to generate the machine language segment using the 'fair' code generator is appreciably larger than the time to perform the CSE or CM algorithm. Therefore, the combined time to perform CSE and CM separately is much greater than the time to perform the combination, because the machine language segment must be generated twice.

The optimization counts associated with each of the optimization states depend on the loop structure of the program. A pre-analysis of the program's loop structure is made after the loading phase. The loop analyser partitions the segments into three classes: innermost segments (loops) consisting of two or fewer basic blocks; outermost segments; other segments. In the loop classifications that follow, the triplet (C0,C1,C2) represents the optimization counts for optimization states 0, 1, and 2 respectively:

1 innermost segments: (0,1,50). Thus innermost segments are fused into 'dumb' machine language if executed once, then totally optimized. The loop analyser initializes the optimization state and count for basic blocks belonging to an innermost segment to 1.

2 outermost segments: (6,15,*n*) where *n*=10 if the length of the segment (in basic blocks) is less than or equal to 10; otherwise 2×*length*.

3 other segments: (6,15,200).

4 entire subprogram: (6,15,*n*) where *n* is the same as in 2. However, CM is not performed as the last optimization; instead CSE is applied to all the basic blocks in the subprogram. It makes no sense to remove invariant quads out of a subprogram because the entire subprogram is always executed when called. Thus the entire subprogram is considered a segment with respect to optimization. What constitutes an outermost loop inside a subprogram depends on whether the subprogram is called from within a loop. It is assumed that this is always the case for if this assumption is not made, experiments indicate that system performance is degraded.

The above optimization states and counts were the result of experimenting with approximately 15 different systems. There is every reason to believe that it is possible to construct other variants which control optimization better and outperform our system. Our system is just one solution whose excellent performance results show that dynamic optimization is a viable technique.

VALIDATION AND EXPERIMENTAL RESULTS

In this section, we present the experimental evidence which demonstrates that dynamic optimization is a workable and valid technique. In order to evaluate Adaptive FORTRAN's performance measurements, it is necessary to compare the results with those obtained by running the same set of test programs under other types of FORTRAN compilers, viz: WATFIV, FORTRAN-IV G, and FORTRAN-IV H.

There are a number of practical problems in making these comparisons. First, not many computers have all three compilers available. Second, the differences in characteristics of various computers (for example, speed, word size, and instruction set) must be taken into account. Finally, the differences between the compilers themselves, for example, the parsing and code generation techniques employed, the type of machine language generated, and the run-time support package must be taken into account.

The ideal situation would be to have all the compiler systems run on the same machine and to use the same compiling techniques, optimizers, machine language generators, and run-time support package. The construction of these compiler systems was considered to be too large an undertaking. Therefore, a more expedient approach was taken in which the Adaptive FORTRAN system (AF) was transformed to resemble each of the other three compilers. It was easy to make the necessary changes because of the way AF was constructed. The main discrepancy between the transformed systems and the actual compilers lies not in the type of code produced, but in the way it is produced. Each transformed system uses the Adaptive FORTRAN compiler to translate FORTRAN source text into quads. After loading the quads, but before starting execution, the quads are translated to the machine language form that most resembles the code produced by the compiler being emulated. We feel this discrepancy in no way alters the validity of the test results, since the use of a consistent approach does not bias the results.

The three transformed systems and the manner in which they produce code are:

1 AFW: resembles WATFIV. The entire program is translated to 'dumb' code before execution starts. A true WATFIV compiler does not produce quads, but compiles machine language directly. Like WATFIV, AFW compiles in one pass directly to core. But whereas WATFIV's machine language is absolute and requires some patching before execution starts, AFW produces relocatable quads which must be loaded. Therefore, the compiler-loader phases of a WATFIV compiler probably would be slightly faster than those of AFW.

2 AFG: resembles FORTRAN-IV G. CSE is performed on all the program's basic blocks and then the entire program is translated to 'fair' code before the start of execution. A FORTRAN-IV G compiler usually produces relocatable machine language directly to a disk file. The absolute load module is created from the relocatable object modules by a standard system loader. Since these modules are on disk, load-time should be greater than that for AFG which uses an in-core loader. The compile-time for FORTRAN-IV G should be comparable to the combined time required by AFG to compile and load the program and perform the translation of the quads to machine language. Therefore, the compiler-loader phases of AFG should be slightly faster than that for FORTRAN-IV G.

3 AFH: resembles FORTRAN-IV H. All optimizations are applied to the entire program which is then translated to 'fair' code before the start of execution. CSE is first performed on each basic block in the entire program. Then the segments are formed via fusion starting with the innermost ones and working outwards. The list of segments and their order of processing is given to the system, not deduced by it. As each segment is formed, CM is performed on it. After all segments are formed, the entire program is translated to 'fair' code. A true FORTRAN-IV H compiler also produces an internal form such as quads which its optimizers process (cf (200)). It performs strength-reduction which AFH does not do. The compiler-loader phases of AFH should be slightly faster than that for FORTRAN-IV H for the same reasons given above for AFG.

These three compiler systems form the basis against which AF is compared. The performance of each system was measured by running the same set of test programs under each.

The test programs

In order to draw meaningful conclusions about the performance of AF, it is necessary to run a number of test programs under it that have different characteristics. Care must be exercised in selecting the test programs to avoid biasing the results. For any compiler system, it is always possible to construct a program that makes it look miserable or one that makes it look good. To ensure that the test programs are representative of the type of programs written in the real world, both the published literature and students were used as a source.

A number of criteria were used to select the test programs from the potential candidates; they were designed to test if the usage of AF is restrictive. The main criterion was to select programs with differing loop structures, for example, a different number of loops, loop lengths (measured in basic blocks), and loop nestings. The reason was that we wanted to test AF's performance both on those class of programs it was designed for (that is, programs for which 5% of the code accounts for 50% of the execution time) and on those that do not fall into this classification.

Second, we wanted programs that have parameter(s) that can be varied to control their execution time. This allows us to study the performance of AF for small, medium and large execution times, and determine performance as a function of the execution time.

Finally, we wanted programs that were compute-bound in order to do a worst-case analysis. I/O-bound programs were not selected because the I/O handlers are not part of the user's program and cannot therefore be optimized by the system, and if the program performs any I/O, the I/O time is a constant for a fixed test point regardless of the version of the experimental compiler system being used. Thus, the analysis of the results is unaltered since it is the difference between the measurements that is relevant when making comparisons.

The four test programs selected and their characteristics are:

1 EE: A student electrical engineering problem.
   a) control parameters: *C21* and *C31*, increments that control the accuracy of the results; for the test runs, *C21* was held fixed while *C31* was allowed to vary
   b) program units: main program unit only
   c) number of statements: 51
   d) number of basic blocks: 9
   e) number of individual loops: 1
   f) loop size: 7 basic blocks
   g) loop nesting: 1 single-level

   This program is to typify the type of program written by a student.

2 SIEVE2: A prime number generator (204).
   a) control parameter: *K*, the number of primes to be generated
   b) program units: main program unit only
   c) number of statements: 86
   d) number of basic blocks:27
   e) number of individual loops: 7

f) loop sizes (in basic blocks): 1,2(2),4,5(2),25*

g) loop nesting:

1 single-level

5 double-level

1 triple-level

This algorithm is a modification of Chartres' algorithm in that it generates the first *K* primes instead of all the primes less than or equal to *M*.

3 LES: A linear equation solver (205, 206)

a) control parameter: *N*, the number of variables

b) program units: main program unit plus 2 subprogram units

c) number of statements: 97

d) number of basic blocks: 45

MAIN:15

DECOMP: 20

SOLVE: 10

e) number of individual loops: 13

MAIN: 4

DECOMP: 5

SOLVE: 4

f) loop sizes (in basic blocks):

MAIN: 1,2,4(2)

DECOMP: 1(2),3,4,18

SOLVE: 1(2),3(2)

g) loop nesting:

MAIN: 2 single-level, 2 double-level

DECOMP: 1 single-level, 3 double-level, 1 triple-level

SOLVE: 2 single-level, 2 double-level

The original algorithm given in the textbook by Forsythe and Moler (205) consists of two subroutines. However, Moler later published new subroutines that were a modification of, and replacement for, the corresponding original routines (206). These were the routines used in the program. The test matrices were generated by the program and correspond to Example 3.6 in the book by Gregory and Karney (207).

4 QZ: An eigenvalue problem (208).

a) control parameter: *N*, the size of the square input matrix

b) program units: main program unit plus 9 subprogram units

c) number of statements: 654

d) number of basic blocks: 323

MAIN: 9	QZVEC: 77
QZ: 7	HSH3: 5
QZHES: 66	HSH2: 5
QZIT: 97	CHSH2: 5
QZVAL: 49	CDIV: 3

---

* *The notation is to be interpreted as follows: for the 7 individual loops, one is of size 1, two of size 2, one of size 4, two of size 5, and one of size 25.*

e) number of individual loops: 51
 MAIN: 2
 QZHES: 19
 QZIT: 12
 QZVAL: 4
 QZVEC: 14
 HSH3, HSH2, CHSH2, CDIV: 0

f) loop sizes (in basic blocks):
 MAIN: 2,5
 QZHES: 2(12),3,5,7(2),21,23,32
 QZIT: 2(7),3,9,10,44,66
 QZVAL: 2(3),42
 QZVEC: 2(6),3(2),5,7,18,19(2),48

g) loop nesting:
 MAIN: 1 single-level, 1 double-level
 QZHES: 3 single-level, 7 double-level, 9 triple-level
 QZIT: 3 single-level, 2 double-level, 7 triple-level
 QZVAL: 1 single-level, 3 double-level
 QZVEC: 3 single-level, 7 double-level, 4 triple-level

This program was obtained from Stewart and is described, but not given in his paper with Moler (208). The test matrices are generated by the program and were suggested by Stewart. This algorithm is interesting in that the intermediate quantities produced by the program may not be the same owing to rounding errors. Consequently, the execution times are theoretically not strictly comparable. However, for practical purposes they are, that is, the timings depend in a uniform manner on the size of the matrix.

The test results

The performance of each compiler system is measured by obtaining the total run time for a test program as a function of its control parameter, where total run time is the sum of compilation time, load time, and execution time. The timings were made on a PDP-KA10 computer system with core having a 1.8 microsecond read/write cycle. During a test run, the computing environment consisted of the monitor, the I/O handlers and the particular compiler system being tested. Identical computer runs produced the same timings so there is no statistical fluctuation in the results. A 10-microsecond clock was used to make the timings, which are given here in seconds.

The results of the test runs are presented in graphical form (Figures 4 to 7). The test programs were also run under F40, the FORTRAN-IV compiler on the PDP-10 and AFI which runs the program interpretively only.

Analysis of test results

Before analysing the position of the AF performance curve relative to the curves for AFW, AFG and AFH, we first analyse the relative positions of the AFW, AFG and AFH curves and see if they conform to expectations.

AFW, AFG and AFH differ only in the amount of compile-time optimization they apply to a program, and thus in the efficiency of the machine language they produce. At the start of execution, the AFH curve lies above the AFG curve which in turn lies above

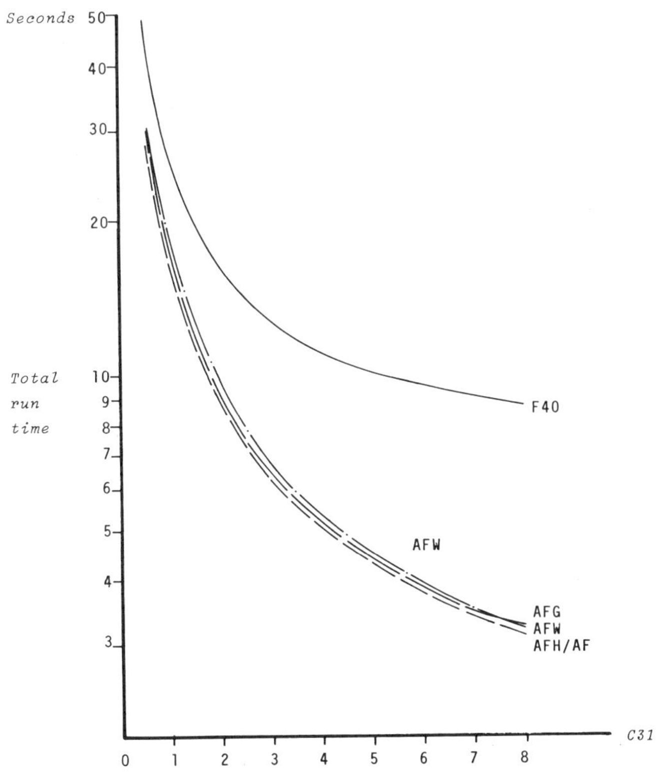

Figure 4: Performance curves for program EE

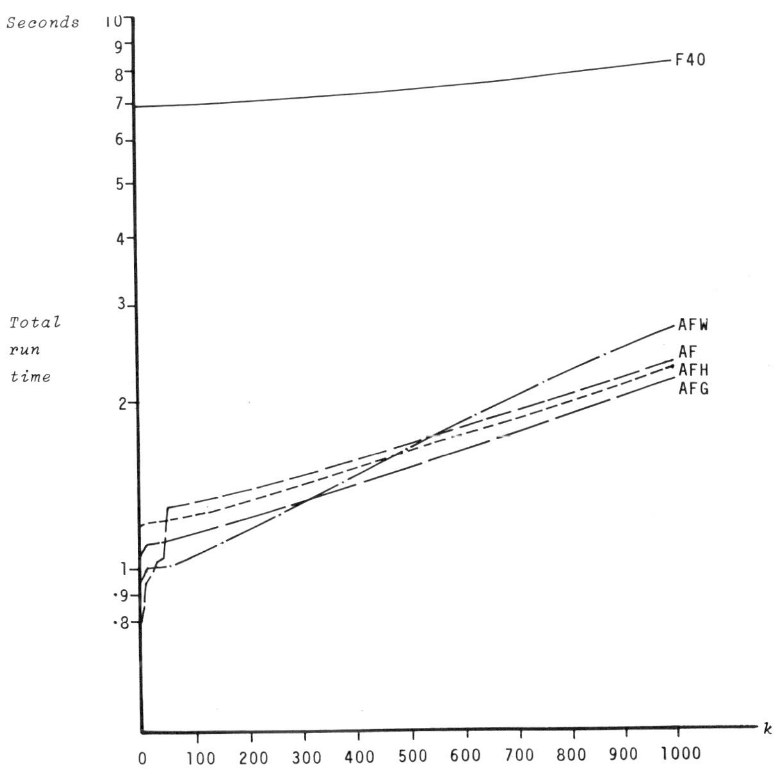

Figure 5: Performance curves for program SIEVE2

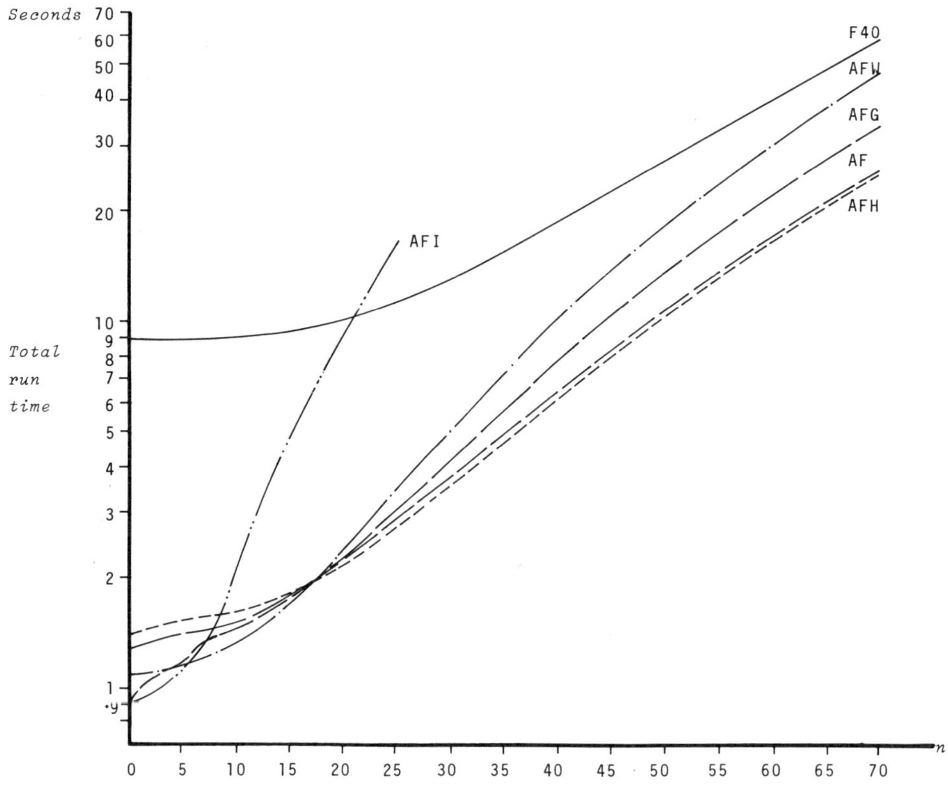

Figure 6: Performance curves for program LES

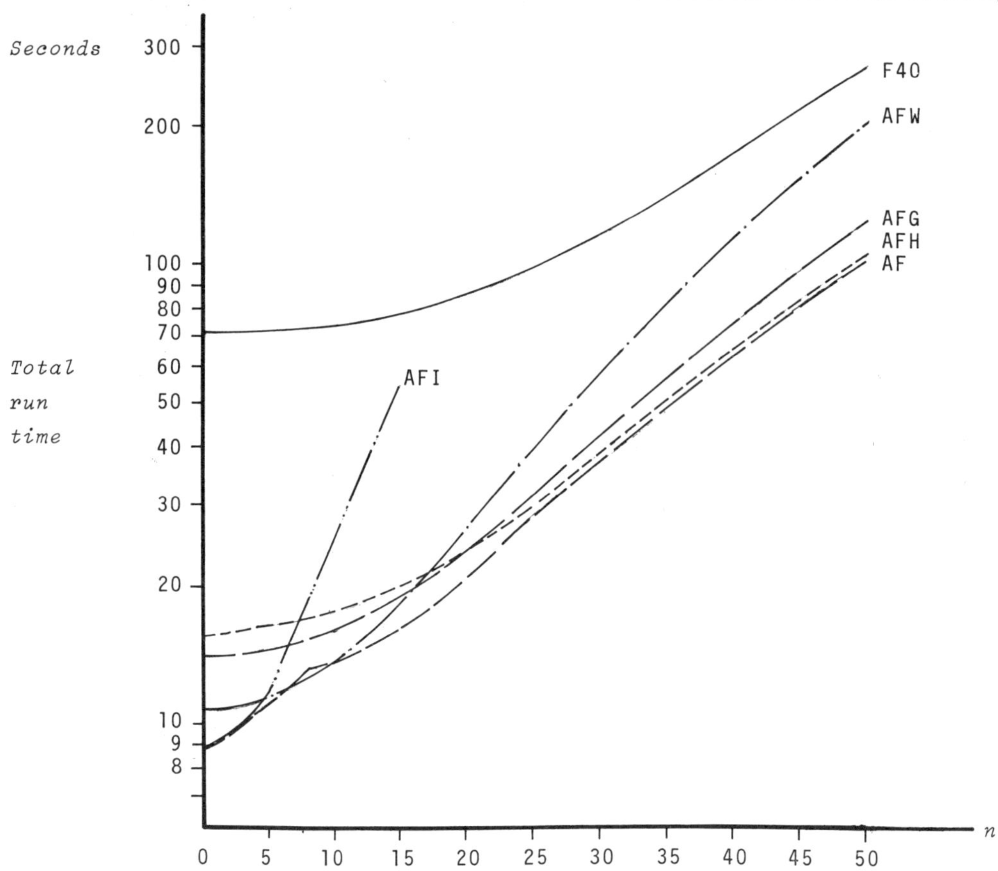

Figure 7: Performance curves for program QZ

the AFW curve. Because of the relative efficiency of the code, the AFW curve eventually will cross the other two, and the AFG curve will cross the AFH curve. These crossover points occur when the difference in compilation time equals the difference in execution time. It is expected then that if a program is run long enough, the AFW curve will lie above the AFG curve which in turn will lie above the AFH curve. If, however, the additional optimization (CM) performed by AFH has no effect, that is, does not remove any invariant quads from any loop, then the effort is wasted and the AFG curve will lie below the AFH curve.

By checking the figures for each test program, it is seen that the curves do indeed follow this behaviour pattern. Only for the test program SIEVE2 does the AFG curve lie below the AFH curve. The reason is exactly that given above, viz: CM has no effect. An examination of the optimization results showed that the loops did not contain any invariant quads.

As for the AF curve, it is expected to lie initially below all the other curves since it performs no initial optimizations. This is indeed the case. If a program is run long enough, the AF curve will asymptotically become parallel to the AFH curve because the executable code becomes identical to that produced by AFH. There are indications that it approaches the AFH curve from above if the time required for the program to be optimized exceeds the compile-time optimization time for AFH; otherwise, it approaches it from below.

There is a range in which the AF curve might cross over one or more of the other curves and then cross back under. This occurs for small execution times. The width of the range seems to depend on the diversity of the program's loop structure. Consider each test program in terms of increasingly diverse loop structures:

1 EE: This short program has one loop which constitutes most of the program. Since this loop is an innermost loop, the only difference between AF and AFH is that AF first translates the loop to 'dumb' code which is executed before being totally optimized. Hence, AF's execution times differ from those for AFH by a constant.

2 SIEVE2: This program contains a main execution loop which constitutes most of the program and gets totally optimized almost immediately. However, it contains a few embedded loops and is therefore considered an outermost loop. Hence its optimization is more gradual than the loop in EE, but not gradual enough because representations are changed before it is necessary. The spike occurring at the beginning of the AF curve is due to CM having no effect on the outermost loop. This optimization time is wasted and the machine language segment is identical to that produced by CSE.

3 LES: This program consists of three program units each containing a number of loops. Each subprogram unit contains a doubly nested loop which accounts for most of its execution time. The one program unit gets called only once so the benefits of total optimization are wasted if the program does not run long enough. The other program unit is called repetitively so eventually the double loop and the entire subprogram get totally optimized. The results are excellent, for only AFW is slightly better than AF for small execution times. The initial part of the AF curve is not smooth due to the optimization perturbations which are more apparent for small execution times.

4 QZ: This program contains the most diverse loop structure and consists of 10

program units. Four of the units constitute the main part of the program, and each is called only once. There are a large number of inner loops of one or two basic blocks whose early optimization probably contributes to the fact that the AF curve is the best of any test programs. This is also the only case in which the time for total dynamic optimization is smaller than AFH's optimization time. The initial part of the AF curve is not smooth for the same reason stated for LES.

The test results indicate that AF does not outperform all the other systems across the entire spectrum of run times, but that for a particular program there is a given range in which one compiler system is better than any of the others. However, AF is better than any other single compiler system over the spectrum. Thus, we conclude that it is better to build one compiler system to cover the run-time spectrum than three separate specialized compiler systems, each designed for a different range of the spectrum.

CONCLUSIONS

Whereas current approaches apply code optimization equally to the entire program at compile time, our approach exploits dynamically the observed behavioural characteristics of programs, viz: that a small part (5%) of the code accounts for a large portion (50%) of the execution time. The effect is gradual optimization of a program, that is, the optimization is applied to one section of code at a time. The longer the program executes, the more optimized a section becomes.

The results were very encouraging. While AF did not outperform each of the other systems at all points in the run-time spectrum, it did perform better over the spectrum than did any other single compiler system. The major remaining problem lies in controlling the rate of optimization. AF's performance curves look worst for small-to-medium run times, indicating too much optimization is being applied too soon. More research is needed to find a better means for controlling the optimization rate.

We feel that we have demonstrated a worthwhile alternative to compiler design that should be considered seriously. The approach makes more sense, from an implementation viewpoint, than building many special-purpose compilers. The system can be built in an incremental fashion because of its modularity. Each step consists of programming and debugging an optimizer module and then adding it to the system. The final product is an adaptive compiler that does not require much more effort to build than a full optimizing compiler. AF was built in this manner: in 3 man-months we had programmed the compiler and interpreter, and had programs running. Then each optimizer was programmed in ½ to 1 man-month, debugged and added to the system. In less than a man-year, the system was completed.

It is clear that such an implementation approach is open-ended up to a point, for one can keep improving the efficiency of the generated code by adding more efficient optimizations until one exhausts all the optimization possibilities. There are other well-defined optimizations that work with the same internal form we produce; they should be added to the system and the performance measurements retaken, for example, strength reduction, opening subroutines, and other machine-dependent optimizations.

PROGRAM OPTIMIZATION IN A SERVICE BUREAU ENVIRONMENT

A J Jones

Unilever Computer Services

A J JONES graduated with first class honours in Mathematics at University College, London, in 1957; from there he went to Babcock & Wilcox Ltd, the boilermakers, joining their newly-formed computer section within the Engineering Department, where he worked on a Pegasus I doing both the analysis and programming for engineering calculations including cost estimation. While there he worked on an Argus 200 being used to control a boiler/turbine unit at a power station. Mr Jones gained commercial systems and programming experience as well as systems programming knowledge on IBM 360s at Babcocks & John Laings. He moved to Unilever Head Office Computer Department in 1968 as Systems Programming manager in charge of systems generation and the programming advisory service. Following the merging of the department into the newly formed UCSL in 1970 he became manager of Programming Support Services, which included the evaluation of programming aids and systems and the performance evaluation and optimization of application systems.

PROGRAM OPTIMIZATION IN A SERVICE BUREAU ENVIRONMENT

INTRODUCTION

What differences in the approach to optimisation should there be between the user of a service bureau and the user of an in-house service? Basically none; what differences there are lie in the division of responsibility between the supplier of the service and the user, and the continuing commercial pressure that is applied to use cost as a measure of efficiency.

The paper will define the different areas of responsibility, the extent of that responsibility and the benefits that the large user community of a bureau brings to each individual user. The benefits include the range of software tools available, the depth of experience that can be shared and the stability of the environment (although it does not remain completely static).

The paper will first detail the resources completely under the control of the bureau and actions that can be taken; then the tools and service that the bureau offers to its users; this leaves the work that must be undertaken by the programming user; and finally, and most important, looks at optimization as the end user sees it.

THE PRESSURE TO OPTIMIZE

If you have justified the expenditure on the installation of your own computer, it will probably be some time before the workload puts pressure on the machine capacity. When that happens, the in-house user thinks of hardware upgrade or maybe program optimization.

For the bureau user, the pressure is on from the start. Each application system has to be justified in terms of the returns on expenditure. It does not matter whether you have written your own programs or use a package or have had a bespoke system written by a software house. Whatever your choice, you have made sure the system processes your information to your satisfaction, that is, functionally the system is correct. So it is put into production on the bureau and you receive the bill for the first month's processing. Rather a shock perhaps! You talk to other users, as within the bureau environment you belong to a large community of like-minded people; many of them offer helpful advice, as can the bureau's experts. The users are presumably non-partisan but not well informed on your problem; the bureau may be well informed and are rather partisan. Whose advice would you accept? Of course, the answer should be no one's until you have measured the various factors involved. Only when you have collected the performance data, for your system, can you plan the right action to take. The advice offered can be helpful in interpreting the data but should not be acted upon blindly.

WHO MEASURES WHAT?

So how do you go about measuring the various factors involved in running your work at a bureau? Let me first list the factors involved; these are grouped into two main areas. There is the user system made up of programs, data, JCL and the manual interface; then there is the system environment made up of various hardware and operating system software components. The first area is the responsibility of the user and his software supplier (who may be the bureau). The environment is the responsibility of the bureau; as this is the larger and more general area, I will start there and work down to the more particular.

The bureau's responsibility

For a user to carry out effective optimization on his own programs, he must first be confident that the work is being run in a stable environment, that the environment does not contain any peculiarities that affect the general user.

To achieve this state with the environment, the bureau has to measure and modify the hardware configuration and/or operating system software so that the average workload is processed cost-effectively. This is a continuing activity as the workload changes with growth and change in the user community. There is a gradual rate of change and the modifications rarely if ever invalidates a user's past optimization. Thus the bureau would monitor the system on a daily basis using built-in measuring such as the operating system accounting mechanism; from the data collected, useful statistics can be drawn, such as: what turnround does each class of job achieve, what general programs are most used.

From these statistics, questions can be anticipated. If a large number of jobs require more than two tape drives, would it be best to increase the number of units or to encourage tapes to be mounted serial on fewer units during the job's execution? This sort of question can be answered by evaluating the alternatives and costing them against the predicted trends of job requirements.

The interpretation of the statistics may indicate the need for more detailed measurements. So periodically a more sophisticated monitor, either hardware or software, would be used to obtain the detailed measurements at the lowest level of resource utilization. These measurements will include the utilization of each channel, device, maybe dataset or even individual program member within a library. From this will stem a reorganization of system components on a disk, or across disks and channels.

For instance, in the 360/65 installation at which I work, a series of performance measurements indicated that the use of a drum for systems residence was justifiable. The throughput improvement was predicted and the system was measured after installation of the drum; when only a 5% instead of the predicted 11% improvement was obtained, a thorough investigation was made in parallel into the hardware, the operating system and the monitor. The investigation unearthed a non-destructive bug in the operating system, that is, the bug did not cause any errors but lost time by treating a fixed-head drum as a moving-head disk. I wonder how many drums are installed and running under the erroneous operating system. The measurements were taken using a software monitor, which is the easiest type to install and use; provided the user is aware of the interference caused by the monitor itself when analysing the results, no false analysis should be made. A hardware monitor could then be used occasionally to confirm the analysis when the expense is justified.

However, whichever is used, the optimization that is effected is for the 'average' job. For many users this will give good enough results; their programs or systems are not too complicated and effort in improving their efficiency is not justified.

The user's responsibility

What about the user whose system is still inefficient? How would he set about the job of optimizing his system? First he needs some tools mainly to measure the resource utilization of his system; with each tool should come advice on how to use it and how to interpret the results. Here the bureau does have some responsibility in that it can obviously provide a service; the user has the prime responsibility to request the service. There are three types of aid the bureau can provide.

1 The bureau can offer some automatic optimizer. This the user applies in a rather blind fashion. This type of tool takes the object code produced by a compiler and optimizes the machine code by removing unnecessary code, such as the reloading of a register with information it already contains. This type of tool suffers from a major drawback in that it is necessary to reapply the treatment every time a program is altered.

2 The bureau can offer sophisticated measuring tools. This type of tool will highlight areas of high resource utilization and conflicts within a program or system. More expertise is required in interpreting the data gathered by such tools; it also requires a deeper knowledge of how the various components of the operating system and possibly hardware work. The final result may be as simple in action as the separation of two files between physical disk volumes or the task of rewriting some high-level language statements.

   In this area quite significant savings have been made with very little effort. For example, a 20% CPU saving was made by expanding seven variable-indexed instructions into twenty-eight fixed-indexed instructions. In another case, a saving of nearly seven hours out of seven and a quarter hours elapsed time was made by repositioning a single indexed sequential file access statement.

   The effort in locating the areas of inefficiency is not very great; the effort involved in removing it can vary considerably. For instance, it would be more difficult to decide to rewrite part of the system when the inefficiency is seen to be built into the design. This is not necessarily the designer's fault; in the systems analysis stage, the user makes categoric statements about record type volumes or some other thing and the analyst makes decisions on this erroneous data and an inefficient system results. An example of this is in the use of indexed sequential access to a file which originally was going to have 5000 entries of eighty characters each. The description (70 characters) was dropped from each entry of which there were finally only 500. In this case it was worthwhile doing a complete sequential file read into an in-core table and using a binary search routine.

3 The bureau can offer advice and education. Here there is some onus on the users to share their experience. The bureau does have a responsibility to gather and then disseminate the experience in a digestible form. This can take the form of a user forum or a seminar or a formal education class. This is aided by everyone concerned documenting techniques and any facts discovered; future work can then draw on the recorded experience. In this area the bureau can often do work of an experimental

nature. For example, in my own environment, measurements were taken of accessing a given amount of data on disk using different blocking factors and access method options; the results were tabulated along with a write-up of the theory involved and presented to users at a seminar. The motive behind this third area is to avoid inefficiencies at the design and programming stage. This also applies to the acquisition of software, either an application package or a more generalized piece of software. It should be a part of the evaluation process to measure the performance of a software product using all the tools available. The measured efficiency should be one of the criteria by which a product is judged as well as the functional capability. I have been involved in such exercises. In one instance, a user requested a performance evaluation of a DBMS given a data base structure he thought would be appropriate to his business need. Some approximate record and key sizes were chosen and the test data base set up. Various access patterns were stimulated using the test data base and measurements taken on individual file activity. The process was repeated using different blocking factors on individual files and altering the order in which the data was loaded onto them.

The main objective was to verify with respect to the possible data base structure the supplier's claims on performance given certain criteria. The claims were proved to be substantially correct. At the same time useful performance data were obtained and experience gained; the information was filed away ready in case the user should install the DBMS.

So now we have a stable environment within which the user has optimized program and systems. Is that where it stops? No, there is one other group of people who are involved in the process, the end user. At times, he is confused with the user who runs the system; often they are one and the same person but not always. When they are separate entities, what does the end user see as optimization?

THE SYSTEM FROM THE END USER'S VIEWPOINT

In terms of the end user there are more factors then just the resource utilisation of the computer; for instance the end user will measure turnaround from the time he hands over the raw data, probably in the form of orders or invoices or some other pieces of paper, to the time he receives the results usually in the form of printed output. Saving seconds, even minutes in computer time will not significantly reduce this turnaround time. Probably, it will be more important to consider different ways of gathering or preparing the data for computer input, or of making available to the user the output from the computer.

More timely information can have significant cost benefits. Much effort has been put into both of these areas in the past few years. Key-to-tape disk systems often have had a remote-job-entry capability added; this has allowed information to be prepared for computer input on site where the information is generated.

For output, COM is being increasingly used. It is neater and more readily scanned.

All of these end user areas are thought of as improvements in working methods and I look on them as a form of optimization. As such, measurements should be taken both before and after system implementation. If the system is being implemented for some estimated benefit, that is, not an overall cost saving, the means of measuring that benefit should be agreed as part of the system specification and the task of measuring should be part of the system implementation. What do you do if the expected level of benefit is not achieved? As in the computer part of the system, measure each activity to determine where the most significant cost savings can be made. In addition, a re-evaluation should be undertaken of the case that the system would produce the benefits; it is pointless to improve the working of a system which cannot achieve the desired result. It is obviously better to expend effort in redesigning the system.

CONCLUSION

When undertaking optimization in a bureau environment, the bureau must provide a stable and efficient system in which each user can optimize his applications for cost and benefit. The bureau can offer expert help to the user in this task but should not confine the area of investigation to the computer part of a system if at all possible; the user may be wasting effort in optimizing the computer part of the system, that is, not making optimum use of resources to solve his problem.

LIVE PROGRAM TUNING: A PRACTICAL METHODOLOGY

D Lankey

Logica Limited

D LANKEY graduated in Mathematics from Southampton University in 1962. He joined Ferranti Ltd/ICT Ltd and worked for three years on the design and production of basic software for Orion and 1900 series systems. From 1965, he was employed by the British Railways Board. Initially he redesigned and implemented the Communications Supervisor for a pilot real-time wagon control and traffic information system run on Honeywell 200 machines. He then became responsible for establishing technical support functions for two new ICL 1900 installations, and subsequently for the management of the Technical Services Branch providing support to some 250 staff at several ICL 1900 and Honeywell 2200 installations and associated system development centres. He led two major technical studies in BR, one concerned with the introduction of modular programming techniques and the production of an ICL/Honeywell compatible test harness. He joined the Computer Performance Analysis team at Logica Limited in 1973 and has led several studies resulting in significant performance improvements in a variety of installations. He is now responsible for this area of Logica's activities as Manager of the Data Processing Economics Division.

LIVE PROGRAM TUNING: A PRACTICAL METHODOLOGY

INTRODUCTION

The design, coding and testing of a computer program is a complex task, which is typically undertaken in the midst of a number of pressures. It is reasonable to suggest that the majority of analysts and programmers are now trained to carry out their work effectively with due regard to the performance characteristics of the end product, the live programs. However, in general it is naive to think that the ultimate efficiency of a program is the prime objective of most data processing departments. Their most demanding requirement is that the systems are made to work on schedule.

It is hardly surprising then that the majority of programs exhibit scope for optimization after being put into live use. How many times have we heard a programmer declaring how much better his program would be if he had a chance to start again? What is needed at this stage in the development of a program is a reliable method for identifying any scope for optimization quickly and quantitatively so that the benefits may be costed and scarce skilled programming staff used effectively.

Most programs, once they are handed over to the computer operations department, do not come under any scrutiny beyond that arising from problems experienced by the user, or maybe, by the computer control and operating staff. Performance deficiencies are, except in extreme cases, not recognized since, in general, there are no yard-sticks on which to base any criticisms. Further, in a large multi-programming system, individual program performance is submerged with all the other operating system and application activities. This combination of circumstances leaves considerable scope for live-program optimization based on selective performance measurements.

The Logica Computer Performance Analysis service has developed an approach to enable the shortcomings of existing programs to be quantified so that optimization costs may be balanced against savings. The techniques have been successfully employed in a wide range of computer installations and have included program optimzation as part of major system performance exercises as well as assignments directed solely at specific programs whose performance was clearly unacceptable. The approach is based on the use of hardware monitoring techniques and is, therefore, machine and language-independent in principle.

Methodology

Figure 1 shows the basic stages in the optimization process. The diagram has been simplified and, in particular situations, some of the activities may prove superfluous and alternative iterations may prove desirable. The chart merely gives an indication

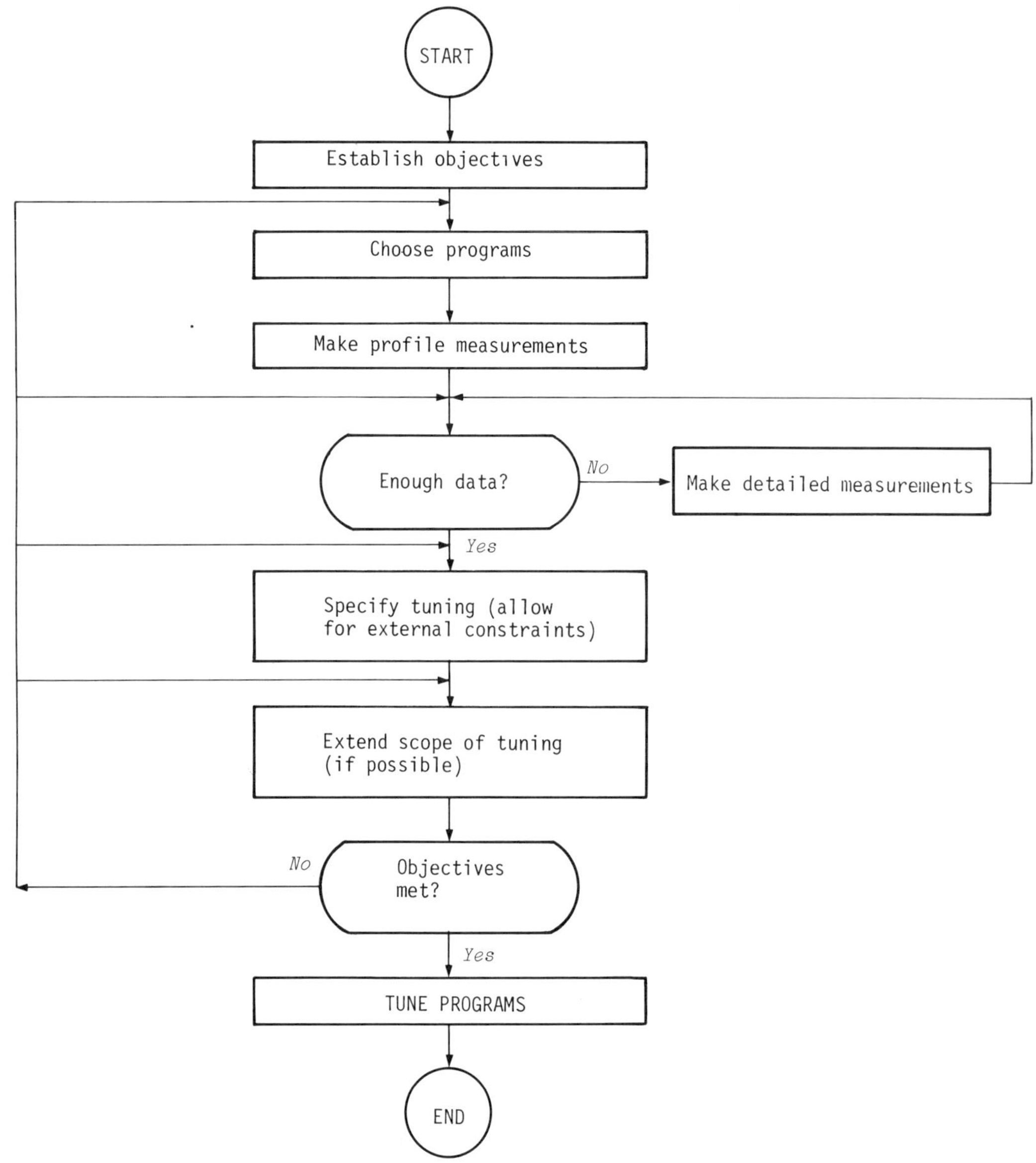

Figure 1: Program tuning methodology

of the usual steps and should not get in the way of a flexible approach to meet unusual situations.

This logical approach has been derived over a long period of time to meet the practical needs of a wide variety of computer users. The major features which we have found to be of particular benefit are:

1 the total concentration on areas offering major scope for optimization;

2 the objectivity afforded by the measurements, which minimizes any dependence on the analyst's prejudices;

3 the reduced need to use the application programmers to plan the optimization effort and the consequent reduction in any disturbance to other programming activities.

The major activities shown in Figure 1 are discussed in sequence in the remainder of this paper. Examples have been used to illustrate the techniques and benefits of the general approach wherever appropriate.

CHOICE OF PROGRAMS

A typical data processing installation will process several dozen application systems comprising hundreds of programs. The optimization of a few programs, each requiring skilled analysis to measure and diagnose inefficiencies therefore demands that the programs are selected carefully.

The criteria for the selection process will, of course, partly depend on the precise objectives of the program performance study. Typical objectives are:

1 the reduction of particular program/suite elapsed run times to meet external deadlines,

2 improvements in overall installation performance from the optimization of major programs;

3 increasing the awareness and skills of programmers so that overall program performance is improved steadily.

In case 1, the choice of programs to be investigated is usually trival and a representative selection can easily be specified.

The general requirement of case 2 requires more consideration however, since the interaction between programs in a multi-programming environment becomes an important parameter. The criteria in this case cannot be simply defined but will probably include:

- programs whose aggregated run times are long (either from periodic long runs or frequent shorter runs);
- time-critical programs which require priority facilities which downgrade overall site performance;
- unsociable programs which degrade overall site performance by virtue of their excessive resource demands (for example, by requiring 5 of the 6 available magnetic-tape decks)
- general-purpose software which is incorporated in many programs so that the benefits of selective optimization effort can easily be shared.

PROGRAM PROFILES

The first stage in the measurement process is the production of the program profile. The hardware monitor is used to measure the chosen programs during a special run in controlled, uninterrupted conditions. The profile simply accounts, in hardware utilization terms, for all the elapsed run time so that the major components are clearly identified. The profile is essentially the same as that developed for the analysis of overall system performance.

If the profile is to be meaningful then it is important that the measured run is:

- truly representative of the normal process, (that is, typical data has been input);
- not affected by external activities beyond essential operating system functions (this requirement usually dictates that the program is run in a single programming environment)

The program profile may be displayed in a variety of ways. However, the conventional bar-chart format shown in Figure 2 is the most flexible for this purpose. The significance of the profile can be simply related to the program by describing the

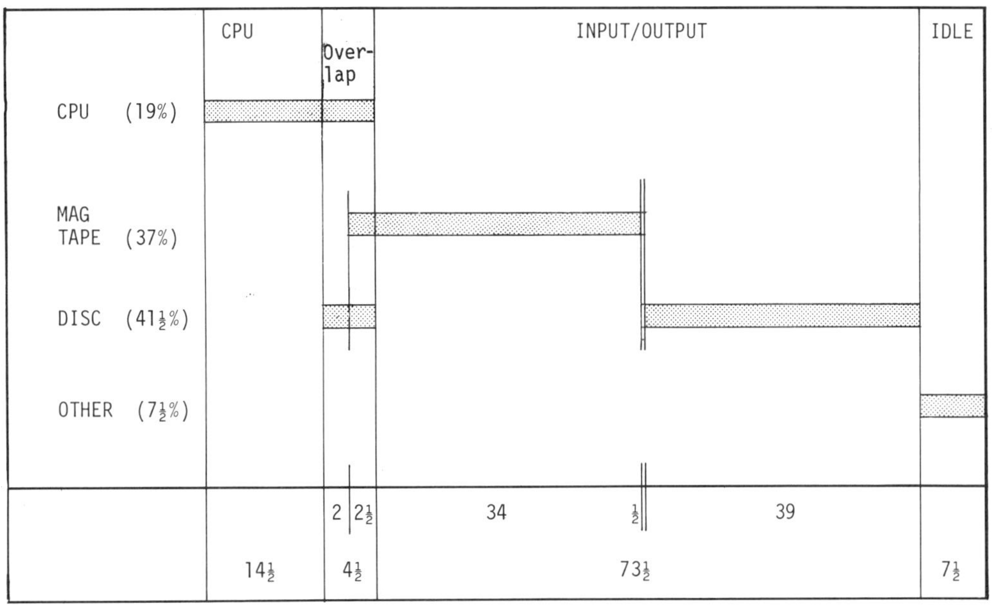

Figure 2: RS03 program profile

the peripherals in applications system terms. This is shown in Figure 3 which relates to the program shown in the system flow-chart in Figure 4.

This example is from an ICL 1904S installation which uses the GEORGE 3 operating system. RS03 is the main update program for two master files:

1 an indexed sequential disc file 'RS-POST', which is updated at random in situ

2 a multi-reel magnetic tape file 'RS-STAFF'.

Transactions are read from a magnetic tape file and the first phase of the program carries out the 'RS-POST' updates which do not affect the 'RS-STAFF' file. The second phase, chosen for optimization since it represented the significant part of each RS03 run, reads the remaining transactions from a small GEORGE filestore file.

CPU busy	**19.2%**
Executive	6.2%
GEORGE 3	5.9%
Program RS03	7.1%
Any magnetic tape	**37.1%**
& CPU Wait	34.5%
B/F 'RS-STAFF' file	18.6%
C/F 'RS-STAFF' file	18.6%
'TRANS-OUT' file	0.7%
Any disc	**41.4%**
& CPU Wait	39.5%
Program RS03 files	1.6%
Magnetic tape/disc overlap	**0.7%**
& CPU Wait	0.6%
Other (for example, Console TY)	**7.4%**

Figure 3: RS03 program profile table

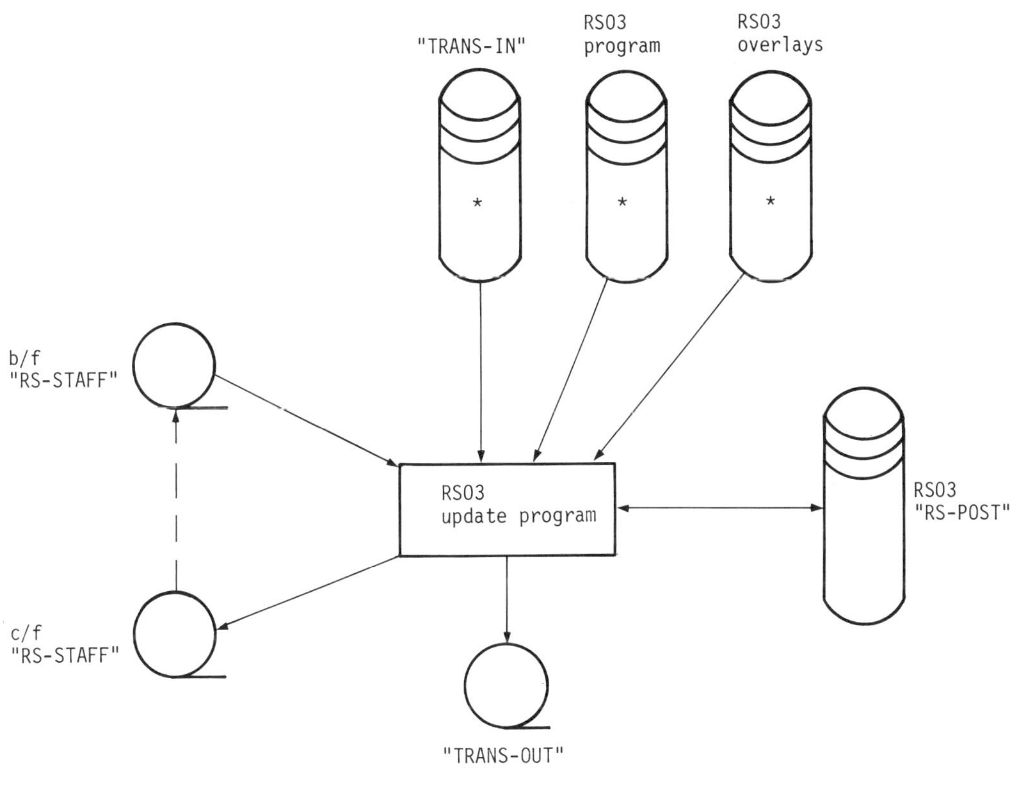

Figure 4: RS03 program flowchart (phase 2 only)

This phase outputs print details to another tape file.

The program profile relating to this single phase is easily obtained by isolating the measurements for the appropriate time period. The start and end times are often externally marked by console messages or the opening/closing of files. If necessary, however, analysis of the monitor output can reveal the switch from one phase to another which is typically delineated by major profile changes.

The profile must include a breakdown of the major file activities. In this case the 'RS-STAFF' files have been isolated. The use of a data-well like the GEORGE 3 filestore, however, presents additional problems since discrete logical files, shown with an asterisk in Figure 4, are not distinguishable in physical terms. Activity in different filestore files must therefore be established from software instrumentation, in this case the GEORGE 3 Monitor File for the job. The filestore transfers are then:

- program file $<$ 100
- overlay file $>$ 18000
- input transaction file $<$ 100

so that the breakdown reveals that nearly 40% of RS03 run time is spent on overlay transfers.

The key areas of the profile are now exposed and the areas which offer most scope for optimization can be considered in more detail. The areas are:

1 overlay file activity 39.5% (disk)
+ processing to handle I/O

2 magnetic tape file 'RS-STAFF' activity
18.6% (input tape)
18.6% (output tape)
+ processing to handle I/O

The next stage of the analysis will depend not only on the nature of the profile, but also on the external constraints.

EXTERNAL INFLUENCE ON OPTIMIZATION

The actual recommendations for optimization of RS03 must take into account:

- the availability of resources to change the program, recognizing the costs and benefits of each improvement;
- any constraints imposed on the program by the computer system, for example, main store size limits, disc file space limits;
- any side-effects of improvements which will mean changes to other programs or systems, for example, as a result of changing file designs.

These three areas were all considered in the case of RS03 and the recommendations for its optimization reflect the environment. Two straightforward modifications to the program were considered:

1 the elimination (or reduction) of overlay transfers by making them (selectively) store-resident

2 the addition of double-buffering facilities for the 'RS-STAFF' files

Both proposals require additional main store and will, therefore, reduce the store available for other programs. The reduction in run time from these changes however (which could be expected to be about 50%) more than justified the increase in store requirement from 17K words to 30½K words. The 1904S configuration included a 192K word store and there were typically 6 active programs loaded so that this isolated change would not prove unduly disruptive.

The total elimination of overlays is, of course, a crude modification and is not often justified. In this case, whilst it was clear that overlay activity was excessive, more detailed information was required to support a selective modification. The recommended action was put forward since it transpired that the program's mean run time was 2½ hours and no restart facilities were incorporated. The urgent need was therefore to cut elapsed run times drastically and any pruning of the store size could then be considered in the longer term.

RS03 was coded in COBOL so that both the immediate changes could be trivially incorporated. Further, the changes were confined to RS03 and no other program modifications were necessary, so that no further analysis was considered appropriate at that stage.

DETAILED MEASUREMENTS

RS03's overlay activity would, as we have already seen, need more detailed measurement to enable selected overlays to be made store-resident. This second level of measurement is often required to break down the predominant activity in a program profile.

Figure 5 shows the profile for another ICL 1900 program, AB08, which ran for over 6 hours per day. The profile directs the performance analyst to the processing activity and does not provide adequate information to support practical optimization effort.

The hardware monitor is used, in this situation, to produce an activity map of the processing so that division of the CPU activity between different routines can be established. Figure 6 shows the instruction address map for AB08. Sections of core without any significant activity have been omitted for clarity in the diagram.

The performance analyst's job is now straightforward in so much as the major sources of run time activity have been isolated to two small sections of code. Both subroutines were, unexpectedly, written in assembly language and were not part of the main COBOL coding. The routines were part of the data manipulation software and incorporated main-store table look-up facilities. Analysis revealed that each entry to the routines involved a serial search through a 200-item list, that is, a mean search against 100 keys. The key fields were in the range 100-999 so that it was possible to access the list via a self-addressed index requiring 450 words (2 pointers per word) in each case.

These modifications were actually coded on the same day that the measurements were produced and, following tests, the program was re-run. The run time had been halved

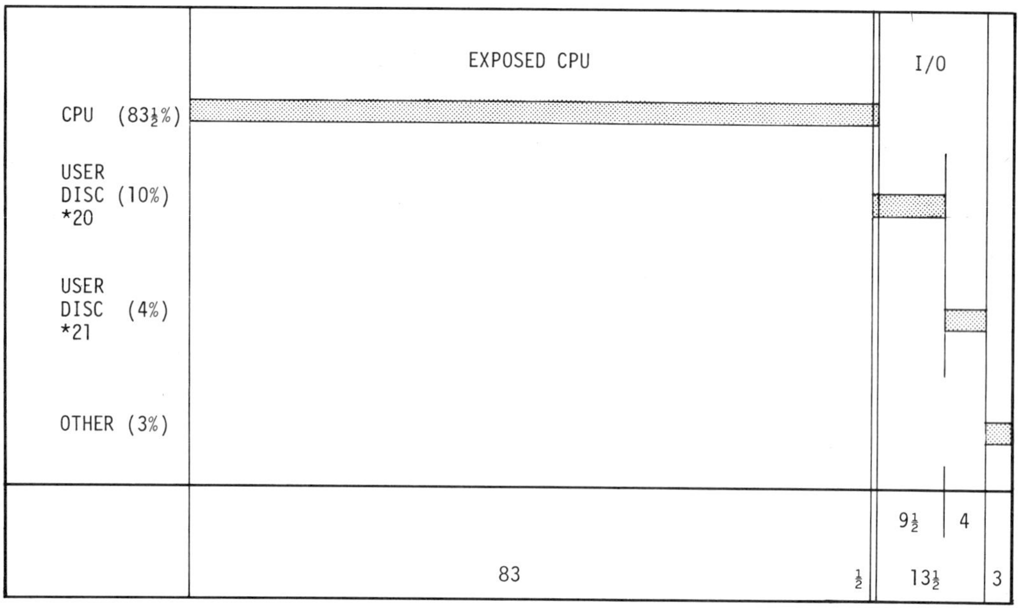

Figure 5: AB08 program profile

COBOL	VET	5%
	CROSSREF	4%
	DATES	2%
PLAN assembler	MOVEGRP1	1%
	GETEL1	1%
	MOVEGRP2	2%
	MOVEL	1%
	GETEL2	5%
	GETELNO	1%
	TABEL *	55%
	CONVELNO	4%
	CONVGRP*	13%
	GETADR	1%
SOFTWARE	DISC H/K	1%

Figure 6: AB08 instruction map (% of user CPU busy)

at a cost of 900 words of main store, which was not significant at the installation in question.

Figure 7 shows the new AB08 program profile. The optimization cycle may be repeated until the benefits no longer justify the investigation effort. In this particular example the revised profile has not revealed any new information which could not have been predicted from the original. The new figures merely then verify the effects of the implemented changes and, in particular, demonstrate that there are no unforeseen side-effects.

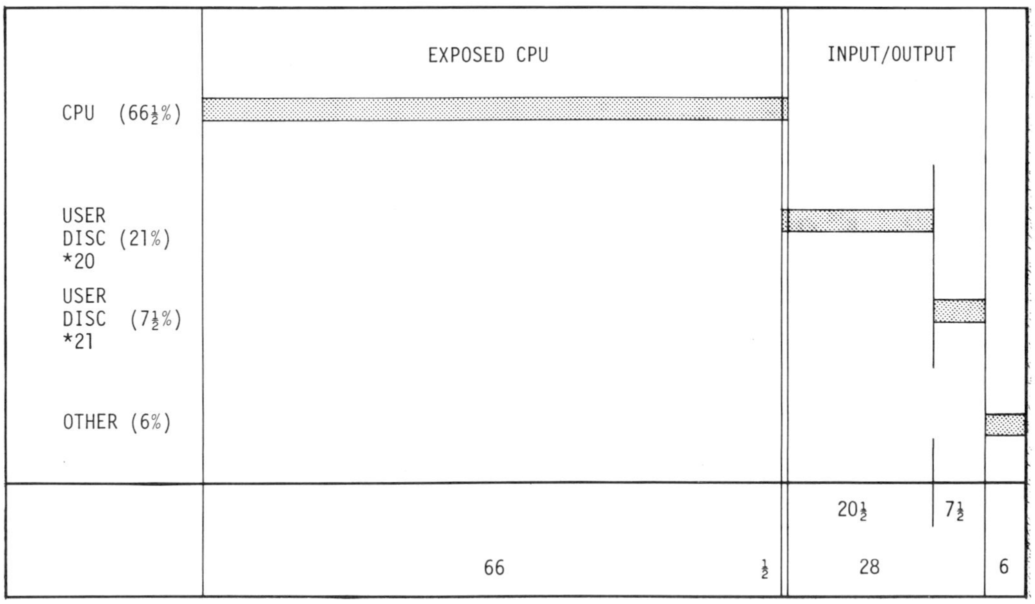

Figure 7: AB08 post-tuning profile

MEASUREMENT OF ON-LINE SYSTEMS

The two examples discussed earlier are both ICL 1900 batch-mode programs. The measurement procedure and the corresponding identification of activities offering potential for tuning (by virtue of their large contribution to overall program activity) is, of course, independent of the computer system and the program type. The methodology can be used in a wide variety of situations although the ultimate recommendations and modifications may demand specialist knowledge of the particular environment.

A recent study contrasts sharply with the previous examples and demonstrates the flexibility of the approach using a hardware monitor in conjunction with the computer manufacturer's modified operating system. The study was commissioned to assess the potential expansion capability of a dedicated on-line monitoring and control system. The remit was complex and included:

1 the quantification of the system's spare capacity

2 the identification of any gross inefficiencies

3 the measurement of exceptional situations generated by an external simulator

4 the calibration of the system's software monitor

5 the detailed measurement of routines believed to generate excessive processing overheads

6 an assessment of the next release of the tailored operating system.

The hardware monitor profile (Figure 8) indicated that the overall CPU load exceeded 60% and that, when no on-line functions were being performed, the tailored operating system still utilised 56% of the elapsed time. Detailed measurements were then taken to break down the operating system activity by:

- an instruction address map
- a 'reason-for-entry' code map.

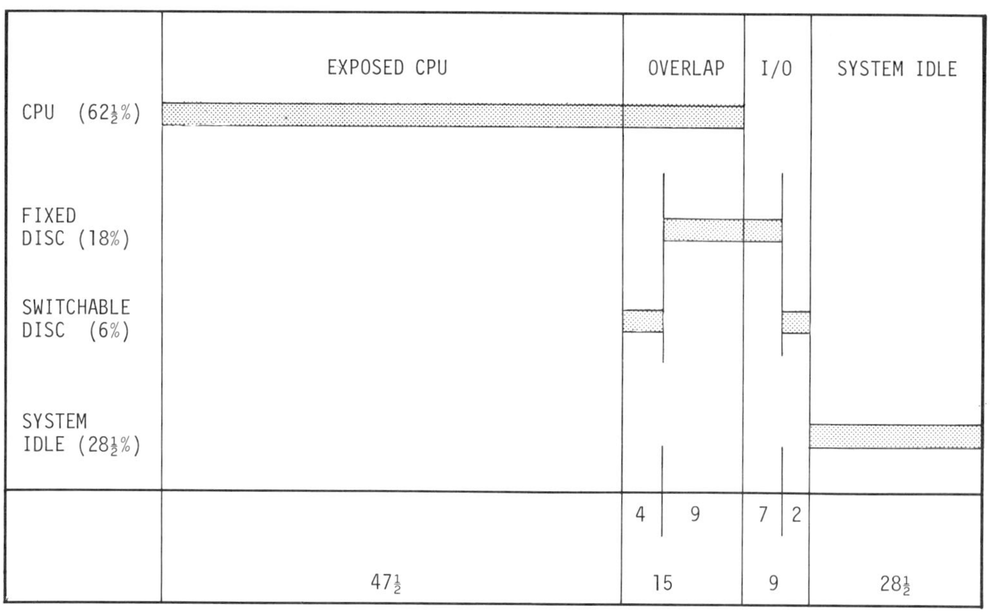

Figure 8: On-line system profile

The instruction address map revealed that the peripheral status-checking routines accounted for most of the processing activity. Redundant functions were eliminated, thus further tailoring the operating system to the installation's requirements. The modifications were undertaken in collaboration with the mainframe supplier's staff.

The 'reason-code' map (Figure 9) derived from the hardware monitor's measurements of a processor highway also proved invaluable and exposed a redundant 10 msec interval entry, which was also eliminated easily.

The modified system was introduced after trials and further monitor measurements showed that the processor load had been halved. Additional measurements, via the system's simulation facilities, showed that the new system was easily capable of handling the projected three-fold increase in the controlled system load so that the

REASON FOR ENTRY	USAGE	
	% OF ALL ENTRIES	FREQ (msec)
Terminate program	24.5%	18
Activate type 1 interrupt program	11.4%	38
Activate type 2 interrupt program	17.7%	25
Special call of interrupt program*	43.6%	10
String handler 1	0.7%	580
String handler 2	1.2%	360

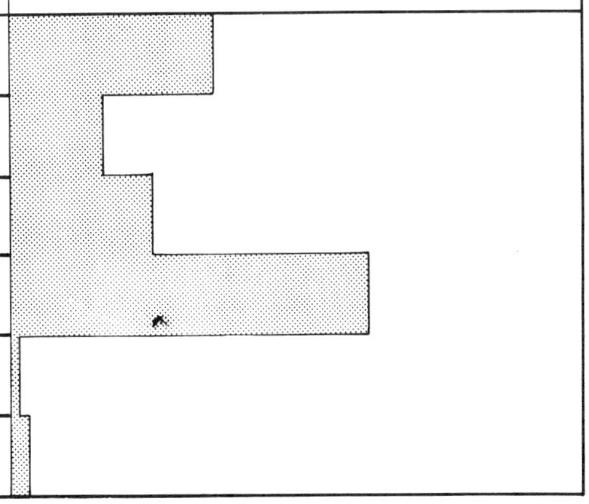

Figure 9: On-line system - supervisor entry "reason-code" map

threat of a possible transfer to new, incompatible equipment, was removed.

Investigation of the instruction-address maps revealed that the suspected routines did not, in fact, contribute significantly to the processor load. The biggest routine required a mere 0.2% of elapsed time in normal conditions and this was incidentally halved as a result of the operating system amendments!

Finally, we studied the specification of the planned operating system and related its facilities to the measured operational environment. It was apparent from high-resolution profile data (one-second intervals) that the control-panel response times were directly related to the disc activity and, further, that at peak times the delays were severe. We therefore analysed a disc activity map (Figure 10) to establish how new disc handling facilities could best be utilized and response times reduced.

TRACK ADDRESS		FILE-IDENTITY	USAGE (% OF ALL ACCESSES)
FROM	TO		
A0	A1	BACKING STORE MAP - SPINDLE A	8.0%
A2	A3	BACKING STORE MAP - SPINDLE B	20.4%
A4	A123	Data & miscellaneous programs	5.1%
A124		DIRECTOR OVERLAYS	14.5%
A125	A196	Data & miscellaneous programs	11.2%
A197	A199	FILE CONTROL ENTRIES	17.1%
B0	B199	Data & miscellaneous programs	22.1%

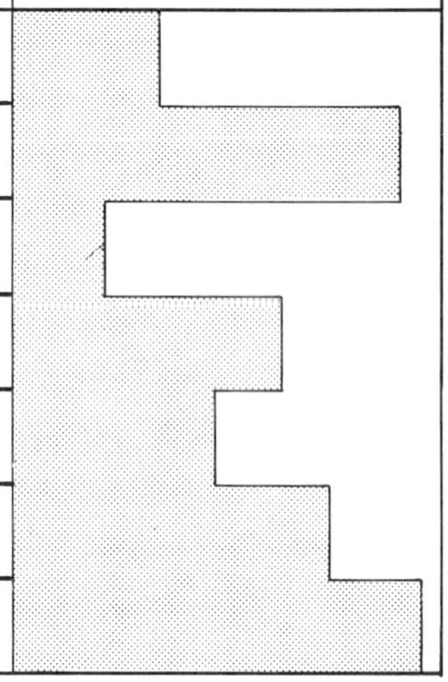

Figure 10: On-line system - fixed head disc summary of disc accesses

Four basic new facilities were considered:

1 the retention of selected File Control entries in main-store to reduce the disc transfers;

2 the declaration of permanent fixed-length disc files so that they could be allocated contiguous physical blocks and chaining via the disc-held Backing Store Map file would no longer be required for these files;

3 the locking of selected operating system overlays in main store;

4 the locking of selected user routines in store.

Item 2 alone does not require additional main store space and all the suitable files can be declared. The remaining options compete for store space and the jigsaw can only be completed from a detailed store layout map and complete disc activity breakdowns to indicate the relative activity between each File Control entry, operating system overlay, and user routine.

The analysis which was carried out in conjunction with the installation system's programming team concluded that almost exactly 50% of all disc traffic could be eliminated whilst retaining limited spare main store for contingencies.

The recommendations were documented in great detail so that each change could be reconsidered at the time the new software became available. The quantified benefits could then be used to assess the priorities and an effective improvement plan could be put into operation to make the best use of limited skilled systems programming resources.

The program profile concept is therefore applicable to the tuning of both batch and on-line systems. A further variation is also useful in the latter case to support the detailed investigation of particular transactions, typically those arising from reported poor response times.

Figure 11 plots the major profile components from our on-line example against time. Individual transactions can, in this specially organized trial run, be clearly seen. Their details were recorded clerically and times were synchronized with the aid of a stop-watch. During the actual optimization study in question, the relationship between response times and disc traffic was originally noticed as a result of profile data displayed in this manner.

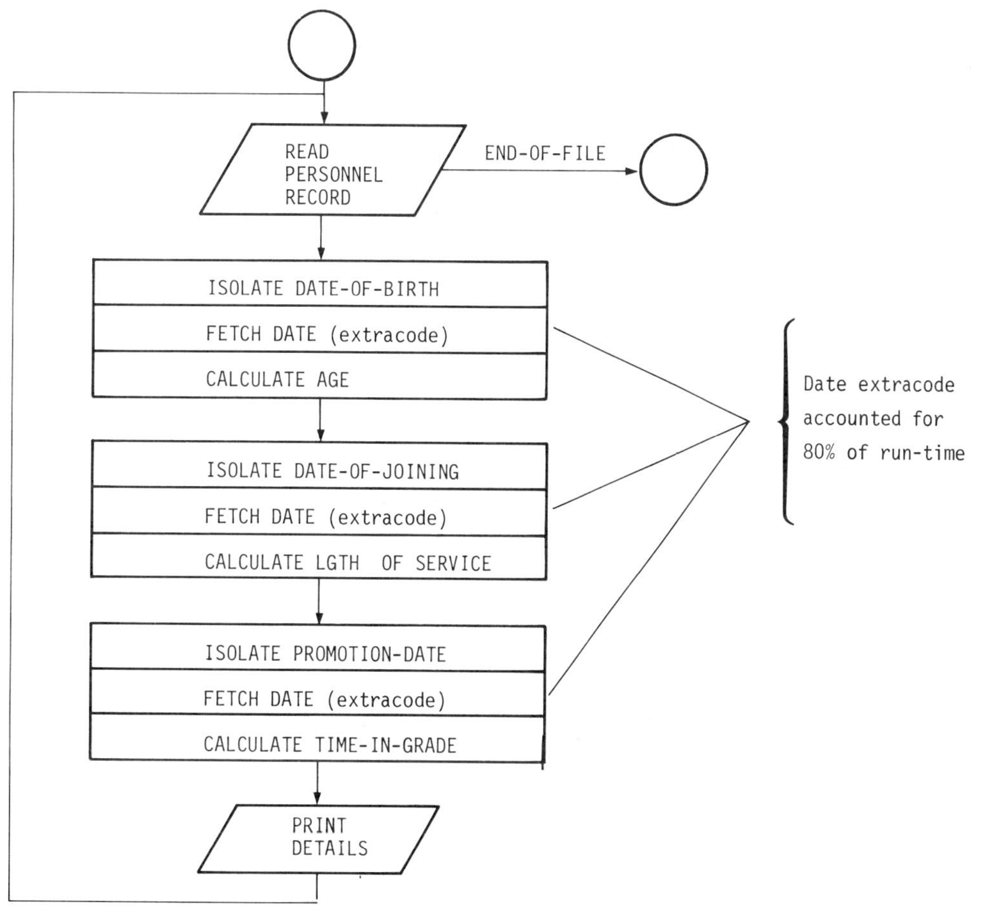

Figure 13: Obvious program inefficiency

EXTENDING THE SCOPE OF THE OPTIMIZATION

We have already noted that any recommendations for program tuning must take account of external constraints, including any side-effects on other programs or systems. In some cases, the side-effects may be beneficial so that, if the scope of the tuning is to be maximized, other programs and systems should be amended.

AB08 provides an exceptional example of this principle. The program formed part of a data base creation suite which was required daily for a period of several months and, at the time of our investigation, could not handle the projected data volumes within each 24 hours. The study was set up to tune AB08 and the next three longest running programs.

The search routine changes had a dramatic impact on all four programs since they all exhibited similar profiles and instruction-address-maps. Figure 12 shows the daily run times before and after the routines were changed and several other minor improvements were made; 15 hours per day had been reduced to 7½ in one day's programming effort! The new routines were subsequently incorporated into the other programs in the suite automatically when they were next recompiled. Our other recommendations to remove some inefficient and redundant COBOL coding were also implemented over the whole system and, within a few weeks, the original 30-hour run had been reduced to just over 7 hours.

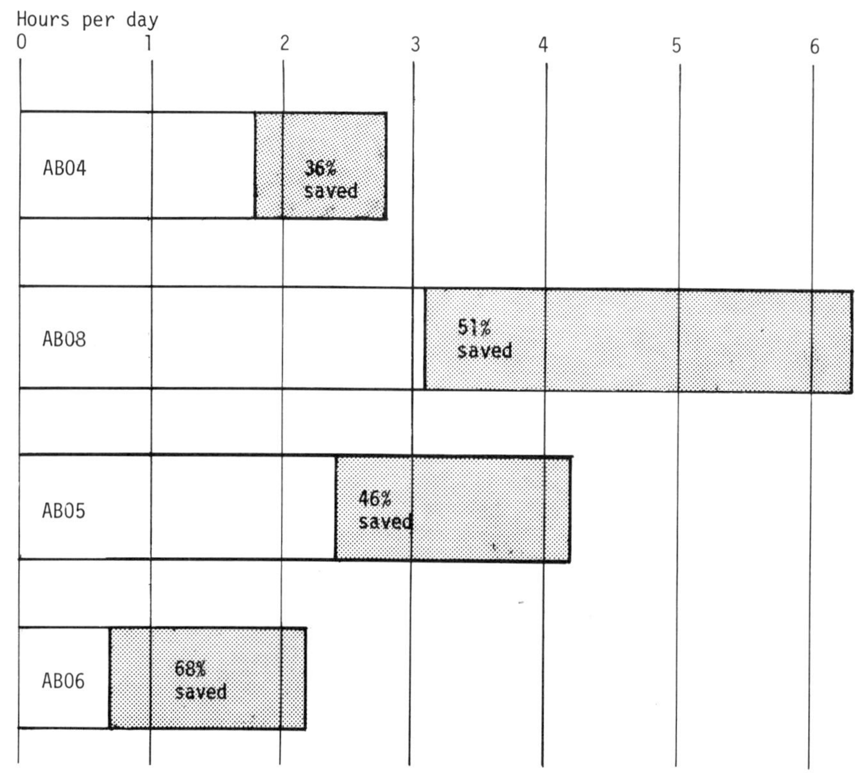

Figure 12: Extensions to AB08 tuning

The other example, RS03, arose at an installation which provided an internal bureau service for user departments. The Computer Manager organized the program tuning study as an adjunct to a major system performance exercise and chose the programs to ensure that each major systems and programming team would be involved. The measurements were undertaken by Logica staff using special GEORGE 3 job descriptions and carefully selected data for each single-programmed run. The results, which comprised:

- program profiles
- instruction-address maps
- disc-address maps (major activity packs only)
- GEORGE 3 monitor files
- GEORGE 3 System Performance files

were briefly analysed and a Workshop was arranged to discuss each program in front of all the interested parties.

Ten programs were analysed 'publicly' in two half-day sessions. The combination of our analysts' experience of monitor output, the application programmers' knowledge of their own programs and the competitive spirit between different programming teams combined to produce a wealth of tuning recommendations and a new awareness of live program performance. The exercise was completed quickly and all the optimization ideas were effectively advertised with, hopefully, long-term benefits to the client.

The techniques described in this paper are designed to highlight major areas of potential tuning. The rewards are often substantial and it is easy, with hindsight, to believe that no special measurements were really necessary. In general, however, the recommendations could not be arrived at quickly and could not be quantified without the overview provided by the program profile. Some exceptions do arise and on several occasions our measurements, carried out at the client's request, have only confirmed inefficiencies which should have been apparent if the operating system signals had been noticed.

Figure 13 shows the outline block diagram of a simple program in a personnel information system. It was run in a dual-programming environment and had a reputation for 'stopping' the other stream. The single-programmed monitored run was observed, by Logica performance analysts, and it was noted that the 'supervisor-state' console indicator was lit continuously. The operators confirmed the observation but had never seen fit to draw attention to the phenomenon.

The cause of the excessive supervisor activity was quickly discovered. There were three entries per input record to fetch the date, each requiring the activation of a

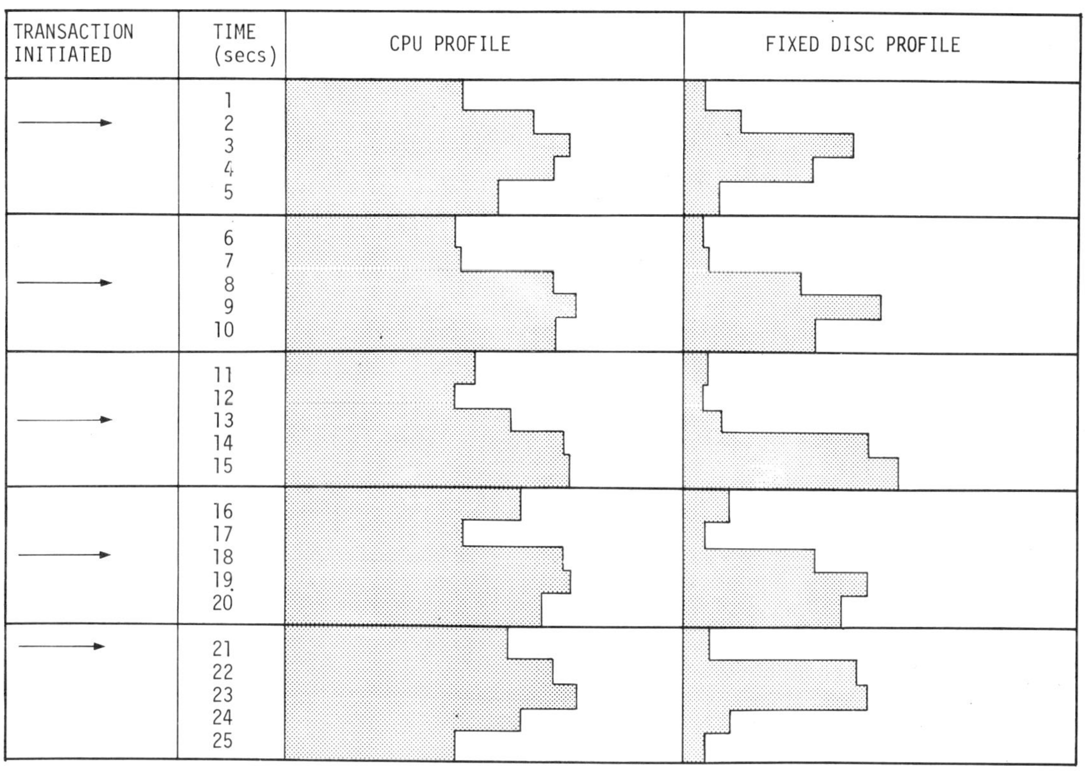

Figure 11: On-line system profile v. transactions

software extracode. Simple modifications reduced this activity to one entry per run and the date was easily retained in the program's data storage area.

The profile contributed little since it was not produced until the program had been recompiled! It did, however, enable us to predict confidently that the program would now run some five times faster than before, and this was proved the following day.

Observation and simple analysis of available statistics can therefore detect some gross inefficiencies. Single programming runs are, of course the most revealing, and our experience has already detected the following categories of inefficiency in this way:

- excessive supervisor calls (as just described)
- lack of input/output multiple buffers (observed from magnetic tape deck movements)
- bad disc file random hash algorithms (observed from clustering of disc accesses).

Other potential problems can be identified from operating system logs. Disc accesses in particular deserve some 'reasonability' checks to verify that each logical access generates a reasonable number of physical accesses. Two typical faults can be traced from such analysis:

- excessive overflow
- imbalanced file indexes designed so that at least one level requires multi-block searches.

CONCLUSIONS

The techniques described in this paper and summarized in Figure 1 provide a proven framework for the efficient identification of live program optimization potential. The methodology is particularly attractive since each potential optimization area is quantified at an early stage and no effort is wasted on the investigation of other, less critical, functions.

Few installations can afford not to consider carrying out the simple reasonability checks on all their production programs. Most will find scope for investigating selected programs more closely. This activity will, at the very least, increase the general awareness of program performance with consequent benefits in the future. At best, the level of savings illustrated by the examples in this paper can be sought and the costs of the investigations will be repaid with full interest.

HIGH LEVEL PROGRAMMING: LANGUAGES AND OPTIMIZATION

J G Laski

Associate Professor
University of Rennes

J G LASKI obtained a starred first in mathematics and a PhD in Mathematical Logic. Subsequently he was engaged in Operation Research and Corporate Planning in the Steel and Oil Industries. For a control project in 1961-62, in association with John Buxton, he designed and implemented an early simulation language, CSL, which became fairly widely used, and may even, somewhere, be still in use today. He then returned to academic life in order to try to understand what he had been doing; since then, he has been engaged in doing so, not only in respect of his own computing work, but also for a more general range of computing activities. He has taught at various universities in the UK and USA, is principally interested in the semantics of programming languages, is a member of an IFIP working group on this subject. He has been called the Peripatetic Gadfly of British Computing.

HIGH LEVEL PROGRAMMING: LANGUAGES AND OPTIMIZATION

INTRODUCTION

I hold the thesis that, contrary to popular belief, all program optimizations can be expressed in a suitable programming language and do not require explicit use of machine code; furthermore, powerful programming constructs make it easier rather than harder to achieve optimal code.

Below, we will discuss in detail examples to support this thesis, but, first we acknowledge three bounding limitations of optimizations that may be possible and which may require attention to the actual machine code. We would emphasize that this point of view in no way excludes examining the machine code that some particular construct translates to and improving it by hand. But we should also consider why the better code was not reached and improve our compilers and languages for next time.

These limitations are:

- choice of a slow algorithm and/or a space-consuming algorithm where a less costly one is available;
- dealing with space constraints caused by timing discontinuities in the architecture of the target machine, for example, not over-running page-boundaries;
- punning, that is, the use of the same bit-string to represent two different kinds of information, such as an instruction and an integer constant.

We must all, of course, have the humility to admit that we are, as yet, beginners in language design, compiler design and machine design, and those we have and use have weaknesses that we do not yet understand well enough (will we ever?) to avoid, so that, with present technology, optimal code is not always achieved and it is worth combing the target code our compilers generate from our programs, to see where, how and why better code could have been achieved.

Nevertheless, it is a corollary of my main thesis that what one discovers by so examining generated code is, in our present state of technology, most often of more value as input to compiler designers, language designers and machine designers than for the additional economy it provides to the user of the program in which it was found.

For it is equally, if not more, important for the user to recognize the two following facts if he wants to use his computing resources efficiently:

- An insecure and unmaintainable program is inefficient and security and maintainability follow from the expression of the program in a humanly understandable form.

- A minute proportion of the program text will occupy the CPU for much the greater part of the running time, and programmers will rarely pinpoint accurately where this is before the program runs.

MACHINE CODE AND PROGRAMMING LANGUAGES

We make a very precise distinction between a *machine code* and a *programming language*. The former, as everyone knows, is the set of instructions that change the state of the machine. It is quite wrong, and vastly confusing to regard the latter, as is instanced by the survival of the early terms 'automatic programming' and 'autocoder', as shorthand for machine code. This mistaken notion, natural enough in the historical context of the early pioneers of high-level languages, has stuck around for far too long and, even today, is still widespread in the computing profession.

A programming language is a vehicle for man-machine, man-man and man-self communication.

It follows that the choice of constructs within a programming language is bounded by, and in any context should be informed by, an appropriate balance between:

- what these constructs enable to be expressed;
- how easily programs that use them can be understood by their human users;
- how easily these programs can be translated to code of available machines;
- how efficiently the resulting code can be evaluated.

that is, this choice is governed by the tasks, the programmers, the compilers, and the machines.

Assembly code is an example of a programming language in which ease of translation takes absolute precedence over human understandability; in the present state of compiler technology, the languages that are in current use seem to me to be too heavily weighted to enable programs written in them to be translated by compiler technology of the last generation rather than to enable programmers to clearly express powerful programs.

TRANSLATION AND OPTIMIZATION

At this point, we must introduce the notion of optimizing, as opposed to straightforward translation. Our compiler technology has advanced to a point at which many feasible optimizations can, at a price and sometimes a heavy price, be performed automatically.

We must therefore distinguish, for some proposed programming construct, between the code that it would be conceivable to generate as its translation (or, more precisely, its influence on what is generated as a whole for programs in which it is used, by an ideally clever compiler), and what the compilers we can afford (where we are limited not only by the cost of applying present-day compiling technology, but also by present knowhow of optimizing techniques) will generate. This is yet another point at which to repeat that security is more necessary to overall efficiency than local optimization, so that we should avoid optimizing techniques for which any doubt exists as to whether they may, in circumstances that are not clearly understood, alter the essential meaning of the programs to which they are applied.

There is a general rumour that all high-level language programming constructs reduce the efficiency of the code that can be generated and increase the difficulty a compiler will have in generating an adequate translation. From this it follows that one should only allow in one's programming languages the minimum of high-level constructs that are needed to pander to the wishes of weak-minded programmers who would do a better job if they used assembly code anyway. Unfortunately, this rumour is false.

Adding a new high-level construct to a programming language may have one of two entirely distinct effects; it cannot have both and it is always perfectly clear which of the two is the case.

The first kind of construct (of which allowing the size of vectors to be decided at run time rather than compile time will serve as an example here and below), increases the run-time space overhead of representation and the time and space overhead of subroutine calls in order to buy increased flexibility. Optimization, in this case, comes from allowing the programmer to specify no more expensive a flexibility than he in fact requires and to enable that expensive overhead to be confined to that subpart of the running program within which it is necessarily required.

The second kind of construct (of which allowing conditional expressions as well as conditional commands will serve as an example here and below) always has beneficial effects both on the source program, and on the practical achievement of optimal code. Its only harmful effect is to require a very slight increase in basic compiler size, say 30-100 words per construct, and a proportionally smaller decrease of compiler speed; this latter effect is almost certainly more than compensated for by the fact that a given algorithm can be expressed by a more concise source program which, more importantly, can be more easily conceived, understood and maintained by programmers to whom the construct is a familiar part of their language and thought.

The effect of these second kind of constructs is to enable a translator to achieve optimal code with less analytic effort. In practice, this means either that better code will be produced for the same amount of optimizing analysis or that similar code will be generated by a compiler which does less and costs less; this disjunction expresses two points on a continuum on which the compiler designer will make his choice.

The only good reason not to include such constructs in a modern programming language is when it is to be compiled in a machine with a small store whose designers have made it technically impossible to add to; the reader will notice that management ignorance of the advantages of buying more store at today's prices for a machine that is to be used for compiling is not included in this good reason. An acceptable reason is that language and compiler designers do not yet know what constructs will enable certain cases to be dealt with. (cf the section *Pointers and problems* below). The usual (and bad) reason for excluding such constructs from the majority of languages used at the majority of installations is the ignorance, timidity and conservatism of elderly obsolescent programmers; amongst these I include beginner programmers who have been taught obsolescent ideas on the job, in programming schools, and a substantial proportion of universities.

OPTIMIZING AND SUBOPTIMIZING

Omitting the second kind of construct from our languages on the grounds that each syntactic construct will as a result compile more slowly is, as we pointed out above, a sub-optimization that, crudely, can be shown to disoptimize since the same algorithm will as a result require fewer syntactic units for its expression. This serves as a warning of the danger of obsessive naivety in the choice of what to optimize, which should be guided by the overall economy with which we deploy our total resources.

Even reading this paper, let alone allowing any of its prescriptions to influence one's programming approach, is, at best, a waste of time for someone exclusively concerned with an I/O-bound application. Let him wait until he has bought faster channels and disks or restructured his use of backing store. However, when he is compute-bound or development-bound, and for those who already are, we must recognize that our suboptimizations may result in improvements or disimprovements on other suboptimizing measures. We do not, in this paper, offer more than the platitude that one must think through the strategic implications of one's choices and the non-platitude that strategic thinking is a scarce resource that should be concentrated where the pay-offs can be expected to be greatest.

We list the dimensions of suboptimization with which we are concerned and which should be considered in the examples below. Some, clearly, are easier to measure than others; unfortunately ease of measurement seems in practice to run counter to importance.

1 program conception, maintenance and modification
2 program security
3 compiler speed
4 compiler size
5 compiled code security and accuracy
6 compiled code speed
7 compiled code size.

It is accepted practice to sacrifice a little of points 6 and 7 for 2 and, with optimizing compilers of dubious validity, for 5. There seems a general consensus among leading computing scientists that it would be worth doing so too to discover the most frequently executed part of a program in order that it can receive concentrated attention both by the programmer on the local polishing of the source program and by the compiler's applying locally additional expensive, elaborate optimizing techniques which it would not be economic to apply to the whole program. The experimental FORTRAN System of Wulf and Hansen (page 185), in which the frequency with which regions of the program are entered at run time is monitored and triggers their partial recompilation with more sophisticated optimizing already beats both WATFOR and optimizing FORTRAN H by the measure of compile + execution costs. Although blue-sky, this is certainly not beyond the horizon. Personally, I am of the opinion that, for a less archaic language than FORTRAN for which known and not excessively expensive techniques can produce near optimal code from well-expressed source programs, the results of focusing programmer attention will have a better pay off than mechanical optimizing technique however crafty.

Simple redesign of machine architecture, for example, cache stores, enables optimization to take place at run time on the actual computation path and makes elaborate analysis at compile time to achieve the same effect almost, but not quite, without value. In fact, run-time optimization operates in terms of the single relevant computation path, whereas compile-time optimizations may only be applied if they are valid on every one of the many potential run-time computation paths.

This illustrates dramatically the effect that developments of machine architecture may have on the economic value of particular optimizing techniques.

We will, below, speculate briefly on some possibilities for optimization of a radical redesign of machine architecture, the so-called tree machine, which should more properly be called a graph machine, conceived independently by Suffrin and Wulf – and doubtless many others.

EXAMPLES

We treat in this section a few examples in sufficient detail to illustrate specific points and refer briefly to others which enable us to make related points. We attempt neither an exhaustive catalogue of syntactic forms, nor of possible optimizations and attendant high-level language constructs that enable a compiler to achieve optimal code without undue difficulty; as indicated earlier, we take the view that it is not yet, and may never be, possible to complete the latter. Nevertheless, there is a substantial amount already known and the reader is expected, by the exercise of his reason and imagination, to extend the instances below by analogy and generalization.

We assume a target machine with multiple multi-purpose registers and the assembly code we use should not confuse; we also use three macros DO C, LD E, LA E, which correspond respectively to sequences of assembly code that perform the command *c*, load the value specified by the expression *e* to a standard accumulator, load the address specified by the expression *e* to a standard accumulator. We write, for example, LD I X rather than LD X when we are concerned with more than a single standard accumulator.

Restriction of flow-paths through labels

Consider the two following sequences of machine code:

```
......LD  E ;  JFLS  L1 ;  DO C1 ;  JUMP L2 ;  L1:DO C2 ;  L2 .......     (1)

...L1:LD  E ;  JFLS  L2 ;  DO C  ;  JUMP L1 ;  L2: ........              (2)
```

Without a full flow analysis of the surrounding program to ensure that there are no other occurrences of jumps to L1 or L2, which is expensive to perform, especially if we bear in mind that the LD and DO macros may stand for arbitrarily long sequences of code, we can make no assumptions about the machine state when we arrive at L1 and L2.

Thus we can take no advantage of any knowledge we might have that some fast register has the same value, since it had been loaded thence, as some word of store or that the value that should be in some word of store is presently in some fast register and has not yet been stored where it should be. We must therefore, to account for possible flow-paths, perform the delayed stores before any jump and, after any label, make no assumptions that the value of any word of store is already in some fast register.

However, from the source **if** *e* **then** c_1 **else** c_2 and **while** *e* **do** *c*, we know without further analysis that there is no non-local flow to the labels our translator will generate. More, from what we know of the state of the registers and stores before the code sequence, we can deduce directly and simply what we may assume both within any part of it and at the start of whatever follows it.

Note that, even with a one-armed conditional command **if** *e* **then** *c* a FORTRAN-like construct that only allows a simple command in an **if**-construct is adequate to directly express the flow-structure required.

Conditional expressions and code motion

Consider the source: **if** *e* **then** $l := e_1$ **else** $l := e_2$. A naive translator would achieve (in skeleton)

```
... STORE L ;  JUMP L2 ;  L1:.... STORE L ;  L2 ....
```
(3)

whereas we would much prefer to coalesce the two store instructions after the jump and reach:

```
... JUMP L2 ;  L1:..... ;  L2 :  STORE L ; ...
```
(4)

This would be achieved without any analytic effort had the source read (using for conditional expressions a LISP-style syntax): $l := (e \to e_1 , e_2)$.

We find a vast range of analogous constructs in, say, those PL/1 programs we have examined. Note that we might have begun with: **if** *e* **then** $l_1 := e_1$ **else** $l_2 := e_1$ and not even ALGOL 60 has syntax to express the required meaning so that the expression is to be thought of as assigned to alternative locations or, equivalently, that in the target code LD E occurs only once, preceding JFLS L1.

Loop constructs and code folding

Suppose one knows that, in every case, the body of some loop is to be repeated at least once. Rather than the code 2, one would wish to achieve:

```
... L1:DO C ;  LD E ;  JTRU L1 ; ...
```
(5)

One could write: *c* ; **while** *e* **do** *c* but some analysis would be needed to recognize that the command preceding the loop is the same as that that forms its body and most compilers would not take the trouble and would generate:

```
... DO C ;  L1:LD E ;  JFLS L2 ;  DO C ;  JUMP L1;  L2:....
```
(6)

However if the source construct: **repeat** *c* **while** *e* is available code 5 will be achieved without any analysis.

Unless the average number of times the loop body is expected to be repeated is less than one, a better translation than 2 of **while** *e* **do** *c* is:

```
... JUMP L1 ;  L2:DO C ;  L1:LD E ;  JTRU L2 ; ...
```
(7)

and we have, in not using this loop code in 6, unfairly exaggerated slightly how hard it is to get from this likelier version of 6 to 5. Our doing so was deliberate; we wished to be able to illustrate that the optimal target code for some construct may differ according to its run-time pattern of use, which no amount of compile-time analysis (apart from simulation of execution paths) can discover, but may very well be knowable to the programmer.

The constructs we have so far discussed, and, indeed, many more, not only simplify the generation of optimal code but also enable the programmer to move more easily in his mind between the source program text and the algorithm it expresses. We again re-emphasize that we regard this effect on the programmer as far more conducive to overall efficiency than the effect they have on target code.

Nevertheless, it is worth having constructs in one's language that only enable the programmer to direct the translator as to the context within which it should choose what the code it generates should aim to achieve, provided that using such constructs does not get in the way of the programmer's apprehension of the source text.

In the instance of loop frequency we are considering, one might expect **while** *e* **do** *c* to translate to 7, whereas, if one had good reason to wish 2 to be generated, one would write: **while**, **rarely**, *e* **do** *c*; **rarely** is an example of what has been called a *pragmat*. It may well recall to old hands the FREQUENCY statement of early FORTRAN. No modern programming language would repeat FORTRAN's treatment of its DO-loop which translates not to 7 but to 5, assuming that in every instance of every loop, its body is to be executed at least once.

In the context of arrays, which was what FORTRAN was designed for, this assumption is valid; it only begins to fail when we use FORTRAN to process possibly empty lists. This should serve as a warning to language designers today not to assume that their language will necessarily always be used for the kinds of programs they expect and, more importantly, for language choosers to be aware of the language designer's assumptions and their consequences.

Programmers and computers

We said above that the kind of target code to aim at was knowable by the programmer. Before the program runs he will, sometimes, be certain, and correctly so, that the conditions hold under which **rarely** will yield what is, for a certain loop in a certain context, better code, or equally certain that they do not. More often he will be doubtful, and rightly so.

It is for this practical situation that the run-time monitor that we advocated earlier comes into its own. We envisage some such sequence of events as the following.

Initially, the programmer should include **rarely** in those loops where it needs little thought to be certain of the worth of doing so, allowing himself to think a little more deeply about those parts of the program that he suspects to be executed most frequently.

After the program has been run often enough for the monitor's report of execution patterns to be accepted as valid, he will know where he can usefully think deeply about his program; he may, as a result, add or delete **rarely** from loops, and, most probably, will remain doubtful about certain loops. These he can qualify by writing **possibly rarely**. A second stage of monitoring takes over to report the average number of repetitions of the body each time the loop is encountered, and, in due course, the programmer knows enough to be able to delete **possibly**, since he knows whether or not **rarely** should be deleted. If he can use the qualifier **possibly** with or without the pragmat **rarely**, the translator can, during this second bout of monitoring, take account of what the programmer regards as more probable.

We described a development/maintenance process in terms of a single pragmat, but, of course, such a system applies for as many kinds of pragmats as there are in use, and that we gain experience of using such a system. For clarity of exposition above, we separated the two kinds of monitoring into two distinct stages. This is not necessary and even a little harmful; we need some other pragmat to specify over what regions of the program we want frequency monitoring to take place.

Programmer versus computer

In the system outlined above, the responsibility for deciding what optimal code the compiler should aim for is left entirely to the programmer; all that is automated is the provision of the evidence on which he acts. The question arises at once as to whether or not more should be automated. In part, the answer to this question depends on an economic judgement of the relative cost-effectiveness of programming talent against machine costs, tempered by a judgement of the relative value of a programmer's unreliable intuition against a machine's exhaustive reliability.

Unlike **rarely**, **goonas**, whose meaning we shall discover below, is a pragmat which can be shown, by compile-time analysis, either to apply or not to apply. Also unlike **rarely**, it will, if used where it does not apply, result in incorrect code being generated. Discussing this, Wulf put the extreme view that all should be automated and pragmats not used. He gave as his reasons not only that optimizing analysis was reliable whereas not all programmers were, but also that their use obscured the ease of apprehension of the algorithm from the program text. A similar argument made him wish to call a halt to a proliferation of constructs in a programming language of the kind we have turned aside for a moment from examining, admitting these only if they simplified the expression of algorithms and not for the fact that they enabled simple compilers to generate optimal code.

These arguments are cogent and cannot be ignored. They are not completely persuasive to the author for two equally cogent contrary arguments. The first, for which **rarely** serves as an example, is that, in some situations not only can the programmer be better informed than some mechanical system, but also, if he makes an incorrect decision, the consequences will only be non-optimal code and not an invalid program. If an incorrect use of a pragmat may lead to an insecure program, that pragmat should only be used where it can be established to be correct and we fully accept that an automated system is the only method of doing so in which we may have complete confidence. However, we claim that, where potential optimizations have contrary effects on independent desiderata, only non-local considerations can mediate and these are available solely to the programmer.

The second argument in favour of leaving to the programmer an involvement in achieving optimal code, even where this is possible automatically, is psychological, since it will engage him more with the program, which helps its maintenance. Moreover, if the system gives him adequate feedback to feel proud of his successes and aware of his misjudgements, he will educate himself as a programmer.

Curiously, as a programmer develops, there is both more and less reason to automate more. More reason since the simpler optimizations no longer challenge and engage him, less reason, since doing so distracts his attention less from considering deeper possibilities. Finally, invention of high-level expressive constructs and discovery of optimizations from study of machine code are activities that reinforce one another and together add to the power of the programmer's conceptual apparatus.

An interesting optimization is possible if some subroutine b, called by a, calls c and, on c's return, itself immediately returns to a. In this case we can arrange that c

when called overwrites the space used by *b* and can return directly to where *b* returns to, that is, *a*. The author proposed that code to do this could be generated if the call of *c* involved the pragmat **goonas** *c*( ). Conversely, Wulf proposed that an optimizing compiler could recognize such cases. Perhaps Wulf's approach is to be preferred since **goonas** *c*( ) would translate to invalid code if incorrectly used. Nevertheless, the author believes that the programmer should be aware of this possibility – which combines the economy of loops with the clarity of recursion – so that he can design his programs to take advantage of its possibilities.

Common sub-expressions and local declarations

We would like the source *a*[3 × *i* + 1] := *b*[3 × *i* + 1] + *c*[3 × *i* + 1] to generate:

```
LOAD      2  I
MULTI     2  3
ADDI      2  1
LOADIND   1  B,2
ADDIND    1  C,2
STOREIND  1  A,2
```
(8)

and not recalculate the value of the index on each of the three occasions it is required.

If the source construct :

a[*x*] := *b*[*x*] + *c*[*x*] **where** *x* = 3 × *i* + 1 ; ... (9)

is available, code 8 can be achieved without any analysis.

Code 9 has precisely the same meaning as:

begin let *x* = 3 × *i* + 1 ; *a*[*x*] := *b*[*x*] + *c*[*x*] **end** ; ... (10)

so that, as far as program structure is concerned, we do not need the **where** construct. Comparison of the texts 9 and 10 illustrates the pragmatic value of allowing synonymous structures to be available in a single language. In fact, pragmatically, we might well restrict **where**-declared locals to be constant so that they cannot appear on the left hand of an assignment, etc, unlike **let**-declared locals. Such considerations are, of course, logically subsequent to those we are mainly concerned with in this paper; from this it does not follow, of course, that they are any the less important for the design of an efficient system for the programmer.

Our final point in these examples is a little difficult to make since we do not have familiar syntax to do so, and necessarily so because it is precisely to observe that we may not necessarily have syntax available to express what we may conceive of as expressible and to examine the consequence of this fact.

In 9 we did not avoid reduplicating the largest possible subphrase, but only the largest possible expression subphrase within it. In a clumsy syntax we wrote an analogue of:

a **sub** *x* := *b* **sub** *x* + *c* **sub** *x* **where** *x* = 3 × *i* + 1 (11)

rather than the shorter:

a x := *b x* + *c x* **where** *x* = **sub**(3 × *i* + 1). (12)

Even with a suitable syntax, this latter form does not, in fact, make it easier to reach the optimal code of our imaginary target machine. Suppose, however, that this had a special register SB, such that if a word were a vector descriptor, any operation whose effective address was that word would, in fact, work on the element by using the contents of SB as a subscript selector — this could be useful if, in the style of the Burroughs machines, this involved hardware bounds-checking, etc.

Then, from the source texts 9 or 10, a simple-minded compiler might only generate:

```
LOAD 2   I ; MULTI  2 3 ; ADDI 2 1 ;
LOAD SB  2 ; LOAD   B ;
LOAD SB  2 ; ADD    C ;
LOAD SB  2 ; STORE  A ;                        (13)
```

rather than the optimal:

```
LOAD SB  I ; MULTI SB 3 ; ADDI SB 1 ;
LOAD  B    ; ADD    C   ; STORE A ;            (14)
```

which will be generated without optimizing analysis from the source text 11 (assuming programming syntax allows the programmer to give any common subphrase and not just those given phrases that are also expressions). This example illustrates a number of very important principles of language design, compiler design and machine design which, if ignored, will inhibit efficient computing. Consequent upon our experience of language and thinking, our programming languages do not necessarily allow the expression, and hence hide from us, unfamiliar yet meaningful structures; putting in syntax to allow us to be aware of them, as the source text 11 illustrates, seems, within our traditional ways of thinking, inherently clumsy, unless and until we have absorbed them into our intellectual tools; moreover, as code 8 illustrates, our existing machines, whose design assumes that they are not part of our language and our thought, cannot take advantage of their use, whereas they suggest new and useful machine designs, as shown by the code in 13 and 14.

The question is whether or not they should be included in the programmer's language; if they are, learning to use them is a burden which may or may not reward the programmer; if they are not, certain optimizations may be missed.

We take the view that the programmer should be made aware of them by providing them in the language that provides him with his tools of thought but not necessarily in that part of it which his compiler accepts. This implies, if we want to reach optimal code, that the compiler requires to retain common subphrase optimization, etc. If a program involves these optimizing phases, it is vital to discover why and take note of what and why as input to language and machine design.

ENVIRONMENT SCOPE AND EXTENT

The optimizations and language constructs we considered above are wholly advantageous except in exceptional circumstances. We could continue similar examples indefinitely, but prefer to encourage the reader to do so for himself. BCPL has a vast range of constructs and the author's forthcoming paper on escapers discusses some less familiar constructs. The language constructs we now consider more briefly are very different. Their employment has relatively global effects rather than purely local; they buy flexibility at the cost of run-time overhead.

To achieve optimal code from the use of such constructs requires a precise understanding of the implications of their use in order that:

1 no more expensive a construct is used than is necessary to provide the flexibility that is necessary to the problem;

2 given the cost of that flexibility has to be paid. We too use all the consequently available flexibility rather than just the particular construct that entailed the additional cost;

3 we restrict this additional overhead to as small a context, dynamically, as possible.

We can best examine the situation with the aid of an example.

If we compare ALGOL 60 with FORTRAN IV, we see that, at compile time, all identifiers can, in each language, be mapped into address pairs which, at run time, can be mapped to offsets relative to corresponding bases.

In FORTRAN, at run time, two bases are required, one for COMMON, the other for the variables of the routine in which we find ourselves; moreover, the value of these bases is known, and can be added into the code at load time.

In ALGOL, by contrast, as many bases are needed as the depth of blocks in the program; moreover, since the size of arrays is not known until their declaration, the position of these bases in the store at run time is unknown until block-entry.

Thus ALGOL addressing uses up modifiers; since these are normally general-purpose registers, this reduces the degree to which the value of expressions can be calculated without involving the cost of putting and retrieving intermediate values in the store.

BCPL, BLISS, and no doubt many other systems programming languages, observed that a useful compromise between addressing costs and flexibility could be achieved by restricting addressability of locations to either the most global (whose address could be absolutely determined at load time) or the most local. Thus only one modifier need be tied up by addressing needs at run time.

If, further, the size of any objects declared at run time was known at compile time, the items of the innermost routine, rather than just those of the innermost block could be addressed with the aid of that single modifier and the overhead of changing environments (that is, changing the value of this modifier and arranging to be able, if appropriate, to restore it) need occur only for each routine applied and not at the more frequent block entry/exit.

Moreover, temporaries could be stored, when fast registers were not available, at known offsets to these same local pointers.

Thus the overhead of simulating the required addressing regime is reduced to the use of one modifier at all times and five instructions and one location for each routine application and return.

Unfortunately, there are many circumstances in practice where it would be a good thing to delay until block entry time the decision as to how much space is needed for some local data structures; consider for instance some general-purpose routine that, each time it is run, can read parameters that give it the size of data for this run.

The discussion above indicates that any solution requires two pointers, one to the top and the other to the bottom of the locals, although if we know how many temporaries are in use at any stage, we need not use up a fast register for this latter, but reserve space with the locals for any that the fast registers cannot hold.

The key notion required for optimizing programs requiring this more complex run-time representation of their environment is to provide interfaces that enable a routine with these additional complexities to be called by a standard (more efficient/less flexible) routine and itself to call a standard routine, without these latter altering what they do at, respectively, call and return; we leave the extra overhead to the non-standard routine. In that way, the overhead required by the additional flexibility does not spread outside a single routine which the programmer can make as compact as possible.

The author designed such an extension to BCPL. To the normal 5-instruction sequence this added one instruction when it was called, and two to the call of any routine within it. A further feature of the design is that space for the bodies of dynamic data structures was not handed back when the block in which they were declared was left, and subsequently declared structures do not overlap. This space-inefficiency is preferred to the time-overheads involved in giving space back as soon as it is available. Clearly, the programmer should avoid declaring large data objects in non-nested blocks; in particular such declarations in the body of a loop will cause the program rapidly to run out of space.

It was suggested that the system should be modified so that such declarations could only be made in the outermost block of a routine, so that no space-inefficiency would be possible; this is clearly mistaken since, frequently, in some external block we read or calculate parameters for the data structures we declare in an inner block. A possible restriction would be to disallow declarations of dynamic data structures in blocks such that they were in the body of a loop, or that other blocks existed in the routine that neither enclosed it nor were enclosed by it.

The author is against such restrictions in principle. It seems better to explain very fully the way such a system works. Then efficiency comes from the programmer making an informed choice between possible alternative systems and programming to fit best with the best available. If none is available to the programmer, he will reinvent the wheel – which will take a lot of effort before (if ever) it runs true, and may very well be the wrong size since the programmer has not had available for study a range of standard sizes with advantages and disadvantages.

Analogously, the cost of representing the run-time environment may be increased to allow more addressing flexibility; an interesting level between BCPL/BLISS on the one hand and the full static chain of ALGOL 60 is to allow **own** variables, which in turn allows **coroutines**. In the author's opinion there is often much to be gained in close-matching such choices to the needs of algorithms and, more generally, knowing how to do so.

PRESERVING PROGRAM STRUCTURE AT RUN TIME

We earlier observed that cache stores enabled savings of store accesses for values which were repeatedly needed on *some* computation path, perhaps even making puts redundant, whereas an optimizing compiler could only organize register use to aim at avoiding those that would be valid on *all* conceivable computation paths. We have also observed that optimizing compilers can arrange code motion so as to avoid recalculation of common sub-expressions whose value remained constant on all computation paths.

It is interesting to consider whether one could have a machine organization that could avoid this recalculation in every instance of common sub-expressions whose value was unchanged on the particular computation path of each individual run.

Suffrin and Wulf have separately proposed that an interpreter that worked directly on the parse-tree rather than on a linearized version of it could achieve this and other optimizations.

More precisely, common sub-expressions would be merged to appear only once in the structure so that, say, **if** $a+b$ >0 **then** x := $a+b$ would appear as in Figure 1. Then at each expression node one can add an associative register which holds the last value calculated for that sub-expression.

The situation is complicated by the fact that a or b might have been updated between the time that $a+b$ was first calculated and when it is then needed. We, therefore, at compile time, have to string a chain of pointers from each identifier to all sub-expressions of which it is a component so that values that are no longer valid can be cancelled. A further difficulty is that the component identifiers may refer to different locations if the sub-expression is referred to in different environments, for example in different subroutines. The associative match, therefore, has to be on the current environment as well as the sub-expression itself.

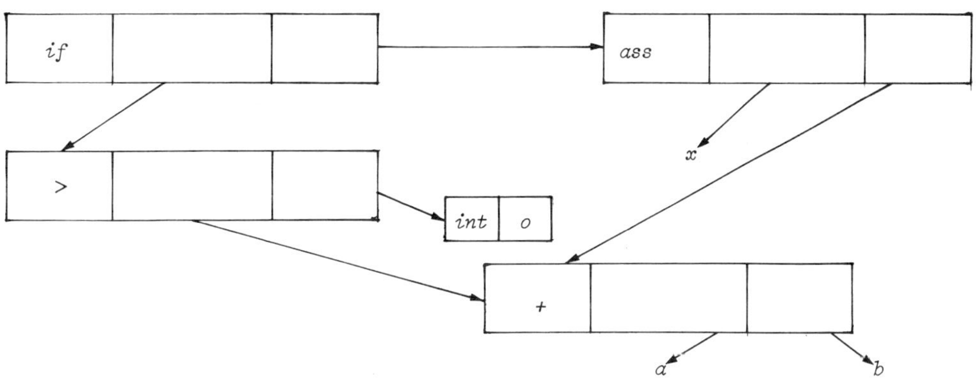

Figure 1: Optimized representation of **if** $a+b > 0$ **then** $x := a+b$

Wulf has gone further, suggesting that the value of $p > q$ should not change if p increases or q decreases and analogously for other connectives. Additionally he has suggested that, with several interpreters sharing arithmetic units, one could set one's spare interpreters to recalculate any expressions whose associated valu^ has been lost. We would then get a run-time analogy of those compilers that look for potential parallelism in the program.

Such a fragmented representation of a program can be stored in about the same number of bits as the usual linearizations, so that there is no space penalty; in fact slightly the reverse. The interpreter has to be a set of mutually recursive routines rather than a repeat loop of a switch to a choice of alternate routines; the interpreter would require a stack of resumption points, and the overhead of providing this would have to be weighed against the potential advantages.

There are more of these advantages than the saving of evaluation of common sub-expressions. Consider the conditional command. If its expression evaluates to '*false*', there is no point in bringing its command into fast — and expensive — storage. Again, if we are expecting to execute a command, there is no possibility of the sub-tree being interpreted representing an expression, so there is no need for the instruction set at command nodes to be able to represent expressions, or *vice versa*. Then the instruction set at each mode can be smaller, and hence need less decoding.

We do not suggest that such a machine design and its possible efficiencies is more, at the moment, than blue-sky speculation over the far horizon. We have indulged in it a little to show that careful consideration of precisely what is involved in interpreting the high-level languages that we use to express our algorithms, can reveal interesting opportunities for optimization that have hitherto been obscured by unconscious constraints that are implicit in our traditional coding languages and our traditional machine designs.

POINTERS AND PROBLEMS

If the value in some location is interpreted as some other location, all bets are off. We cannot guarantee that the contents of a location are unchanged if its identifier has not appeared in the program on the left-hand side of an assignment, since some pointer expression can also refer to it, and we can't necessarily find out whether this is so at compile time.

Hence pointers in a language have a devastating effect on possible optimizations.

The author is of the opinion that languages could be designed to reduce the devastation, by considering the precise purpose of any pointer use. For example, pointers may be used to construct a representation for some complicated kind of data types. In this case these pointers cannot refer to other data in the store with respect to which, therefore, store-shadowing optimizations can still be carried out. Conversely, if the pointers are used to represent forms of indirect reference, all bets are still off.

One solution, explored by APL for example, is to pass to the compiler the program as an algorithm about the higher-order data, so that the compiler knows the use to which the pointers are put. This is not always possible particularly if new or unusual data structures are needed.

The author is of the opinion that declarations could be used to express whether a pointer was being used for the former or the latter purpose and to allow or disallow pointer access to some data for reading or updating.

These use-type and access-type declarations could therefore restrict the all-bets-are-off effect that pointers have on optimization possibilities to see what it would be advantageous to include in high-level programming languages.

CONCLUSION

We have illustrated ways in which programming in high-level languages makes easier rather than harder the recognition of what optimizations are possible and where. Existing high-level languages reveal possible efficiencies that are rarely obtained with present programming languages and compiling practices, and could be obtained today without difficulty. They also reveal areas where new programming styles, language to express new programming ideas or new machine designs could, possibly, in the future, lead to further optimizations.

Finally, we would reiterate that a simple-minded choice of criteria for optimization can often lead to sub-optimization, that incorrect programs are not optimal, and that the clarity of correctly chosen high-level programming constructs adds reliability to programs as well as their simple translatability to faster, shorter code.

INSTRUCTION SET ENHANCEMENT

W D Manville

GEC Computers Ltd

W D MANVILLE obtained a BA degree in mathematics at Wadham College, Oxford, in 1969. In 1970 he obtained a distinction in the Diploma in Computer Science at the University of Cambridge Computer Laboratory. He then spent 3 years working for a PhD on microprogramming support for programming languages under the supervision of Professor M V Wilkes at Cambridge. During this time he contributed to 2 papers, on microprogrammed support for the language AL-1, and on the use of a writeable control store in a multiprogramming environment. Since 1973 he has been working as a Senior Programmer for GEC Computers Limited, at Borehamwood, Herts, where he has been involved in the design and production of a Coral 66 compiler and other software for the GEC 4080 computer. He is currently working on the design and implementation of new systems for the 4080.

INSTRUCTION SET ENHANCEMENT

INTRODUCTION

Conventional means of improving run-time efficiency of programs include the use of highly optimizing compilers and the coding of the most critical parts of the programs in machine code. The efficiency of the resulting program is, however, limited by the fixed instruction set of the computer. One way of improving the efficiency further is to add to, or modify, the instruction set of the computer to make it more suitable for the tasks being performed.

To modify the instruction set of a computer which used special-purpose hard-wired logic is so formidable a task that few would consider it a practicable proposition.

However, many computers are microprogrammed, that is, the instruction set that the programmer is presented with is interpreted by a lower-level microprogram which generates the control signals in the processor. This general-purpose instruction set is usually a small subset of the operations which could be performed on the same hardware and will not be ideal for any particular application. Thus, a possible way of improving the performance of particular programs or sets of programs on a microprogrammed computer is to add to, or modify, the microprogram to interpret additional, or alternative, instructions. When the microprogram store is writable, the proposition is more attractive than when special read-only memories have to be produced. It also permits dynamic changes to the microprogram to support different programs at different times.

This paper examines the ways in which special-purpose instructions can improve program performance.

Example

Consider, as an example, a program which frequently searches an ordered array by means of the 'binary chop' technique. Expressed in Coral 66, the main loop of this procedure could be:

```
for i := (bottom + top)/2 while i ≠ bottom
do if a [i]>value then top : = i
   else if a[i] < value then bottom:= i
   else goto found;
```

The code generated by the single-pass Coral compiler on the GEC 4080 is such than an average of 13½ instructions are obeyed each time round the loop. The best that could be achieved by writing the loop in machine code, or by using a perfect optimizing compiler, would be an average of 8½ instructions each time. Thus, the greatest reduction in execution time possible by the use of conventional techniques would be about 40%.

If there was a single machine instruction to perform this operation, considerably greater reductions would be possible. It would be feasible to implement such an instruction on the microprogrammed 4080 and I estimate that it could execute about 8 times faster than the Coral version or 5 times faster than the optimum machine code program.

GAINS FROM INSTRUCTION SET ENHANCEMENT

Various gains are possible when a sequence of orders is replaced by a single special instruction with the same effect.

Reduced execution time

Consider the sequence of operations performed for a typical instruction (for example, add from store to an index register):

1 Fetch program counter

2 Increment program counter

3 Decode instruction

4 Fetch data from store

5 Gate operands to adder

6 Perform addition

7 Gate result to index register

8 If interrupts have occurred deal with them, otherwise go to 1.

Firstly, by using a special instruction in place of a sequence, the time spend on fetching and decoding instructions is reduced. Stages (1) to (3) and (8) may be regarded as a necessary overhead for each obeyed instruction. By replacing a sequence of *n* instructions by a single one, the time spent on these stages should be reduced by a factor of about *n*.

A second way in which time can be saved by the use of special instructions is by the elimination of unnecessary operations from the processing parts (4) to (7) of the instruction previously used. For example, it may be unnecessary to gate a result from a processor register to an index register at the end of one step and then to retrieve it at the beginning of the next.

A general-purpose instruction set often restricts the full range of operations that the underlying hardware is capable of. By implementing a special instruction it may be possible to use a method which could not be done easily with the regular instruction set even though the processor could do it simply. For example, implementing arithmetic of a different precision from normal is likely to need strings of instructions for each operation, especially for dealing with signs and carries. A special instruction may be able to use 'hidden' registers and facilities not available directly to the programmer and thus reduce considerably the processing time required.

Finally, it may be possible to perform some operations in parallel which had been constrained by the nature of the regular instruction set to be done sequentially.

The extent to which these gains can contribute to a real gain in speed of the program will depend on what the limiting factor in the computer is. Where the store is slow and the processor could work faster than it can be supplied with instructions and data, the elimination of instruction fetches will have a direct result and the other gains will not contribute much. If, at the other extreme, the processor is continually busy and never has to wait for instructions or data from store, the savings in stages (2) and (3) and those due to the elimination of redundant operations and the use of parallelism will have the most effect.

Reduced storage requirement

The amount of store required for the program will be reduced and in cases where this reduction is significant, it can also have an effect on the performance of the program. On a paged system, the program would probably occupy fewer pages and therefore the overhead of dealing with page faults would be reduced. If a slave, or cache, store is in use, there is a greater probability of finding the desired instruction in the slave.

AREAS FOR ENHANCEMENT

The most effective way of enhancing the instruction set of a computer depends on the application for which it is being used.

For example, if most programming is done in a particular high-level language, provision of special instructions to perform the primitive operations and to operate on the data types of that language could produce worthwhile improvements. This would be especially true for languages like APL which operate on whole arrays at once.

Alternatively, if most of the work done is scientific calculations, then provision of additional instructions to perform trigonometric functions, logarithms and square roots could produce beneficial effects.

In many systems, total throughput could be improved considerably by providing additional instructions to support the most common operations of the operating system. Thus, on a multiprogramming system in which processes typically only run for a short time it would be beneficial to provide support for the operations required in process change. For example, the designers of the GEC 4080 realized that this could be particularly useful for real-time applications and implemented process scheduling, inter-process message handling and other operating system functions in microprogram, with the result that process change takes about 10% of the time needed on computers where software is used.

In systems where one program runs for long periods of time (for example, a weather forecasting program, or a sorting program), then it is appropriate to consider support for that particular program, provided that the program is limited by processor or store speed and not by the speed of some peripheral device. The parts of the program which account for most time can be determined and special instructions implemented to perform the required function, as in the binary chop example considered above.

Thus, we have four possible areas for enhancement of instruction sets:

1 instructions to support a particular programming language

2 instructions to support a particular application area

3 instructions to support operating system functions

4 instructions to support individual programs

The four types of support can well exist in parallel. A particular program could benefit from special instructions suited to the language in which it is written, others which support the application area and some which are used to speed up sections of this particular program. The throughput of the system in which it runs could be improved by support for its operating system.

The next sections of this paper concentrate on language support because this is the area in which the author has done most work (162). The later sections of the paper are relevant to all types of support.

PROGRAMMING LANGUAGE SUPPORT

Since programming in high-level languages has much to recommend it, viz transferability, maintainability and programmer productivity, it is a good idea to tailor the instruction set of the computer to suit the language being used, thus reducing the run-time overheads of using the language.

If one looks at the code output by a high-level language compiler for a conventional computer, one will frequently find that quite long sequences of machine orders have to be generated for single operations in the high-level language. Also, there are frequently calls on library routines to perform functions which would require too much code to be generated in-line. Thus, one approach to instruction set enhancement for programming language support would be to identify the most common order sequences and library calls and to replace them by special instructions.

An alternative strategy is to abandon the standard instruction set and to implement, in microprogram, an interpreter for a code designed specifically for the high-level language. The relative merits of the two approaches are considered later.

Examples of programming language support

The possibility of changing a computer's instruction set by changing its microprogram was recognized as early as 1951 by Wilkes (163) when he first introduced the idea of microprogramming. While microprogram stores were read-only, only a few experiments were carried out because of the cost and difficulty involved. With the advent of computers with writable control stores, in the early 1970s many more experiments were made.

Conversational Programming System

An early example of an extension to a microprogrammed computer's standard instruction set is that developed for IBM by Allen-Babcock Computing Inc for the IBM system/360, model 50. 18 of the 25 instructions developed were used in the conversational programming system (CPS), a system designed to read, translate and interpret statements written in a subset of PL/1 in an interactive environment (164). This is an interesting example as it combines support for PL/1 language features, for compilation and for multiprogramming.

Five of the new operations microprogrammed were instructions working on floating-point decimal numbers. These were included to reduce the transformations required during input and output as these were expected to be relatively frequent operations in an interactive environment. Two other instructions were of use in recognizing delimiters etc during lexical analysis. Eight were used for list handling and searching and, perhaps the most powerful, EVAL, was provided to evaluate an arithmetic expression held in a compact reverse Polish form.

The standard control store of the model 50 has 2816 words of 90 bits. The new operations used by CPS used 645 words of which EVAL accounted for 184 and the floating decimal instructions for 320.

Figures for the performance of the CPS system are not available but it was predicted that the use of these special instructions would speed operation by a factor of 5 over an equivalent implementation using the standard instruction set.

The EULER machine

An interesting example of the use of a microprogrammed interpreter for a high-level code is provided by the experimental implementation of the programming language EULER on the IBM System/360 model 30 computer by Weber (165).

EULER (166) is a block-structured language which requires dynamic type-checking of operands and includes dynamic storage allocation, list processing operations etc. Use of conventional machine code to carry out such operations would result in programs either being very long or containing many calls to subroutines to do the type-checking etc. Such a language is clearly a good candidate for the use of an interpretive code at a higher level than conventional machine code. The code used by Weber was a form of reverse Polish notation, each operator being represented by one byte. It was estimated that the interpreter would require 2500 words of microprogram, excluding input/output handling. A further 500 words were needed for the translator from source to interpreted code, which used a simple precedence technique.

Weber estimated that at run-time his system would be about a factor of 10 faster than a system using 360 machine code compiled in-line for operations requiring considerable type testing. It would also be quicker, but by smaller factors, for other operations such as real arithmetic.

Other language interpreters

Following the above experiment, a number of other microprogrammed interpreters for high-level, language-oriented instruction sets were produced, APL and SNOBOL, being frequent candidates for support.

With their B1700 series, Burroughs have produced machines designed specifically for the multi-programming of interpreters of high-level codes (167). Typically, the codes are compact and object programs require less than half of the space required on other computers. It was claimed that, on a suitable configuration, COBOL programs would run 60% faster on B1700 than on an IBM 360/30, and at about the same speed as on the COBOL-oriented B3500.

Levels of support: BCPL

When considering the use of microprogramming to enhance the run-time efficiency of programs written in a particular language, one must choose between the use of an interpretive code and the implementation of special instructions. In the former case there are a number of levels of code, from source code to conventional machine code, that may be used. In the latter case, the degree of support will depend on the mismatch between the language and the computer's basic instruction set and may include replacement of standard order sequences by a single special instruction and the use of special instructions in place of library routines.

A study was made (162) of various actual codes and possible extended machine codes and interpretive codes for a particular high-level language: BCPL (168). BCPL was chosen for this study because it is not an obvious candidate for microprogram support! Unlike those of APL and EULER, the operations and data types of BCPL are simple and can generally be mapped efficiently onto conventional computers. Thus, gains for BCPL will be less than those for many other languages.

A number of the possible interpretive codes arise in the normal course of compilation. Conceptually, the compiler works in 4 stages, although, in practice, the first two are done in parallel:

1 The first stage is lexical analysis: the source program is converted into a string of lexical tokens, operators and reserved words are identified, names are looked up in a dictionary and comments and non-significant layout information are discarded. For BCPL and similar languages, this stage can account for over half of the compilation time.

2 In the second stage, syntax analysis, the lexical tokens are fed in order to a syntax analyser which creates a tree form of the program, taking account of operator priorities and parentheses.

3 The third stage is the translation of the tree into a machine-independent intermediate code, OCODE (169), which is similar to a machine code for a simple stack machine.

4 The fourth stage is the only one which is machine-dependent: transformation of this machine-independent code into machine code. The code generator normally performs a certain amount of optimization, taking account of any special features of the target computer's instruction set. It also has to generate some standard order sequences to correspond to one OCODE instruction for the more complicated operations such as function entry.

For a language such as BCPL, it would clearly be both difficult and costly to attempt to interpret the source code, or even the lexically analysed form, directly. Such high-level codes can be considered for languages with a simpler syntax, such as APL, but are not worth further consideration for BCPL.

A comparison was made between various other interpretive codes:

TREE - a compacted form of the tree produced by the syntax analyser.

OCODE - with the assumption that the top 3 stack elements would be held in processor registers.

INTCODE - an interpretive code, produced from OCODE, which is used in bootstrapping BCPL onto different computers.

IACODE - a slightly higher-level version of OCODE, using single-address instructions instead of reverse Polish.

These codes were compared on the assumption that they were all implemented on the same 24-bit machine with the instructions being interpreted by a microprogram held in a fast store so that the speed of execution would be approximately proportional to the number of main store accesses. The comparison was carried out using software interpreters for the various codes to gather statistics for a standard set of programs.

IACODE was found to be the best. It was the only one which required fewer store accesses than any of the actual machine codes studied. The program length was also less than for any of the machine codes, by as much as 52%. It also required about 25% less compilation time to produce it than to produce conventional machine codes.

It was found that by implementing special instructions in place of certain standard order sequences that were generated for the Titan (ATLAS 2) computer, the execution time of BCPL programs, measured in terms of storage accesses, would be reduced by about 18%. The length of the compiled code would be reduced by about 30% by these changes. The operations supported were function entry and exit, SWITCHON blocks (which are similar to, but more flexible than, ALGOL 68 CASE clauses), and access to elements of arrays. On a machine with a much simpler instruction set (DEC PDP7), on which some arithmetic operations had to be done by subrouting call, special instructions used in place of standard order sequences could reduce the storage accesses by about 38% and the program length by about 21%.

The implementation of special instructions in place of standard library routines, in addition to those above, would result in typical reductions of about 36% in store accesses on Titan. These instructions would be used for functions such as input/output of numbers and string handling.

Levels of support: other languages

Similar studies were made of other languages. For AL-1, an experimental language using a tabular data structure and associative links (170), considerable improvements were possible because of the repetitive nature of operations such as searching columns of tables for particular values. Replacement of standard order sequences and library routines by special instructions led to savings of 50-60% in the number of store accesses. Program lengths were reduced by about 40%. The use of an interpretive code, considerably more compact than Titan machine code, resulted in greater gains: around 70% in storage accesses and 50% in program length.

For FORTRAN, the main places where support would be valuable are input/output, mathematical functions (SQRT, SIN, etc), subroutine entry and exit, COMPLEX and double-precision arithmetic and type conversion operations. For a sample set of programs on the Titan computer, it was found that using special instructions for all the above functions could lead to savings of 66% of store accesses and 35% of program length. The formatted input/output package accounted for the major part of these savings. A compact interpretive code close to source language, such as that proposed by Melbourne and Pugmire (171), would require quite a complicated interpreter and would result in average figures similar to those produced by the use of special instructions.

For ALGOL 68C, a special instruction set supporting procedure call, entry and return, type conversion, mixed mode arithmetic and those operators which had no corresponding orders in the Titan instruction set was investigated. For a sample set of programs, up to 20% of storage accesses and 10% of program length was saved. If input/output library routines were supported as well, the saving of store accesses could be as much as 50%. Interpretation of high-level codes would be comparatively difficult for ALGOL 68 because of the complexity of the language. An interpretive code on about the same level as the extended instruction set considered, but more compact, would produce savings of about 33% in program length over the Titan version.

From the above results it would seem that on a machine with a large basic instruction set the implementation of a few extra instructions to cater for aspects of particular languages which normally require standard order sequences or library routines can result in savings of around 20% in execution time, if language primitives only are supported, or of about 50% if standard library routines are also supported. In addition, space requirements may be cut by around 20%. The use of interpretive codes at a higher level can reduce the space requirements further.

The languages chosen were all, except AL-1, languages which are commonly used and map quite efficiently onto conventional computers. If more exotic languages had been investigated the gains would have been greater. Also, if the basic instruction set with which comparison was made had been less powerful more special instructions could have been used and the improvement in performance would have been more noticeable.

INTERPRETIVE CODE OR EXTENDED INSTRUCTION SET?

The principal advantages of an interpretive code are as follows:

1 It can be more compact than a standard machine code because instruction formats can be designed to suit the language directly.

2 It is closer to the source language. This means that it takes less time to compile into the interpretive code than into standard machine codes and that in a program development environment diagnostics can be given in terms which can more easily be related to the source code.

3 The code can be machine-independent. Compatibility between implementations on different machines can be ensured more easily.

On the other hand, special instructions have the following advantages:

1 Less microprogram is required. It is possible to implement a language initially using the basic instruction set only and then to add support later when the need

has been identified.

2 There is a degree of uniformity in the code produced by compilers of different languages. Routines written in different languages can be mixed more easily.

3 There is greater flexibility in the support given. Support can vary from just a few special instructions to support particular features of the language to special instructions used to speed up the inner loops of an individual program.

4 Hardware support for instruction fetch and decode can be given more easily for a standard instruction format than if a variety of interpretive codes are in use.

5 The standard instruction set can be used to give a standard interface with the operating system.

6 Although compilation of extended machine codes will generally take longer than compilation of higher-level codes, optimization may result in the program running faster than an interpretive code version would.

7 It would be easier to share microprogram between different language systems.

Given that an entire interpreter could be implemented as one special instruction, the advantages of the special instruction approach probably outweigh the disadvantages.

PER-PROGRAM SUPPORT

As indicated by the example at the start of this paper, support for the inner loops of a particular program can produce significant improvements in speed. These are often greater than the improvement factors obtained by the support of the language in which the program is written. There are two ways in which the support could be arranged. The first is for the programmer to identify the areas where support is most needed and to write the appropriate microprogram himself. This has the disadvantage that the programmer has to be competent to write the microprogram. A more attractive possibility is the automatic generation of the microprogram by some super-optimizing compiler. In the current state of the art, this is an extremely difficult task, particularly for those machines which have very complex micro-instruction sets, but it does have the advantage of maintaining the machine-independence of the program and of hiding the details of the processor from the programmer.

STATIC OR DYNAMIC ENHANCEMENT

Extensions to a particular computer's instruction set could either be static, where the extension is permanent, or dynamic, where different programs running on the computer use different extensions. The former may be acceptable for a computer which is dedicated to a particular small set of programs and it would require less expensive hardware than the dynamic method. For static extensions a read-only memory may be used to hold the microprogram but dynamic extension would require a writable microprogram store. The dynamic method is more flexible and allows a greater range of support to be given with a particular size of microprogram store. It would also permit the transfer of programs using particular extensions to other similar computers as the microprogram could easily be transferred as well.

In a non-multiprogramming environment the loading of microprogram would need to be done only once for each run of a program. In a multi-programming machine, different programs might require different microprograms. Wilkes (172) proposed a method by which the overhead of reloading microprograms could be minimized in such an environment, by sharing the available storage between the various users and loading the microprogram for a particular special instruction whenever the instruction was used and the microprogram was absent.

DIFFICULTIES IN ENHANCING INSTRUCTION SETS

On currently available computers it is not an easy task to extend the instruction set. An increasing number of machines have writable microprogram stores but they have not generally been designed with user extensions in mind. To enable instructions to be added to a basic set, there should be sufficient free space in the microprogram store, or else it should be possible to add extra store to that required for the basic set. Also, there must be some unassigned operation codes which can be used for the new instructions.

The task of writing the microprogram is not an easy one for most machines, particularly those in which the microprogram is at a very low level. Micro-instruction sets vary from those which resemble the instruction sets of small computers, with operation and address fields which are transformed by decoding logic into the control signals required, to those in which a wide word is used and very little decoding need be done to produce the control signals. The latter are most often used for the faster machines and when microprogramming them it is very necessary to know in detail about the operation of the processor hardware, its timing constraints, and which operations can be carried out in parallel.

Most manufacturers are reluctant to support user microprogramming and will not provide the details of the micro-instruction set and processor hardware which are required. Some manufacturers would even withdraw normal engineering support if the user were to modify the microprogram. The tolls available for the development of microprograms are often primitive and are not often available to the user.

A problem which must be faced when considering the use of microprograms supplied by users is that, on currently available computers, the microprogrammer can usually bypass protection systems. Thereby, whether accidentally or maliciously, he can interfere with the operation of the system as a whole or with other user's programs or data in a multiprogramming machine. Protection may be enforced at the microprogram level either by building it into the underlying hardware and disallowing certain operations when the machine is in non-privileged mode, or by restricting the set of micro-instructions that a user can cause to be executed.

CONCLUSIONS

The technique of instruction set enhancement can be used to improve the run-time performance of programs as an alternative to, or in addition to, other techniques. Special instructions can be implemented to support individual programs, all programs written in a particular language or doing a particular application, or the operation of the system as a whole. The performance improvement obtained depends on the degree of the original mismatch between the program and the machine on which it was being run. In certain cases of language support the improvement may be as great as a factor of

10 in speed. Support of conventional high-level languages on computers with a rich instruction set can produce a factor of 2 improvement. Support for programs which spend most of their time in one section of code can produce large improvements.

To use the technique to the full in anything other than a machine dedicated to running a particular program requires that the enhancement be done dynamically. There are various problems in achieving this on currently available computers but none are inherently insoluble.

BEHAVIOURAL ASPECTS OF PROGRAM OPTIMIZATION

P R Newsted

Assistant Professor of Business Administration
University of Wisconsin

P R NEWSTED is an Assistant Professor of Business Administration at the University of Wisconsin in Milwaukee. Trained as a cognitive psychologist at Carnegie-Mellon University, his interests and research have broadened to include computer programming as a problem-solving activity. Most recently, he has published an introductory programming text exclusively using the SNOBOL string-processing language.

BEHAVIOURAL ASPECTS OF PROGRAM OPTIMIZATION

INTRODUCTION

Efficient computer programs are traditionally viewed as those that compile most quickly, execute as swiftly as possible, need the least core, and run with no significant bugs. It should be a truism that efficient programs are also well documented, easy to understand, simple to use, and straightforward to modify. Unfortunately, the great bulk of operating software does well to meet the first 'hard' set of these efficiency criteria, and only infrequently meets the second, 'soft' set. All DP managers and users clearly want both but, until recently, programming was considered such a mystique and an art that almost any running program was considered acceptable. To use Wirth's term (123), programmers relied on 'trickology' to create efficient programs. Fancy overlays, code that modified itself, and other such non-transparent strategies were looked up to — even if not always understood. Programming was truly an art. It may still be an art, but the point that is becoming increasingly apparent is that it should also be a profession.

Optimization through professionalism

Kraft and Weinberg (124) point out not only that would-be members of the profession stand to gain higher salaries and restricted entry into the DP field by the certification and licensing inherent in a profession but also that the consumers of data procession should be guaranteed a professional product. But as they also note, the real difficulty with professionalism in programming is not the controversy and ramifications of certification and/or government licensing but the criteria of professionalism itself. They did a brief but telling survey to find examples of professional and therefore optimum programming.

Sadly, they found just the opposite. They obtained nine typical programs that had been in industrial production at least six months (that is, real software). They asked programmers for better rather than poorer examples of their work. Of the nine programs they received, one was in FORTRAN, one in ALGOL, three in COBOL, and the remaining four in PL/1. They totalled 6110 lines of code for an average of 679 lines per program. They gave each program a critical two-hour reading, after which an average of 16.8 hours was spent in revising and rewriting to overcome previously unknown deficiencies. 42 serious errors were discovered in just these nine programs (an average of 5 per program). Serious errors were considered to be those that would result in costs exceeding a month's salary for the programmer who wrote the program. Among other things, the errors they discovered in these supposedly 'clean' programs caused reruns, inefficiencies, operating difficulties, lost business, underbilling, incorrect paychecks, and false predictions. In so many words, the real reason programmers are not professionals is that they are not behaving like professionals. Just using the hard dollars and time criteria, these nine *real* production programs selected by the programmers were significantly improvable. When Weinberg and Kraft modified these programs, they were generally faster and shorter with a 19% reduction in core usage and a whopping 45% reduction in running costs.

Thus it is clear that optimization is still possible in programming. As almost all computing centre billing systems make hard criteria easily measurable by detailing core usage, CPU time, I/O accesses and the like, hard efficiency is easily measurable – even if not easy to change.

What is less easy to measure and even harder to optimize is the behavioural or psychological aspects of programming. Such optimization leads not only to improvements in the so-called soft criteria cited above but also to increased dollar and time efficiencies – which obviously result (though often indirectly) when it becomes clearer what a program and its programmer(s) are about.

CRITERIA FOR BEHAVIOURAL OPTIMIZATION

The criteria for behavioural optimization of programming can be divided into two groups. First are the common-sense guidelines that almost all programmers and managers say they accept and try to follow. Second, there is an increasing group of behavioural rules which have been experimentally substantiated and cannot be ignored whether they appeal to common sense or not.

Common-sense standards

The volume of lore, legend, and manuals that exist attest to the fact that programmers at least believe they know how to behaviourally optimize programs. Few are the programmers who have not stared in horror at the huge documentation and standards manuals with which they are confronted as they start their first programming job. What are these things that many *believe* are right? A simple starting point is to examine a published manual on documentation. Van Duyn (125) has written a manual that is typical. It is full of clerical-like tables, careful checklists, exact and consistent file specifications, and guiding flowcharts. None of this is to be faulted and if followed it probably works. But the catch here is the "if followed". Programmers are notorious for taking short cuts and documentation is typically the first. Regrettably, most programs and systems are only documented after the fact and then quite poorly. In so many words, documentation manuals do not take human nature into account. Documentation will not be done unless it has to be done prior to some other step – perhaps even the coding itself. Fortunately, this human side of programming is becoming more obvious and hence there is real hope of behavioural optimization of programming.

The psychology of computer programming

With the advent of an interest in the human side of programming, especially (126), greater emphasis has been placed on both the actions of programmers as individuals and as they behave in a group. The concept of egoless programming from Weinberg has been accepted by many. According to this view, programs should not be viewed as paintings or sculpture, which are extensions of an artist's ego. But rather programs (even if primarily created by one individual) should benefit from the comments and insights of the programmer's colleagues. This should take place throughout the development of the program. Hence, not only is a highly idiosyncratic program avoided, but also the programmer feels less personally criticized when the code is reviewed by a supervisor. An additional benefit claimed for this strategy is that specific programmers become less indispensible. If a particular programmer leaves, gets sick, is transferred, or becomes pregnant, there are other programmers who at least have some familiarity with the original programmer's work.

The suggestions from other knowledgeable observers and investigators are increasing. Brown (127) cautions programmers and analysts to be 'lookers' and not 'blunderers'. His five rules of thumb are undoubtedly true with their strong appeal to one's sense of the "right way to do things given human frailities". He suggests that we:

1 keep putting ourselves in the shoes of others such as the user, the manager, the manual reader, and the person who takes over the project when we get promoted;

2 document everything, continually assuming we are going to have an attack of amnesia next week;

3 verify and test and repeat this every time the smallest detail is changed;

4 plan for a changing environment;

5 imagine everything in terms of what happens when it goes wrong.

Rogo (128) details the need for functional specifications for any proposed program or system. This is very much like a turn-key system for software. Users are queried in detail as to what they need and how their desired system should *function* irrespective of how it is coded. Crucial interests of the users include report formats and frequencies, types of runs (in non-jargon terms), input descriptions, and descriptions of the clerical tasks the system can perform. When such specifications are detailed (that is, documented) before programming commences, negotiation and discussion can take place and a desired system as well as one that is possible (given software and hardware) can result. Functional specifications can eliminate most of the "that's great, but what I really wanted is" requests by getting them out in the open to begin with.

Attractive as functional specifications are, they do not get to the actual programming – though following them makes it safe to proceed with coding. What guidelines are to be offered in the actual writing of statements? One can depend on amusing and often helpful proverbs (129,130). Detailed – if not experimentally supported – books on 'style' can be consulted (for example (131)). There is much in such a book of style to lead to professionalism:

- a prologue definition of a program and its variables
- logical indenting (especially with ifs)
- use of blank lines and carefully set-off comments
- mnemonic names and labels
- standard abbreviations and punctuation
- generality
- use of pre-programmed modules
- non-repetitious calculation of constants
- optimized ordering of arithmetic operators
- non-mixing of data modes or types
- efficient looping (where as much is outside the loop as possible)

- few **gotos**, and then only those that jump short distances
- minimal subscript usage
- a full knowledge of all language and system features

And the list can go on.

Care must be taken in following this lore and style when confronted with the need for hard efficiency. Knuth (132) correctly points out that the hard optimization of code has been overstressed. He notes that

> "most of the running time in non-I/O bound programs is concentrated in about 3% of the source text. We often see a short inner loop whose speed governs the overall program speed to a remarkable degree; speeding up the inner loop by 10% speeds up everything by almost 10%. And if the inner loop has 10 instructions, a moment's thought will usually cut it to 9 or fewer."

Thus Knuth is suggesting that too much tinkering under the guise of achieving hard efficiency should not be done because tightening in all but small sections of code will lead to a less transparent program that is difficult to read and hard to debug.

Structured programming

In addition to the assortment of published and underground wisdom that exists about optimizing programming, there has been one specific thrust (which is still without much experimental validation) that, if nothing else, is proving a rallying point for those concerned with the behavioural aspects of programming. This is structured programming. Structured programming is as much an attitude as it is a series of techniques. Top-down programming, logical code blocks, **goto**less code, and modularity are all part of it, but it is more than this. Structured programming is a realization of the limited information-processing capabilities of human programmers. Wirth's definition (123) sums it up quite well. To him, structured programming is

> "the expression of a conviction that the programmer's knowledge must not consist of a bag of tricks and trade secrets, but of a general intellectual ability to tackle problems systematically, and that particular techniques should be replaced (or augmented) by a method. At its heart lies an attitude rather than a recipe: the admission of the limitations of our minds."

Specifically, one's mind cannot be expected to understand ridiculously tight or 'tricky' code. This view is strongly reinforced by Knuth's comments on the usefulness of the **goto** statement (132). Though **gotos** are viewed as harmful, most programmers still feel the need for a statement that in fact 'goes to' without saying **goto**. Short jumps with **gotos** are acceptable; branching over many statements is not, because easily grasped abstractions are not possible. All levels of a program (with or without **gotos**) should be easily 'chunked' or abstracted into one basic concept or function. 'Chunked programming' is really what is meant by structured programming – it is not simply **goto**less coding.

Elimination of **gotos** can lead to better and more easily understood abstractions or program chunks. Though such code may be harder to write, it should certainly be within the grasp of the real professionals envisioned by Kraft and Weinberg (124).

Experimentally supportable standards

The experimental evidence on the behavioural optimization of programming can be divided into three areas:

1 the work in the area of planning and understanding a program using a flowchart

2 guidelines for actually writing code

3 studies on debugging.

The usefulness of flowcharts

Flowchart it! The admonition of many a manager to a beginning programming. The beginning programmer will probably do so. He or she has to start somewhere in the complex task that has been assigned. A flowchart is as good as any placc to start – or so it seems. It is a way to bring order out of chaos. Typically, such a flowchart is highly useful to the beginning programmer because it is a way of organizing what is to be done. If the flowchart is reasonably correct and straightforward, it may also serve as documentation.

This is all well and good for the neophyte, but what of the experienced programmer who balks when asked to write a flowchart? Such a programmer may often jot down a few notes but frequently feels a full flowchart is a waste of time. "I know how to write this program; don't put paper work in my way" is the lament of the senior programmer intent on the job at hand and wishing to ignore documentation standards that require initial flowcharts.

Who is right in this very real scenario? How can it be determined whether flowcharts are truly useful or not. The obvious answer is well-designed and carefully controlled experimentation. Statistical techniques exist so that it can be stated with a known level of confidence how correct one or another technique is. The difficulty with experimentation on programming, however, is finding the appropriate setting. If real DP personnel are to be studied, the productivity of the group cannot help but be affected. Few managers would let an experimenter use a technique that might be bad just to have it actually proven to be bad (at the expense of the department's performance).

This problem is well seen in the study of flowcharting. To have a programming department stop flowcharting their work just to prove a point is not very appealing – even to higher management who can be apprised of the long-range goals of such a study. Hence, a different population of subjects under different conditions must be used even risking some inapplicability of results.

Using the setings of two universities, Shneiderman, Mayer, McKay, and Heller (133) have done five carefully thought-out experiments, which all reach the conclusion that flowcharts are essentially useless. Their compelling results are almost certainly applicable outside their educational setting and probably to languages other than FORTRAN (which was used in all of their experiments). In their first experiment, they required two groups of students from an introductory programming course to write a short program. One group received instructions to write a flowchart prior to the code; the other did not. The correctness scores of each group (normalized to 100%) were insignificantly different: 94% for the flowchart group, 95% for the non-flowchart group.

In an experiment in comprehension rather than program composition, the results were the same. Two groups again from an introductory course were each asked questions about two programs (27 and 24 FORTRAN statements respectively). One group had a flowchart for the first program; the other had one for the second. The result on the untimed test of comprehension indicated that students had more difficulty understanding the second program whether they had a flowchart for it or not.

When comprehension and debugging were required in a third experiment, flowcharts again did not help. In this experiment, intermediate FORTRAN programmers participated in a two-factor design. Either subjects were familiar with flowcharts and were using them in their courses *or* they were not. Alternatively, they had a general macro flowchart, a detailed micro one, *or* none at all. The task of subjects in each of these six cells was to discover and correct three bugs in a FORTRAN program, which was supplied with output. Results showed that familiarity with flowcharts did not matter. Past work with flowcharts did not help or hinder debugging. In addition, the kind of flowchart provided (if any) made no difference. Finally, no interactions between kind of flowchart and familiarity were seen.

When students were confronted with a program to modify, Shneiderman *et al* again showed flowcharts to be ineffectual. In an elegant three-factor study they compared: Indiana University students with those at Purdue University, types of modification, and three levels of descriptive flowcharts (macro, micro, and none). Their results were significant in all areas except flowcharting. Purdue students did significantly better than Indiana students; the second modification was harder than the first, but flowchart type or presence (or its statistical interaction with other factors) were insignificant.

In a final experiment on comprehension (designed to be more difficult than the first experiment on comprehension), students were questioned about the logical characteristics and execution results of a two-way array-merging algorithm. The algorithm was presented in one of three ways: as a flowchart, as actual FORTRAN code, or as flowchart and code together. An analysis of variance indicated that all groups performed equally well. The way the algorithm was described made no difference to students' ability to figure out its operation and properties or to determine what it would print.

Thus when dealing with FORTRAN programs (less than 100 statements long), Shneiderman and his colleagues have found that students are neither helped nor hindered by flowcharts. The question remains, however, as to the validity of these results and their applicability to large business systems.

As to validity, the easiest way to show that a condition or treatment has no effect is to do a sloppy experiment where variability is bound to be high and significant differences non-existent. Evidence that this is not the case with Shneiderman's work comes from at least two fronts. Significances in areas other than flowchart/no-flowchart comparisons were found (such as between different kinds of students and between different kinds of problems). Secondly, Shneiderman has done other experiments on programming of a similar quality (to be cited below) with comparable variability, which do show significant effects of the main variables under investigation.

With respect to applicability, the conclusions cannot be as positive. On an absolute scale, conceptualizing Shneiderman's small programs is easy compared with systems of several thousand lines. Clearly some help is needed in understanding large systems; probably flowcharts can do this. But Shneiderman's work certainly questions whether flowcharts are the best solution. A carefully written description may do as well if not better. As yet, the experiments in a real DP shop remain to be done. That these experiments will come to the same conclusion as those of Shneiderman *et al* is partially suggested by the limited use of most automatic flowcharting programs. The fancy starred boxes and intricately drawn lines are easily generated and sometimes serve as documentation, but are usually too confusing to be of much real use (134,135). The same may well be true of large manually drawn flowcharts. Thus the best conclusion to be drawn about planning large systems has probably already been given when structured programming was defined. At whatever level a system is viewed – in its entirety or at the lowest level of assembler code – it must be 'chunkable' into understandable parts. A flowchart may do this as may a clearly written description – or even a well-structured program itself.

Rules for coding

There have not been a great many experimentally substantiated rules for actual coding, but a number of things are becoming clear. Statement constructions that follow the 'structure' inherent in structured programming are easier to understand than those that do not. Sime, Green, and Guest (136) demonstrated that subjects naive to programming (that is, similar to beginning programmers) found the **if** (*condition*) **goto** construction harder to use than **if-then-else** phrasing. Miller (137) also showed that simpler language constructions are easier to understand and can be followed more quickly than involved formats. His work suggests that conditional statements with conjunctive ANDing are easier to understand than disjunctive statements with ORing (especially ORing coupled with negation).

Logical **ifs** in FORTRAN, which are representative of a structured technique have been shown, by Shneiderman and Ho (138), to make FORTRAN programs easier for student programmers to understand than arithmetic **ifs**. Further support for the chunked, **goto**less style of structured programming again comes from Shneiderman and Ho. They showed that FORTRAN statements organized into a logical flow are easier to memorize and thus understand than statements in a random order. Regrettably, the interesting experiments of measuring understanding via memorizing code with and without **gotos** (and/or other questionable constructions) have not been done.

In terms of documenting while coding, it has been shown that on short FORTRAN programs (less than 30 lines), comments and mnemonic names may actually interfere with attempts to understand the program (139). This seems to happen because different things are connoted to the programmer and the program readers by the comments and variable names in the program. In large programs it is imperative that the programmer select comments and mnemonic names and labels that have appropriate meanings not only for the programmer himself but also for anyone who might be expected to come into contact with the program.

In addition to different ways of doing coding, there are two commonly used mediums for coding: the interactive teletypewriter terminal and the batch processing environment. Advantages of each easily come to mind, but an extensive study has been done by Sackman (140) with students using ALGOL at the US Air Force Academy. Though his results are more than five years old, they are still timely and worth study by any DP manager who is in the position to effect how much coding his programmers do in a batch-processing environment versus a time-sharing one, Briefly summarized, his conclusions are:

1 *Computer costs*
A consistent and statistically significant finding was that to solve the standard experimental problems almost twice as many computer runs of cadet programs were required under time-sharing than with batch. Direct computer time costs are inferred to be significantly lower under batch.

2 *Man-hours to complete problems*

Time-sharing generally required 12% more man-hours for completion of test problems for the entire sample. Although this result is statistically significant for the entire sample, it was not consistently significant for individual courses and problems. No reliable mean difference between time-sharing and batch were found in the correlated measure of elapsed time to complete problems.

3 *Problem grades*
Although there was an overall tendency toward 4% higher grades (that is, better programs) under time-sharing, this trend was not statistically significant.

4 *User preference*
Time-sharing was consistently preferred by cadets over batch with respect to overall ratings throughout the course of the experiment. However, the margin of preference, which was substantial at the beginning of the experiment, was significantly reduced by the end of the experiment to a relatively small edge in favour of time-sharing.

5 *Positive attitudes toward batch*
The batch mode was viewed as easier to learn and use, better for coding, and more conducive to individual organization of work and for problem analysis, particularly for well-defined problems.

6 *Positive attitudes toward time-sharing*
The time-sharing mode was perceived as posing a greater challenge, allowing greater exploration of the problem, and as leading to a greater insight and heightened creativity, particularly for open-ended problems and for more skilled users; it was the preferred mode for program debugging.

7 *Computer system service*
The above findings are contaminated to an unknown extent by less reliable service under time-sharing (which was installed just before the start of the experiment), and by short on-line console sessions (15 minutes, reserved in advance) which were associated with very heavy demands for time-sharing.

8 *Individual differences*
As in all previous on-line/off-line experimental studies, very large individual performance differences overshadowed computer system differences, often by an order of magnitude.

Thus in terms of coding, it can be recommended that a structured approach is best; appropriate names and labels a must; and the programming environment (batch or time-sharing) should be selected with cost in mind given individual programmer differences and the needs for creativity as opposed to routine, tightly defined problems.

Experimental results on errors and debugging

If not the most time-consuming of a programmer's activities, debugging is certainly the most onerous. Fortunately, this may change as there is an increasing variety of work, surveyed below, that has started to unravel the process of debugging and provide some tentative aids for the programmer attempting it:

1 *Individual differences in errors and debugging*

Not surprisingly, veteran programmers make fewer errors than beginners. But surprisingly not that many fewer. Youngs (141) found that in programs averaging 50 statements (in a variety of languages: ALGOL, BASIC, COBOL, FORTRAN, and PL/1) veteran programmers made an average of 15 errors in getting their programs to run as opposed to 19.4 for neophytes. Interestingly enough, there were no differences in the number of errors on the first run of each group.

Part of these results may be explained by small sample size (30 beginners and 12 veterans), but there were also large individual differences in errors made and found by the programmers – hence leading to large variability and obscured significances. Large individual differences in debugging are a real phenomenon, however, as Gould and Drongowski (142) have also found. This may suggest that many people can be taught to code and even to program but that only very few should ever go on to be 'professionals'.

An interesting examination of debugging practice, which sheds further light on individual differences, was done by Weinberg (126). In describing the different results to be expected based on different instructions to programmers, Weinberg noted two different debugging strategies, which he denoted as "assertive" and "humble", Among the assertive debuggers (1/3 of the group), there were many more short looks, quick corrections and immediate resubmissions. In the humble group, there were few quick looks; in effect, the humble group never made syntactic errors after their first run because they made all additional modifications without mistakes. The assertive programmers, however, invariably had to go back and make corrections in their corrections. Weimberg goes on to suggest that programmers in the humble mould are best suited for a batch environment, whereas their more assertive colleagues may best use their impulsiveness at a time-sharing terminal.

2 *Kinds of errors*

In a study of several hundred programs (divided between PL/1, Assemble, and FORTRAN) in a time-sharing environment, Boies and Gould (143) found that only 15% of the programs had syntactic errors at all. Semantic errors were by far the most common – thus leading them to stress the need for better understanding on the part of the programmers of the task(s) and language(s) with which they are involved. As might be expected, beginners have been shown to make more semantic errors than veterans (141).

A variety of semantic errors have been classified by experimenters. Using Youngs' classification (141), the following types of semantic errors were found, (the list being ordered from most to least frequent):

- assignment
- allocation
- I/O
- iteration
- parameter/subscript
- conditional execution

Gould and Drongowski (142) reported a similar ordering. The preponderance of assignment errors again suggests poor comprehension of algorithms if not goals on the part of the programmers.

3 *How errors are corrected*

The *who* and the *what* of errors is interesting, but the crucial question to a programmer is *how* should the debugging be done. Though Youngs (141) has shown that errors are removed exponentially, more specific things need to be said about how debugging takes place. Several investigators have suggested that it is a process of scanning code rather than studying listings of output (other than to note that an error has occurred). In the work of Gould (144) as well as Gould and Drongowski (142), subjects made little use of output – essentially ignoring even correct output when it was provided. In addition, Gould has demonstrated that an available on-line debugging system will receive little use even by experienced programmers while they are debugging.

Further confirmation that debugging is not very sophisticated comes from Nagy (145), who has shown via a sophisticated on-line error collection program that students make one-line changes in programs both with respect to compilation and execution errors. They work on a further error only when they have corrected an old one. Clearly, more use should be made of good diagnostic compilers. WATFIV exists for FORTRAN; COBOL can be compiled with WATBOL. It has been suggested by McCracken (146) that even experienced programmers can benefit from the compilation and execution diagnostics of such non-production compilers. Nonetheless, the picture is emerging of often unsophisticated, one-step-at-a-time debugging – with each step involving a new run.

Again the call for professionalism and chunked programming is appropriate. Chunked code is easier to understand and should thus be less prone to errors and should allow easier detection of those errors that are made. And obviously, professional programmers should do this better than anyone else.

CONCLUSION

Thus behavioural optimization returns to the need for professionalism in programming. How are professionals to be found (or trained)? A preliminary attempt (147) at predicting ability and grades (which would seem to be obvious correlates of professionalism) indicated the following two regression equations for introductory programming students:

GRADE = ·46(ABILITY + ·30(COLLEGE GPA) - ·17(TIME SPENT)

ABILITY = ·34(GRADE) + ·31(DP CAREER) - ·23(GROUP WORK) + ·16(EXPERIENCE)

The surprising thing about these equations is the negative loadings given "time spent on the course" and "working with others". One can conclude that programming ability (as measured as self-perceived ability by the questionnaire used in this study) may be more innate than business training course 'spiels' would have one believe. Poor students may spend much time on programming and ask many questions of their instructor and fellow students, but it does not improve either their grades or perceived programming ability.

Thus the best advice a DP manager can be left with in his hunt for professionals is to hire people who write chunked, readable programs. And it may turn out that though most students can be taught to 'code', only those with Wirth's "general intellectual ability to tackle problems systematically" can be truly taught to program and produce programs that meet both the criteria of hard and soft efficiency.

MACHINE EFFICIENCY VERSUS PROGRAMMING EFFICIENCY

J Palme

National Defence Research Institute
Sweden

J PALME is Head of the Datology Section of the Research Institute of National Defence in Stockholm. He has been employed at the Research Institute since 1963. He became a Master of Technology at the Royal Institute of Technology (Stockholm) in 1964 and a Licentiate of Technology in 1968. His most significant experience has been in discrete event simulation, simulation languages, high-level languages, and systems for answering natural-language questions. He has written the following books (in Swedish): Beware of MRA (1962), Free Abortion (1964), FORTRAN for the ALGOL user (1970), Programming languages (1971), and several crime novels.

MACHINE EFFICIENCY VERSUS PROGRAMMING EFFICIENCY

ABSTRACT

This paper discusses the different kinds of trade-off which can be made between programmer efficiency and machine efficiency. Subjects treated are how to reduce programming cost, whether advanced programming tools can help, how a programming language can increase reliability and lower debugging costs, what kind of language will give the most efficient object code, the trade-off between memory usage and CPU time, why certain high-level languages have problems with the efficiency of the object code.

INTRODUCTION

By machine efficiency I mean reduced hardware costs: doing the same job while using less hardware resources like memory units, CPU time, etc. By programming efficiency I mean reduced cost of development and maintenance of the software.

The purpose of this paper is to discuss whether these two goals are compatible or not; do we have to make a trade-off between incompatible goals, or can we find solutions which satisfy both goals at the same time?

Since programming languages and their implementations are important in this respect, the discussion will be centered around those subjects.

PROGRAMMING COSTS

The actual time to write a computer program usually represents only a small fraction of the programming cost. The costly and time-consuming parts are debugging and maintenance. Making the software safe, reliable and dependable is costly, but in most cases necessary, since the losses caused by unreliable software are often even larger.

Since errors will always occur with large computer applications - machine errors, human operator errors and software errors - good software products are expected to protect against disasters which these errors may cause. Such products are called fail-soft, and all except very small computers contain at least some fail-soft capabilities. For example, an error in a user application program should not destroy the operating system in the computer. Getting fail-soft capabilities contributes significantly to the programming cost.

Maintenance of a software product does not only include correction of errors, but also development of extended capabilities and program changes. In many cases, the total programming effort spent on such development is much larger than that of the initial development. If the initial design of the software is such that the new capabilities are difficult to accommodate, maintenance becomes especially difficult and costly.

REDUCTION OF PROGRAMMING COSTS

To some extent, programming costs can be reduced by good programming techniques, well-trained software development personnel etc, but that aspect is not of primary interest in this paper.

In addition, there is a trade-off between four cost factors:

1 buying or developing general-purpose software (compilers, software analysis tools, application packages, etc)

2 hardware costs during the development of programs

3 hardware costs during the production runs

4 personnel costs for program development, maintenance and use.

The balance between these cost factors depends on the application.

If the cost of production runs is high compared to the development cost, then it might be worthwhile to spend more money on the other three cost factors. One might then choose to use an expensive, highly optimizing compiler. Such a compiler may be more expensive to buy or develop; it will use more hardware resources during program development and it will also often increase the personnel costs for program debugging, since highly optimizing compilers tend to be less reliable than other compilers. Another solution is to use a programming language which closely mirrors the architecture of the machine - assembler language or a machine-oriented language of the PL/360 kind. Such languages yield more hardware-efficient object programs, but are less secure and therefore cause higher debugging cost.

However, I will show below that the use of such machine-close languages may very often not give as hardware-efficient object programs as people tend to believe.

By using more advanced program development tools, personnel costs are saved at the expense of hardware costs and general-purpose software costs. This will often give a net saving, since the cost of developing general-purpose software can be shared between many users.

In many applications, the hardware cost for production runs is actually a small part of the total cost, and it may be profitable to use more advanced program development tools even if these given higher hardware costs during production. The more advanced programming tools may for example give increased reliability and reduce the time to develop and modify the software. Low reliability can be very costly, and having to wait a long time before software can be modified can also be very costly.

ADVANCED PROGRAMMING TOOLS

Important tools to reduce the program development cost are a secure operating system, preferably one which allows time-shared conversational program development and debugging, good programming language systems and certain other utility programs, for example for text editing, semi-automatic documentation and file maintenance and back-up.

The same computer may not at all be the best for program development and for production runs, and therefore different computers are more and more often used for these purposes. Sometimes cross-compilers and simulators are used to develop software for small machines on bigger machines, more suitable for software development.

However, there is also a risk in using very complex program development tools. Since these tools are very expensive to develop, most users have to use tools they have not developed themselves and are not maintaining themselves. If these tools are not sufficiently reliable, they may bring more trouble than help.

Software tools which are supported by large manufacturers or software houses are not necessarily more reliable. In practice, users have often had difficulties with such 'well-supported' software, where the support includes new releases once or twice a year such that often old programs do not run any longer with the new releases! My personal experience, for example, is that PL/360 is much more reliable than OS assembler for the IBM computers, in spite of, or perhaps because of, the support given to OS assembler by IBM.

If manufacturer support is not a good criterion for the reliability of software development tools, which criteria should then be used?

- The structure of the software should be simple and natural, without a lot of added-on baubles which are not necessary and which just decrease the reliability. The size of the compiler may be a good criterion.

- The software should be secure by definition. By this I mean that the software should be defined in such a way that, when you use it, nothing can happen which does not follow from the definition of the software. This point is best illustrated by counterexamples, and FORTRAN is a good choice since FORTRAN is such a very insecure language. The following are some examples of what can happen in FORTRAN:

- If there is a lack of correspondence between two subroutines, then funny things can happen, usually with little, or unhelpful, diagnosis. Examples are non-similar COMMON statements, and the lack of correspondence between actual and formal subroutine parameters. Consider for example why the following program will often output 2 instead of 1:

```
SUBROUTINE SUB(I)
...
I = I + 1
RETURN
END
CALL SUB (1)
J = 1
WRITE (6) J
```

- If your program depends on the fact that certain compilers initialize all un-initialized data to zero, or that certain compilers keep local data in subroutines between different calls to these subroutines, then you are in for a surprise when you change to a new version of the compiler or the operating system.

- FORTRAN has few data structures except dimensioned variables, and FORTRAN programmers are therefore encouraged to use dimensioned variables. These are however very insecure. The array bounds are easy to exceed, and there is no checking against using the wrong index in the wrong array.

Please note that these examples do not primarily indicate faults in bad FORTRAN implementations. They indicate faults in the FORTRAN programming language itself. A good compiler can seldom improve very much on a bad language.

A way to protect against insecure programming languages (like FORTRAN or PL/1) is to develop special check-out compilers. This is however not usually a good solution, since it is difficult with an insecure programming language to get adequate compatibility between the check-out and the optimizing compilers. Also, the cost of developing two compilers reduces the choice of manufacturer.

A good programming language should therefore be secure in its own definition. Examples of such languages are SIMULA and SNOBOL. SIMULA and SNOBOL do not need any check-out compilers, since every compiler is by definition also a full verifier that programs are within the language.

THE BENEFITS OF A GOOD PROGRAMMING LANGUAGE SYSTEM

The most important ways in which good programming language systems can lower the development costs are by encouraging well-structured programs and by automating as much of the check-out as possible.

A well-structured program is a program which is divided into modules with well-defined interfaces. There are two main ways of dividing a program into modules. One way is to have different modules for different parts of the task. Another way is to let lower-level modules define more advanced concepts to be used in higher-level modules.

An example of the latter may for example be graphics packages or data base systems. They define more advanced concepts, to be used higher-level modules of the program. It is important that each application project should itself be able to develop such lower-level packages for its own use.

The person who writes the program for a module should also be allowed to tell the programming language system what kinds of uses of his module are legal and illegal. The compiler should then automatically check that all other modules of the program use his module in the correct way.

There are strong arguments for using general-purpose languages for large applications, but general-purpose languages have to give the programmers freedom to do many different things. And the more freedom a programmer is given, the less checking the compiler can do of the correctness of his programs. The solution to this dilemma is to allow the programmers to tell the compiler what kind of checking to do. If the programmer tells the compiler that the variable v is used to store a velocity, the variable s to store a distance and the variable t to store a time, then the compiler can itself catch a bug such as $v:=t/s$.

If the programmer tells the compiler that the variable p should always be positive, then the compiler can catch statements where p may become negative, and force the programmer to put in some special statement to indicate that he is aware of the possibility.

The ideal language for one module of an application is a language which only allows the constructs necessary for writing that module and nothing else. A good language should therefore allow the user to put in statements into the program to restrict the language so that the compiler can do a better job of checking the program.

POSSIBLE INEFFICIENCIES OF ASSEMBLY LANGUAGE

There are several reasons why assembly language programs sometimes do not turn out to be as efficient as people tend to believe.

Every large software product has to contain a lot of internal checking. When a program is executed, then there is usually at least two levels of checking. One level is the checking done by the module 'programming language system' on the module 'applications program'. And the second level is the checking done by the module 'supervisory system' on the module 'programming language system'. In large systems, these three main modules are divided into submodules with further checking in-between them.

If a large application package is written entirely in assembly language, then much of this necessary internal checking goes into the run-time code. The different modules of the large application will thus contain a lot of code, often as much as 50%, just to check that other modules are not misusing it. This checking code is executed at run time, requiring both memory and CPU time.

If a good high-level language is used instead, a language that allows the compiler to do this checking as discussed in the previous section, then a lot of this internal checking can be moved from run time to compile time, thus giving more efficient object programs. (This was first pointed out to me by C A R Hoare.)

There are other related reasons why assembly language programs sometimes tend to be less efficient. For example, since assembly language is tedious to write, programmers in assembly language tend to write their programs as interpreters, which interpret commands stored in tables, text strings or other data structures. This may be a good way of structuring the programs, but such interpreters can be very inefficient in terms of CPU time in comparison with the code derived from a high-level language.

COMPARING PROGRAMMING LANGUAGES

One often hears comparisons of the 'efficiency' of two programming languages of the following kind: one or two so-called 'typical' small programs are written in the various languages, and the CPU time and memory needed for running the programs is measured. The main fault with this is that no small program can ever be typical of a large applications program. Small programs need little internal checking, while large packages are critically dependent on the integrity of the language itself and of the internal checking within the package. Since high-level languages can move part of that checking from run time to compile time, they may actually give more efficient code for large packages.

In practice, I have noted that these so-called typical programs are atypical in other respects also. For example, often the so-called typical programs are more CPU-bound, and contain less I/O, than actual user programs. The 'typical' programs are also often too small to be able to take advantage of the better data structuring facilities in high-level languages.

PRE-COMPILERS

A pre-compiler is a compiler which outputs code to be compiled once more by another compiler. A pre-compiler can be seen as a program structuring device. Instead of writing a large program in a low-level language, the program is instead written in a high-level language which the pre-compiler translates. The pre-compiler is thus an example of the kind of module which defines high-level concepts and checks that they are correctly used by the high-level programs.

It follows from this that pre-compilers, which are very simple to write, should actually be specially geared to one special application. By defining a specialized high-level language just for that application, and writing a pre-compiler you can get more readable programs and make the computer to do more of the checking.

Since most existing programming languages today are not very secure and do not allow the users to instruct the compiler to do very much extra checking on their programs, pre-compilers can often be a good way of structuring programs. However, there are some problems, such as when the ordinary compiler gives error messages about the code generated by the pre-compiler.

A pre-compiler takes as input a specification of a program in a higher-level language and translates into a lower-level language, and the program is then compiled using the standard compiler for this lower-level language. Most often, the lower-level language are common ones like FORTRAN, ALGOL, COBOL, or LISP.

MetaCOBOL and the many well known 'structured FORTRAN' compilers try to overcome weaknesses in COBOL and FORTRAN. However, the same technique can also be used to write a pre-compiler for a very restricted specialized language. I once produced a set of computerized lessons and, instead of writing the lessons directly in ALGOL, I invented a rather simple, very restricted and specialized language suitable for writing my lessons. I then wrote, in one month, a pre-compiler from this specialized language to ALGOL. Thereafter, I could write the lessons in the specialized language in two months. If I had written them directly in ALGOL, it would have taken much longer than three months. Note that the writing of the pre-compiler itself was very easy, because

1 it compiled a restricted language

2 it produced ALGOL code, not object code (211).

MEMORY VERSUS CPU-TIME TRADE-OFF

There is often a trade-off to be made between memory usage and CPU time. For example, an open subroutine (= a macro) requires lower CPU time but more memory. Packing of data requires less memory for data storage, but more CPU time and more memory for the code that does the packing and unpacking. Compiling into some kind of very compact code, which is interpreted at run time, can often reduce memory usage considerably, but usually requires more CPU time.

In a particular situation, one of the resources may be much scarcer than the other.

For example, on many minicomputers, memory is much scarcer than CPU time; on large time-sharing systems, the opposite may be the case.

Within most programs, 90% of the code is executed 10% of the time, and 10% of the code 90% of the time. Thus, the optimal trade-off between memory and CPU time will vary between different parts of the same program. By using performance measurement tools (212), it is often easy to find out which parts of a program are specially demanding of CPU time. Some compilers can be told to generate either CPU-efficient or memory-efficient code for different parts of a program. Such compilers tend, however, to become very large and complex. A better solution may be to use a memory-optimizing compiler, and recode intensively used code in assembly language. In such cases, it is best first to debug the code completely in the high-level language, and always to keep a working version of the program written entirely in the high-level language. Recoding into assembly language of a program which has been fully checked out in a high-level language first is usually astonishingly simple to do. It is in fact so simple that some program development groups always code in high-level language first, even if their programs have to be entirely recoded into assembly language afterwards.

COMPILERS GENERATING HIGHLY-EFFICIENT CODE

As I have noted above, compilers generating highly efficient code may not necessarily give the highest run-time efficiency.

There are basically two kinds of compilers generating highly efficient code. One kind is the optimizing compiler. Typically in my experience, such compilers are often not very reliable. The optimization code seems to be very error-prone, as in the following simple FORTRAN example, where an optimizing compiler produced code that output a thousand times more lines than the user wanted:

```
IF((I/1000 * 1000.EQ.I) WRITE...
```

Another typical property of highly optimizing compilers is that their ability to optimize will vary much depending on the kind of program they are compiling. A compiler which optimizes array accesses in loops may not be at all good at optimizing list structure handling or I/O. Generally, optimizing compilers tend to optimize better on benchmark programs than on really typical programs.

One way of avoiding the problems of optimizing compilers is to allow programmers to give information to the system which aids in optimization. A programmer might for example indicate whether a certain data item should be highly packed (more object code, more CPU time, but less data space), medium packed or not packed (less object code, less CPU time, but more data space). This seems acceptable, but we do not yet know how much can be gained with this method. Certainly it will make the compiler much more complex, since the number of cases to be handled in the compiler increases, often with the product of all such kinds of programmer-defined variations.

The second way of having a compiler generate highly efficient code is to let the programming language closely mirror the hardware architecture of the machine. An example of this is PL/360. Such compilers have the drawback that this machine architecture is not always well-suited to good programming. The ideal solution to this dilemma would of course be to design the hardware in such a way that good high-level languages can be easily and efficiently implemented, and today much research is aimed at this solution (213).

EFFICIENCY PROBLEMS WITH HIGH-LEVEL LANGUAGES

The following paragraphs discuss some well-known causes of poor efficiency within existing high-level languages.

Memory allocation

Automatic allocation and deallocation of memory is a facility which is very useful to a programmer. The reason for this is that the programming of memory allocation and deallocation is very error-prone, and automatic handling of this can thus help to prevent common programming errors. However, automatic systems for memory allocations are costly. Very advanced systems, like those in languages like SIMULA or SNOBOL, will usually require about 10% extra CPU time for typical programs and about 20% extra memory compared to efficient hand-coded memory allocation.

On the other hand, hand-coded memory allocation may use more fixed data areas, with less overlaying of data in the same parts of memory, and in such cases hand-coded allocation may give less memory-efficient programs. (This will for example often happen in FORTRAN).

Block structuring

Structuring data into blocks can often save memory and give more secure code, but the access time to the data will be longer, and the display vectors (internal data structures used to access blocks) will occupy core.

Inefficient parameter transmission

The transmission of parameters to procedures is often not handled very efficiently Transfer by name and by value can both be very inefficient. I personally feel that the two most important parameter transmission modes are by reference and as constants. They are efficient and useful. A constant is a parameter whose formal parameter cannot be assigned to, the actual parameter may however be a variable. Thus, a compiler can often choose to implement constant parameters either by value or by reference.

Difficulty of choosing between CPU-efficient and memory-efficient code

The fact a compiler does not always know which parts of a program are most efficiently coded as CPU-optimizing or as memory-optimizing is one common reason why high-level language compilers sometimes produce less than optimal code. The solution is to let the programmer convey this information to the compiler, although that will make the compiler much more complex and bulky, since the number of special cases to be handled in the compiler will multiply with the number of different settings of this programmer-controlled switch.

Separate compilation

Many compilers defer to run time many program checks which could actually have been made at compile time. This is especially true of errors which can only be diagnosed by looking at two separately compiled modules at the same time. (Most FORTRAN systems do not diagnose such errors at all.) However, a compiler can store interface information between the modules on disk, to transfer information between the compilation of the various modules and thus make these error checks at compile time. This is for example done in the DECsystem-10 SIMULA compiler. That compiler makes a full check of all such module interfaces, and the efficiency of the code will be the same whether the code is divided into separately compiled modules or not.

CONCLUSION

There are obviously trade-offs to be made between different requirements when choosing how to write a program package. But the trade-offs are not always immediately obvious; for example, machine-oriented languages may not always give the most efficient code. In future, we may be able to develop systems of hardware and software such that the compiler can generate very efficient code (because of good hardware architecture) and so that many of the checks now often done at run time can instead be done at compile time (because of good programming language design).

SYSTEM PERFORMANCE OPTIMIZATION IN A VIRTUAL STORAGE ENVIRONMENT

Dr M R Patel

International Computers Limited

M PATEL graduated with First Class Honours in Electrical Engineering, from Manchester University in 1961. He completed his PhD in Control Systems Engineering, at Cambridge, in 1964, and followed this with a period of lecturing at the University of East Africa, Nairobi. In 1966, he joined English Electric and worked, first, on research into Digital Control Systems at the Nelson Research Laboratories, and then as a design engineer at Kidsgrove. From 1969-1971 he was based with ICL in Manchester, working mainly in system design. During the last three years at Kidsgrove his work has been largely in the field of Operating Systems Design, and he has been involved in both hardware and software considerations.

SYSTEM PERFORMANCE OPTIMIZATION IN A VIRTUAL STORAGE ENVIRONMENT

INTRODUCTION

In order to talk about system performance in a virtual store environment, one needs firstly to define how the system performance is to be measured, and secondly what is it primarily a function of. To this end, the paper proposed a model of the computer system and an expression to describe its throughput. From the system throughput expression, it is then possible to determine the necessary condition for an individual program performance optimization. Attention is also drawn to the fact that conflicts do occur between measures taken to increase run-time efficiency and maintainability.

A MODEL

A uniprogramming system has maximum throughput capability of $1/E$ jobs per second or transactions per second where E is the existence time in seconds of the average job or transaction in the system, as shown in Figure 1.

This model can be extended for a multiprogramming system in which all the programs require the same amount of resources, as illustrated in Figure 2. The maximum throughput T of the system can then be expressed as

$$T = \frac{C}{E} \text{ transactions per second}$$

where C is the concurrency that the system can support.

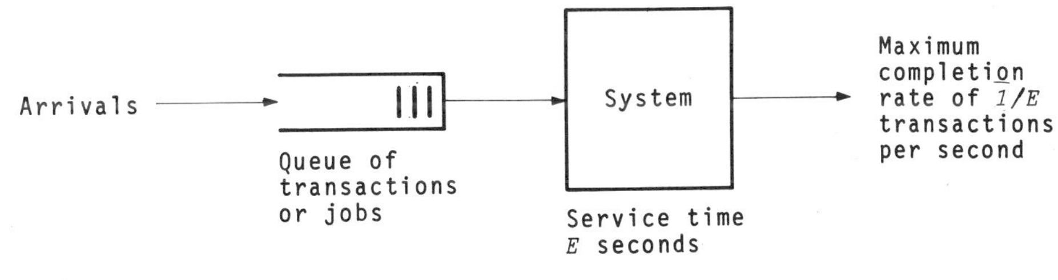

Figure 1: Uniprogramming system

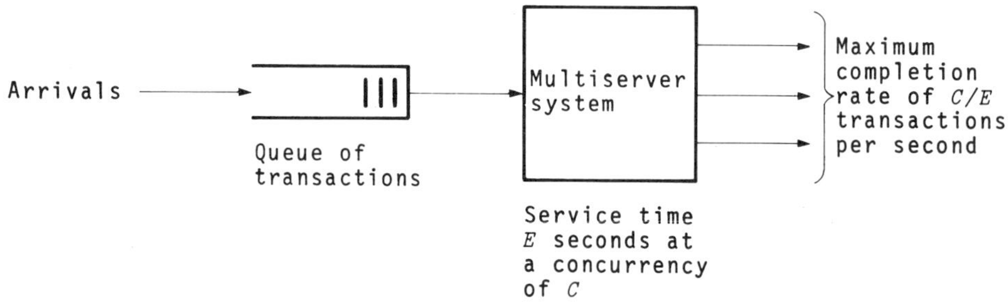

Figure 2: Multiprogramming system

The concurrency C that the system can support is a function of the allocatable store size. Let S be the total store size on the installation. Let Z be the store size taken up by the operating system (including public programs). Let Q be the store size to be allocated to one instance of a program to be multiprogrammed at a concurrency of C. Then concurrency C that can be supported for the program under consideration is given by

$$C = \frac{(S-Z)}{Q}$$

Thus the maximum throughput T of the system is given by

$$T = \frac{(S-Z)}{(Q \times E)} \quad \text{transactions per second or jobs per second}$$

So far, we have been considering multiprogramming systems that multiprogram several instances of the same program. In order to extend the use of the above expression, we assume a mix of M programs to be multiprogrammed each of which requires store of size Q_i for a duration of E_i. The average store resource required by these M programs is the average of $(Q_i \times E_i)$ over all i. The maximum throughput the system can support is then given by

$$T = \frac{(S-Z)}{(Q \times E)_{\text{av}}} \quad \text{transactions per second or jobs per second}$$

Another way of looking at the derivation of the above expression is as follows. Of the total main store size S at the installation, a size Z is taken up by the operating system and the public programs. The remainder $(S-Z)$ store size is available for allocation to programs. Each of the programs which is a candidate for the use of main store has normally a different requirement for the amount of main store it needs; and equally each program's need for the main store is for different durations of time. Thus balancing the resource availability with the sum of the resource requirements, one obtains:

$$(S-Z)E = \sum_{i=1}^{T} Q_i \times E_i$$

where T is the number of transactions or jobs executed in time period E.

It is also possible to express this as $T \times R_{\text{av}}$, where

R_{av} = average of $(Q_i \times E_i)$ over all i. Combining the two expressions one obtains

$$\frac{T}{E} = \frac{(S-Z)}{R_{av}} \text{ transactions per unit time}$$

If the time period chosen is a second (that is, E = 1 second), then we obtain the same result as before.

It is now necessary to examine the implication of the above expression on an individual particular program of a mix. The program mix is a representation of an average workload. But an actual installation would in fact experience a wide variety of workload conditions. One of these conditions is the multiprogramming of the same program in the mix. Thus in order to maximize the throughput capability of the system it is necessary to minimise the average of $R_i = Q_i \times E_i$ for all the jobs in the mix. This is achieved when each of the jobs in the mix minimizes its R_i. R_i is, in fact, the amount of store resource used by the program, measured in Kilobyte-seconds.

In order to examine the components of existence time, it is now necessary to extend the model a little further, to include I/O devices as in Figure 3.

The I/O device of primary interest here are the discs or drums holding files or virtual storage for which there is no room in main store. On some systems, the files are accessed by programs through the virtual store interrupt (VSI) mechanism. In the following, the file store and virtual store on discs or drums will be accounted for separately, so that the significance of merging them can be examined later.

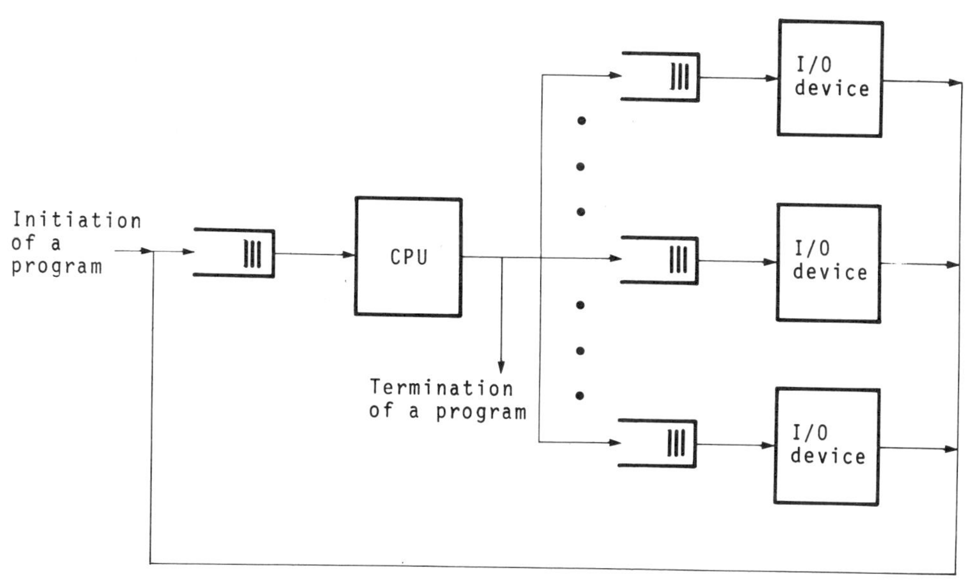

Figure 3: A model of a multiprogramming system

The existence time *E* of a program can now be expressed as

$$E = (CPUT + FSTT + VSTT) + (CPUQT + FSQT + VSQT) - OVERLAP$$

where:

CPUT = Number of instructions executed × time taken to execute an instruction
FSTT = Number of file store input/output requests × time taken to service a request
VSTT = Number of virtual store interrupts × time to service a VSI
CPUQT = Number of times awaiting allocation of CPU × average process queuing time
FSQT = Number of input/output requests × average queuing time for such a request
VSQT = Number of VSIs × average queuing time for a VSI request
OVERLAP = Overlap time between initiation of a filestore request and a wait on its completion by a program

Note that for a uniprogramming system, the queuing times are zero, and for a multiprogramming system the sum of the queue lengths of each of the queues for the I/O devices and the CPUs is the concurrency *C* of the system.

Let us now examine the relationship between existence time and the main store size in which a particular program is executed.

Several studies (176 to 180) have shown that almost all programs behave in the manner shown in Figure 4. The amount of store resource *R* used by the program, as a function of the allocated store size to it is therefore as shown in Figure 5. Note that maximum system performance is obtained with finite virtual store traffic and not zero traffic

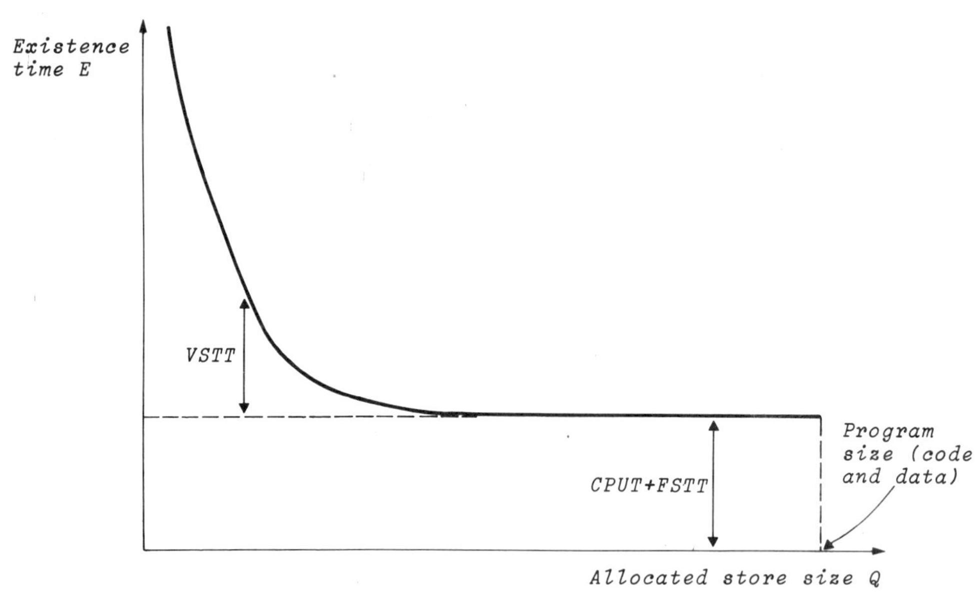

Figure 4: Existence time vs allocated store size (uniprogramming)

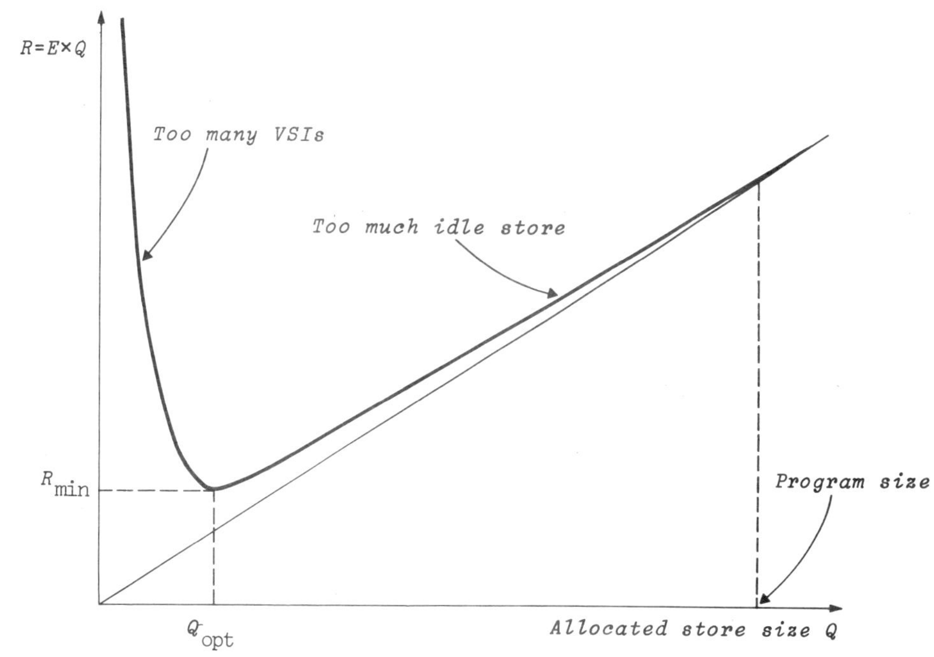

Figure 5: Store resource used vs allocated store size (uniprogramming)

It is interesting to examine the influence of backing store speeds on the existence time and the resources used by a program, as shown in Figures 6 and 7.

Note therefore that the optimum store size to be allocated to a program is a function of the speed of backing store for virtual store access.

Let us now examine the effect of multiprogramming on existence time and resources used by a program, as shown in Figure 8.

Note that in Figure 8 there are in fact two causes for increased existence time of the program. Firstly because of this particular program having to join a queue formed by other programs for the CPU, file store and virtual store. And secondly because of allocated store size to this particular program causes additional virtual store interrupts with decreasing allocated store size. But near the optimal operating regime the contribution to the existence time due to the second factor in practice is much smaller than that due to the first factor.

Note that the optimum store size to be allocated to a program is slightly greater under multiprogramming than under uniprogramming, due to the additional queuing times, as shown in Figure 9.

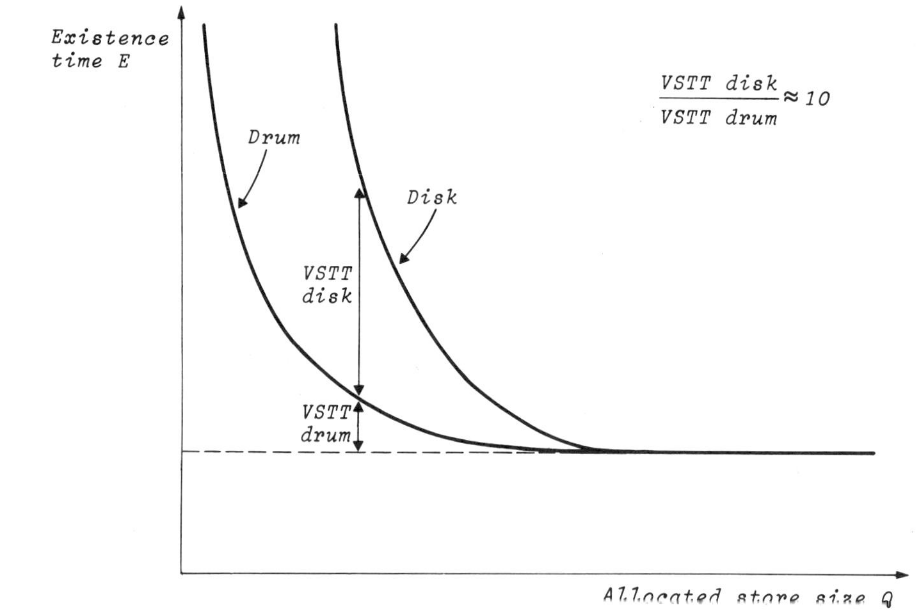

Figure 6: Existence time vs backing store speed for virtual store

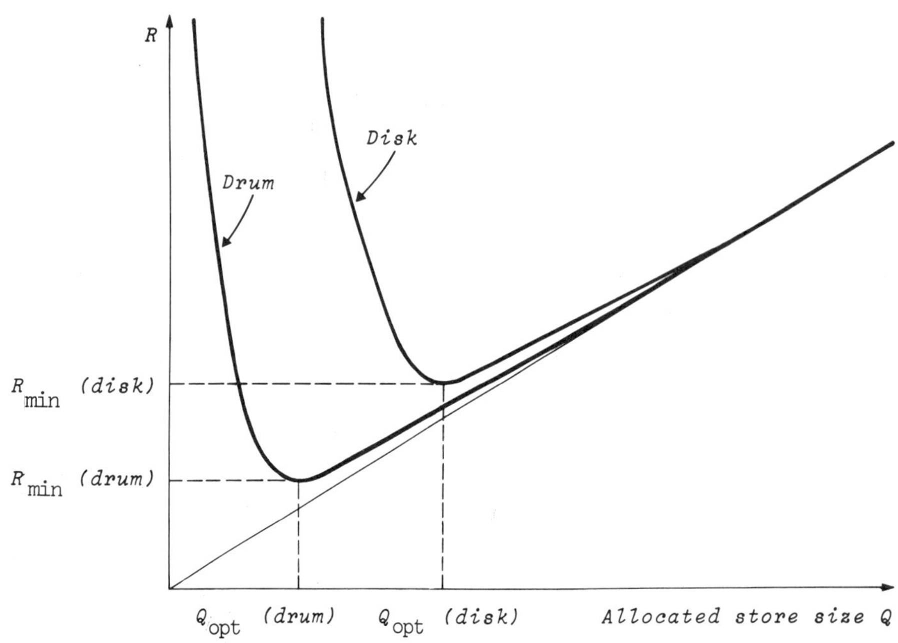

Figure 7: Store resource used vs backing store speed for virtual store

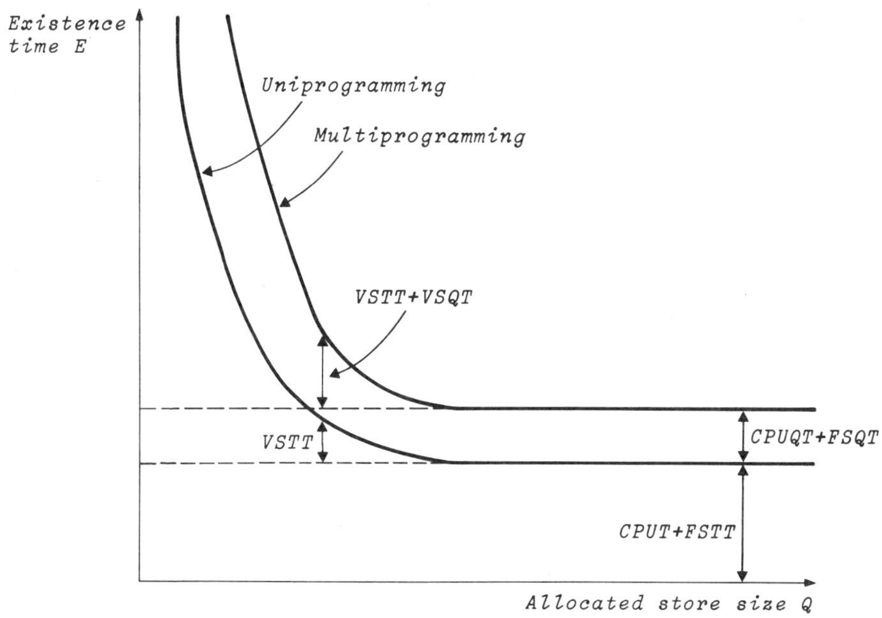

Figure 8: Existence time vs allocated store size (multiprogramming)

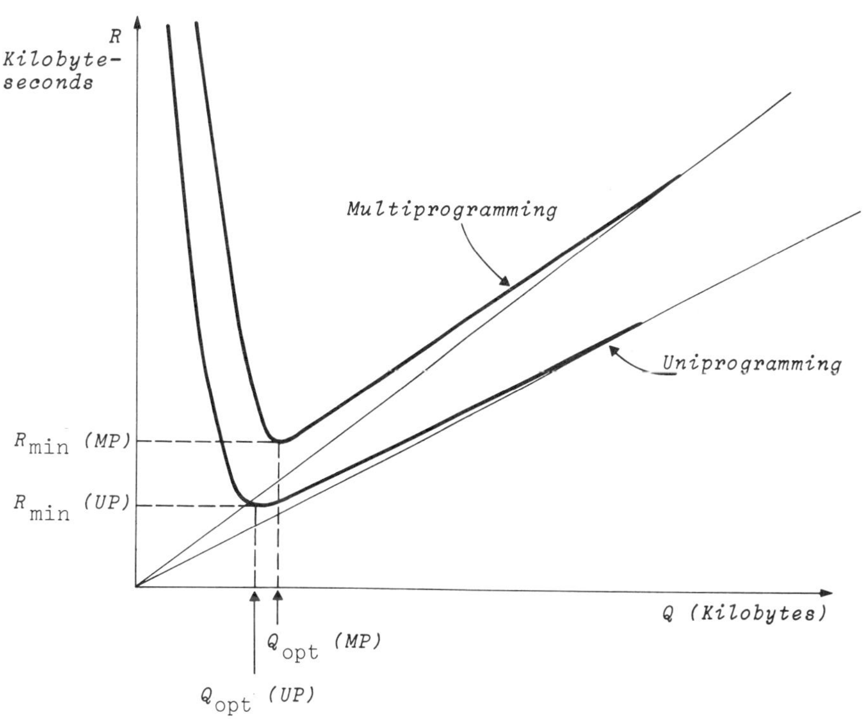

Figure 9: Store resource used vs multiprogramming

STATEMENTS ON VIRTUAL STORE SYSTEMS

The model developed above can be used to explain some of the statements made in the technical literature about the behaviour of virtual store systems. The following are a few of them:

- *System performance improves as the main store size of an installation increases.* This is explained by the increase in concurrency.

- *System performance improves as the execution time of the programs in the work-mix decreases.* This is explained by the decrease in the existence time.

- *The elapsed time required to execute a program is longer in multiprogramming than in uniprogramming systems.* This is explained by the increase in the existence time arising from the queuing times for the CPU, filestore requests and virtual store requests.

- *For a given peripheral system configuration on many systems, there is a level of multiprogramming beyond which the system performance decreases, assuming that the main store size is increased to match the increased concurrency.* At first, the increase in concurrency increases the system throughput because the increase in existence time resulting from queuing for the secondary store transfers is small. At some stage, the increase in existence time resulting from long queues caused by increased concurrency and the consequent inter-program interference offsets the benefits of increased concurrency. This, however, need not be so, and can be avoided by local discard policies instead of global discard policies.

- *System performance improves as the speed of the backing store peripherals increases, given a constant configuration.* This is explained by the reduction in the existence time, a major component of which is the I/O request transfer times.

- *System performance improves as the speed of the processor increases, given a constant configuration.* This is explained by the reduction in the existence time. Normally the CPUT of a program is a small fraction of its existence time (about 12% for commercial programs), and therefore the system performance improvement from a faster processor is quite limited, unless more and faster peripherals are added to the configuration as well.

- *System performance improves as the number of channels to the backing store peripherals is increased.* This is explained by the reduction in queuing times as a result of a spreading the load over more channels.

A GOOD VIRTUAL STORE SYSTEM DESIGN

We are now ready to examine the implications of the above model in terms of what constitutes a good design for a virtual store system. In all the examinations of the model above, we have assumed that the store size allocated to a program during its existence time is constant. In practice, however, it is found that the store requirements of most programs for minimum store resource utilization measured in Kilobyte-seconds, is a function of process time (181). In other words Q_{opt}, the optimum allocated store size to a program, is a function of process time. Thus emerges the first requirement of an operating system supporting virtual storage:

1 The operating system should be capable of assigning main store to a program, such that the amount assigned is near optimal, and is variable during the existence time of the program.

In order that the above capability be provided by an operating system, it is necessary for the operating system to detect changes in working set sizes of the program being executed. This now leads to the second requirement of a good operating system:

2 The operating system should be capable of detecting changes in working set of the programs being executed

Although there are many ways of detecting changes in working sets of programs by operating systems, this needs to be done at low cost in instructions executed by trading some loss of main store. A very accurate measurement of working set costs a lot of executed instructions, but utilizes main store more effectively; a less accurate measurement of working set incurs less cost in instructions executed, but leads to some loss in store utilisation. This capability therefore requires some assistance from hardware, leading to our third requirement:

3 The hardware of the computer system should be capable of providing information on which segments or pages of the program have been referenced during an interval of time.

In order to minimize the cost of changing the working set, derived from the reference bit set by the hardware, it is important for the operating system to know which segments or pages have been changed or written to during an interval of time. This leads to our fourth requirement for a good system:

4 The hardware of the computer system should be capable of providing information on which segments or pages of the program have been written to during an interval of time.

We will refer to the 'reference bit' and the 'written-to bit', collectively as 'use bits'.

The operating system should be capable of examining these very useful use bits perodically at low cost in instructions executed in order to detect changes in working sets, derive the working sets, and therefore determine the near optimal working set sizes, and thereby assigning the right storage size to each program. In order to perform this function at low cost it is important that the use bits are not examined or scanned too frequently. This implies that the scan rate for the use bit should be adaptive to the needs of such a scan (182):

5 The scan rate for the use bits should be a function of the rate of change of working set. In other words, when the change in working set is slow, the scan rate of the 'use bits' should be low; and vice versa. The most convenient measure of the rate of change of working set is, of course, the VSI rate for the program.

There are times in practice when programs do change their working sets very fast indeed, but only during a very short period of time. In that case, it is not worth optimizing the use of main store by such a program over this short interval of time, since this would incur heavy CPU costs. This leads to our sixth requirement of a good system:

6 When the rate of change of working set for a program is very high indeed, the operating system should turn off the scan until either the rate of change (that is, the VSI rate) has dropped, or until some sort of store constraint has been hit by the program.

In the above we have been talking about the rate of change of working set or the VSI rate, but we did not identify the measure of unit time. This turns out to be very important. The working set principle as defined by Denning applies to the behaviour of programs when observed in process time and not in real time for a multiprogramming system. What this really means is that the working set of a program is not a function of the execution of other programs. Thus, the extension of the working set size of a program should not decrease the working set size of another program. Each program thus needs a high degree of isolation from the behaviour of other programs. It is obvious though that complete isolation between programs cannot be provided in practice, since even the device queues which we have talked about are a means of slowing down other programs by one program. However, this is a second-order effect and so the likely level of interaction between programs can be severely restricted. Therefore, we can formulate our seventh requirement of a good system:

7 The scan rate and the VSI rate should be measured in process time and not in real time.

In order to minimize the effect of a misbehaviour program on other programs, it is also necessary to provide this isolation by particular attention to the discard algorithm used in virtual store systems. With global discard policies what can happen is that a program with a very high VSI rate will diminish the working set sizes of other programs below the Q_{opt} value thereby inducing thrashing (183). In order to avoid thrashing it is necessary that:

8 The operating system should adopt local discard policies, and not global discard policies; this will maintain the required working sets in main store and so provide the Q_{opt} store size to each program.

With a local discard policy, one would expect the overall average VSI rate of a system to be linearly related to average concurrency, it being at any time limited by the sum of the working sets of the programs under execution at that time. However, for a system based on a global discard policy, the VSI rate of the system increases more rapidly than linearly with concurrency, because of the tendency of some programs to execute with a store allocation below their Q_{opt} value.

There have been proposals that the discard algorithm should be activated at regular real-time intervals to examine the main store usage as a whole and remove programs that are unused. It is fairly simple to see why this does not work well by examining the impact of the algorithm on the lowest-priority program in main store. Since the lowest-priority program in main store will only be allocated a CPU if all other programs are waiting for peripheral transfers to finish, there will be occasions when it will not have executed for some long time. If the discard algorithm is activated on a regular real-time interval basis, it will therefore find the main store holding the lowest-priority program unused, and will therefore discard it. Thus the lowest-priority program has been given less main store than its working set size requirements. The program when next allocated the CPU will cause a large number of VSIs, because it is working below its optimum store requirements. This consequent additional traffic between the secondary store and main store will produce longer queuing times for all other programs. Thus the eventual outcome is that all programs in main store run slower because one program in main store is thrashing. It is therefore important that none of the programs in main store get less main store than it needs. It is better for the lowest-priority program not to execute at all, than for all programs to execute slowly on its account. This is illustrated in Figure 10.

The use of global discard policy in virtual store system is one of the main causes of thrashing. A slightly different way of looking at this problem is to examine the cost per activity against activity rate, as shown in Figure 11.

Economies of scale which are applied in other contexts need to be applied to virtual store as well. Global discard policies act contrary to the principles of economies of scale; but in conjunction with the ability to share code between activites, it does provide a means whereby the cost per concurrency can be reduced with increasing

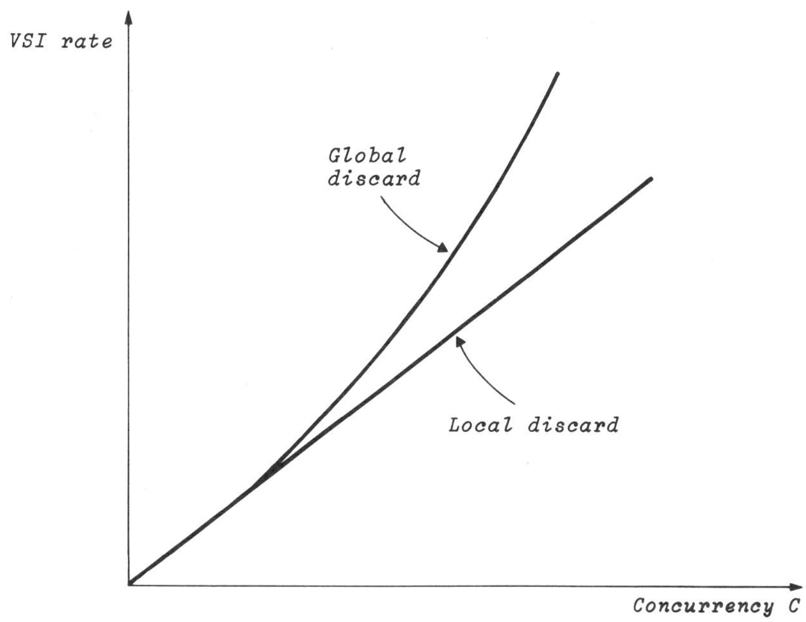

Figure 10: VSI rate vs concurrency

concurrency.

I believe this principle needs to be applied much more vigorously in the design of computer systems. Very often when the cause of performance limitation of a particular system is identified, it turns out to violate the principle of economies of scale. At the design - or audit - stage it is therefore well worth asking the question: does the cost per activity increase or decrease with the activity rate? This leads to the question of what happens when the sum of the working sets will not fit into the available store size. The answer is:

9 It is better to reduce the concurrency *C*, by removing a program from store, than to multiprogram with a higher concurrency but with non-optimum store allocated to each program.

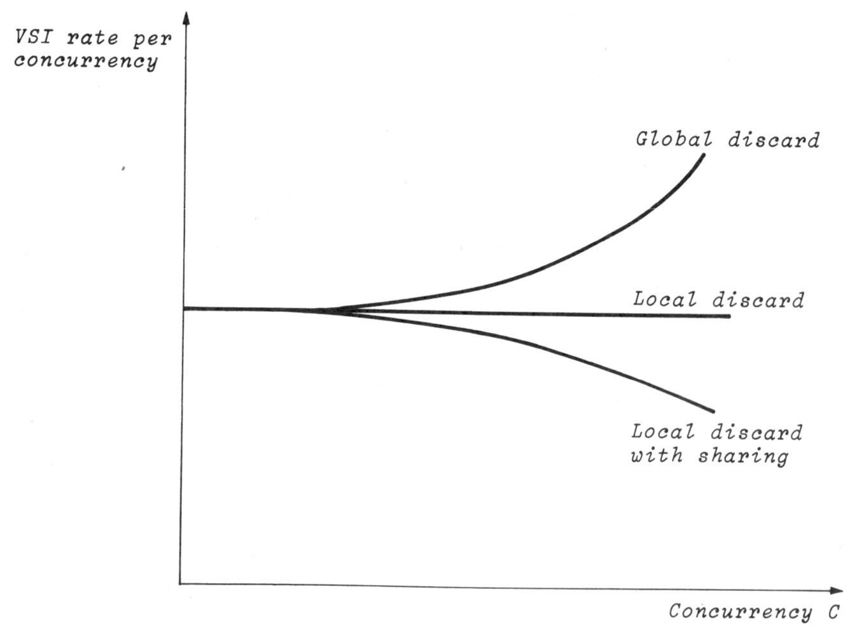

Figure 11: VSI rate per concurrency vs concurrency

One obtains higher system throughput by operating a smaller number of programs at Q_{opt}, or slightly above, than by executing a larger number of programs with store sizes slightly less than Q_{opt}. This is because the slopes of curves of R versus Q on either side of Q_{opt} have very different slopes. It is therefore necessary for an operating system to be able to adjust the concurrency, such that each program executes near but above and not below its optimum value of store quota. The ability to alter concurrency implies the following capability in the system:

10 The operating system should be capable of rolling in and rolling out the working set of a program (virtual machine).

The roll-in or roll-out capability of the operating system would be triggered as a result of

a) the completion of a program

b) there being not enough main store to house the sum of the working sets

c) explicitly by a program indicating a long wait such as in multi-access sessions.

11 The operating system thus needs to provide a procedure which can be called to indicate a desire for the program to be waited a long time (> 1 second).

This procedure may in fact be called implicitly as a result of the program calling snother procedure to output a message to a terminal. This is really taking advantage of prior knowledge of the behaviour of some programs.

There are certain programs, such as compilers and utilities, whose dynamic behaviour is well-understood and a lot is known about their requirements. It is important to make use of this knowledge in virtual store systems, rather than let the virtual store system determine, at considerable cost in the number of instructions executed, the behaviour of such a program every time it is executed for discard purposes. This implies the following requirement:

12 The operating system should provide a procedure which can be called upon explicitly (instead of via a VSI), to indicate a desire for a change in working set (that is, an overlay). Such a procedure call would thus bring some information from backing store into main store, and will discard some information from main store - which may or may not require a transfer to backing store, depending on whether the information had been altered since it was last brought into main store.

Such a scheme allows the use bit scan rate for such a program to be kept to the very minimum, thereby incurring very low costs in the administration of the program's virtual store. This procedure may, in fact, need to reschedule the use of main store, that is, alter the concurrency, if it finds there is not enough free main store available to service the call.

Since object programs produced by a translator from a high-level language source cannot contain such explicit overlay calls, based on the static nature of the program rather than the dynamic one, it is important for virtual store systems to provide another route through which the system can be informed by the program writer about the expected dynamic behaviour. Thus arises the need for:

13 a collector, which should provide the programmer with the ability to map translated areas onto logical segments or pages, as shown in Figure 12.

It is important that the collector should not be a mandatory pass, because, in a program development phase, it is a nuisance to have to provide mapping commands to the collector, since the relative frequency of retranslation to execution is very high.

Having established the need for a collector, one needs to drive it intelligently, and that means good feedback from the operating system on the behaviour of the program being executed:

14 The operating system should provide feedback on the resource *R* used by the execution of a program and, if required, the trace of the VSIs caused when executed in a given fixed main store quota.

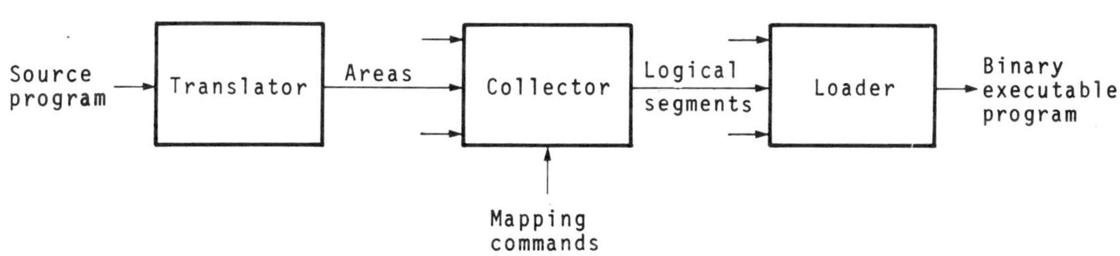

Figure 12: The role of a collector

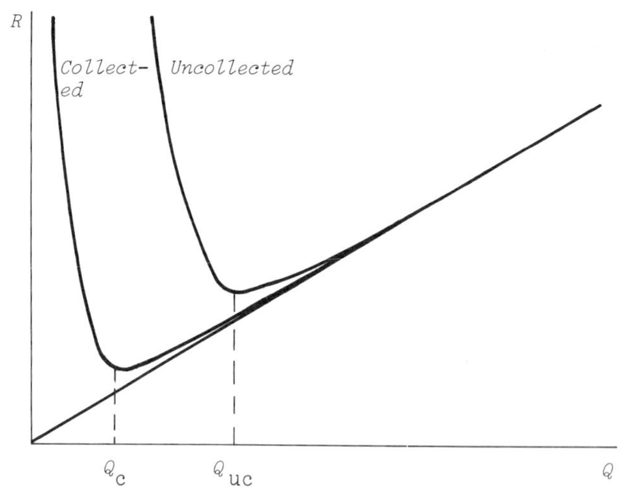

Figure 13: Effect of collection on a program

This information allows the programmer the ability to experiment with his program in order to reduce the value of ($Q \times E$) required for its execution. The experimentation may involve merely placement of translated areas onto logical segments, or may involve new algorithms for such programs as sorts. The effect of collection on a program is illustrated in Figure 13.

Logical segments created by the collector creates a need for a distinction between segments and pages, the former being variable-length and the latter fixed-length. In order to cater for this distinction:

15 The operating system should normally use segments as units of transfer on a VSI, and paging as a means of minimizing external storage fragmentation. Paging therefore helps the main store management but does generate internal fragmentation, which can be kept down by selecting an appropriately small page size.

LIMITATIONS OF THE MODEL

The model of Figure 3 assumes one channel per I/O device. In practice, several discs or drums would share a channel. Thus a more accurate representation of the I/O device is required, such as given in Figure 14.

These models have been analysed in fair depth (184,185). It is possible to collapse the model of Figure 14 to that of Figure 3, with the I/O device timing reflecting the total timing of a request in Figure 14.

Although different queuing systems have different relationships between the response time (that is, the sum of request service time and the queuing time) and the utilization of the resource under consideration, there is a general tendency that exists in all of them. This generalization can be expressed as follows:

$$\frac{\text{Response time}}{\text{Service time}} = \sigma \left\{ \frac{1}{1 - \text{utilization}} \right\}$$

This is illustrated in Figure 15.

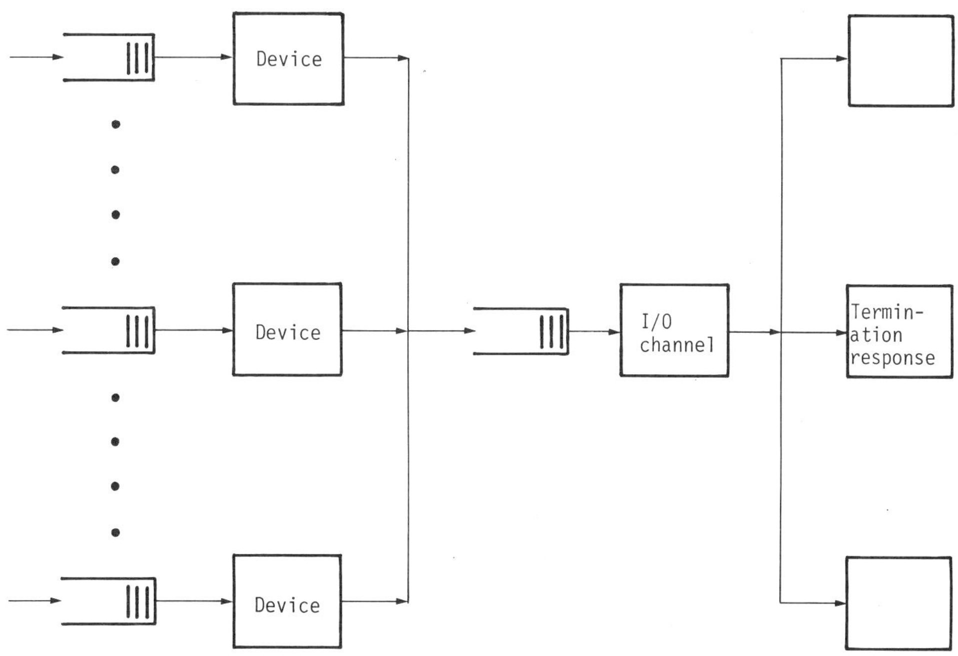

Figure 14: A model of the backing store

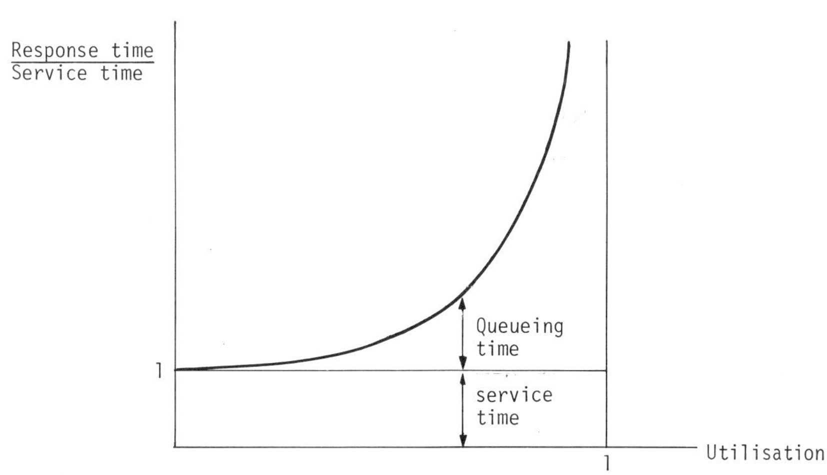

Figure 15: Response time vs utilisation

COMPILERS FOR VIRTUAL STORE ENVIRONMENT

Compilers for real-store addressing environments provide a capability for overlay generation. Compilers for virtual-store environments need to provide a similar facility for segmentation. A module of code would be capable of independent compilation and would map on to a segment. When all the modules necessary to form a program are compiled, they are either 'collected' or 'loaded'. The process of 'collection' or 'loading' would establish the linkages between the compiled modules. The code generated by compilers for execution in a virtual store environment needs some special considerations.

The code generated for a real-store environment was not normally required to be sharable between several processes. For compilers in a virtual-store environment, there is the additional consideration, however, of code sharability. There are two ways of sharing code in a virtual-store environment:

1 The code and data are at the same virtual addresses in several processes or virtual machines, as illustrated in Figure 16. The segment table entries for code would point to the same physical main store location, while the segment table entries for data would point to different instances (one per process) of the data.

2 The code and data are at different virtual addresses in different processes, as illustrated in Figure 17. The segment table entries for code would point to the same physical main store location, while the segment table entries for data would point to different instances (one per process or VM) of the data.

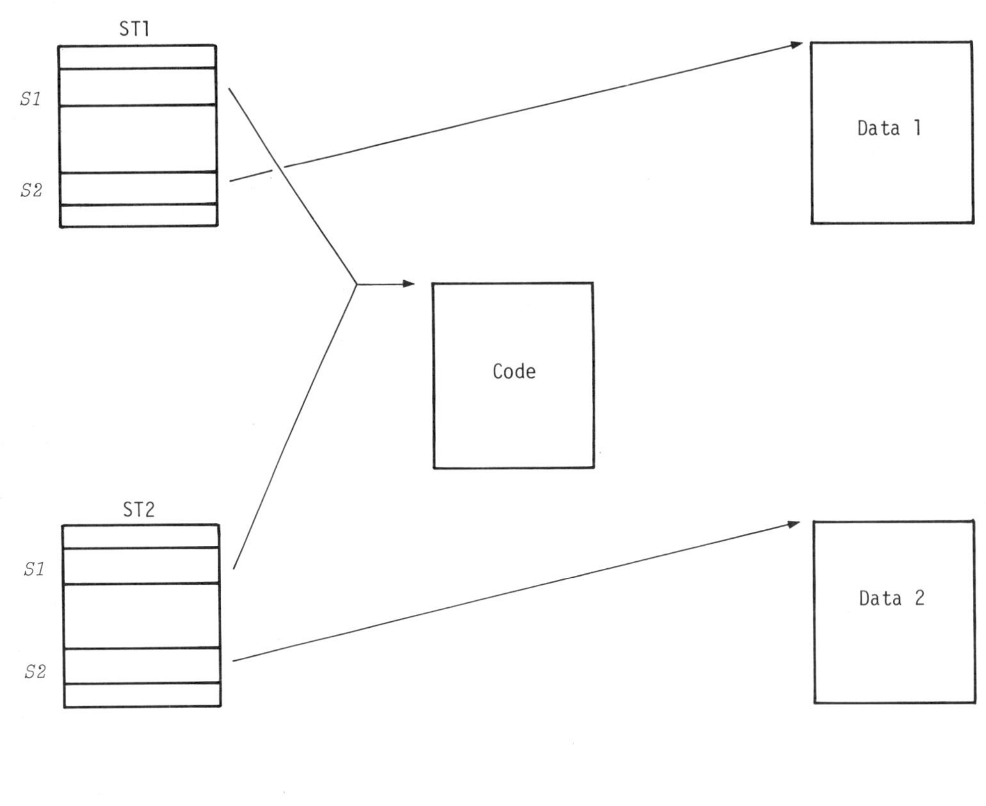

Figure 16: Common address sharing

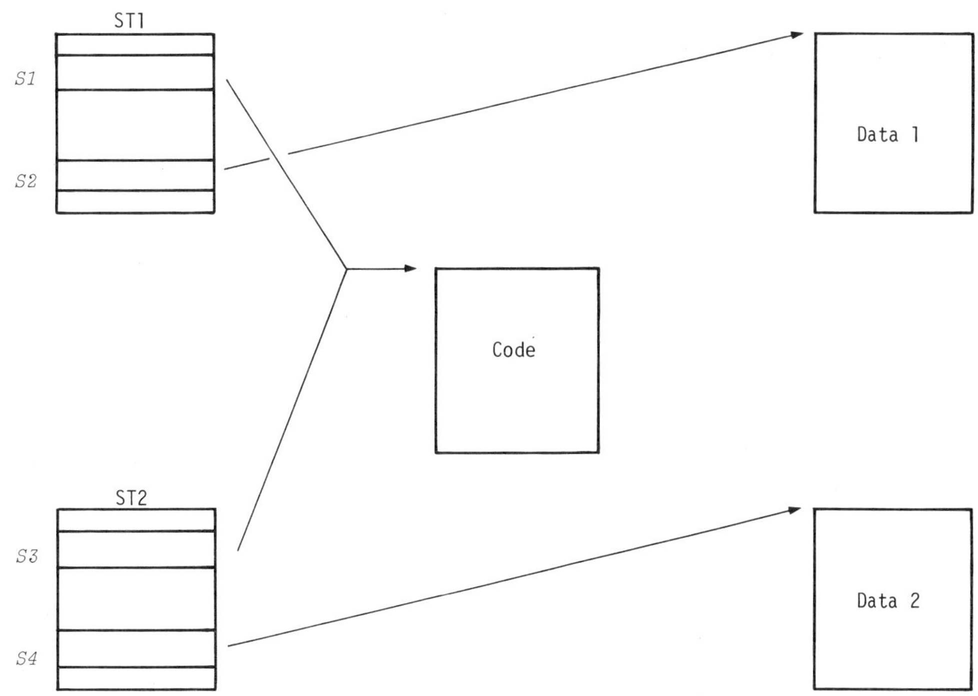

Figure 17: Unplanned sharing

Superficially, there is very little difference between the two methods, but for a compiler it makes an enormous difference. In the first case, there is no constraint on the compiler as to where it places address locations; either the code segment or the data segments will do. In the second case, there is a constraint on the compiler; it cannot place address locations in code.

Thus in the first case the code and the linkages are shared, whilst in the second case only the code is shared whilst there are multiple instances of linkages and data, as illustrated in Figure 18.

CONFLICT BETWEEN PROGRAM PERFORMANCE AND MAINTAINABILITY

Notice that the addresses pointing to data segments in the common address sharing scheme are scattered throughout the code segments. What is the impact of such a mapping produced by a compiler?

Development of large programs requires the ability to compile independently several modules that form the totality of the program. These compiled modules are then collected or consolidated together for subsequent loading and execution. When a bug is found, as is inevitable, in one of the modules, one is happy to recompile that module, but not the rest of the program. The mappings proposed in Figure 18 are adequate for that purpose. Similarly, one would be happy to recollect/reconsolidate the module that is recompiled, but not the totality of the program. The proposed mappings of Figure 18 are in that case not adequate for that purpose, because the recompilation will have changed the position of the entry points to code procedures.

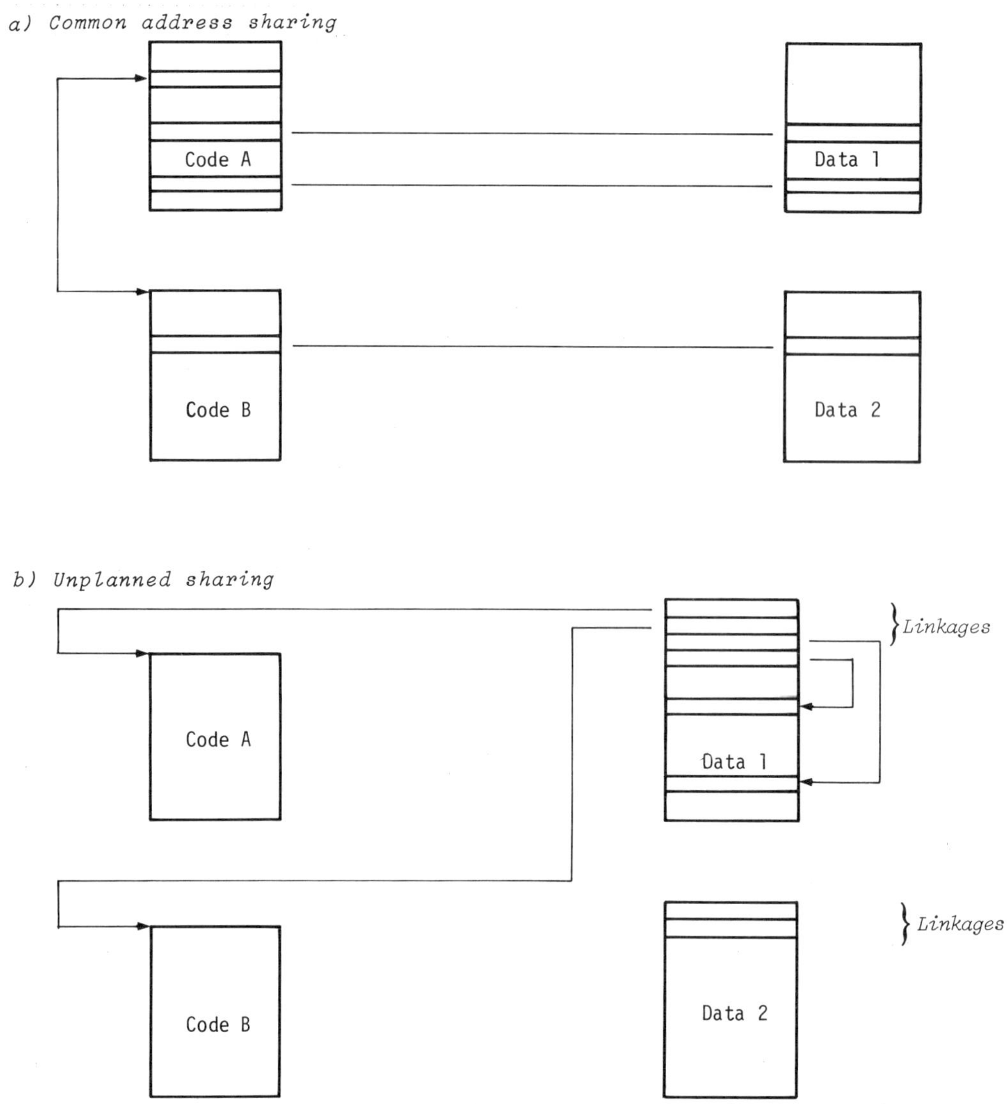

Figure 18: Compiler mappings

It would thus be necessary to recollect/reconsolidate the entire program, even though only one module has been changed.

The first change that is needed to the mapping, therefore is, that the various addresses in the code segment need to be grouped together rather than scattered throughout the segment. But the placement of the grouped linkages within the segment is significant; it cannot be placed at the end of the segment. That is because the recompilation of the segment will involve a change in the size of the code area, which will shift the position of the linkage table. Thus the grouped linkage table needs to be placed at the beginning of the segment in order to avoid changing its position on recompilation.

The second change that is necessary to the mappings is to transfer control only via the pointers in the linkage table at the beginning of the segment. This now ensures that when a module is recompiled and recollected, no other segment needs recompilation or recollection, most of the time. There are times when the interfaces between modules are changed, and in those cases it is necessary to recompile and recollect all the affected modules (see Figure 19).

Notice that one has traded off some of the program performance by using an extra level of indirection in order to achieve a greater degree of maintainability. Such trade-offs are necessary in view of the high costs of program development and maintenance.

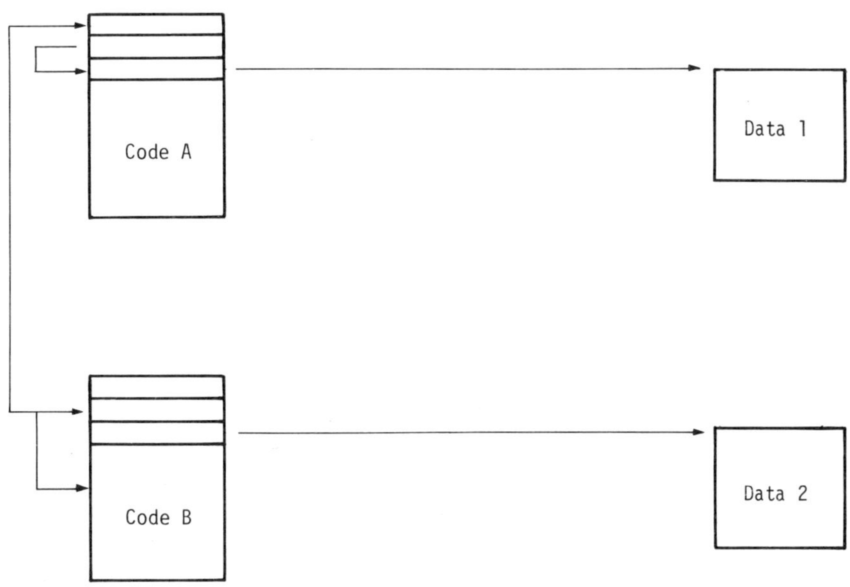

Figure 19: Common address sharing with independent compilation/collection

RECOMMENDATIONS

A site experiencing performance problems with its virtual store system does not have all the above variables to manipulate. It has a much more restricted choice. However, there are ways in which these problems can be minimized:

- Place virtual store on a disc volume with very little other traffic to other files on that volume.

- Place the disc drive on a channel carrying very little other traffic from other drives.

- If possible, place virtual store on a faster device such as a head-per-track disc or drum.

- Obtain VSI traces for programs that are executed often. Use the results of the traces to rearrange the programs in order to reduce the number of VSIs caused, or the amount of store required, or both, through the use of a utility such as a collector.

- If necessary, perform space/time trade-offs on the program. It is most important to remember, however, that these should be in terms of *real* store Q and *real* time E, and not in terms of *virtual* store.

EXPERIENCE IN PROGRAM AND SYSTEM OPTIMIZATION

I L Ramage

British Rail

I RAMAGE studied applied physics at Durham University, before going to work for Rolls-Royce Ltd as a computer programmer. His interests developed in the direction of System Software and he transferred to their Systems Programming Group. In 1970, Mr Ramage left Rolls-Royce to take up his present position of Head of Systems Programming at British Rail in Derby.

EXPERIENCE IN PROGRAM AND SYSTEM OPTIMIZATION

ABSTRACT

On first acquiring a IBM System/360 or 370, one is given a generalized operating system, which offers a very wide range of facilities but, because of this, it can have serious inefficiencies. This paper will cover the methods used to identify these problems, and the techniques employed to overcome them in an attempt to optimize throughput, both at the level of the user program and more extensively at the system software level.

At the user program level, problems are identified and specific software in the form of assembler inserts written either to speed up existing facilities or to offer new ones. For system software, the technique used is to find out how the system works and then design monitors to assess the performance and identify possible areas of improvement. If these improvements are feasible, and can be cost-justified, they are made and the monitors are then re-run to confirm that the expected benefit has been obtained.

The measuring tools used are described in some detail and compared with some of those commercially available and a guide is given to interpreting the output by considering a performance analysis case study.

INTRODUCTION

IBM operating systems offer essentially the same facilities for all machines from 360/30 or 370/135 to 360/195 or 370/168; covering a performance ratio of 36:1 and a possible real core size ratio of 125:1. This is a tremendous achievement and great credit is due to IBM for obtaining the success that they have, but there is undoubtedly still considerable scope for improvement. Because of the very general nature of the operating system, each installation will discover bottlenecks and inefficiencies peculiar to their own methods of working, but there are a number of these which will exist in all IBM systems and I intend to describe some of the methods we used at British Rail to identify and overcome the more serious hold-ups that we encountered.

The machine that I am considering is based at the Railway Technical Centre in Derby. It is used for research work primarily by engineers writing small programs to solve specific problems. In addition to this there are a few large packages that are run many times, including stress analysis and train simulation. About 90% of the work is written in FORTRAN and the remainder is written in PL/1 or assembler. The machine I shall be talking about is a 370/145 with 768K of storage and the operating system is VS/2, release 1.6. Also installed is the IBM Time Sharing Option (TSO). This services up to 12 terminals used by the engineers for interactive development of programs. The machine is very overloaded and both total throughput and terminal response time is always a problem. We are therefore very conscious of the need to improve performance both by encouraging the users to write efficient programs and to make the system function as fast as possible.

OPTIMIZATION AT THE USER PROGRAM LEVEL

Most programs are written in high-level languages because this is much easier for the average programmer to write and debug than basic assembly languages. They are, however, almost invariably less efficient but now, as machines are relatively much cheaper and people more expensive, if a program takes 10% longer to run or 10% more store, that is acceptable.

All high-level languages have several Achilles heels and if your program happens to make heavy use of these, a serious performance problem can arise. On many occasions, the problem can be by-passed by coding the program slightly differently, for example, one failing common to all high-level languages is the large execution time for arithmetic involving conversions between fixed and floating point. These can be avoided by careful programming. Other things may be not so easy to avoid, for example the somewhat fundamental act of input and output in FORTRAN is quite time-consuming. If one is reading or writing large amounts of data, firstly the obvious, unformatted I/O should be used in preference to formatted, but even this leaves much to be desired because of the manner in which this is performed (see Figure 1).

A block of data is read into the buffer and then moved to the program storage locations

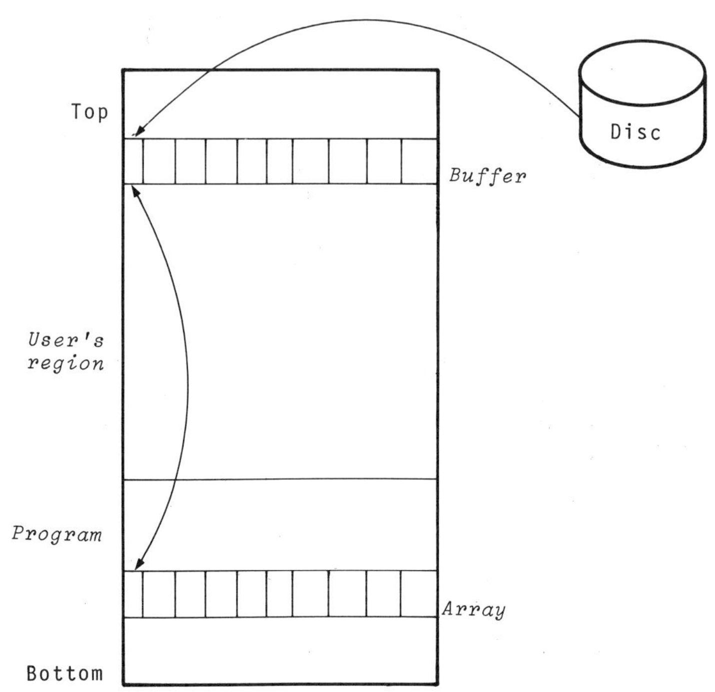

Figure 1: FORTRAN indirect I/O

element by element with a loop even if these areas are contiguous as, for example, with an array. A considerable performance improvement can be realized by providing routines which will read directly into the arrays without going through intermediate buffers. At the Railway Technical Centre, the first encounter with this was on a 360/44. This is a 'scientific machine' with its own programming system. We ran the normal OS/360 on it using an emulator to complete its instruction set. These emulated instructions are therefore very slow; for example, although the basic instructions take only about one or two microseconds, MOVE CHARACTERS takes about 250 microseconds and DIVIDE PACKED up to 1800 microseconds. The effect of this is that the normally high overhead of moving data about becomes intolerable and it was found that on introducing routines that would read the data directly into the storage areas, some programs had their CPU time reduced by as much as 80 to 90%. Even on other machines, the savings are considerable though not quite so dramatic.

Many users seek advice if they think their programs are taking too long to run and we find that the same mistakes occur again and again. Some of the common improvements are listed below:

1 The most frequent fault is, as already mentioned, the time-consuming FORTRAN I/O, which where possible is replaced by calls to this assembly routine. There are further improvements that can be made to I/O, such as putting larger block sizes on data sets or recoding the actual statements to use array reads and writes instead of subscripted transfers.

2 Mixed mode arithmetic was eliminated wherever possible.

3 Array subscript calculation was kept to the simplest possible, and single-dimension arrays were used in preference to multi-dimensional.

4 Excessive use of function subprograms was replaced by 'in-line' coding thus eliminating the overhead involved with invoking any subprogram.

5 Arithmetic IF statements were replaced by logical IF statements because they generate more efficient code.

6 Large numbers of named commons can restrict the optimization techniques of the compilers as it unnecessarily ties up base registers so these should be combined into as few as possible.

7 Unnecessary DO loops (for fixed counts of 2 or 3) were removed and written out in full.

There are also many other minor causes of inefficiency but these cover some of the most time-consuming ones that have been found so far.

Overlayed programs were other potential sources of poor performance. There can be marked differences, not only in elapsed time but also in CPU time, caused by poor overlay structure. A program has been developed to intercept all overlay branches and produce a report of which subprogram is being called and where the call has come from, both in chronological order of calls and sorted by frequency. Use of this tool has given considerable improvement to the run time of several programs.

Data set integrity is another area where there is scope for improvement as the in-built method bears a strong resemblance to sledge hammers cracking nuts. If a job requires to read a data set, it specifies DISP = SHR in its JCL and has shared use of the data set for the entire duration of the job. Any number of tasks may share one resource simultaneously, but if a job requires to write to a data set, it specifies DISP = OLD and is given exclusive control of the resource and no other program may use it for either reading or writing for the entire duration of the job.

This is far too drastic a protection as usually, a job is only updating a file for a small percentage of its total run time, and only needs exclusive control for this period. Furthermore, for partitioned data sets, there is no reason why jobs should not read the data set while another one is writing. This problem was tackled by providing an assembly insert which a program could call when it required exclusive use of a data set, and release it when it had finished. The use of this removes quite a few hold-ups and makes the job of scheduling the machine much easier.

There are many such assembly routines existing in our installation; for example, one offers BPAM support for FORTRAN and PL/1 and another offers dynamic variation of array sizes at execution time. These have been in use for some time and the Systems Group is always willing to offer advice or write specialized assembly routines to overcome any specific inadequacies or inefficiencies that we or the users may find.

VIRTUAL SYSTEMS AND THE USER PROGRAM

With the advent of virtual systems came a whole new 'code of good programming'. Many of the earlier points applicable to non-VS systems remain valid but there are also a few new ones to add to the list. The new system overheads introduced by virtual storage include:

1 *Dynamic address translation*
Dynamic address translation is a remarkably small overhead because of the efficient hardware implementation, in particular the Look Aside Buffer, which resolves the translation in a very high percentage of cases.

2 *Paging*
The overhead incurred by paging depends partly on the programmer to keep it at a minimum and partly on the scheduling, being careful not to over-commit the machine. In non-VS environments, the program needed to have enough main storage to accommodate the maximum required but in VS environments it needs only enough main storage to accommodate the working set of the program.

The working set is a somewhat nebulous quantity, but for our purposes, we will define it as the amount of main storage required to run the program with a paging rate of not more than 3 per second.

The programmer must make efforts to keep his working set to a minimum. Some of the things he can do are as follows:

- Avoid having too many I/O buffers or there is a good chance of their being paged out before they are used.

- Organize the program so that the program's usual path is sequential and if certain subroutines are used in only two or three places, repeat the coding in-line.

- Error or other exception routines should be kept out of the main line through the program with other little used subroutines and page-aligned at the end of the program.

- Associated routines should be grouped together on the same page.

- Overlays should, in general, be removed, although in one or two programs in our installation it was found that the unoverlayed versions actually took longer to run. This was because the very efficient overlay structure that had been generated was in fact reducing the paging in comparison with that of the unoverlayed version. This was certainly found to be the exception rather than the rule.

In general, one should aim to reduce paging wherever possible using whatever techniques may happen to be appropriate.

3 *CCW translation*
CCW translation is a very considerable overhead on I/O operations. This is one area where the VS implementation could be said to be done on the cheap. The channels have not been modified for VS operation and are therefore unable to deal with virtual addresses in CCWs, therefore the supervisor must convert these to a series of real CCWs in work space before starting the I/O operation. On average, this involves the execution of some 1500 extra instructions per data transfer over a non-VS system. Because of this, it is imperative to keep I/O down to a minimum.

Another method to improve performance is to reduce mistakes, and many mistakes arise in handling of card decks, both in their being incorrectly modified by the programmer and, occasionally, being dropped/shuffled by those who handle them. This is almost entirely eliminated in our installation by having a very comprehensive and easy-to-use source and load module library system, thereby keeping decks down to small dimensions and more immune from such errors.

The system used is described below.

Three communal libraries are set up for use by all or, in a very large installation, a group of programmers:

1 the source library, which is a partitioned data set holding the programs in card image format;

2 the test load library, which contains the programs in partially link-edited form for later inclusion and full link-editing to create an executable load module;

3 the production load library, which contains tested programs in fully link-edited form for immediate execution.

The *modus operandi* is that the programmer adds his programs to the source library, compiles them and partially link-edits them onto the test load module library. Then for testing, he includes the routines for a full link-edit onto a temporary data set for execution. Thereafter, he only submits the modifications to the source programs and these are merged with the original member, then compiled as before. Programmers are encouraged not to update the source library every time they do a run but to create a temporary version on work storage and compile it from there. This partially overcomes the biggest problem of partition data sets, that is, the need for frequent reorganization, and also, the programmer finds it easier as he is usually changing the same areas several times and it is simpler to do this when the original source has not been updated.

The update, compilation and link-edit for as many members as are required are all done as one step, thus eliminating the system overhead of scheduling each step individually. Furthermore, the link-editor is executed as a sub-task concurrently with the next update giving further performance improvements.

Apart from these basic functions, the system has many other facets to make life easier for the programmer, for example, Print, Punch, Scratch, Re-name, merging of several members into one or vice versa, automatic conversion from sequential to partitioned organization as required and vice versa, and many more.

Since the source library is partitioned, it is compatible with all the system-catalogued procedure libraries and therefore the same program can be used to update these also. This is very useful in that programmers only have to learn one method of library updating and this method is far superior to any of the standard methods. In particular, it will not destroy a partition data set directory if misused. Full data set integrity is maintained by the program using techniques compatible with the assembly routine already described.

SYSTEM TUNING

In the case of tuning user programs, the intention was to make individual jobs take considerably less time, but in system tuning, the aim is to make events that occur exceedingly often take a few seconds or even milliseconds less in an attempt to increase total throughput.

Over the life time of OS/360, a considerable amount of expertise has been gained by the System Programming fraternity in tweaking the system to the highest possible pitch. Some of the more significant areas are described in the following paragraphs.

Data set placement

Data set placement basically means adjusting the system libraries to suit one's hardware configuration. Most installations have only disks for direct access storage, drums and fixed-head disks being owned only by some of the largest systems. The first step in optimizing disk I/O is to spread the load as evenly as possible over as many devices as possible thus allowing the maximum degree of concurrency. Reading a record into core involves the disk in three distinct processes:

1 moving the head to the correct cylinder
2 waiting till the start of the record is opposite the heads
3 reading the record.

The first component, seek time, is approximately proportional to the number of cylinders moved. Therefore steps should be taken to locate frequently used data sets together in the centre of the disk. The arm will then tend to home on the centre and therefore have only up to half the disk to traverse in order to reach the periphery. The aim of the tuning is to achieve a usage curve like that shown in Figure 2.

Notice that the VTOC is not at the beginning of the disk but more towards the centre of the pack. It is placed far enough in so that data sets may balance around it.

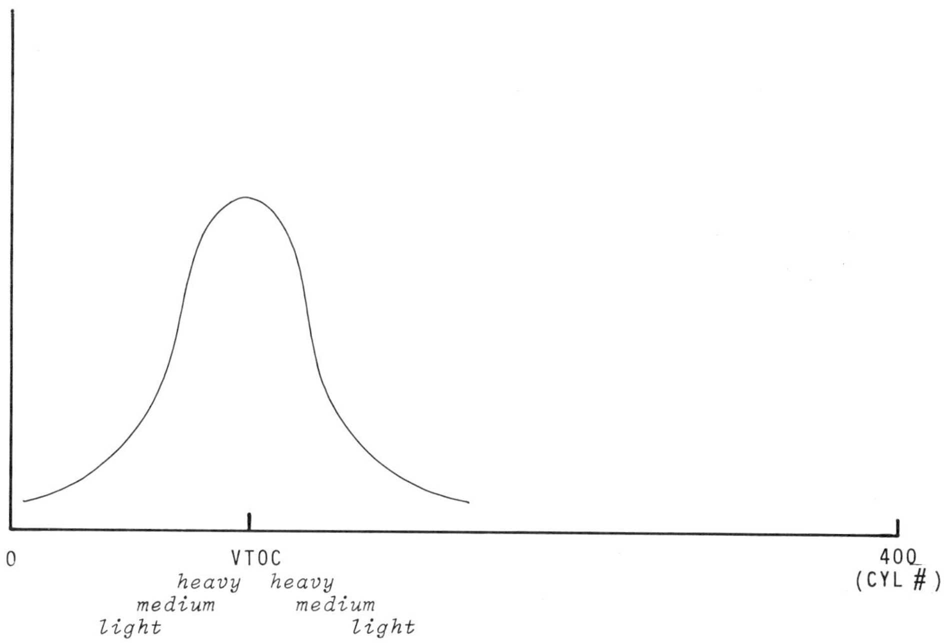

Figure 2: Disc usage graph

SVCLIB placement

In a standard OS system, there are two libraries that are used more than any other. The first of these is SVCLIB, which contains most of the system's transient modules and should definitely be given special consideration. It is a partitioned library containing about 1000 members of which typically 5 to 10 are used per second. The directory occupies about 7 tracks of a 3330 disk and the whole library about 5 cylinders. Of this library, about 240 members will make up over 97% of the activity and if these are put on the same cylinder of the library, this 97% can be resolved without moving the arm. In practical terms, the time taken for the rotational delay and reading the record is about 10 milliseconds. The time taken to move the head is about 10 ms + 0.1 ms per cylinder, so if the head has to move to a nearby cylinder, the data transfer takes twice as long as if it does not move – a clear saving. In practice, there is not room for the 240 members on the first cylinder because of the directory, but most of the members are addressed directly by disk address without reference to the directory. Therefore the solution is to identify these routines and put them on the second cylinder and those that require access to the directory in order to locate them are placed on the first cylinder. For those after the last ounce of efficiency from SVCLIB, the placement can be carried even further by considering the position on the track. Many of these routines are used in sequence with one transferring control to the next and if they are placed so that by the time one has finished processing, the next is just arriving at the read heads, the rotation delay can be almost eliminated!

The idea of ordering members within a library is not as simple as may first appear. The standard utility for copying libraries is IEBCOPY and upon reading the user's guide, one discovers that members can be selected for copy using SELECT cards. One may think it is only necessary to punch up these cards in the correct order, run the job, and then one has a library with everything in the desired order, but this is not so. The current version of IEBCOPY has been optimized for maximum speed and it functions by first reading all the SELECT cards, reading the old directory entries, sorting these into increasing track order to minimize arm movement and copies them. In other words, the output ends up in exactly the same order as the input! In our case this was circumvented by the monitor program described later. Having created a list in the desired order, it punches out a COPY card and then inspects the directory entry for each in turn. As long as the disk address increases, it punches out a SELECT card for each. When the address decreases, a new COPY card is produced before the next SELECT card. The effect of this is that the program copies the group between copy cards in its old order, which is now the desired order for the new library, and each copy is treated as a separate operation giving a final library in the correct order.

The JOB QUEUE library

The other most heavily used library is the JOB QUEUE. This is a data set of chained groups of records called logical tracks and when a job wishes to write to the JOB QUEUE, it first tries to fit the record into the most recent logical track; if there is no room, it gets one from the free queue and uses that. The first tuning step is to put it on a separate device to SVCLIB, the next is to select the right size for the logical track so that, on the one hand, it is large enough so that tracks are not being allocated too often, and on the other hand, it is not so large as to waste space. This is something that each installation must calculate from a knowledge of the characteristics of their own work. The second point, often overlooked, is to keep the size of the JOB QUEUE down to the minimum required because, as jobs finish, their tracks are added to the end of the free queue thus resulting in a chain going at random all over the data set. If the data set is kept as small as possible, the average seek distance and therefore the average access time is also minimized.

The LINKLIB library

The next most active library is LINKLIB and ideally this should be on yet another disk. The members contained therein should be placed in frequency of use as for SVCLIB. Although one cannot hope to localize the activity to only one or two cylinders, it can be kept within as small an area as is possible. Members that are used frequently can have their directory entries in core to obviate reference to the directory (resident BLDL list).

Reduction of system overhead in VS systems

The tuning covered so far is simply the shuffling of the standard system to accommodate the hardware limitations. The next aspect is to change the method of operation to minimize system overhead. One good way of doing this is to use dedicated work data sets. The sort of jobs run at the Railway Technical Centre are mainly short jobs allocating and scratching many small work files. By allocating some permanent files for them and using the initiated dedicated work files feature, the time for scheduling each step can be dramatically reduced.

With virtual systems, tuning is even more important. The ground rules still apply but some of the emphasis needs to be changed. Data set placement and disk load balancing are still relevant but now SVCLIB is a library of no consequence, being used extremely rarely, and LINKLIB is also used much less. The JOB QUEUE is heavily used, as before, but the largest area now is that used for paging. It is possible, and indeed essential, to split this area over several devices. One of these must be designated to the primary page data set and it holds the pageable link-pack area. This library contains all the transient modules that were previously loaded from SVCLIB and a large proportion of the more heavily used ones from LINKLIB. Thus it is an area of potentially very high activity. Fortunately, the working of VS is such that the most heavily used modules tend to remain in core for long periods, the actual content at any one time depending on the particular work the system is doing. Therefore one has the effect of a heuristic dynamically changing link-pack area. Because of this high activity, it is desirable to separate it from all other paging. There is no direct method of achieving this, so one has to resort to a subterfuge. When the system desires to page out, it writes to the page data set that has the maximum number of free page slots. Therefore, to use three-page data sets, if one makes the primary data set just large enough to hold the link-pack area, and the other two about the same size as each other, all paging activity other than PLPA will be equally distributed between the other two.

Apart from this general manipulation of the system, it is also possible to achieve considerable gains by actually changing the system code so that it functions differently and happens to be much more effective for one's own system. The biggest difficulty here is the identification of the areas where improvement will give most effect. Some of the typical examples of this follow:

1 When doing OPEN, CLOSE or EOV processing, the system does a series of transfer controls between strings of modules. They are supervisor-assisted linkages, which do the following processes.

   a) perform SVC interrupt handling
   b) obtain in new request block and initialize it
   c) scan the active queue for the required module (it is very seldom there)
   d) scan the link-pack area directory for the required module
   e) complete the request block
   f) issue an exit SVC
   g) remove the previous request block
   h) branch to the new module.

   A modification to the supervisor linkage has been done to eliminate steps a to c, f and g, thus giving a considerable saving, this saving being made 2.5 times per second on average.

2 The SVC routine associated with the accounting routine (SMF) was found to be about the tenth most frequently used module in the system. This was investigated and a considerable overhead was discovered. Statistics were being collected on which data sets were being used. Certain ones that were of no interest were being filtered out by a standard exit routine but by that time, most of the work involved in obtaining the data had been done. The result of this was that every time a file was closed, the following steps were executed:

   a) the normal route through CLOSE processing was diverted to include two further transfer controls to modules which constructed a record;

   b) the SMF was issued with all the resultant SVC overhead;

   c) this fired up the accounting routine task, which let the exit routine decide that in 95% of the cases, the record was not needed.

A modification was made by inserting code into the CLOSE routine to inspect the data set name and to decide if the record was required before starting any of the additional code. This also made considerable savings.

There are many such system modifications that one can make to improve performance and the biggest job is, as has already been said, finding them, and the performance tools described below can help in that respect.

SYSTEM MONITORING

Now I should like to turn to the system programmer's stock-in-trade, the monitor programs. There are many monitors about; some can be purchased from software houses; some are available free, but with strings attached, from IBM; and a very wide variety go from hand-to-hand between system programmers of different installations. These performance analysis tools fall into two broad groups:

1 those which monitor the execution of a specific program
2 those which monitor the system as a whole.

The monitors in the first category can help to pinpoint sections of the user program where improvement might be possible. The output is usually in the form of histograms showing the area of the program in which most time is spent, thus enabling the programmer to direct his efforts to those areas which will give greater improvement. Very real savings can be obtained using this technique. In general, it is not worth writing one's own program to do this as there are several available, for example PPE from Boole and Babbage or the Instruction Execution Analyser by Geoff Brown, which does these functions admirably and is, I believe, considerably cheaper.

The monitors in the second category enable one to tune the operating system. Basically, I do not think it is a good idea to buy system performance tools if one has the time and resources to develop one's own. The main reason is that one is never supplied with source code and this restricts all extensions to the monitor to be done only at the pleasure of the marketing body, and at a further price. With constantly developing software, new features are continually required to be monitored and, if one has the source, it may only be a few hours work to incorporate the required code, but if one has to return to the suppliers, the work may be done much later, or not at all. At any event, it is likely to be too late for the timescale required. After installing VS/2, new areas of potential system bottlenecks are constantly being unearthed as one learns more about the system, which makes the ease of modification to the monitor a very real advantage.

Another shortcoming of not having the source is that one does not know exactly what is being measured. An example of this is the fundamental measure of the percentage CPU utilization. There are at least four methods of measuring this when using a timer-driven sampling technique:

1 inspect the TIMER OPSW to see if the WAIT BIT was ON;

2 scan down the Request Blocks of all tasks to see if they have the WAIT BIT ON;

3 run a 'soak program' at low priority to count all CPU time left over after servicing the other tasks;

4 if TSO is active, inspect the driver status flags which state whether a time-sharing task, system task, batch task or WAIT task was last despatched.

All of these give slightly different results and one needs to know which method was being used. Similar comments can be made about some of the other entities measured.

Having collected the figures, there is then the problem of data reduction. This is usually where commercially obtained tools score heavily as they have various options producing many informative reports and lots of graphs giving instant pictorial representation of the system. Whereas the usual home-grown monitor produces a few simple tabulated listings. Probably the reason for this is that most system programmers enjoy writing monitors, but find the task of editing the data a somewhat mundane and tedious task and it therefore tends to be neglected. IBM are in a somewhat difficult position with regard to monitors as they are bound hand and foot by the anti-trust laws of America. Their monitors are available free, but not the source material. They may only be used in a 'marketing environment' by a systems engineer and all print-out produced is spirited away by the SE and he gives you, the customer, a written report of his conclusions. Fortunately, most SEs follow the spirit of the law rather than the letter and therefore considerable benefits can be obtained using the IBM monitors.

Undoubtedly the best results are obtained from one's own tools and, at British Rail, we have developed a powerful monitor which records more than any other single monitor and at considerably less overhead. The monitor is made up of two main areas:

1 a time-driven routine to collect statistics on many system activities and produce reports at regular intervals

2 several event-driven routines to collect information on such things as paging, module loading and disk activity.

The monitor runs virtual, to the best of my knowledge the only one to do so, and fixes only four pages (16K) in core. The overhead on the sampling is 1-1½% on a 370/145 and a similar quantity for the intercepts.

System monitoring is, in many ways, a very imprecise science with no hard and fast rules. The policy that we have adopted is:

1 Monitor the system regularly using our own tool.

2 When a particular problem arises, develop a special-purpose software tool which can be quickly made to work and get immediate results, then incorporate the new features at leisure into the main monitor.

One must be very careful when testing system monitors, as, when the data is obtained by interrupts in the supervisor, any program checks or mistakes in the monitor code are catastrophic. It is a good policy to do as much as possible with sampling, as this can usually be run 'enabled' and very seldom affects the integrity of the system. Such monitors can actually be developed and run in the foreground region of a TSO system.

The first problem is to identify what needs to be measured, and, if it needs to be done by means of intercepts, by far a greater problem is deciding on the correct location for these hooks to be placed.

Having then collected the figures and produced the reports, the next stage is the analysis of the results. One has to decide which of the figures represent bottlenecks in the system and how to use the data to decide what action may be taken. It is exceedingly difficult to give precise rules on how the results should be interpreted as this is largely a matter of experience with a particular system.

A SURVEY OF COMPILER OPTIMIZATION TECHNIQUES

P B Schneck

Goddard Institute of Space Studies

<u>*Note*</u>

A version of this paper first appeared in Proceedings of ACM Annual Conference, August 27-29, 1973, pp 106-113; copyright 1973, Association for Computing Machinery, Inc.

P B SCHNECK has been senior computer scientist on the research staff of the Goddard Institute for Space Studies, NASA, in New York for the last four years. His primary interests are in operating systems and compilers; he is currently examining optimization and parallel compilation techniques, and was previously responsible for the design of a specialized operating system for NASA/Goddard's 360/95 – 370/165 computer complex. Prior to joining NASA, Mr Schneck worked as Manager of Systems Programming for Computer Applications Inc., a New York Software firm; he subsequently joined Programming Methods as Manager of Systems Programming. Mr Schneck has written a number of technical articles and has also presented papers at several ACM National Conferences. Mr Schneck received his BS and MS degrees from Columbia University in the field of Engineering Mathematics; he is currently a PhD candidate at New York University in Computer Science.

A SURVEY OF COMPILER OPTIMIZATION TECHNIQUES

ABSTRACT

The major optimization techniques of compilers are discussed, and grouped into three categories: machine-dependent, architecture-dependent and architecture-independent. Machine-dependent optimizations tend to be local and are performed upon short spans of generated code, making use of particular properties of an instruction set to reduce the time or space required by a program. Architecture-dependent optimizations are global and are performed while generating code, taking into account the structure, though not the detailed instruction set, of a computer. Architecture-independent optimizations are global in nature. They are based on analysis of the program flow graph and the dependencies among statements of the source program. Recent advances in optimization are discussed.

The concept of a universal optimizer, performing architecture-independent optimizations at the source code level, is reviewed.

INTRODUCTION

Most computer systems support a multiplicity of programming languages. For a particular language, the translators or compilers often exist in three versions. First, there is the small and fast compiler intended for program development, which has extensive diagnostics and debugging aids. Second, a re-entrant conversational compiler with comprehensive editing facilities is used for on-line development of programs. Finally, a third compiler, the optimizing compiler, larger and slower than the others, is used for translating production programs into efficient object code. In this paper, we examine the techniques employed in optimizing compilers and make some quantitative comparisons between programs produced by them and by other compilers. The FORTRAN language has received the greatest amount of attention because it is the most widely used production programming language. Consequently, a large number of the references given concern FORTRAN.

The history of optimizing compilers dates back at least as far as FORTRAN I (221). At that time most programming was done in machine language and a compiler which offered convenience at the expense of machine time would not have been acceptable. The following quotation from the IBM specification reveals that the convenience of the new language was believed insufficient to cause its widespread acceptance.

> "...FORTRAN may apply complex, lengthy techniques in coding a problem which the human coder would have neither the time nor inclination to derive or apply. Thus, in many cases, FORTRAN may actually produce a better program than the

normal human coder would be apt to produce."

Even in that very first FORTRAN compiler, 25% of the instructions were for optimization.

OPTIMIZATION TECHNIQUES

The following three sections describe various optimization techniques which have been used in compilers or have been suggested. As yet, very little has been done to classify optimizations; they are grouped here by function.

Compiler optimization techniques operate on three levels: machine-dependent, architecture-dependent, and architecture-independent. *Machine-dependent* is used to describe the instruction-level sensitivities of a compiler. *Architecture-dependent* denotes those parts of a program which relate to the general hardware implementation but not to a specific machine. *Architecture-independent* is used in lieu of the more familiar phrase 'machine-independent' to indicate those aspects of program formulation which do not depend on a particular computer system, or even on a type of implementation (for example, pipe-line processing). Optimizations originating in the academic and scientific community tend to be global, while until recently manufacturers have concentrated on local and machine-dependent techniques.

Machine-dependent optimization

One of the earliest references on compilation techniques concerns PACT (The Project for the Advancement of Coding Techniques), an experimental compiler. The target machine was the IBM 701, and the PACT Compiler described by Miller and Oldfield (222), produced code sensitive to the register placement curiosities of that machine. No formal techniques were employed, rather a set of rules was coded in tabular form to control code generation. To a large extent this same technique is applicable today for machine-dependent code optimization. The FORTRAN I compiler contained a sophisticated arithmetic translator, by Sheridan (223), which performed association and commutation in order to take advantage of the AC/MQ relationship on the IBM 704. For example, a string of multiplications and divisions was reordered to minimize the number of register transfers ('exchanges') that had to be performed. McKeeman (224) proposes a post-processing technique for optimization. One may consider a window traversing the sequence of generated (unoptimized) code. If the instructions visible in the window match one of a number of patterns, then the code is transformed. In this manner, redundant stores, multiplications by two, and register transfers can easily be optimized. Bagwell (225) describes a set of clever coding tricks (special cases) which may be implemented for almost any machine. This is essentially McKeeman's approach, though performed during code generation. We stop at this point, having cited the most descriptive techniques.

Architecture-dependent optimization

Three optimization techniques are classified here as architecture dependent. These techniques are used for machines having the following general characteristics:

1 the computer has n accumulators;

2 the computer can execute several independent instructions in parallel;

3 the computer executes arithmetic and logical instructions upon multiple data streams.

The evolution of computer architecture has followed a path from the single-accumulator IBM 704 to the multi-accumulator CDC 6600, capable of executing several instructions in parallel, to the ILLIAC-IV which operates on up to 64 data items simultaneously. There has been a parallel evolution in optimization techniques.

The n-accumulator computer

Straightforward code generation of expressions involving non-commutative operations poses a special difficulty for a one-accumulator computer. In an expression such as $(a+b)/(c-d)$, the denominator should be computed first so that it is available for division when the numerator is computed and is in the accumulator. Anderson (226) discusses a technique which implements this procedure and does away with the need for storing and recovering the values of many subexpressions. This is accomplished by looking ahead and delaying code generation for the left side expression of a non-commutative operator until code generation for the right side occurs. On a multi-accumulator machine the technique is also valuable because it decreases the number of registers required to evaluate an expression.

Nakata (227) has extended the procedure to handle n accumulators. The procedure is enhanced by the fact that some heuristic observations are included to make the output similar to ordinary coding practices. The programming problem of using a minimum number of accumulators is equivalent to a graph-theoretic tree transformation proposed by Redziejowski (228). An algorithm for performing the tree transformation is proposed, proved, and shown to be equivalent to that of Nakata. An investigation into the properties of tree-structure representations of arithmetic expressions by Schneider (229) yields the number of registers required. In particular, for k nested parenthetical subexpressions with n operator precedence levels, $(k+1)\ n+1$ registers are required.

Finkelstein (230) describes a technique, aptly named 'deferred store', which eliminates much unnecessary storing and loading of partial results within loops on multiple-register machines ('register' is used here to indicate either an accumulator or index register). When an assignment statement is executed, the accumulator is not actually stored in the result variable. Instead, other registers are use in place of those containing data for deferred stores. If a result variable is to be modified before the deferred store has been performed, the value of the variable is in place and need not be fetched. The following example indicates a common situation where the deferred store saves a significant amount of time:

$$\sum_{i=1}^{n} a_i$$

```
      DO 1  I = 1,N
    1 SUM = SUM + A(I)
```

A special case of the n-accumulator machine is one where the accumulator is the top element of a push-down stack. The Burroughs 5000 and English Electric KDF9 are examples of such a machine. Randell and Russell (231) describe a one-pass procedure for translation of arithmetic expressions into Reverse Polish form suitable for a stack machine. An interesting point is their architecture-independent optimization of calculating a constant during compilation when both operands are constants. Generalizations of this technique are discussed in the next section.

Parallel instruction execution

The CDC 6600 computer was the first commercially available machine able to overlap the execution of several instructions. This class of computer, capable of parallel instruction execution, has independent functional units which are able to operate simultaneously. The programmer (or compiler) need not be explicitly aware of the parallel execution capability. It will be used when possible. However, if the instructions are ordered to maximize parallel execution, a performance advantage of up to a factor of three can be obtained. Allard, Wolf and Zemlin (232) describe the parallel capabilities of the 6600 and briefly mention the speed advantage gained by reordering instructions. Thorlin (233) describes the technique used in CDC FORTRAN, based on a PERT-like analysis of dependency and timing for ordering 6600 instructions. The independent functional units of the machine are kept busy by placing unrelated instructions together and by sequencing the longest activities first. A similar instruction scheduling technique was implemented by Blum *et al* (234) in the IBM FORTRAN-H compiler. A dependency array is constructed which defines the area within which each instruction may be moved. A weight is assigned to each instruction by adding a base weight (a function of the instruction time) and the weight of every instruction which is dependent on it. Instructions are then ordered by decreasing weight.

The improvement attainable by instruction reordering is limited by a parallelism inherent in the original instruction sequence. Stone (235) summarized techniques which may be used to translate arithmetic expressions to achieve a high degree of inherent parallelism. The process corresponds to a tree structure with minimal height. This is the opposite result from that of the previous section where minimizing the number of registers increased the tree height. Figure 1 shows two different trees for evaluating the expression

A*B*C*D*E*F*G*H.

The first tree employs only one register for evaluating the expression, while the second results in the minimum evaluation time on a machine with at least four simultaneous multipliers. Because of the effects of data store/load instructions, this tree may not result in minimum time on machines with fewer multipliers. Figure 2 shows two different sets of instructions for evaluating the expression corresponding to the two trees, and resulting in serial and parallel execution.

The general problem of minimizing the tree height of a set of expressions has been examined by Han (236). He describes a procedure for determining the minimum tree height of an expression. This can be used by a compiler as a measure of the degree of parallelism that can be obtained in a program. A method for attaining the maximum amount of parallel execution on a machine with a fixed number of processing units is given by Ramamoorthy and Gonzalez (237). They present a method for ordering subexpressions which indicates those expressions to be delayed in the event that not enough processing units are available to perform all computations in parallel.

Multiple data streams

The previous section discussed some techniques relevant to computers whose architecture permitted parallel execution of instructions while maintaining the standard instruction set. This section concerns the techniques applicable to computers where the instruction set reflects the computer's capacity to perform a single instruction on many data items. Two computers, the CDC STAR and the Burroughs ILLIAC-IV are both in this category. The STAR is a pipeline computer, processing operands sequentially

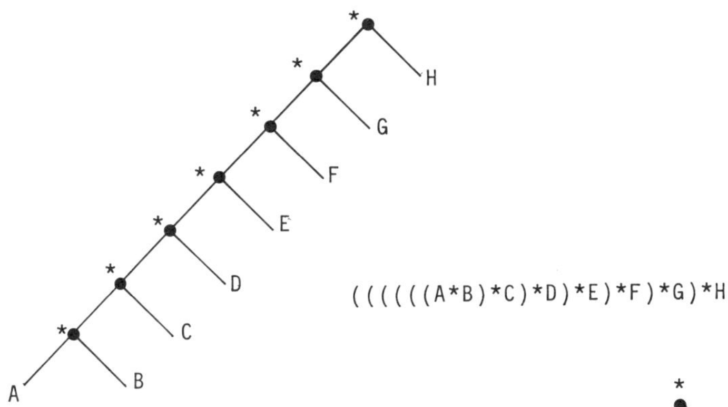

a) Tree yielding minimum number of registers

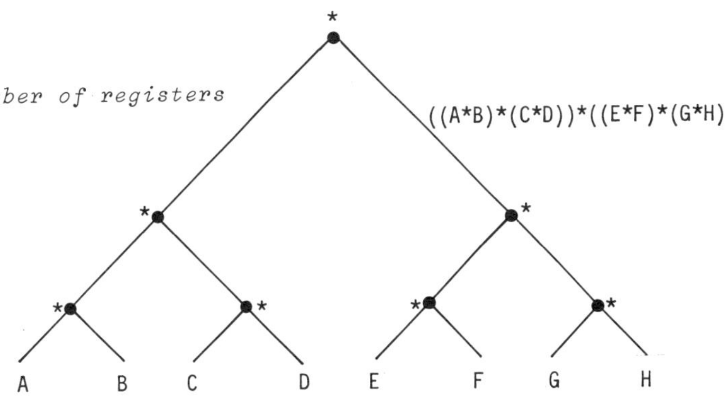

b) Tree yielding maximum inherent parallelism

Figure 1: Tree structures for serial and parallel computation of an expression

```
1L   1,A
2*   1,B
3*   1,C
4*   1,D
5*   1,E
6*   1,F
7*   1,G
8*   1,H
```

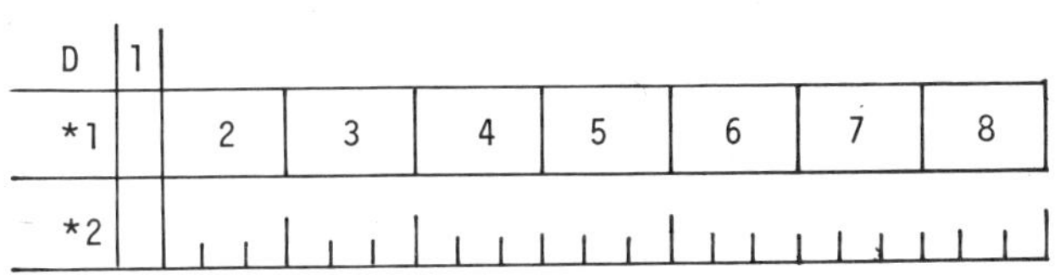

a) Serial execution, time = 22 cycles

```
1L   1,A
2*   1,B
3L   2,C
4*   2,D
5*   1,2
6L   2,E
7*   2,F
8ST  1,T
9L   1,G
10*  1,H
11*  2,T
12*  1,2
```

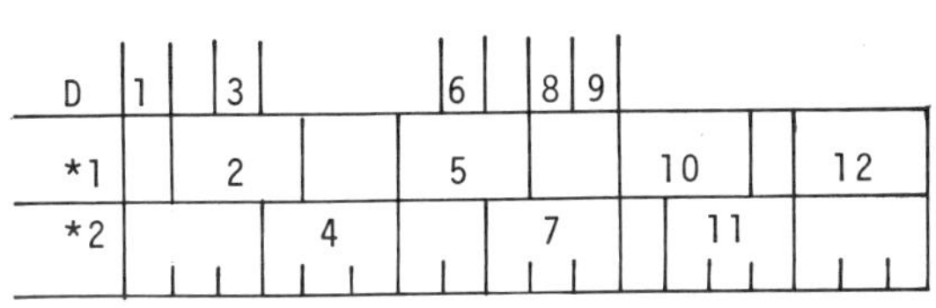

b) Parallel execution, time = 18 cycles

Figure 2: Resource use in serial and parallel computation of an expression

but with a high degree of overlap. The ILLIAC is a parallel computer, processing up to 64 operands simultaneously. The instruction sets of the two machines bear remarkable similarity, and high-level language programs must be designed from the same viewpoint for either machine.

Burkhardt (238) describes some occurrences of inherent parallelism in programs written in a procedural language. He points out that parallelism may occur from the arithmetic expression level, through independent iterations of a loop, up to parallel task execution within an operating system environment. Millstein (239) reports on the design of a FORTRAN compiler for ILLIAC IV. The compiler will detect parallelism in the use of subscripted variables in DO-loops. The 3-step procedure first determines data dependencies, and if there are more between loop iterations, examines flow within the loop and determines an expression ordering. The first two steps are analysed by graph-theoretic techniques, the last by *ad hoc* methods. A later report by Lamport and Presberg (240) gives a detailed description of the algorithms and techniques used to permit parallel execution of DO-loops.

Schneck (241) has developed a simplified algorithm for the detection of parallelism in standard FORTRAN programs. The concept of 'feedback' which prevents parallel execution, is defined. Testing for feedback involves a flow analysis of the source program and a search for subscript forms which cause feedback. In the absence of feedback, statements are rewritten to indicate parallel execution. Additionally, scalar variables which might bar parallel execution are expanded to vectors. Thus,

```
          DO   1 I = 1, 20
          A = (B(I) + B(I+1))*.5
          C(I) = C(I) + A
    1     D(I) = D(I) - A
```

may be performed entirely in parallel.

Kuck, Muraoka and Chen (242) have performed a similar analysis. Their orientation was to define a machine architecture which would be of value in processing 'ordinary' programs. They conclude that even for simple programs a multiple-processor organization consisting of 16 processors is of value.

The deliveries of commercial vector processor computers in 1974, the Texas Instruments ASC (Advanced Scientific Computer) and the Control Data STAR (String and Array Processor), have resulted in intense interest in practical use and effectiveness of these systems. Cohagan (267) continues the development of techniques to detect and generate vector operations from standard FORTRAN code. The ASC compiler implements these techniques and is able to discover virtually all code which may be processed by vector instructions. The compiler must consider not only the vector architecture, but also the fact that 1, 2, or 4 processors (pipelines) may be available on a system. Treatment of multiple pipelines is similar to the treatment of parallel instruction execution discussed earlier. Wedel (268) describes the organization of the ASC compiler and gives results obtained from it. The STAR is supported by extensions to FORTRAN which permit simple expression and handling of vector operations as described by Zwakenberg (269).

Architecture-independent optimization

Optimization techniques which are categorized as architecture-independent are global in nature and perform a flow analysis upon the source program in order to obtain necessary information. A summary of the major architecture-independent optimizations follows and is illustrated in Figure 3:

- The most widely applied optimization is *common sub-expression elimination*. When a calculation is performed, a search is made to determine if the calculation was performed previously and need not be repeated. If so, the prior result replaces the calculation.

- *Dead variable elimination* removes statements which assign values to variables that are not used in the program. This most frequently results from program modification, but may also be due to common sub-expression elimination.

- *Code motion* refers to the rearrangement of expressions permitting a calculation to occur in a low-frequency program segment and to be available for use in a high-frequency segment.

- *Constant propagation*, removes calculations containing only known constants from the program and performs them in the compiler. This is certainly code motion to a low-frequency segment.

Sample program:

```
    A=B+C
    Y=Y+1
    Z=C
    Q=(Z+B)*SIN(.7854)
    DO 1 I=1,100
1   P(I)=P(I)*(A+B)
```

Optimized program:

```
    A=B+C
    (1)
    (2)
    Q=A*.7071   (3)  (4)
    T00001=A+B  (5)
    DO 1 I=1,100
1   P(I)=P(I)*T00001
```

1 Elimination of dead variable
2 Elimination of dead variable, caused by 3
3 Common sub-expression elimination
4 Constant propagation
5 Code motion

Figure 3: Architecture-independent optimizations

Frequency analysis

The original FORTRAN compiler (243) contained an optimizer which gathered information on the source program's structure as described below. The source program was analysed and broken down into a set of basic blocks*, and a table listing the predecessors of each basic block was created. This table was then used in a Monte Carlo simulation, to find the relative frequency of execution of each basic block. A random number generator, augmented by programmer estimates supplied in FREQUENCY statements**, was used to traverse paths in the program flow graphs, and a count was kept for each basic block. Figure 4 shows a program flow graph used as an example throughout this section and Figure 5 the relative frequencies, obtained by simulation. Blocks were then optimized in order, from highest to lowest frequency. The target computer, an IBM 704, had only three index registers and much of the compiler's

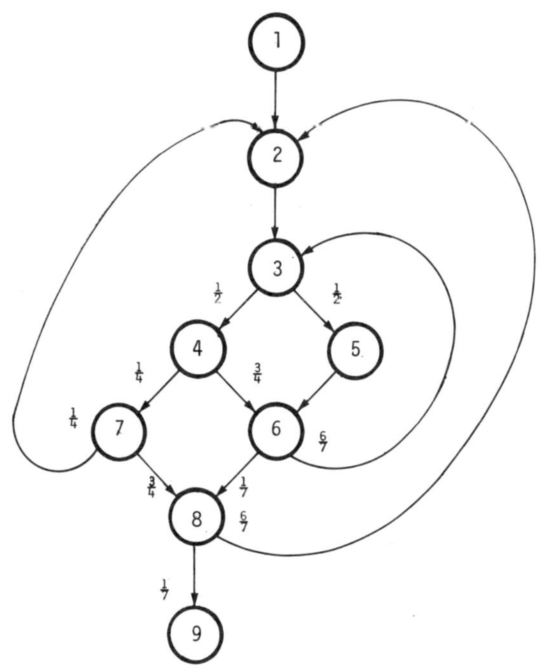

Figure 4: Program flow graph with branch probabilities

optimization centred on assigning them efficiently in the most frequently executed blocks of the program. Code generation was performed for a machine assumed to have as many index registers as required. The optimizer then assigned the 704's three index registers efficiently within the highest frequency block of the program, interpolating instructions to save and restore index register values when necessary. As other blocks were processed, index register assignments were made to match those of 'adjacent' (immediate predecessor or successor) higher-frequency blocks. When no

---

* *A basic block is the fundamental program flow unit; it is a segment of code with only one entry and one exit point.*

** *According to John Cocke, the FREQUENCY statement was removed from the language after it was discovered to have been incorrectly implemented, causing frequencies to be assigned inversely, without any user reaction.*

Block	*Relative frequency*
1	1.0
2	8.2
3	33.0
4	16.5
5	16.5
6	28.9
7	4.1
8	7.1
9	1.0

Figure 5: Relative frequencies obtained by simulation

adjacent blocks had already been processed, no matching of index registers was necessary. When just one adjacent block had already been processed, it was only necessary to choose a matching permutation of the index registers. If two or more adjacent blocks had already been processed it might not be possible to match all index registers. It then became necessary to add instructions to load index registers with the values required by adjacent blocks. The progression of processing from high-frequency to low-frequency blocks caused the added instructions to be located in the later, low-frequency blocks.

Horwitz (244) described a graph-theoretic procedure for index register allocation. An optimal index register allocation may be obtained for straight-line (loop-free) programs. The algorithm described is a practical procedure for carrying out the highly combinatoric assignment process similar to that employed by FORTRAN I. Luccio (245) provides a further reduction of the enumeration required to arrive at an optimal allocation. The program graph is partitioned, and the allocation problem may be solved separately for each subgraph and then combined.

An alternate, linear programming approach for assignment of registers is given by Day (246). He demonstrates an optimal algorithm and gives two others which provide good approximations but are fast enough for use in a compiler.

Matrix analysis

Prosser (247) described a Boolean matrix approach to flow graph analysis which made it possible to avoid the lengthy Monte Carlo techniques used in FORTRAN I. The predecessor information obtained by analysis of the program is used to construct a 'connection' matrix, shown in Figure 6. The connection matrix C has a 1 at C_{ij} if and only if program block j is a direct successor of program block i. By repeated matrix multiplication, the connection matrix may be used to determine the sets of blocks participating in loops. Prosser also introduces the 'dominance' relation to indicate that a particular block (dominator) must be traversed before another block (dominee) can be reached. This construct is extremely valuable, for when a calculation is moved out of a block it must be moved to a dominator block, to assure that it will be performed. These matrix operations yield valuable, if lengthy, methods for obtaining program flow information. Warshall (248) described a simplification of multiplication of $n \times n$ Boolean matrices which reduced the time required from $O(n^3)$ to $O(n^2)$, making matrix techniques practical.

Ramamoorthy (249) gives some general results on what may be obtained from the connectivity matrix of a program flow graph. In particular he presents algorithms which identify inessential nodes, enumerate maximal strongly connected regions (that is, loops) and partitions the flow graph into disjoint subgraphs. These matrix manipulations are all basic in obtaining the information required for program optimization. Inessential nodes may be discarded from a program, because they will never be executed. The identification of maximal strongly connected regions permits locating relative constant expressions and moving them to lower frequency regions, as well as indicating on which blocks the optimization process should concentrate. Partitioning the flow graph into disjoint subgraphs permits working with smaller units

		Successor block								
		1	*2*	*3*	*4*	*5*	*6*	*7*	*8*	*9*
Predecessor block	*1*	0	1	0	0	0	0	0	0	0
	2	0	0	1	0	0	0	0	0	0
	3	0	0	0	1	1	0	0	0	0
	4	0	0	0	0	0	1	1	0	0
	5	0	0	0	0	0	1	0	0	0
	6	0	0	1	0	0	0	0	1	0
	7	1	0	0	0	0	0	0	1	0
	8	1	0	0	0	0	0	0	0	1
	9	0	0	0	0	0	0	0	0	0

Figure 6: Boolean connection matrix C

at a time, resulting in a significant decrease in the combinatoric efforts expended in optimization.

Matrix methods for the analysis of a program's flow graph were used by Allen (250) in a FORTRAN optimizer. The connection matrix is used to obtain a set of 'strongly connected regions' (that is, loops) which the optimizer processes from the inside out. Within a basic block, redundant expressions are eliminated and evaluated only once. Constant propagation is performed and expressions are replaced by their computed values. Within a loop, invariant instructions are moved out, strength reduction is performed and tests are simplified. Unused definitions and computations are eliminated where the flow information indicates this is possible. The procedures to effect these optimizations take advantage of the bit parallel operations found in most machines, and perform logical operations, a word at a time. The article is extremely comprehensive and shows the details involved in applying each of the techniques listed.

Following Allen's optimization techniques, Kleir and Ramamoorthy (251) describe optimization procedures for microprograms, which may be viewed simply as another source language, requiring translation to machine language. The connectivity matrix is used to find strongly connected regions which are processed innermost to outermost, and code motion is performed to decrease instruction execution frequency. Within a basic block, common sub-expression elimination and dead variable elimination (referred to by the authors as redundant actions and negated actions) is performed.

Gries (252) devotes an entire chapter to discussion of code optimization techniques. He discusses optimization at three levels: within a basic block, within a loop, and globally. The global optimization techniques are patterned after Allen.

In FORTRAN I, subscript calculations were performed at any definition of a variable used in the subscript, leading to inefficient code when many definitions occurred with few uses. Most other compilers simply recomputed a subscript for each use, or kept track of local multiple uses of a subscript (for example, within an assignment statement). The problem of determining where a common subscript (or any common expression) may be computed with minimum frequency in order to be available when required, was considered by Ryan (253). The algorithm may be used with a multipass compiler and permits locating computations within a lower-frequency region at a distance from the point of use.

In the 1960s, the advent of new hardware brought a new class of compilers and optimization techniques. In an IBM Technical report, Medlock and Lowry (254) describe the optimization techniques which are the foundation of the IBM FORTRAN H compiler.

The dominance relationship introduced by Prosser is extended. In addition, a new defining relationship makes it possible to replace the dominance array with four vectors and reduce the space required. Frequency information is obtained by inverting the probabilistic connection matrix p, where p_{ij} indicates the probability that program block j will succeed block i. Figure 7 shows the probability connection matrix for the example flow chart, and its inverse. Row one of the inverse indicates frequency relative to block one.

Determination of relative frequencies again permits ordering the processing of blocks, from highest to lowest frequency. Within that order, common sub-expressions may be eliminated and expressions may be moved from a high-frequency to a low-frequency block. The dominator relations are used to ensure availability of an expression when needed. When profitable, strength reduction will be performed, with initialization

P — Successor block (columns), Predecessor block (rows)

	1	2	3	4	5	6	7	8	9
1	0	1	0	0	0	0	0	0	0
2	0	0	1	0	0	0	0	0	0
3	0	0	0	1/2	1/2	0	0	0	0
4	0	0	0	0	0	3/4	1/4	0	0
5	0	0	0	0	0	1	0	0	0
6	0	0	6/7	0	0	0	0	1/7	0
7	1/4	0	0	0	0	0	0	3/4	0
8	6/7	0	0	0	0	0	0	0	1/7
9	0	0	0	0	0	0	0	0	0

$(I-P)^{-1}$ — Successor block (columns), Predecessor block (rows)

	1	2	3	4	5	6	7	8	9
1	0.00	8.00	32.00	16.00	16.00	28.00	4.00	7.00	1.00
2	0.00	7.00	32.00	16.00	16.00	28.00	4.00	7.00	1.00
3	0.00	7.00	31.00	16.00	16.00	28.00	4.00	7.00	1.00
4	0.00	7.02	30.65	15.33	15.33	27.57	4.08	7.00	1.00
5	0.00	6.98	31.35	15.67	15.67	28.43	3.92	7.00	1.00
6	0.00	6.98	31.35	15.67	15.67	27.43	3.82	7.00	1.00
7	0.00	7.14	28.57	14.29	14.29	25.00	3.57	7.00	1.00
8	0.00	6.86	27.43	13.71	13.71	24.00	3.43	6.00	1.00
9	0.00	0.00	0.00	0.00	0.00	0.00	0.00	0.00	0.00

Figure 7: Probability connection matrix P and its inverse

instructions placed in a dominator block. Subsumption, or substituting one variable for another if they are equal at each reference, minimizes the number of simple replacement operations in a program. The FORTRAN H production compiler is again described by Lowry and Medlock (255). Information on the compiler's implementation is given, and several additional optimizations are suggested. An interesting point about the compiler is that it is written primarily in FORTRAN. First run on the IBM 7094, the compiler was used to create a new version of itself for the IBM 360. When the optimizer had been tested, it was used to translate the compiler, resulting in a decrease in size of 25% and a decrease in compilation time of 35%. To achieve a reasonable processing speed the compiler uses bit-vectors which can be processed by the bit-parallel logical instructions available on the System 360. Additional techniques concerned with register assignment and code generation are discussed later.

Graph-theoretic analysis

The UNIVAC 1100 series employs a three-pass optimizing compiler (256). The first pass encodes all operations into a uniform tabular format. In order to achieve maximum recognition of common sub-expressions, redundant information may be added to the table. Flow information is maintained in a list containing all statement numbers and references. The second pass scans the code in reverse order and performs common sub-expression elimination and movement of loop-invariant computations. The compute point of each expression is determined and the expression evaluation moved to that (lower-frequency) point. In contrast, the IBM FORTRAN H compiler will successively move a computation out of each level loop until it can no longer be moved. The determination of an expression's compute point permits high-speed compilation because an expression need not be moved more than once. The second and third passes of the compiler are also concerned with register assignment and code generation, and are discussed later.

The ALPHA automatic programming system (257,258) for the M-20 computer in the USSR, produces object code in some cases nearly the equal of hand coding. The major architecture-independent optimizations performed include optimization of subscripts within **for** loops, and the elimination of redundant sub-expressions within a basic block.

A feature of the ALPHA compiler not found elsewhere is the attempt to minimize the number of locations occupied by data within a program. While many optimizations result in a decrease in the size of a program because fewer instructions are generated, ALPHA specifically minimizes the storage requirements for data and variables by permitting several variables to share a storage location if their uses do not interfere with one another. This is a generalization of subsumption, which coalesces two variables into one if they contain the same value whenever used.

Much of the work in the past two years has centred around the use of the Cocke-Allen interval analysis technique, first described by Cocke and Schwartz (259). This technique is based on the 'interval', a partially ordered set of basic blocks with the following properties:

1 an interval is a set function of a distinguished block called the head,

2 all blocks in an interval, except the head, have all their immediate predecessor blocks in the interval.

Intervals are easily and rapidly constructed, and readily identify inner loops, and a possible processing order within each loop. The ordering induced by the inverval construction is valuable because dominators always precede their dominees. Common sub-expression elimination is simplified in this context because the redundancy of a computation is indicated by its presence in a dominator block. The interval construction process may be iterated, treating intervals as basic blocks and higher-order loops will then be identified. Most program graphs will be reduced to a single node by repetition of this procedure. Those few program graphs which are not reducible may be transformed into reducible graphs by the process of 'node splitting' after Cocke and Miller (260). Figure 8 shows the intervals obtained from the example flowchart and how they may be used to compute relative frequencies. In the proceedings of ACM SIGPLAN'S Symposium on Compiler Optimization, Allen (261) indicates that over 90% of the program graphs subject to analysis were reducible. Algorithms are given which determine the back dominator of each node in an interval, the

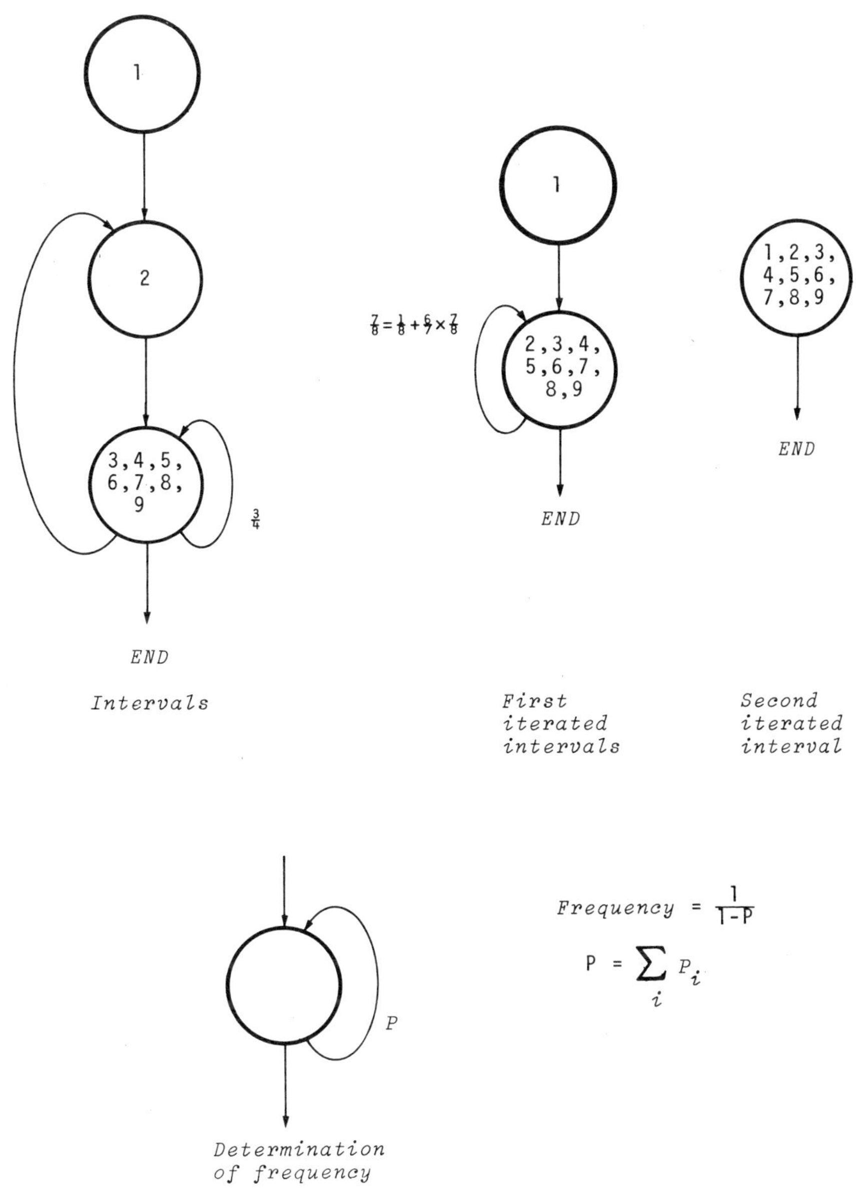

The relative frequency of a loop may be determined from the probability of a loop-closing branch.

Figure 8: Interval analysis and frequency determination

articulation blocks of an interval, and the maximal strongly connected region within an interval. The use of interval analysis for global optimization is shown with an example that demonstrates how information is relayed through successive iterations of the interval construction. In the same proceedings, Cocke (262) describes a method for common sub-expression elimination based upon interval analysis. The information required to determine whether a computation is redundant may be coded as a large system of Boolean equations. The interval technique permits solution of this system without having to perform a tedious Gauss elimination. Only two passes through the system of equations are required. A later paper by Allen and Cocke (263) summarizes techniques for identifying intervals and properties of blocks within intervals. The concept of node splitting, to permit reduction of an arbitrary program flow graph, is discussed in detail. Kennedy (264) has built upon this work. He has divided questions concerning data flow into two classes:

1 those referring to the status of variables on entry to a block;

2 those referring to the effect of computations within a block on later computations.

The first class of problems have been solved, and an approach to the second is given. An algorithm for the identification of dead variables is shown, which, like Cocke's common sub-expression elimination algorithm, requires only two passes. The two passes perform logical operations on bit-vectors, which may be performed in parallel on most machines, resulting in a very high-speed algorithm.

The *value number* technique described by Cocke and Schwartz assigns a unique identifier to each calculation in a program. Whenever a calculation is to be performed a table look-up determines whether it is currently available. Because a numeric identifier is associated with each calculation, formal identity is not required to find a common sub-expression as shown in Figure 3. Program flow properties rendering a match impossible are reflected by assigning new identifiers at statement labels.

Schneck and Angel (265) have combined the interval analysis and value number techniques in an optimizer which accepts and produces FORTRAN programs. All of the techniques referred to at the beginning of this section have been implemented and new optimizations are also introduced. Strict ordering of nodes within an interval permits the value number technique to be globally applied and eliminates virtually all common sub-expressions. A second pass over the program, in the manner of Cocke and also Kennedy permits global constant propagation to be performed. The efficacy of optimization at the level of a programming language is also discussed.

A recent paper by Hecht and Ullman (266) introduces a pair of transformations which may be used in flow graph analysis. Transformation T_1 removes an edge which begins and ends at the same node. Transformation T_2 condenses a node a into its unique immediate predecessor b resulting in a/b. A flow graph is called *collapsible* if and only if repeated application of T_1 and T_2 result in a single node. Figure 9 indicates the collapsibility of the example flow graph. Collapsibility is shown to be equivalent to interval reducibility. The time to determine collapsibility is $O(n \log n)$ while the time to determine interval reducibility may be $O(n^2)$. Information obtained by interval analysis may also be obtained by application of T_1 and T_2.

Another graph-theoretic superstructure has recently appeared. In order to produce reasonable code for the ILLIAC system optimization is a necessity: the computations removed and improved by global optimization are often the scalar expressions which

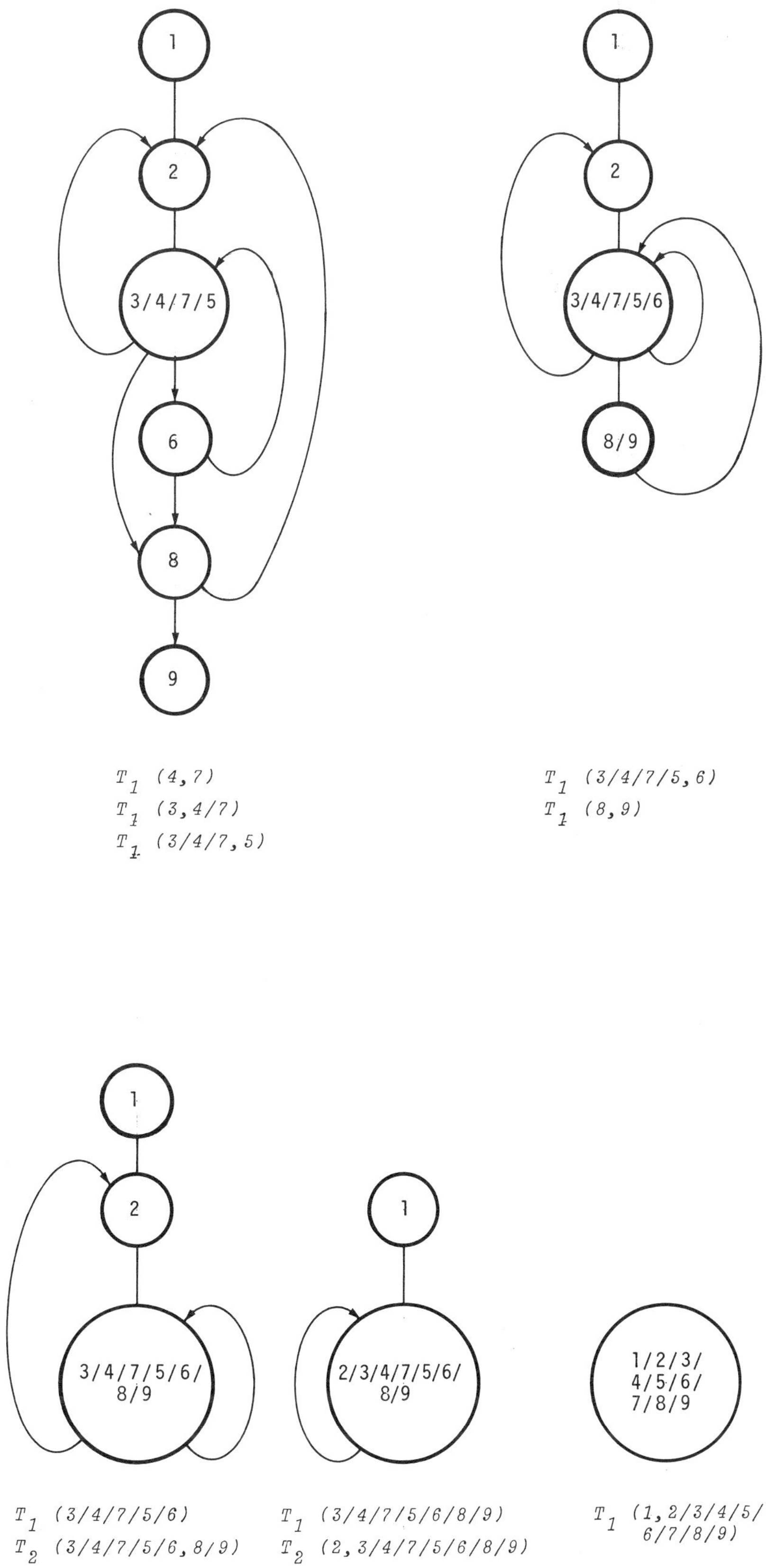

Figure 9: Collapsibility; repeated applications of two transformations yield a simple node in O(n log n) steps

degrade ILLIAC's performance. Loveman and Faneuf (270) introduce the '*P*-graph' algorithm and its application to the standard optimization techniques.

Finally, an idea of Knuth's (271,272), the semantic attribute, has recently received attention as a means of performing global optimization. The technique has been employed in the one-pass removal of invariant expressions from loops and in the elimination of unreachable calculations from programs by Neel and Amirchahy (273, 274).

CONCLUSION

The powerful architecture-independent optimizations are responsible for most of the speed increase obtained by an optimizing compiler. Schneck and Angel (265) have shown that these optimizations may be applied before compilation, and achieve almost all that a compiler can. With IBM's FORTRAN H, architecture-independent optimization accounts for 80% of the speed increase. With the CDC compiler for the 6600, external optimization produces faster code than the compiler can. In summary, an external architecture-independent compiler, supplemented by a machine-oriented compiler is the most cost-effective technique. This is true for the manufacturer who may devote less time to the compiler, as well as for the programmer who will find debugging easier in this environment because he can see what changes have been effected.

FUTURE DEVELOPMENTS IN PROGRAM PERFORMANCE OPTIMIZATION

P B Schneck

Goddard Institute of Space Studies

FUTURE DEVELOPMENTS IN PROGRAM PERFORMANCE OPTIMIZATION

I have had my say; if I am wrong it is your business to take up the argument and refute it.

Plato

INTRODUCTION

The history of program optimization techniques begins with the attempt to show that high-level language compilation can result in code comparable to that of a human programmer. The FORTRAN I compiler (274) devoted approximately one fourth of its code to optimization, in order to achieve a standard of efficiency acceptable to the programming community. At that time (1954), that meant an efficiency comparable to that obtained by human programmers. In those early days of computing, costs were centred on the hardware and so programmers spent much of their time and effort aimed at achieving high efficiency and good use of the system. Today, the division of capital has been reversed: the majority of a computing installation's budget is now spent on programming and software costs. The technological forecast indicates that this imbalance will increase in the future as hardware costs continue to decrease and labour costs continue to increase. Thus, optimizing compilers have been successful in making it possible for programmers to write in high-level language (such as FORTRAN and ALGOL) and obtain the productivity advantages of such languages without a significant penalty in terms of efficiency. Because of the continuing impact of technology on hardware prices, there is ever more pressure to increase the programmer's productivity. Optimizing programs* will permit an extension of the availability of computers to large classes of unsophisticated users in much the same way as decreased hardware costs have permitted the utilization of computer systems in more widespread and commonplace applications.

Examination of the capabilities of optimizing programs shows that acceptable performance may be obtained at significantly lower cost by simplifying the rules of programming languages and subjecting the resulting programs to the optimization process. Thus, at some point in the not-too-distant future it will be possible for a non-programmer (the end user) to create a description of his problem and have that transformed into a reasonably efficient program.

A BRIEF REVIEW OF COMPUTER SYSTEM ECONOMICS

The introduction of early (*circa* 1952) computer systems gave rise to a situation which was imprinted upon the new-born industry. Because the mammoth machines were so expensive, and labour so inexpensive, all attention was focused on keeping the machines busy.

---

* *The word 'compiler' has purposely not been used at this point as it is to be stressed that compilation, which is a technique for the professional programmer, may disappear as we know it today.*

Software was primitive. The comprehensive systems which are in common use today were not yet conceived. Bootstrap loaders, machine language programs, and 'hands-on' debugging were the programmers' tools. Despite these conditions, the major costs in a computing centre were hardware.

Those first-generation machines each used thousands of vacuum tubes. As technology improved, newer components were employed. The introduction of transistor circuits permitted speed increases of two orders of magnitude without a major increase in cost. Those second-generation machines were more adaptable and they were used in a much wider variety of applications. Software was developed for the programmer and the operator. The programming effort required for a machine was no longer concentrated upon a single program; it was divided among a collection of smaller programs. The introduction of third-generation hardware and software reversed the traditional ordering of their costs. Fast and inexpensive hardware, coupled with the general-purpose software it had made possible, began a new era. The widespread use of computers in new areas resulted in a mismatch between programming speed and computing capability. While computing capabilities have grown by a factor of one thousand, programmer productivity has not kept pace. The latest machines available, the STAR, ASC, and ILLIAC, extend the trend further. Their increases in speed are accompanied by a loss in programmer productivity due to their unusual architectures.

Realization that programming costs are now a majority of most computing budgets has resulted in attention to programmer productivity and the introduction of new techniques which have received general acceptance. The structured programming movement has shown considerable success in raising programmer output and simultaneously reducing programming errors. Management techniques, such as the chief programmer team, have proven to be effective for large and lengthy software projects once thought to be untenable. The following sections of this paper address future areas of program performance optimization, programmer productivity, and hardware and their relationships to each other.

DIRECTIONS IN CLASSICAL PROGRAM PERFORMANCE OPTIMIZATION

Current program optimization techniques may be classified as machine-dependent, architecture-dependent or architecture-independent. The most natural part of a compiler to modify to obtain increased performance is the code generator and thus the earliest optimizations were machine-dependent. Next, attention was turned to formal methods. Consideration of flow graphs and program structure leads to architecture-independent optimization, such as common sub-expression elimination, or code motion. Finally, development by manufacturers of families of machines with similar architecture (for example, IBM 360/370, CDC 6000/7000, HIS 6000, RCA Spectra) and the appearance of architecturally similar machines by different manufacturers (for example, the multiple-register CDC 6000 and IBM 360, the vector processor CDC STAR and Texas Instruments ASC, the array processing ILLIAC IV and STARAN) led to development of a level of optimization techniques, called architecture-dependent, that lies between machine-dependent and architecture-independent techniques.

Extensions to current techniques

Architecture-dependent and architecture-independent optimization techniques are fertile areas for development of additional optimizations. Current work, centred on parallel and vector processors, was recently presented at an ACM SIGPLAN conference on *Programming*

Languages and Compilers for Parallel and Vector Machines. Techniques are being developed for recognition of parallel/vector processable sequences of instructions (architecture-dependent) which may be handled efficiently by specialized machines. The theme common to much of the work in progress today is that current programming languages do not permit expression of the concept of parallel or vector processors. Future work will be based upon programming languages which permit these constructs in a natural form.

The most thoroughly investigated area is that of architecture-independent optimizations. The history of optimizations in this area can be traced back to the handling of 'relcons' (loop invariants) in the FORTRAN I compiler. Analysis techniques have evolved from Monte Carlo simulation to determine execution frequencies of program blocks, through lengthy matrix techniques, to current graph-theoretical techniques (for example, the Cocke-Allen interval analysis).

Fuller utilization of the flow information will permit additional optimizations to be effected. For example, the back dominator relation has been widely used in optimizing compilers to assure that a computation must have occurred. Figure 1 illustrates the back dominator relation and its use. Until recently, the forward dominator has been ignored. It may be used to assure that a computation must occur, and that it is safe to move a redundant sub-expression from a conditional path to an unconditional path (275), as shown in Figure 2. Recent work by Allen (283) combines control flow information and data flow information in order to determine when it is possible to remove common sub-expressions, propagate constants, etc.

Compilers have become adept at optimizations *within* program units. There is probably little which will be added in the future. The return obtainable with current techniques will be increased significantly when it becomes possible to optimize across program units.

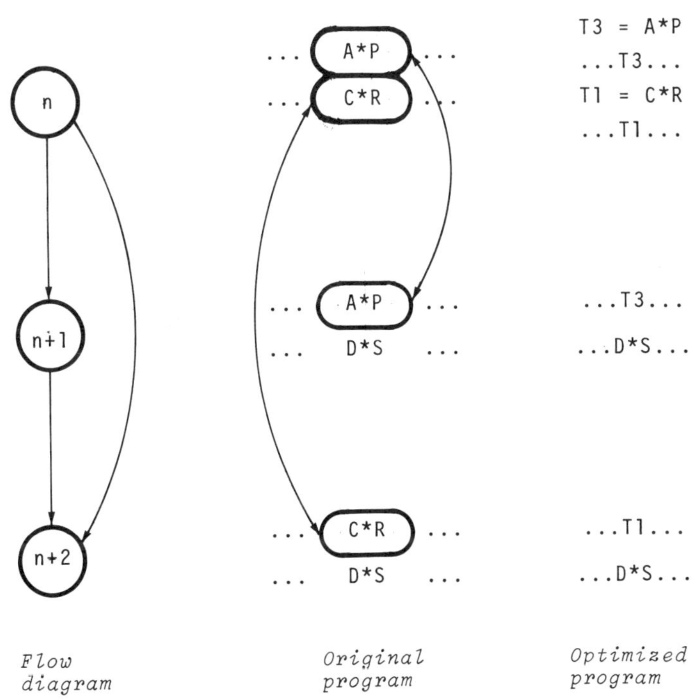

Figure 1: Classical 'back dominator' common subexpression recognition

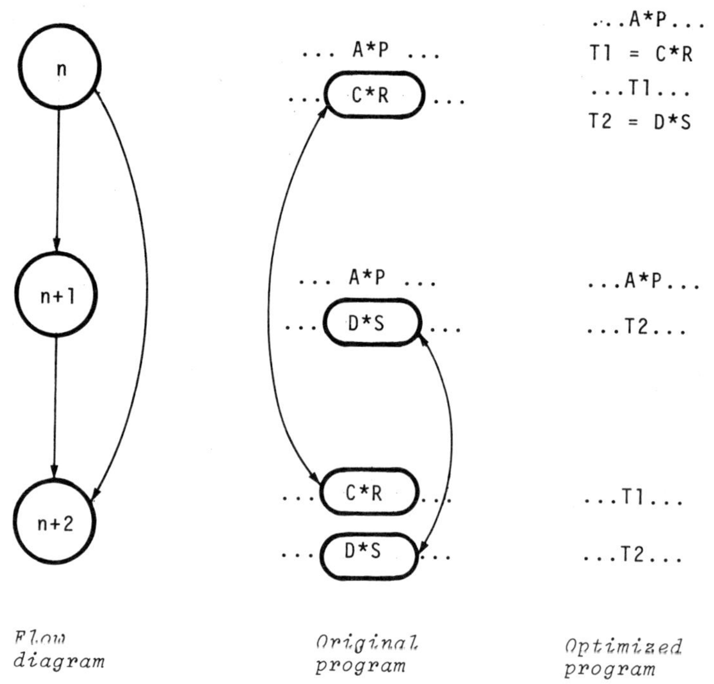

Figure 2: 'Forward dominator' common subexpression recognition

Each step which has been taken, from a single arithmetic statement (276), to a basic block, and then to a program unit, has resulted in a higher level of optimization and better performing programs. Inter-procedural optimization will have a similar effect. General-purpose routines will operate as efficiently as if they had been coded for a special case.

Semantic preprocessing

Current program optimizers are usually found as part of language translators. An independent optimizer, used as a separate program to improve source programs, has recently been implemented (277). This use of an optimizer permits a significant simplification of the programming/debugging task while also providing efficient programs. The optimizer is able to perform its restructuring on the source program level. This has three major effects:

1 The programmer is able to see the restructured program. Debugging is simplified because the restructured program represents the program in actual use and all changes made by the compiler are in evidence.

2 The programmer need not spend time searching out and performing optimizations. Programs may be written in a form close to the problem statement which is easily maintained, and the optimizer will be used to create efficient versions. Changes or additions may be applied directly to the optimized program.

3 The benefits of sophisticated program optimization techniques are available even for machines which have no optimizing compiler.

An external optimizer may also be used in an inverse mode. The goal of such a 'semantic preprocessor' (278) is increased language capability and its corresponding increase in programmer productivity, without a decrease in performance. A frequent effect of increased language capability is a decrease in program efficiency. A semantic preprocessor based on program optimization techniques permits introduction of extensive language facilities without penalty. Figure 3a illustrates the convention view of an optimizing compiler: a program which transforms a given high-level language program into an efficient lower-level language program. Figure 3b illustrates that a semantic preprocessor results when optimization techniques are used to expand the facilities of high-level language.

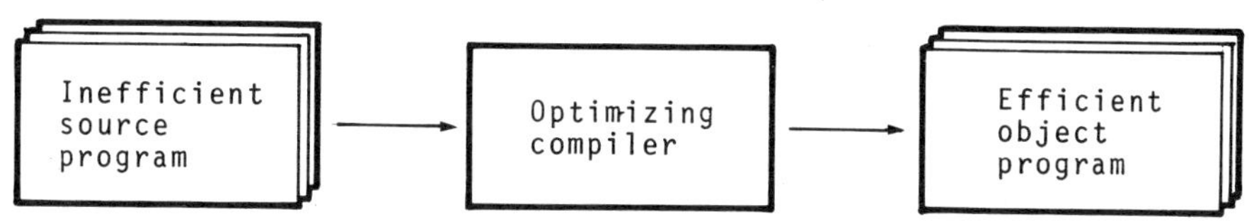

a) Conventional use of an optimizing compiler

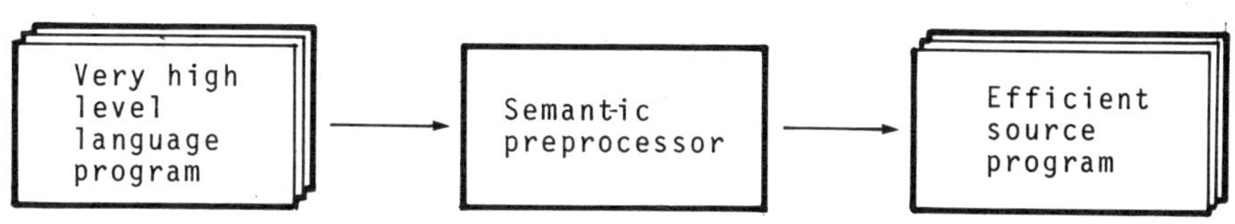

b) Use of an optimizing compiler as a semantic preprocessor

Figure 3: Two views of program optimization

HIGH-LEVEL PROGRAMMING LANGUAGES

Future developments in high-level languages are tied to advances in optimizing compilers. The first programming languages were one-to-one assembly codes, transliterated into machine language. The purpose of assembly code was to permit use of mnemonic names in place of absolute machine locations. Strange as it may seem, optimization was required even at that level of language availability. The IBM 650, a popular drum-oriented system, was extremely sensitive to the placement of instructions and data on its storage drum. Revolving at 12 500 revolutions per minute, a single revolution required 4.8 miliseconds. If instructions were carefully placed, no time delay was incurred; in the worst case, a full 4.8 milliseconds would be wasted waiting for the appearance of the next instruction on the drum. When storage assignments were performed by hand, placement of instructions was taken into account. When an assembler took over the task of performing the storage assignments, it was necessary to account for the drum rotation in order to produce a program that would run in a reasonable time. This was one of the earliest machine-dependent optimizations.

The creation of the FORTRAN language and compiler introduced another degree of freedom in the process of creating a machine language program from a source program. At the assembly language level the preparation of a machine language program is merely *transliteration*; apart from storage allocation, few choices are left to the assembler. The *translation* process from FORTRAN to machine language takes place at a much higher level. The compiler determines how effectively various features of the target machine will be utilized:

- Does the compiler generate 'accumulator' instructions for a multiple-register machine?

- Does the compiler utilize the special loop increment/test instructions found on the target machine?

- Does the compiler perform instruction scheduling for a machine with autonomous execution units?

- Does the compiler utilize indirect addressing?

The list could be extended significantly and would still merely scratch the surface of the range of implementations available to the compiler writer. Despite the great number of questions which might be asked concerning the operation of a compiler for FORTRAN (or ALGOL, PL/1, or COBOL), the output of such a compiler is fairly predictable. The language has left the generation of machine instructions to the compiler, but not the approach or choice of algorithm.

Very high-level languages such as SETL (279) introduce another degree of freedom into the compilation process. The compiler will be charged with deciding *how* to accomplish a program's objective, and then producing machine language instructions to carry out the objective. The very high-level languages will not require that the programmer pay attention to details which are not relevant to the solution of his problem. Instead, the programmer must carefully control the use of data structures and type of variables or he will inadvertently prevent the compiler from being able to perform the reduction from worst-case to best-case coding necessary for efficiency.

A simple example suffices to illustrate these ideas. To obtain the smallest value of a set, the FORTRAN programmer must create a loop and search on an element-by-element basis for the minimum value. Not only is the programmer forced to indicate explicitly the search process, but he must also specify an order for carrying out the search. The programmer may not have any knowledge or interest in the storage of the elements of the set, and the entire process is best left in the care of the high-level language compiler. In circumstances where the extreme elements of sets are repeatedly referenced, the compiler may choose to maintain, for example, the maximum, minimum and cardinality of sets as attributes which are easily obtained when required.

In his introduction to SETL, Schwartz states:

> "It is this fundamental difficulty with which the language designer struggles, attempting to invent dictional patterns which are highly expressive and yet can be compiled into reasonably efficient running code... Improved optimization techniques therefore form an essential part of an overall attack on the problems of programming."

A PROBLEM SOLVING DIALOGUE

The boundary between procedural and non-procedural languages continues to grow ever more vague. As procedural languages grow to 'higher-level' languages, they become non-procedural. The difficulty with non-procedural languages is in ascertaining that the resulting program meets the requirements. Even more difficult is determining whether or not a non-procedural program* is correct. The answers to both questions may be obtained together if additional descriptive information is made available to the compiler by the programmer (280). The programmer indicates the course of a computation at each block in a program, and the compiler determines whether or not the description agrees with the actual status of the program. The result of this processing is a summary of points where the description of the program and the program itself were (potentially) not in agreement. The programmer is able to examine the output, modify the program (or the description) and submit the amended program for further analysis. If the descriptive information is a part of the initial program package then few, if any, extra iterations will be required to achieve a successful compilation. When a successful compilation is attained, there is reasonable assurance that a large number of potential errors involving incorrect program preparation, shuffled cards, or careless mistakes, are not present. If the syntax required of descriptive information is chosen carefully, then a beneficial side effect of the verification and correctness analysis is the use of that information for documentation purposes.

Knuth addressed the concept of an iterative system in his ACM Turing Lecture (281):

> "All that we have been giving programmers is an optimizing compiler, which mysteriously does something to the programs it translates but which never explains what it does. Fortunately we are now finally seeing the appearance of systems which give the user credit for some intelligence; they automatically provide instrumentation of programs and appropriate feedback about the real costs. These experimental systems have been a huge success, because they produce measurable improvements, and especially because they are fun to use, so I am confident that it is only a matter of time before the use of such systems is standard operating procedure."

We suggest that this will be carried further. Future programming systems will carry on a dialogue with the user. Additional information will be requested to enable the system to choose a problem-solving strategy from among the many which may be possible. In order to accomplish this, a true dialogue will be necessary, not merely a sequence of batch job submissions. The compiler will request information which is required (for example, for determination of correctness), or which is desirable (for example, for choosing an optimization strategy). The questions will not be 'standard', or prepared as in today's programmed instruction material, they will relate directly to the program in development. By supplying the requested information, the programmer will aid in obtaining major performance increases.

Will it work? Today's interactive compilers which operate in a timesharing mode are already performing some of these activities. They are concerned solely with creating a program, and therefore check for syntactic and logical errors. By offering immediate feedback, it becomes attractive for the programmer to examine and measure the effect of alternative problem formulations. This sort of system offers the opportunity for immense

---

* *The term 'non-procedural program' is irksome, as the Oxford English Dictionary lists one of the definitions of 'program' as: a definite plan or scheme of any intended proceedings.*

productivity increases – the programmer can offer guidance to the compiler on the job of performance optimization – the computer will act as an agent of the programmer and carry out the optimization.

Increased computational capabilities coupled with inexpensive conversational terminals will encourage a programmer/computer dialogue as a means of program development and optimization. The effectiveness of the programmer and computer in this symbiotic relationship will far surpass that of the isolated batch-oriented programmer.

THE IMPACT OF HARDWARE

The technological advances which have made possible the hand-held programmable calculator will find their way into large-scale systems as well. The cost and speed of computation reflect recent advances in technology. Soon, the ability to perform a computation will reflect these advances as well.

Historically, software has focused attention on critical problems and hardware has been designed to eliminate the problem. The history of a hierarchy of store levels goes back to Atlas and recently reappeared with hardware support in the form of the buffer memory and virtual storage systems in the IBM 360/370 computer lines. Programmers have always been fascinated with optimal scheduling of traffic for disk or drum, and the Burroughs disk controller solves that problem. Recently there has even been a suggestion for a hardware optimizer facility to locate and remove common subexpressions during program execution (282).

As described earlier, one of the major problems facing language designers and implementors is the handling of diverse data types. The large number of possible combinations of operands makes it difficult to apply any optimizations. Current hardware requires the programmer (or compiler) to distinguish among the various possible data types by using the proper instruction (for example, on a 360 a load operation specifies one of the following data types: full-word integer, half-word integer, full-word floating-point, double-word floating-point, or character). If the compiler is unable to determine the data type then execution must proceed interpretively. Future hardware will be sensitive to data type, and not require advance selection of a particular instruction class. A descriptor (hidden from the programmer) will be used to carry information on the format and mode of data. The hardware will have the ability to perform complex operations, usually requiring many instructions. (The Texas Instruments ASC can perform a matrix multiply in a single instruction.) Functions will migrate to the hardware, and the compilation optimization process will be greatly simplified.

CONCLUSION

Future developments in program performance optimization have been forecast, based upon the present states and prospects of software and hardware technology. The promise of a future technological breakthrough is always present in the hardware realm. Software is founded upon abstractions, and while breakthroughs do occur, there are no undiscovered physical properties (such as semiconductor behaviour) about to bring orders of magnitude changes.

Thus, software of the future will do a better and more complete job of analysis and

and optimization. The more important impact will be the improvements in programmer productivity due to more effective software. Small, fast, and inexpensive hardware devices will be used to fill the gaps left by software. Thus, the use of computers for problem solving will become easier, and available to the general community without severe problems of efficiency.

PROGRAM BEHAVIOUR AND ITS IMPROVEMENT

J R Spirn

Computer Science Department
The Pennsylvania State University

J R SPIRN received a Batchelor's Degree in Electrical Engineering in 1969 from the Massachusetts Institute of Technology. He then entered Princeton University and obtained a PhD degree in Electrical Engineering in 1973. His thesis, entitled Program Locality and Dynamic Memory Management, *prepared under the direction of Professor Peter Denning, dealt with some program models and their analytical implications. Dr Spirn was Assistant Professor of Engineering at Brown University, Providence, Rhode Island, USA, in 1972-1975. Also in 1974-1975 he was a Visiting Professor of Electrical Engineering at the University of Hawaii. In 1975, he assumed his present position, Assistant Professor of Computer Science at the Pennsylvania State University.*

PROGRAM BEHAVIOUR AND ITS IMPROVEMENT

ABSTRACT

'Locality' is the basic effect in the behaviour of computer programs that determines the efficiency of virtual memory computer systems. In this paper, its properties are studied and a stochastic model (which can be used in simulation/analysis studies of operating and computer systems) is proposed. The model has been experimentally validated. The 'degree' of a program's locality is discussed within the context of the model, and two practical methods for improving the degree in real programs are described.

INTRODUCTION

In virtual memory systems, with paged and/or segmented storage, the memory reference behaviour of programs is of basic importance. Such systems work at all because programs exhibit certain patterns in their references. For example, in a paged virtual memory system, programs run with only some fraction of their total set of pages in memory at any given time. If an instruction or data item in some page not in main storage is referenced, the missing page must be fetched from an external memory device, typically a drum. Since current such devices are perhaps 10000 times slower than main memory, it is essential that missing page references (known as page faults) be rare. Page fault rates exceeding one in about every five thousand references lead to intolerable drum fetching overhead. Yet typical programs can achieve better than this rate with many pages missing. The (intuitively reasonable) conclusion is: in the vicinity of any given time instant, a program uses only part of its total set of pages. Others are not referenced at all about this time. This is called the principle of locality. Note that this is an empirical, not a formal effect; it is certainly possible to succeed in writing a program that uses all of its pages in any reasonably short time interval. Locality is a consequence of the way people tend to consider a complex problem part by part.

For efficient virtual memory operation, the set of pages* in use at a given time must be loaded into main memory. For convenience, we refer to this set as the locality set, or simply as 'the locality'. Successful paging algorithms attempt to estimate each program's locality set, and to retain it in memory. When a page must be removed from main memory, the one selected is one that is supposed to be no longer in the locality. In general, we can only estimate a locality with some error, since we cannot know exactly what a program will do next (without actually executing it). The

* *In a segmented memory with no paging, the memory management units are segments instead of pages. Segments are essentially variable-length pages; hence most of the discussion here applies.*

effectiveness of various paging algorithms generally depends on the accuracy of their locality estimators.

For example, two commonly used paging algorithms are Least-Recently-Used (LRU) and First-In-First-Out (FIFO). When a page is to be displaced from main memory, LRU chooses the page referenced least recently by the program, whereas FIFO chooses the page first fetched into memory. It seems reasonable (and there is some statistical basis) to assume that the page not used for the longest time is least likely to be used again in the near future. Much less reasonable is the supposition that a page is no longer in the locality set simply because it was fetched a long time ago. The page may in fact have been heavily referenced in the near past. Consequently, we expect that LRU leads to a lower fault rate than FIFO, as has been shown by experiment (148,149).

It is possible to be more specific about the nature of the locality phenomenon. In order to define it formally, we must propose one or more mathematical models for it. Such models may be used as program behaviour models to drive analyses or simulations of memory management systems. Once we understand the properties of locality, we may attempt to improve a program's behaviour by increasing its degree of locality. Specifically, if a program's locality sets are made smaller, and if it changes locality sets less frequently, it will exhibit improved virtual memory performance.

MODELS FOR LOCALITY

The expectation that a program will have a favoured set of pages may require elaboration. We may wish to know how large the set is, for example, and perhaps a description of the pattern of reference among its pages. But the dynamic aspects of locality are at least a significant, since the locality set clearly changes with time, albeit slowly. This slow variation is of interest since it accounts for many of the page faults generated by a program (the remaining page faults are due to inaccuracies in locality estimation). Localitities can change gradually as a single page enters or leaves the favoured set; occasionally the change will be to an entirely new, disjoint set as when a program begins a new phase of its execution. If a program's locality set size increases, the memory space allocated to the program should be increased correspondingly, or the page fault rate will rise sharply. Likewise, if the size contracts, the memory allocation should be reduced or the extra space will be wasted. The important issues are the static aspects of locality set content and patterns of reference, and the dynamic aspects of changing set size and content.

We have defined a locality set to be the set of pages used in the vicinity of a given time; however, this is a bit vague. To be precise, we must choose an interval of time around the given time instant and include all pages referenced during that interval in the locality set at that instant. Since the set will depend on the method of choosing the interval, there is usually no unique locality set. It is more realistic to rank the pages of a program by the extent of their usage at a given moment; the locality set is merely the first few pages of the ranking. We call this ranking the locality list at time t. For example, using $\underline{L}(t)$ to denote the locality list at time t, we might have

$$\underline{L}(t) = [2, 1, 3, 0, 4]$$

for a program of five pages. This would indicate that page 2 is most heavily in use, page 1 is next most heavily in use, and that page 4 is in use the least (perhaps not at all) in the vicinity of time t. In general, if the locality list of a program of n pages is:

$$\underline{L}(t) = [X_1, X_2, \ldots, X_n]$$

where the X_i are page numbers, then the locality set of ℓ pages $L(\ell,t)$ is defined to be:

$$L(\ell,t) = \{X_1, X_2, \ldots, X_\ell\}.$$

Using the locality list, we define a locality set of each possible size at a given instant of time. The one actually chosen to be retained in memory is (hopefully) the smallest set for which the page fault rate is acceptably low.

Under this formal structure, we can define methods of identifying a program's locality list and locality sets. There are two possible approaches: one can observe the behaviour of a program externally, or one can model the internal behaviour of the program. The external observer is incapable of determining exactly what a program is doing; he can measure only the effects of doing it. In particular, his only knowledge about a program is an observed sequence of emitted page references $r(1), r(2), \ldots, r(t)$, ... Locality information is inferred from the observations. We call such an externally observed locality an extrinsic locality (150).

The best-known extrinsic locality definition is the *working set* of Denning (151). We define $W(t,T)$, the working set at time t, to be the set of distinct pages appearing in the T most recent references $r(t-T+1), r(t-T+2), \ldots, r(t)$. Parameter T is called the window size and is usually of the order of 10^4 or 10^5 in practical implementations. Since the working set is the set of all pages referenced recently, we can reasonably define $W(t,T)$ to be an (extrinsic) locality set at time t. By varying T, we vary the number of pages in the working set at each given time instant. In this way an entire locality list $\underline{L}(t)$ can be specified:

$$\underline{L}(t) = [X_1, X_2, \ldots, X_n]$$

where $X_1 = r(t)$ is the page referenced at time t, X_2 is the page referenced next most recently, X_3 is the third most recent reference, and so on. *All* pages of the program are included; any which have never been referenced are simply grouped in an arbitrary order at the right end of the list. This particular locality list is often called an LRU stack (152-154), and we shall return to it. Note that for any value of window size T, the working set is the several left-most elements in the locality list; that is:

$$W(t,T) = \{X_1, \ldots, X_{w(t,T)}\}$$

where $w(t,T) = |W(t,T)|$ is the working set size at time t. Since the working set is an extrinsically defined locality set of $w(t,T)$ pages, we arrive immediately at the working set algorithm (151) for memory management: retain each active program's working set in main memory.

Extrinsically defined locality would be entirely satisfactory if it were not for the physical requirement of realizability. A realizable extrinsic measurement is one which at time t assumes knowledge only of references $r(1), r(2), \ldots, r(t)$. The working set measurement is realizable; thus it tends to lag somewhat behind the most current operation of the program. Best possible paging is accomplished with Belady's

Optimal Algorithm (148,153), which is the 'reverse' of working set in the sense that the pages are ranked in the locality list by time of next *future* (rather than past) reference. However, Belady's algorithm requires knowledge of all future references and is thus the 'most unrealizable' algorithm.

We can realizably produce more current measures of a program's locality than the working set by knowing something about the structure of the program. While we cannot know for certain what a program will do unless we actually execute it, the possibilities can at least be narrowed and perhaps assigned likelihood estimates. For example, once a program begins a long tight loop, all pages in the loop may be considered to enter the locality immediately. They may all be dropped as soon as the loop terminates. Graph (or Markov) models, such as that of Figure 1, have been used to model this type of behaviour. Here page 4 is referenced, then a loop of pages 2 and 3. The numbers on the edges are probabilities, so that the loop will iterate an average of 100 times before terminating.

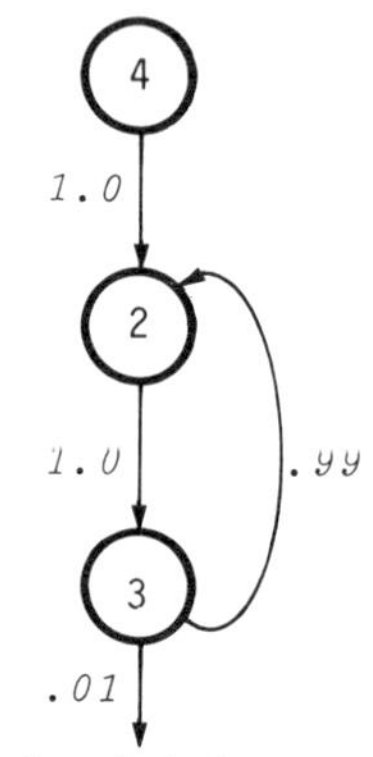

Figure 1: Graph model (vertices are pages)

Graph models of this type have drawbacks, however. In the first place, although any particular program might be modelled this way, it is difficult to use the method to model general behaviour. In a program of n pages, there are n^2 possible edges which must be labelled with probabilities; this is very many parameters to estimate. Moreover, only the most recent reference is remembered, whereas reference $r(t)$ made by a real program usually depends on more than just $r(t - 1)$. Nevertheless, to the extent that a model such as this is realistic, locality information based on probably behaviour in the near future can be obtained. If the model is accurate, the derived information will be a truer picture of the program's current locality than a realizable extrinsic measurement. We call such a model intrinsic locality model since it is based on knowledge of the program's internal state, rather than on an external measurement.

The concept of the locality list can be used as the basic of an intrinsic locality model. The state of the model is the list itself, so that a program of n pages is assumed to have $n!$ possible states corresponding to all permutations of the pages. This has the advantage that knowledge of the state gives us immediately the locality list. We are now assuming that the next reference (and next locality) is determined by the current locality list, which appears to be more realistic than assuming that the sequence of page references is a Markov chain. To complete specification of the model, we must specify the mechanism for locality transition when the locality list changes.

Using each locality list as a state in a Markov chain, there are $(n!)!$ transition probabilities to specify. We can reduce this number considerably by disallowing many of the transitions. Several alternatives have been proposed (154), but among the most empirically realistic is the LRU Stack Model (150,152,154) in which successive states are the working set locality lists mentioned earlier. Suppose

$$\underline{L}(t) = [X_1, X_2, \ldots, X_n]. \tag{1}$$

Then in this model, there are n possible choices for the next list, depending on which page is next referenced. If $r(t + 1) = X_i$, then

$$\underline{L}(t + 1) = [X_i, X_1, \ldots, X_{i-1}, X_{i+1}, \ldots, X_n].$$

(Note that if $r(t+1) = X_1$, the list is unchanged).

Since the locality lists of this model are those of working set, and since the working set algorithm is one of the most successful paging alrogithms, it is intuitively reasonable that the LRU Stack Model will be a good mirror of reality. This has been confirmed by experiment (150).

The Markovian locality transition probabilities in the LRU Stack Model are specified most easily by assigning a reference probability to each position of the LRU Stack. Specifically, there are stationary probabilities $a_1, a_2, \ldots, a_n$ such that $a_1+a_2+\ldots+a_n=1$, and such that if $\underline{L}(t)$ is as given in equation 1, then

$$\text{Prob}[r(t+1) = X_i] = a_i, \quad 1 \leq i \leq n.$$

The probabilities a_i are called the stack distance probabilities. Although these probabilities are fixed, the likelihood of reference to a given page depends on the locality list in effect, and is thus time-varying.

This model has several practical applications, other than its position as a formal model of the locality phenomenon. Since it emits memory references, it can be used as a model of a program in simulations or analyses of operating/computer systems. It also provides a method of testing a real program's degree of locality. Consider two programs A and B. Let the stack distance probabilities of program A be $a_1, a_2, \ldots, a_n$, and let those of program B be $b_1, b_2, \ldots, b_m$, and suppose $m \geq n$. Then we say A has a higher degree of locality than B if for all i, $1 \leq i \leq m$:

$$a_1 + a_2 + \ldots + a_i \geq b_1 + b_2 + \ldots + b_i$$

and if for at least one i, the relation is strictly 'greater than'. If the inequality is reversed, then B has greater locality than A. The motivation is that for any possible locality set size, the more highly-local program will have a higher probability of referencing pages in the locality set. Since we require that the inequality hold for all i, degree of locality is a partial order, so that there exist pairs of programs whose degrees of locality are incomparable. Depending on the locality set size either one will reference intra-locality pages more often. In general, a program with fewer total pages cannot have a lower degree of locality under this definition, since if the locality set size equals the program size, all references will be from within the locality (however, the larger program can still be *approximately* more local).

This particular measure of degree of locality is useful in practice since it is possible to measure the (maximum likelihood) stack distance probabilities of any program by interpretively executing the program, maintaining the LRU stack, and counting the number of references to each stack position. See (150,154) for a detailed description of the method.

CHARACTERISTICS OF THE STACK DISTANCE PROBABILITIES

If we choose a locality set size ℓ for an LRU stack model program, references to pages in stack positions $1, 2, \ldots, \ell$ are intra-locality, and those to positions $\ell + 1$, $\ell + 2$, $\ldots$, n are extra-locality. By the nature of locality, pages within the locality set should have a higher probability of reference than those outside, a condition to ensure this is:

$$\min\{a_1, a_2, \ldots, a_\ell\} \geq \max\{a_{\ell+1}, a_{\ell+2}, \ldots, a_n\}$$

where 'min' and 'max' denote minimum and maximum, respectively. To ensure that pages within locality sets of all sizes are favoured to be referenced, the stack distance probabilities must be monotonic:

$$a_1 \geq a_2 \geq a_3 \geq \ldots \geq a_n. \qquad (2)$$

We call this the locality condition on the a_i. The implication is as follows: when a page x is referenced, it moves to stack position 1 and becomes the page most likely to be referenced next. If some other page y is referenced, however, page x moves to position 2 and its reference becomes somewhat less likely. If the page continues unreferenced, it will migrate slowly towards the right-hand end of the stack (locality list), becoming less and less likely to be used. Experiments (150) have shown that the locality condition (2) strictly holds for real programs up to about the fifth stack position or so, and holds approximately thereafter.

A more specific condition on the a_i arises from an empirical effect known as Belady's Lifetime Function (155). Figure 2 shows a typical observed relationship between a program's mean locality set size ℓ and its mean time (number of references) between extra-locality references $e(\ell)$. Since paging algorithms attempt to maintain in main storage the locality set equal in size to the allocated storage space, if ℓ equals the memory size then $e(\ell)$ is the mean time between page faults. The following relationship (Belady's Lifetime Function) was seen to be an adequate fit to observed data:

$$e(\ell) = a\ell^b \qquad 1 \leq \ell \leq n'$$

for parameters a and b with b equalling approximately 2. The expression fits well to the observed behaviour only for $\ell \leq n' < n$, for some n' usually quite close to n. Denote the rate per reference (or probability) of extra-locality page references by $f(\ell)$; then as a close approximation*

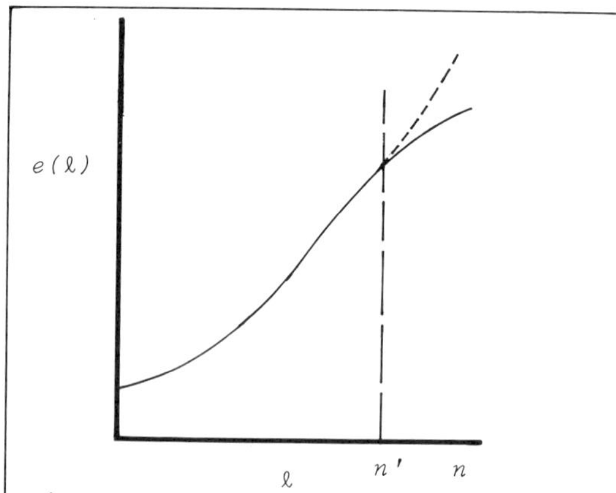

Figure 2: Example e(ℓ) curve

$$f(\ell) = 1/e(\ell)$$

so that

$$f(\ell) = \alpha\ell^{-b} \qquad 1 \leq \ell \leq n' \qquad (3)$$

for parameters $\alpha = a^{-1}$ and b. But in the LRU stack model:

$$f(\ell) = a_{\ell+1} + a_{\ell+2} + \ldots + a_n$$

so that, in the region of good fit of equation 3:

---

* *The approximation is asymptotically exact if extra-locality references are a renewal process* (156), *which they are in the LRU stack model.*

$$a_i = f(i - 1) - f(i)$$

$$= \alpha[(i - 1)^{-b} - i^{-b}] \qquad 1 < i \leqslant n'$$

$$\alpha b i^{-b-1}$$

for moderately large ℓ. Thus, a realistic sequence of stack distance probabilities can be specified with only two parameters, α and b. Sample program models can in this way be conveniently prepared for use in system simulation or analysis.

PROGRAM RESTRUCTURING FOR LOCALITY IMPROVEMENT

Since locality is the phenomenon which allows paging to occur with acceptable efficiency; it follows that if the degree of locality of a program can be improved, its performance in a virtual memory system will improve. Two alternative approaches are:

1 pack the program code and data into as few pages as possible (that is, compile tighter code, reformat the data, etc.)

2 rearrange the instructions and data so that individual localities occupy as few pages as possible.

We shall consider the second of these alternatives, often termed program restructuring. Note that while the first alternative produces smaller programs, the second may not (in fact, the number of pages may increase) because parts of pages may be left empty by the reordering procedure. As a simple example, consider three subroutines X, Y, and Z as follows:

Name	*Size (in words)*
X	800
Y	1400
Z	1100

The page size is 1000 words. If the subroutines are arranged in alphabetical order in virtual memory space as in Figure 3a, then X, Y, and Z will span respectively 1, 3, and 2 pages. Thus, 3 pages may have to be in main memory for efficient execution of Y. If the routines are re-ordered as in Figure 3b, the page span of Y drops to 2, and the average locality size will probably be smaller. Note the wasted space at the end of the second page.

If the programmer has a reasonably good idea of the localities in his program, he might specify them as part of a programming language. Define a block to be a logical program unit, such as a loop, short subroutine, array, etc. Blocks may be indicated by the programmer, or the compiler may calculate them from a flow analysis of the program (optimizing compilers do such flow analyses in any case). The compiler could attempt to rearrange the blocks to increase the degree of locality. In our example, we have assumed three blocks, routines X, Y, and Z, but in general a routine may consist of several blocks.

The simplest restructuring approach is to begin each block on a page boundary, guaranteeing that each will occupy the fewest number of pages. This is not a good scheme for several reasons: First, there will be much wasted space in the last page of

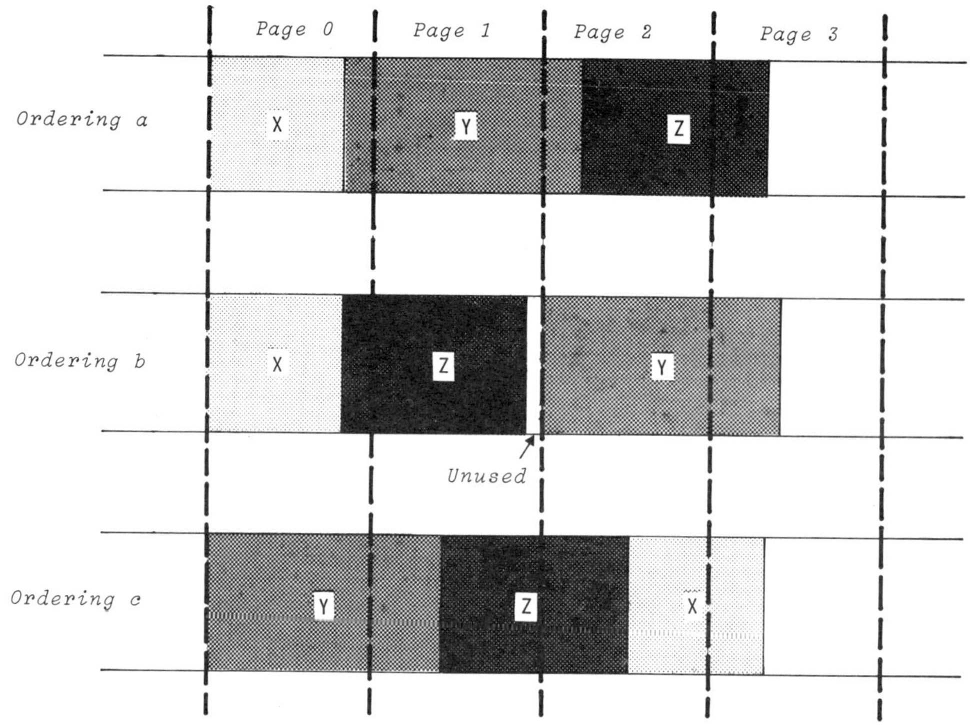

Figure 3: Three page orderings

each block, especially if the blocks tend to be much smaller than pages. Second, a locality set may consist of not one, but several blocks. In that case, we may actually increase the size (in pages) of the locality set. Third, even if each block does happen to be a locality, we have made the locality sets disjoint. Every locality transition will require a completely new set of pages to be loaded into main memory.

A better method is to use the wasted space in the last page of a block to contain all or part of neighbouring blocks; that is, blocks which tend to be used in adjoining time intervals. The re-ordering of Figure 3b is excellent if *X* and *Z* tend to transfer control to one another frequently. For instance, if routine *X* calls routine *Z*, no page fault will occur. Figure 4a shows a possible graph for this program. The vertices are blocks. The edges will in general denote transfers of control or data references; however, in this example vertices corresponding to data blocks are omitted. According to this

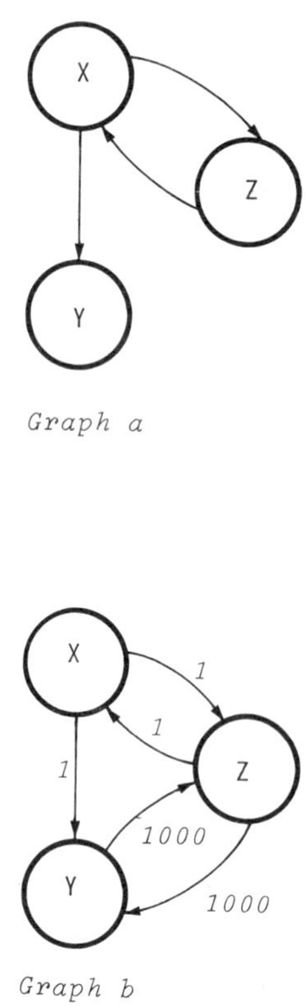

Figure 4: Two program graphs

graph, the rearrangement of Figure 3b is effective; apparently *X* and *Z* form a locality set together, with *Y* a separate locality. A restructuring algorithm should use the connectivity information in the program graph, attempting to place neighbouring blocks in overlapping page sets.

Now, consider Figure 4b, which is another possible graph for this program. Blocks *Y* and *Z* now have the capability of transferring control to each other. The numbers on the edges of the graph are the counts of each control transfer during execution. Clearly, it is more important to combine blocks *Y* and *Z* than *X* and *Z*. Thus, the page assignment of Figure 3c will be best for this task. In this assignment, the dominant locality of *Y* and *Z* together spans 3 pages, as compared to 4 pages in the other orderings. Block *X* also shares a page with *Z* (*X* calls *Z*), but this is a relatively minor consideration.

This example shows that the connectivity of the program graph is not enough to find a good assignment of blocks to pages. The weight of each edge in the graph is crucial. The compiler cannot determine this information; neither, very often, can the programmer. The only reliable method is to measure the task as it executes. For frequently used tasks, in particular for system routines such as editors, compilers, etc., this is practical. It has been shown that restructuring according to measured edge weights reduces the page fault rate by as much as ten to one (157).

Hatfield and Gerald (157) base their restructuring techniques on a measured nearness matrix $B = [b_{i,j}]$, where $b_{i,j}$ is the number of times a reference to block j immediately follows a reference to block i. This is an alternative way to represent the weighted program graph. In our current example, it is:

$$B = \begin{array}{c} \\ X \\ Y \\ Z \end{array} \left[\begin{array}{ccc} X & Y & Z \\ - & 1 & 1 \\ 0 & - & 1000 \\ 1 & 1000 & - \end{array} \right]$$

Hatfield and Gerald assumed that blocks were small compared to the page size, so that several blocks could be completely inserted into a single page. (This is of course not true in our example.) Under this assumption, the following heuristic was shown to yield good page assignments: Reorder the blocks in such a way that the large matrix entries fall close to the diagonal. Since entries on the diagonal would correspond to consecutive references to the same block (hence the same page), those near the diagonal correspond to consecutive references to blocks in nearby (perhaps the same) pages. The blocks are entered into the virtual memory space in the order which gives the strongest diagonalization. Since this is a heuristic and not usually optimal, the procedure can be iterated if measured page reference frequencies are available as feedback to the programmer.

Ferrari (158) has proposed the method of critical working sets (CWS) for use with working set memory management. Working set $W(t, T)$ is called critical if $r(t)$ is not an element of $W(t, T)$, causing a page fault. A critical reference is one causing a fault. The procedure is to measure the CWS matric $C = [c_{i,j}]$, where $c_{i,j}$ is the number of times a critical reference to block i occurs with a critical working set containing j. If restructuring were to place blocks i and j into the same page, $c_{i,j} + c_{j,i}$ critical references would no longer be critical. Thus, we may assign weight $c_{i,j}$ to the edge of the program graph from i to j (this may entail adding new edges to the graph). Optimum graph clustering algorithms can then be used to find the page assignment maximizing the sum of weights of edges between blocks in separate pages. Alternatively, a heuristic such as that of Hatfield and Gerald can be used.

While the CWS method is not always optimal, experiments (158) have shown it to improve over Hatfield and Gerald's method when the memory is working set managed.

We have discussed only the re-ordering of program code, not data. If data is divided into blocks such that there is no required positional arrangement among the blocks, it can often be treated in the same way (but instruction operand addresses will have to be changed). However, it is difficult to partition a large array or other data structure into blocks because the elements must retain certain relative orderings. This kind of restructuring must usually be done by the programmer. For example, McKellar and Coffman (158) give efficient methods of organizing matrices. Alternatively, a change of algorithm to one making more local use of its data will achieve the same effect, as has been demonstrated for sorting algorithms by Brawn, Gustavson, and Mankin (160).

CONCLUSION

We have discussed the properties of the phenomenon of locality, and have constructed the LRU stack program model as a stochastic representation. Among other things, the model provides a way to measure the degree of locality of a program. Two heuristic ways to improve the locality of a program's instruction code have been reviewed; these procedures have often been spectacularly successful for frequently used programs. Virtual memory is a great convenience to the programmer, but it presents new questions of program and system optimization that we have tried to address.

The LRU Stack Model is in fact the simplest of a class of models, called Stack Distance Models, which are the subject of current research. There is actually some correlation between the stack positions of successive references, although in the LRU Stack Model they are assumed to be independent. An example of a more sophisticated model has been proposed by Shedler and Tung (161), who assume the stack distances to be generated by a restricted form of Markov chain. Unfortunately, there has not as yet (to this author's knowledge) been an attempt to validate this model experimentally against real programs; hence its realism is questionable.

Program restructuring can be formulated as a mathematical programming problem if a program model of sufficient accuracy can be found. Barring this, heuristic methods, such as we have described, seem to be necessary to keep the problem tractable.

INTER-RELATIONSHIPS BETWEEN OPTIMIZATION AND STRUCTURED PROGRAMMING

M V Zelkowitz

Department of Computer Science
University of Maryland

M V ZELKOWITZ graduated from Rensselaer Polytechnic Institute with a BS degree in Mathematics in 1967. He went to Cornell University where he obtained an MS in Computer Science in 1969 and a PhD in 1971. He joined the faculty of the University of Maryland in 1971 as an Assistant Professor of Computer Science, and became an Associate Professor in 1975. He is currently a member of the Association for Computing Machinery, of the IEEE Computer Society, and was elected to membership of the Pi Mu Epsilon and Phi Kappa Phi honoraries. His current research interests include: compiler design, diagnostics systems, program optimization, and distributed computer networks.

INTER-RELATIONSHIPS BETWEEN OPTIMIZATION AND STRUCTURED PROGRAMMING

ABSTRACT

Within the past ten years, two aspects of programming have had significant impact upon both language and compiler design – program optimization and structured programming. The purpose of this paper is to review briefly both developments and to discuss the relationship between the two. The fact that there is any relationship at all between these ideas is itself quite interesting since, as we shall see, there is no reason for any such relationship to exist.

OPTIMIZATION

The need for program optimization extends back to the earliest compilers. Backus (100) mentioned that he had little doubt that the first FORTRAN compiler would work; however, he was concerned about the efficiency of its code compared with that of hand-coded assembly language. In those days, with only a few expensive and relatively slow machines, poor code produced by a compiler would have doomed it to failure, since the decreased program preparation time attributed to a compiler was not considered significant.

Therefore, considerable effort was spent in translating as efficient code as possible. In addition, since the FORTRAN language was being defined at the same time as the compiler was being written, the language was tailored to fit the architecture of the target machine (IBM 704). This resulted in some strange anomalies, which still remain in present-day FORTRAN. Such constructs as the arithmetic IF

IF (*expression*) *n1*, *n2*, *n3*

have their beginnings in the three-way branch of the 704.

Today the situation for the compiler writer is not so simple. While languages are mostly fixed (for example, FORTRAN, ALGOL, PL/1), the goal is still to compile code that is as efficient as possible. Of course, from experience with languages like FORTRAN, essentially two approaches towards optimization have developed – peephole optimization and global flow analysis.

Peephole optimization minimizes the program size or execution time of a small section of the program without analysing the entire program. For example, the statement

N := N+1

would result in the following assembly language instructions from a straightforward compiler for a typical register-oriented computer:

```
LOAD N
ADD  1
STORE N
```

However, for certain computers the above could be shortened to:

```
INCREMENT N
```

In general, peephole optimization is machine-dependent in that the changes generally utilize special instructions in the hardware of that particular computer.

Global flow analysis attempts to reorganize the entire program so that redundant calculations are not performed. Most global flow analysis algorithms are based on the assumption that the major part of the execution time is spent within loops. Two major global flow techniques predominate: elimination of common subexpressions and removal of loop-invariant calculations. The first method ensures one-time-only computation of a single expression in a loop by storing its value in a temporary location, instead of recalculating the expression, each time the value is needed. The second method moves expressions whose value does not change in the loop to outside the loop. Thus, if common subexpressions are first eliminated within a loop, and loop-invariant calculations are then eliminated, the loop should be shorter and also take less time to execute.

From this discussion, the reader should be able to see how most global flow analysis algorithms operate. As shown in Figure 1 a program is first divided into its basic loop structure (diagram 1A). The innermost loop is processed first (diagram 1B) and loop-invariant calculations are placed into a block preceding this innermost loop (diagram 1C). These loop-invariant calculations are now candidates for further removal in the next block. By also keeping track of which variables were altered by the innermost loop, the next level of loop structure can be similarly optimized (diagram 1D). This process can be iterated until the entire program has been optimized (diagrams 1E and 1F). The major difference in the various strategies are in the formal definitions of a loop (101,102,103).

Several other optimization techniques also exist. Two examples are folding (performing calculations at compile time instead of during program execution time) and strength reduction (changing multiplication to repeated addition within a loop, such as changing

```
M := I*K
```

to

```
M := M+K
```

when the loop iteration variable is I). These techniques will not be covered in detail here. See Allen (101) for a more complete description of these.

Register allocation also plays a role in program optimization. By keeping certain expressions (especially common subexpressions) and variables in several of the registers available, many LOAD instructions may be eliminated, and significant code improvement can be made. This will be discussed in greater detail later.

In discussing these techniques, it is important to realize that most global flow analysis algorithms modify source language constructs, that is, program variables are merely

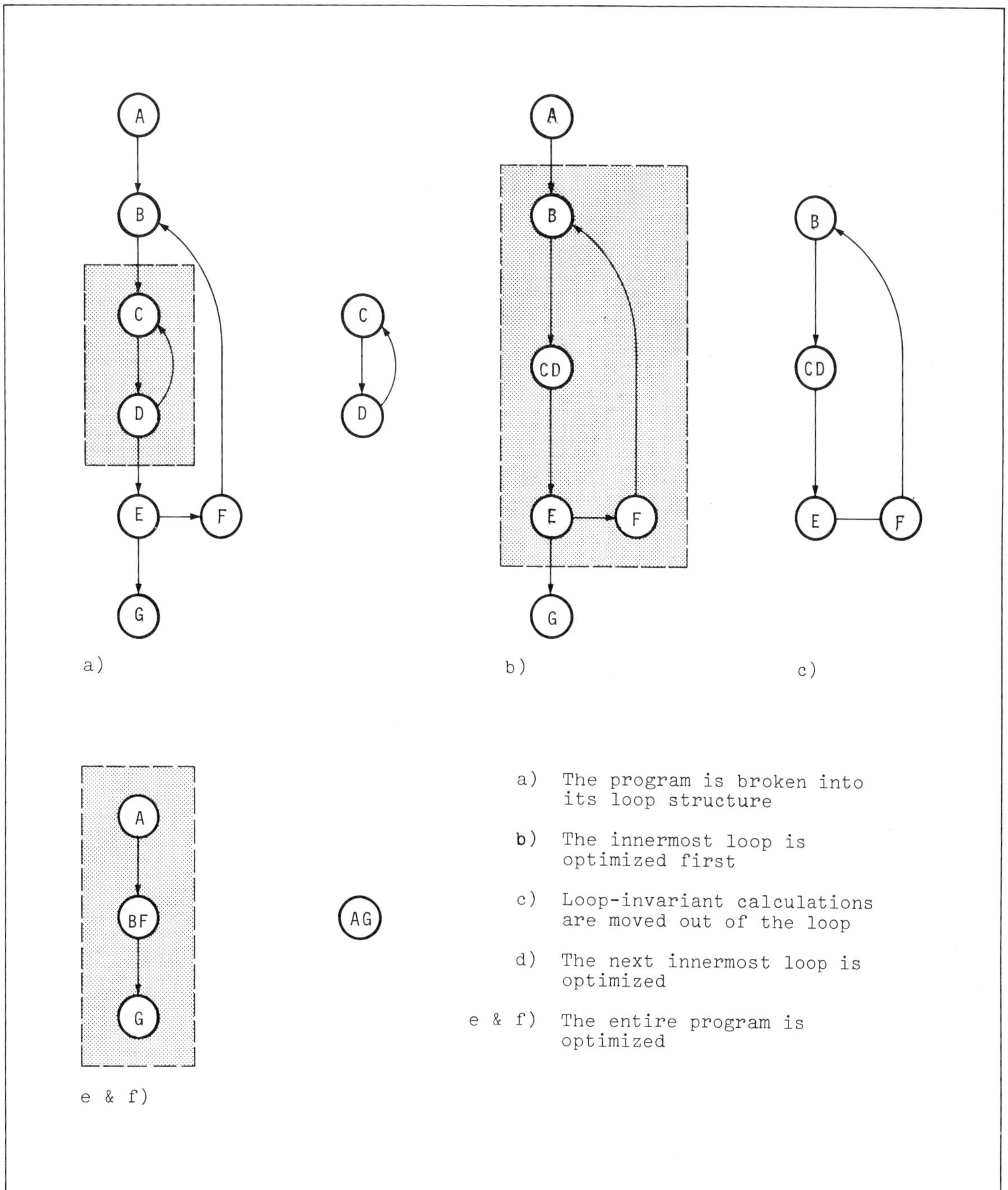

Figure 1: Standard global flow analysis

moved around. Thus a truly careful programmer could hand-code routines that come close to optimized code. The question that must be answered then is why have it?

Optimization does save program execution time. While a programmer could hand-optimize the code, a compiler can generally do a better job at less cost. Although an expert programmer may do as well as an optimizer, in the vast majority of cases the optimizer will do better. Since computer costs are decreasing while programming costs are increasing, it is better to improve a program mechanically than manually.

There are also some cases where a programmer cannot optimize by hand. For example, the expression A(I,J) involves a calculation of the form (Address-of-A + I*N + J). This gets more complex with more dimensions. A global optimizer generally has access to these subscript calculations – expressions that are not available at the source language level.

Since an optimizer does save execution time, a programmer can make use of it to make a program more understandable. Redundant calculations can be added to a program to improve the documentation and readability with the programmer knowing that the optimizer will remove those calculations.

STRUCTURED PROGRAMMING

A more recent development in programming language theory is the development of structured programming. There are probably as many definitions of structured programming as there are papers written about it. The common purpose, however, is to make it easier to write reliable programs, and at the same time make the programs easily understandable and easily modifiable. Structured programming includes all of the following concepts:

1 Program development requires a disciplined approach; for example, the unrestricted use of **goto** statements is frowned upon. Such a requirement has led to the well known result that all programs can be composed of only **if**, **while** and block constructs as shown in Figure 2 (104).

The frequent citing of an earlier paper by Bohm and Jacopini (105) as justification for this result is quite misleading. Their paper shows that any program can be modified by adding appropriate variables so that it consists of only the above three constructs. There is a trivial proof of this, as the following outline demonstrates.

Consider the following *n*-statement program:

```
1: S1;
2: S2;
3: S3;
.  .
.  .
n: SN;
```

This can be converted to the following 'structured' program:

```
I := 1;
while 'true' do
     if I=1 then
        begin; S1; I := 2; end;
     if I=2 then
        begin; S2; I := 3; end;
     if I=3 then
        begin; S3; I := 4; end;
     . . .
     . . .
end;
```

Statements of the form:

```
J: goto K; can be implemented as:
if I=J then
     begin; I := K; end;
```

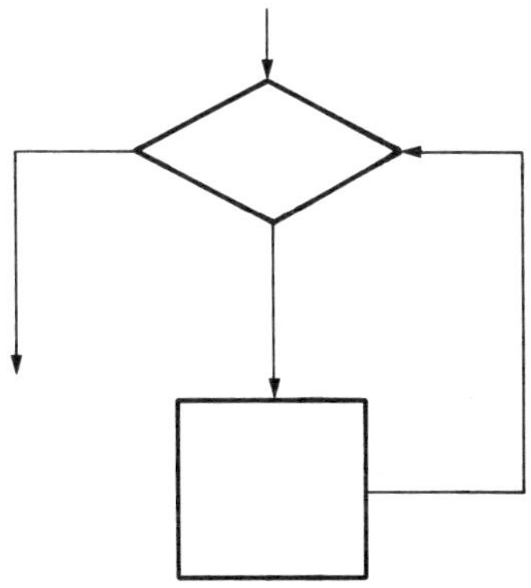

The while construct

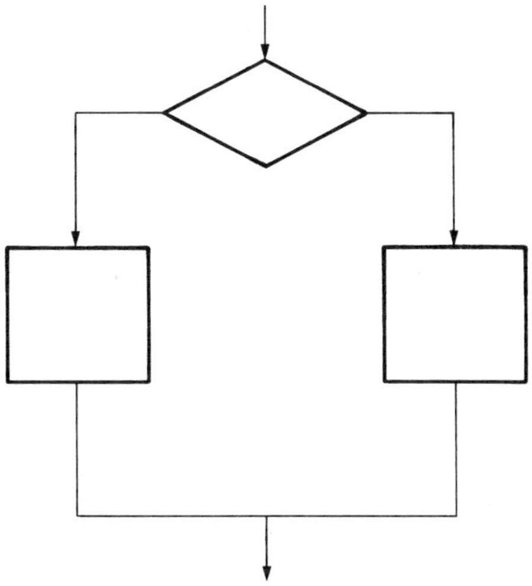

The if - then - else construct

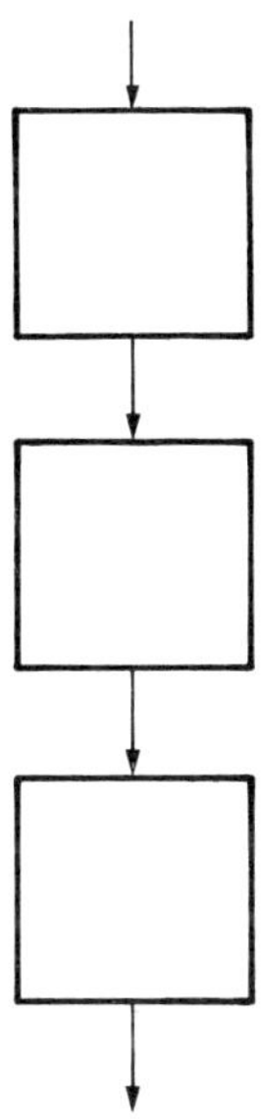

The block construct

Figure 2: The three basic control structures

Loops and **if** statements can be handled in an analogous manner.

Thus, any arbitrary 'unstructured' program can be mechanically converted into a 'structured' program! As should be obvious to the reader, this is not what structured programming is all about. For example, consider the following program:

```
do I := 1 to 2;
     if I=1 then X := Y;
     if I=2 then Z := W;
end;
```

This can easily be decomposed into two **if** statements contained within a loop so that it fulfils some definitions of being structured. However, I don't believe that anyone would consider it to be as clear as the sequence:

```
X := Y;
Z := W;
```

Therefore, structured programming means more than simply using only **if**, **while**, and block constructs. Many other control structures are possible (106). Such constructs as the **case**, **repeat-until** and the event-driven **case** have been proposed. These all have one common property; each is a one-in one-out control structure. That means that control always enters from the top (or from the statement that precedes it) and always exits from the bottom. Thus, the environment of the program (that is, the status of all variables of the program) upon entry into one of these control structures is always the environment of the statement that precedes it. This is not always true for other control structures. For example, with a **goto** statement, the environment at any label in a program may be that of any of the **goto**s that have that label as a target address.

Formal properties of these structures may be developed by restricting programs to one-in, one-out control structures. For example, Hoare (107) has developed a set of axioms that describe the execution of some of these structures and permit proof of formal properties of programs.

This aspect of structured programming can therefore be summarized as follows. A disciplined approach towards program development should be the norm (108). Control structures should be limited to a few well-understood constructs such as the one-in, one-out structures mentioned above.

2 Program development proceeds using a top-down stepwise refinement method (109). The top level of a program is written before lower-level subroutines are implemented. This proceeds until the entire program has been created. The result is that the breakdown of a program into independent sections or modules should proceed in well-defined directions (110).

3 Data structures should be carefully designed. Unfortunately, no simple theory of data structuring yet exists that parallels the control structure results. Several languages are under design that restrict the usage of data according to some of the criteria outlined by Parnas for modules (111).

4 When completed, programs should have a structure that permits a formal, or at least informal (which is better than today's standards), proof to be made certifying the correctness of the program.

Thus, structured programming is a discipline more than an exact set of procedures. The result of following this approach, however, is a system that generally has less errors and is more reliable than systems developed without such techniques (112). Once these ideas are understood, programmers will produce more software with less errors than previously. These programs are generally easier to understand, and more importantly, easier to modify.

EMPIRICAL STUDIES

After the previous discussion, it should be clear that program optimization and structured programming are operating at somewhat cross purposes. Program optimization automatically modifies a program to make it execute as fast as possible. Structured programming, on the other hand, restricts a programmer to the use of certain facilities and so possibly sacrifices speed execution in favour of achieving reliability. What is the effect of this rigid structure on program speed?

At first glance, it appears as if structured programming burdens the user by restricting the programming possibilities available. Although this is true, it does have a beneficial effect. A programmer cannot as easily start to code without thinking through a problem since unrestricted **gotos**, represented as arbitrary arcs on a flowchart, are not permitted. This restriction forces the programmer to spend more time in the design phase and less in the coding phase. This approach has generally been found to improve program structure.

One reason for the improvement is that the flow of control through a program is more tractable. Execution flows from top to bottom, except for loops. This is not true for an arbitrary program written in a language like FORTRAN where control at a labelled statement can arrive from any number of statements. Structured programs more easily allow for deducing the environment at any given statement since the previous environment is known. With arbitary jumps, the previous environment may not be apparent.

A programmer looking at a listing sees the syntactic structure of a program; the dynamic behaviour is not apparent. However, with only one-in, one-out control structures, the dynamic behaviour is virtually the same as the syntactic structure. As a result scanning such a listing gives greater insights into how the program will execute.

Several axiomatic systems have been proposed for structured programming languages (107). Axioms have been written for the **if** and **while** statements. A programmer, using these axioms, even in an informal manner, can frequently optimize a program containing such constructs better than one utilizing **gotos**. What is more important is that some of these techniques are algorithmic, and, as will shortly be explained, can easily be programmed into an optimizing compiler.

Unfortunately, the available empirical data on the subject is meagre. In one such study (113) an optimizer was written for a language called SIMPL-XI (114), which generated code for a PDP-11 computer. This language is a variant of the SIMPL language developed at the University of Maryland (115). This language implemented only the **procedure**, **if**, **while**, and **case** constructs. Running the optimizer on several programs showed that the optimizer performed very poorly.

There are several possible reasons for this result. Firstly, optimization was on a procedure-by-procedure basis. However, the top-down design strategy employed in the programs being tested meant that many different procedures were written. Since this optimizer did not optimize any global variables across a procedure call (since any procedure could modify any global variable), not much code was available for optimization.

One major source for optimization is in register allocation. In the SIMPL compiler, a straightforward register allocation strategy was added to the code generator. A round-robin allocation strategy was used to allocate one of the four available registers each time one was needed. Within any block of code, the compiler kept track of which variables still had their current value in one of the registers. If any of these variables were used again within that block, no LOAD instruction need be generated. Upon reaching the end of any block, such as the end of a **while** loop, all registers were assumed to have no values in them. This was due to the fact that the block of code that set the registers (body of the **while** loop) may not have been executed if the expression in the **while** statement was false. This simple strategy saved about 10% of the generated code over the previous version of the compiler, which used only a single register for its calculations. This register allocator, which certainly did not do a global flow analysis of the program and hence was not optimal, did a creditable job and was used for each program whether optimized or not. Thus, register allocation was always optimized and did not count in calculating the effectiveness of the optimizer.

SIMPL also had extensive peephole optimization algorithms built into the code generator. The consequence was that these also did not show up in calculating the effectiveness of the optimizer.

Another possible cause for the poor results was that SIMPL implemented only one-dimensional arrays. As Knuth seemed to indicate (116), much of the available optimization is achieved by optimization of subscript calculations. This optimization is only minimally available for one-dimensional array references. And as Knuth so aptly states, with more complex data structures in future languages, there should be less emphasis on array calculations and hence less possible optimization possibilities.

A final possibility is that most of the test programs were relatively short. This fact enables a programmer to spot common subexpressions before they appeared in the code. Moreover, SIMPL was being used as a systems programming language, and some other results seem to indicate that optimization does not work as well on such programs as they do on numerical calculations, such as in a typical FORTRAN program.

In spite of the seemingly negative results, other more recent experiments with the SIMPL language seem to bear out some aspects of these conclusions. For example, one large numerical analysis program, involving sparse matrix calculations and written in FORTRAN, was recoded into SIMPL for the UNIVAC 1108 computer (117). The UNIVAC FORTRAN compiler has a relatively sophisticated statement optimizer, but performs no global flow analysis. SIMPL for the 1108 is a straightforward compiler with no global optimizer, but good peephole optimization. In spite of that, the SIMPL program ran in 10% less time. Since every effort was made to preserve the original FORTRAN algorithms in the SIMPL program (although some changes had to be made because of the necessity of eliminating the GOTO of FORTRAN), this seems to indicate the efficiency of such a structured programming language.

Since the SIMPL compiler is itself written in SIMPL, an analysis of the compiler reveals certain interesting aspects of programming in such a language (118). Over a two-year period, five different versions of the compiler were evaluated. The number of source statements in the compiler rose from 3404 in the initial implementation to 6350 in the last one studied and the number of procedures rose from 89 to 289. The two interesting facts to emerge from this study were that the number of global variables accessible by a procedure dropped from an average of 52.0 to an average of only 22.3. Also, the percentage of data bindings, usage of a global variable in a procedure set in some other procedure, rose from 1% of all possible bindings to 3% of all possible bindings.

These numbers seem to indicate that the compiler was restructured as it developed and data gradually filtered to the few modules that needed it. This is in line with the writings of Parnas on module development. Since these measures were devised after all five versions were completed, there was no bias on the part of the compiler writers to affect these measures as the compiler developed. Thus, continued development has led to a system that is quite modular and generates code as efficient as any reasonable FORTRAN.

STRUCTURED PROGRAM OPTIMIZATION

The foregoing discussion seems to indicate two basic conclusions:

1 Structured programming, without an optimizer, can often lead to programs that are more efficient than correspondingly unstructured ones.

2 Current optimization techniques are generally inadequate to improve structured programs to any great extent.

This second point deserves further consideration. As mentioned previously, most global flow analysis algorithms work 'inside out'. This is done by constructing the program graph (Figure 1) from the internal parsed form of the program. The fact that this is the usual technique is not surprising, since most experience with optimization has deriver from the FORTRAN language. FORTRAN has no real structure, so any loop or conditional structure had to be built by the programmer out of the more primitive FORTRAN statements.

This meant that the optimizer had to build up this same structure by analysing across several statements. Most optimizers today utilize this strategy. That is, the parser knows the control structure of a program, yet throws it away when the internal parsed form of the program is created. The optimizer then has to recreate the structure to optimize the program.

When looked at from that point of view, a great duplication of effort becomes apparent. If a program uses only **if**, **while**, or the block as the basic control structures, then a single pass through the program is sufficient to produce the flow graph of a program. All loops that are dynamically nested within a given loop during program execution will also be syntactically nested. This knowledge can be utilized by an optimizer, which would be more efficient than present-day techniques.

An early FORTRAN optimizer by Gear (119) was one of the first to exploit this fact. This compiler was a three-pass compiler with optimization being performed during the second pass. Only explicit DO-blocks were optimized; loops created by IF statements and GOTOs were ignored.

At the heart of the optimization algorithm was the concept of a change vector. This vector contained the names of all variables altered within a loop. There was always such a vector that described the variables of the program during the entire compilation process.

During the first pass, as a DO-loop was encountered, the current vector was saved (in a stack), and a new vector, to contain the names of variables altered in the DO-block, was initialized to empty. Each assignment statement added a variable to this vector. Upon exit from the block at the end of the DO-loop, this vector was added to the parsed program. This vector was also merged with the previously saved vector, which described the enclosing block, since all variables altered within the inner loop are also altered within the enclosing loop. This first pass had the effect of placing in the parsed program at the end of a DO-loop the names of all variables altered within that loop.

The second pass was a backward pass through the program to perform the optimization. Upon entry to a loop (backwards), the vector describing the changed variables was obtained. Any expression that contained variables not in this vector was a loop-invariant calculation. A temporary was allocated and the expression moved to a holding location. When the DO statement was processed, all of these moved expressions were added to the enclosing loop.

For example, the code:

```
      DO 10 I = 1,10
10    A(I) = B*C
```

would result in B*C being replaced by a temporary. The program would be restructured as follows:

```
      T1 = B*C
      DO 10 I = 1,10
10    A(I) = T1
```

An efficient register allocation strategy would keep T1 in a register, and since it is never used outside of this loop, would never store its value into memory. This means that even though a new temporary variable was created, no additional storage space or instructions would have to be generated.

The third pass was a straightforward code generation pass.

This shows that with a rather simple scheme, a global flow analysis routine can be written that works very well for well-structured programs.

This technique was extended in the optimizer written for the SIMPL-XI compiler mentioned previously. Since SIMPL only has the **if**, **case**, and **while** constructs, an extension to the above technique for FORTRAN allows for efficient global flow analysis.

The algorithm used for this optimizer was based upon a recursive descent scheme (120). As with the Gear FORTRAN optimizer, three passes were needed. The first two passes were executed sequentially one block at a time, while the third-pass code generator generated code after all optimization had been completed.

In the first pass, every time a block was encounterd (**while** statement, **then** part of an **if** statement, **else** part of an **if** statement, or one of the blocks in a **case** statement), the optimizer called itself recursively to first optimize the inner block. Upon entry, it created a change vector similar to the Gear FORTRAN optimizer. When it reached the end of the block, it immediately scanned the block backwards removing invariant expressions and common subexpressions. After reaching the beginning of the block, the change vector was added to the vector of the outer block and the invariant expressions were added to this outer block for further optimization. The optimizer then continued with the statement following the inner block.

In this case, since SIMPL has no **goto** statement, this algorithm is equivalent to the global flow analysis algorithms mentioned for FORTRAN optimizers. In this case, however, it is not necessary to implement routines to compute the loop structure of the program. This loop structure is apparent by the recursive nature of the nested control structures. This algorithm is both efficient and easy to program.

In order to bypass some of the problems that were encountered by the above project, a new project is underway to improve the optimizer (121). In this case, Hecht is creating a call graph to indicate which procedures call which procedures. If the optimizer then proceeds by optimizing those procedures that call no others, it is not necessary to assume that a procedure can modify any global variable. This method will allow for optimizing most global variables across procedure calls.

The efficiency of such optimizers is leading to the development of new techniques that are tailored to structured programs and to structured programming languages. Rosen (122) has defined a technique that assumes that a program is decomposable into a set of one-in, one-out control structures. That is, his technique assumes that any program may be decomposed into structures of the form

$$C(S_1, \dots ,S_k)$$

where the S_1 through S_k are other structures. (Note that this includes the one-in, one-out structures mentioned previously.) His algorithm computes usage information for each variable within each internal block and then passes it out to the enclosing block. Not only does he keep track of variables that are modified, but he also keeps track of which variables are 'live', that is, will be used again before being modified. This helps in allocating registers and in determining whether a calculation need be performed at all. The basic recursive descent nature of this process makes it quite efficient –

more so than with classical flow analysis procedures. When random jumps (that is, **gotos**) are taken into account, his mechanism still works; however, it becomes progressively less efficient, becoming similar to previously used techniques. However, for a structured programming language, or a well-structured program in any language, the technique is quite practical.

CONCLUSIONS

As Knuth has stated (116), current optimization techniques already come reasonably close to optimal program execution – for a given algorithm – while his experience has shown that modifying the algorithm can improve the program more than optimization. This suggests that optimizers will not get much better than the best ones of today without some major breakthroughs in optimization technology. Better execution characteristics will depend upon more efficient program algorithms.

Structured programming, however, is one technique that can improve the execution characteristics of a program. The disciplined approach forces the programmer to think more about a program that would otherwise be the case. The few examples that do exist seem to indicate that 'restricting' oneself to structured programming does not lead to inefficient programs and, in fact, the exact opposite may be the case.

Another point is that structured programs allow for efficient optimization possibilities. Only two passes through a program are needed to discover the block structure and eliminate common subexpressions and loop-invariant calculations. This would add minimal time onto the normal compilation time. Optimizers would be cheaper to use and easier to implement. As a corollary to this, with standard optimization being cheaper, more exotic schemes can be tried to get still better code than is now possible.

In any case, both optimization and structured programming do not seem to be going at cross purposes. Although the available data is not conclusive, it does indicate that one need not sacrifice one for the other. In fact, structured programming can be seen as an enhancement to existing optimization possibilities.

BIBLIOGRAPHY AND CONTRIBUTORS' REFERENCES

ANNOTATED BIBLIOGRAPHY OF SELECTED PAPERS ON PROGRAM OPTIMIZATION

F E Allen

IBM Thomas J Watson Research Center

F E ALLEN is at IBM's T J Watson Research Center in Yorktown Heights, New York, where she is manager of the Experimental Compiling Systems Project. She has published numerous papers on program analysis and optimization. Ms Allen is a consultant to the National Science Foundation, has been an IEEE Distinguished Visitor and an ACM National Lecturer. She has lectured on program optimization in the USSR at the invitation of the Siberian Branch of the USSR Academy of Sciences and in China at the invitation of the Chinese Academy of Sciences. Ms Allen has an MA in Mathematics from the University of Michigan.

ANNOTATED BIBLIOGRAPHY OF SELECTED PAPERS ON PROGRAM OPTIMIZATION

INTRODUCTION

Program optimization has long been of pragmatic interest to compiler writers and users. More recently it has become the subject of numerous theoretical investigations. These investigations have led to faster algorithms in some cases and in other cases to proof that certain problems are inherently "very hard" (NP-complete) and heuristic solutions should be sought. In selecting the 67 papers in this bibliography, we started from a list of nearly 250 English language documents. Although the selection process was admittedly subjective, we did try to apply some guidelines. We have tried to include all papers describing compilers which perform optimization. Contrary to the apparent results, we culled many more theoretical papers than practical papers out of our original list. (Unfortunately program writers don't seem to be paper writers.) We have emphasized recent work as a means of noting directions being taken but have completely omitted certain subjects. The most notable omission is optimization for parallel processors. We have generally included theoretical papers which illuminate troublesome areas such as register allocation. The style of the annotation is generally non-critical though particularly interesting work is usually designated as such. Most of the entries are our own summary, not the author's. Terms which are widely used in the literature (for example basic blocks) are not defined; hopefully this bibliography will help the interested reader find his way into the literature at points where such terms are defined.

REFERENCE SOURCES

Some abbreviations of journal titles are used in the list of references. The full title is given below together with the address from which the publication is available.

Journal reference		*Full title and publisher's address*
Acta Informatica		Acta Informatica Springer-Verlag D-1000 Berlin 33 Heidelberger Platz 3 Germany
	or	Springer-Verlag New York Inc 175 Fifth Avenue New York NY 10010 USA

Comm ACM	The Communications of the ACM ACM Order Department 1133 Avenue of the Americas New York NY 10036 USA
Comp Jour	The Computer Journal British Computer Society 29 Portland Place London W1N 4AP UK
Comp Lang	Computer Languages Pergamon Press Ltd Oxford England
IBM Jour of R & D	IBM Journal of Research and Development IBM Corp Armonk NY 10504 USA
IBM Syst Jour	IBM Systems Journal IBM Corp Armonk NY 10504 USA
Inter Jour Comp Math	International Journal of Computer Mathematics Academic Press Inc 111 Fifth Avenue New York NY 10003 USA
IEEE Trans Software Eng	IEEE Transactions on Software Engineering Institute of Electrical and Electronic Engineers Inc 345 East 47th Street New York NY 10017 USA
Jour ACM	The Journal of the ACM ACM Order Department 1133 Avenue of the Americas New York NY 10036 USA

Jour Comp & Syst Sciences		Journal of Computer and System Sciences Academic Press 111 Fifth Avenue New York NY 10003 USA
Proc ACM		Proceedings of the ACM Annual Conference ACM Order Department 1133 Avenue of the Americas New York NY 10036 USA
Proc AFIPS FJCC WJCC		Proceedings of the AFIPS Fall Joint/Western Joint Computer Conference AFIPS Press 210 Summit Avenue Montvale NJ 07645 USA
Proc IFIP		Proceedings of the IFIP Congress North Holland Publishing Co Amsterdam Holland
	or	American Elsevier Publishing Company Inc 52 Vanderbilt Avenue New York NY 10017 USA
SIAM Jour Comp		SIAM Journal on Computing Society for Industrial and Applied Mathematics 33 S 17th Street Philadelphia PA 19103 USA
SIGPLAN Notices		Newsletter of the Special Interest Group on Programming Languages ACM Order Department 1133 Avenue of the Americas New York NY 10036 USA

REFERENCES AND ABSTRACTS

001 AHO A V, JOHNSON S C and ULLMAN J D
Code generation for expressions with common subexpressions
Conf Record of Third ACM Symp on *Principles of Programming Languages* Atlanta Georgia pp 19-31 (Jan 1976)

The problem of generating optimal code for a set of expressions is considered in this paper. Optimal code is defined to be the shortest code sequence that can be generated for a set of expressions where the set of expressions is constrained to be the linear sequence of subexpressions constituting a basic block before registers have been assigned. Efficient algorithms exist (055,015) for solving the problem on a wide class of machines provided the set of expressions has no common subexpressions, that is, provided the result of an expression is used only once in the sequence. This paper shows that the problem is NP-complete on two-address machines such as the IBM 360 even when the number of registers is unlimited. The paper then considers a number of fast heuristics for simple and multiple-register machines. The worst-case performance of these heuristics are evaluated against the optimal solution. An algorithm for a single-register machine is given which generates optimal code and is linear when there are no common subexpressions and exponential in terms of the amount of sharing when there are common subexpressions.

002 AHO A V and ULLMAN J D
Optimization of straight line programs
SIAM Jour Comp vol 1 no 1 pp 1-19 (March 1972)

This theoretical paper first considers the problem of transforming a straight-line program into an equivalent one provided no algebraic laws hold. The transformations for which equivalence can be demonstrated when there are no alebraic laws are:

1 removal (or insertion) of useless statements;

2 removal (or insertion) of redundant statements;

3 renaming of variables;

4 flipping independent statements.

The paper then shows that optimization of straight-line code under "reasonable" cost criteria can always be accomplished by applying sequences of these transformations in a prescribed order.

003 AHO A V and ULLMAN J D
The theory of parsing, translation, and compiling
Prentice-Hall (1973)

The second volume of this 2-volume text contains an extensive section (pp 844-960) on code optimization. Optimization of straight-line code is discussed in detail. Examples of transformations on programs with loops are given. Data flow analysis based on the interval [see (005)] partition of the control flow graph is discussed.

004 ALLEN F E
Program optimization
Ann Review in Automatic Programming vol 5 pp 239-307 Pergamon (1969)

Machine-independent and language-independent methods of optimizing the execution times of compiled programs are described. The approach is based on the topological characteristics of a program. A program partitioning into strongly connected regions is developed which permits modular optimization. The principal methods considered are eliminating redundant expressions, constant propagation, code motion, strength reduction, test replacement, and dead code elimination. Many improvements have been made in optimization approaches since this paper was written (1966) particularly in the areas of control and data flow analysis. The interaction of the various transformations are interesting and are illustrated in examples which were run through an experimental implementation of the methods described in the paper.

005 ALLEN F E
Control flow analysis
SIGPLAN Notices vol 5 no 7 pp 1-19 (July 1970)

The interval construct for partitioning a control flow graph of a program was first defined in this paper. The basic motivation for control flow analysis in an optimizing compiler is the need to codify the program control flow relationships so that other relationships and transformations can be found. The interval partition of a program control flow graph and the set of graphs derived from successive partitions, establish an order for processing the instruction sequences in the program. Using this order data flow analysis fast analysis algorithms can be constructed (010). After defining basic concepts and dominance relationships, the paper defines intervals and their properties, and gives algorithms for finding them and other control flow relationships. Graph partitioning is then discussed and the use of this construct in global analysis is sketched.

006 ALLEN F E
Interprocedural data flow analysis
Proc IFIP '74 pp 398-402 (1974)

The data relationships which exist between the collection of procedures which constitute a program are of interest in program analysis and optimization. For example if the data items defined or used by a reference to a procedure are not known then very little optimization can be done across a call. All data items have to be in their home locations, and subexpressions cannot be moved or commoned across the call. In this paper, an analysis algorithm is given which derives the interprocedural data flow relationships. The algorithm does not support recursive calls but has been designed so that each procedure is analysed only once. Since this paper appeared three other relevant papers have been published (007,042,047). Rosen (047) handles recursive procedures and produces much more precise results but at the expense of a more complex analysis. Lomet (042) also handles recursive procedures, produces slightly less precise results than Rosen but still analyses each procedure only once.

007 ALLEN F E
Interprocedural analysis and the information derived by it
Lecture Notes in Computer Science vol 23 pp 291-321 Springer-Verlag (1975)

After reviewing and expanding the interprocedural analysis methods of (006) the information derived by such an analysis on the collection of procedures which comprise a program is given. Five such items of information are:

1 the static call graph depicting the possible invocation relationships in the collection

2 the control flow graph for each procedure

3 the data flow within each procedure

4 the control flow between procedures

5 the data flow between procedures

Four applications for this information are:

1 annotating program listings to document programs automatically

2 interactively supplying information to the user about the characteristics of his program

3 managing programs more systematically

4 optimizing programs

An example of the results of running a PL/1 program through an experimental system which does such an analysis is given.

008 ALLEN F E and COCKE J
A catalogue of optimizing transformations
In *Design and Optimization of Compilers* (editor R Rustin) pp 1-30
Prentice-Hall (1972)

A large number of the optimizing transformations which can be made to a program are catalogued in this paper. Each transformation is informally defined along with some discussion of the advantages and disadvantages of the transformation. Recently a paper by Loveman (043) has been published which contains a more extensive collection.

009 ALLEN F E and COCKE J
Graph-theoretic constructs for program control flow analysis
IBM Research Report RC3923 T J Watson Research Center Yorktown Heights (July 1972)

In (005) the interval construct for codifying the control flow in a program is discussed. This paper reviews this approach, discusses 'irreducible' graphs and 'node splitting'. Graphs with certain forms of multiple-entry loops are termed irreducible and not amenable to complete partitioning into intervals. They can however be transformed into equivalent graphs which can be partitioned by a process called node splitting. This paper gives properties of irreducible graphs and a node splitting algorithm which is guaranteed to produce a graph which is 'simpler' and can be further analysed. The results of applying these analyses to a large number of FORTRAN programs are given. Irreducible graphs and node splitting algorithms have also been discussed in (019,032,034,049).

010 ALLEN F E and COCKE J
A program data flow analysis procedure
Comm ACM vol 19 no 3 pp 137-147 (March 1976)

Data flow analysis as considered in this paper and elsewhere (019,028, 033,038,059) is aimed at deriving the use-definition relationships in a program. Also of interest are the variables 'live', that is, having a subsequent use, at each point in the program. This paper presents a PL/1 procedure which derives the definition-use and live relationships for a program. It is based in an interval partition of the graph and is driven by an interval ordered, edge listing of the control flow graph.

011 ALLEN F E, COCKE J and KENNEDY K
Reduction of operator strength
Technical Report 476-093-6
Dept of Mathematical Sciences
Rice Univ Houston Texas (Aug 1974)

One of the primary goals of the strength reduction optimization is to identify computations in a loop which produce successive values differing by a constant and then replace them by computations which take advantage of this. These new computations use the old value and the constant difference to determine the new value. The main application for this has been to change subscript computations into register instructions which can be implemented by index register increments. This paper presents a new approach which is somewhat more general and systematic than ones that had been given previously in (004) and (019).

012 BACKUS J W *et al*
The FORTRAN automatic coding system
Proc AFIPS WJCC pp 188-198 (1957)
Also in *Programming Systems and Languages* (editor S Rosen) McGraw-Hill pp 29-47 (1967)

This paper describing the FORTRAN I compiler is included in this bibliography for a number of reasons: its historical interest, our stated intention of including papers on compilers which performed optimization and, more than anything else, our evaluation that this compiler produced more carefully optimized code than any compiler developed since. On more than one occasion we thought the object code was in error only to realize after some thought that an exceedingly clever optimization had been performed.

013 BEATTY J C
A register assignment algorithm for generation of highly optimized object code
IBM Jour of R & D vol 18 no 1 pp 20-39 (Jan 1974)

The register assignment algorithm given in this paper permits a high level of optimization at both the local and global levels. In order to achieve this, the process is broken into three steps: local (to a basic block) allocation, global allocation and assignment, and then local assignment. Local allocation claims all the available register resources needed for local communication but does not designate specific registers. Knowing the local requirements, the global allocator can allocate the remaining register resources to carry information across blocks. Specific registers are then selected for these inter-block quantities, with an attempt being made to minimize mismatches. Local assignment then assigns the locally allocated registers and generates code consistent with the assignments. The algorithm includes the ability to selectively move loads out of loops when enough registers are available to carry the information to its use. The paper includes a report on a prototype implementation which permits comparison with the IBM 360 FORTRAN-H implementation.

014 BREUER M A
Generation of optimal code for expressions via factorization
Comm ACM vol 12 no 6 pp 333-340 (June 1969)

Two problems are considered in this paper:

1 given a sequence of expressions, find the maximum number of common 'factors' or 'formal identities';

2 having found the factors, sequence them so as to minimize the total

number of temporary storage cells (or registers) required to hold the results of the factors.

The expressions considered involve only commutative operators. In order to make the techniques considered computationally feasible, heuristic procedures are applied. The results are, as the paper points out, not necessarily optimal. It is interesting to note that later papers (001,016) have shown that the second problem is NP-complete (that is, very hard) on various machine models. We suspect the first problem is also NP-complete.

015 BRUNO J and LASSAGNE T
The generation of optimal code for stack machines
Jour ACM vol 22 no 3 pp 382-396 (July 1975)

The problem of generating optimal (in terms of the number of instructions required to pop a stack) code on stack machines is considered. It is assumed that the stack is finite and that the expressions can be expressed as trees, that is that they have no internal data dependencies. Three algorithms are given, one assumes the operators have no algebraic properties, a second assumes only commutative operators and a third assumes commutative and associative-commutative operators.

016 BRUNO J and SETHI R
Register allocation for a one-register machine
Technical Report no 157 Comp Sci Dept Pennsylvania State Univ (Oct 1974)

The problem of generating minimal length code for a sequence of expressions which share intermediate results is shown to be NP-complete for a one-register machine.

017 BUSAM V A and ENGLUND D E
Optimization of expressions in FORTRAN
Comm ACM vol 12 no 12 pp 666-674 (Dec 1969)

The title of this paper is somewhat misleading. The paper actually describes a three-pass FORTRAN optimizing compiler. The optimizations eliminate redundant calculations, move invariant calculations out of DO-loops, transform subscripts involving DO-variables to efficient calculations and provide efficient index register usage. The method has been used in the development of several FORTRAN compilers. The design presented here provides, in our opinion, an exceptionally good balance between compile time costs and execution time efficiency.

018 COCKE J
Global common subexpression elimination
SIGPLAN Notices vol 5 no 7 pp 20-24 (July 1970)

The object of the method given in this paper is twofold:

1 to delete computations which have been previously performed,

2 to move computations from their original locations to less frequently executed regions.

A system of Boolean equations expressing the local (basic block) computations is solved in order to determine the deposition of each subexpression. The special Gaussian elimination procedure necessary to solve the system of equations is based on an interval partition of the flow graph (005).

019 COCKE J and SCHWARTZ J T
Programming languages and their compilers
Preliminary Notes Courant Institute of Mathematical Sciences New York University (1970)

Chapter 6 (pages 306-523) of these Notes is called *Optimization Methods for Algebraic Languages*. After an initial discussion of possible transformations, the 'value numbering algorithm' for optimizing basic blocks is given. This is followed by the 'linear nested region analyser' method for global analyses. Program flow intervals (005), Boolean redundancy equations (018), strength reduction, subroutine linkage optimization and register allocation are then discussed. While this document is truly preliminary in form, it contains a considerable amount of interesting information.

020 DARLINGTON J and BURSTALL R M
A system which automatically improves programs
Proc 3rd Intl Conf on *Artificial Intelligence* pp 537-542 Stanford California (Aug 1973)

Methods for mechanically converting programs written in LISP-like languages to more efficient forms are considered in this paper. The main transformations are recursion removal, eliminating common subexpressions, combining loops, replacing procedure calls by their bodies, and doing compile time garbage collection. A system implementing these transformations is described and an example of its use is given.

021 DAY W H E
Compiler assignment of data items to registers
IBM Syst Jour vol 9 no 4 pp 281-317 (1970)

What follows is a direct paraphrase of the introduction to this paper.

The assignment of data items to registers is one of the function performed by a compiler during the preparation of a program for execution. The way in which this function is performed affects the execution characteristics of the program. A good register assignment scheme can, for example, reduce the number of movements of data items between main storage and registers and can allow use of the faster register-to-register instructions. This paper considers three related methods of assigning data items to registers.

After establishing some basic definitions and assumptions, and distinguishing between global and local assignment, the three methods of global assignment – one-one, many-one, and many-few – are discussed.

Global one-one assignment associates exactly one data item with each register in the region of assignment. The method is interesting because it is used in commercially available compilers. In this paper, it is used as a standard for measuring the effectiveness of the many-one and many-few global assignment methods.

Global many-one assignment associates at least one data item with a single register in the region of assignment. A branch-and-bound procedure is used to obtain optimal solutions to this assignment problem and to prove that these solutions are indeed optimal. This procedure provides a standard for measuring the effectiveness of assignment algorithms obtaining possible non-optimal solutions.

Global many-few assignment associates at least one data item with each of several registers in the region of assignment. The structure of this problem is identical to that of the global many-one assignment problem, so that the branch-and-bound procedure may be used to obtain optimal solutions to both problems.

Two algorithms are described that obtain possible non-optimal solutions to the many-one and many-few global assignment problems. For the problems analysed, these algorithms are considered fast enough to be considered for inclusion in an optimizing compiler. In addition, the solutions generally obtained by them are close to the optimal solution and are significantly better than the corresponding global one-one solution.

Finally, certain extensions in the use of the global many-few assignment method that may increase the profitability of the final assignments are discussed. In particular, ways in which this method may be used to effect the assignment of a data item to more than one register in the region of assignment are considered.

022 EARLEY J
High-level iterators and a method of automatically designing data and structure representation
College of Engineering Memorandum ERL-M416 University of California Berkeley (Feb 1974)

Very high-level languages such as SETL, APL and VERS operate on abstract data structures. This paper first catalogues the high-level language constructs called 'iterators' which yield streams of values. Important examples of iterative operations are set formers, and existential and universal quantifiers. Thus $\exists x \varepsilon S | P(x)$ is an iterator with the existential quantifier $\exists$ as an operator. Having established an interesting catalogue of such iterators, the paper then considers how iterators can be implemented more efficiently than by a straight forward implementation. The basic idea is similar to the technique used for data bases in which an inverted file is kept to permit fast accesses. This paper is an early paper in what is becoming an increasingly important area (026,052,053).

023 EARNEST C
Some topics in code optimization
Jour ACM vol 21 no 1 pp 76-102 (Jan 1974)

Cocke and Schwartz (019) and Cocke (018) give an algorithm for discovering when the computation of an expression is redundant and when it can be moved to a less frequently executed region of the program. This paper reviews their methods and extends it to treat the safety constraint, handle multi-entry loops, detect additional commonality and code motion as well as making other improvements.

024 ERSHOV A P
ALPHA — an automatic programming system of high efficiency
Jour ACM vol 13 no 1 pp 17-24 (Jan 1966)

The ALPHA language, a variant of the ALGOL 60 language, is compiled by the system outlined in this paper and detailed in (025). The principal objective of the ALPHA system was to produce fast compact object code. The paper reports a production compiler that had been operational for some time and the results of comparing its output with hand code and earlier ALPHA compilers are given. Two transformations are of particular interest:

1 neighbouring **for** statements having identical **for** clauses and arising from component-wise operations on

arrays are combined;

2 global memory economy.

Since the target machine had only 4096 45-bit words the ALPHA system attempted to minimize the use of memory. An inconsistency matrix is constructed showing which variables cannot occupy the same cell at the same time. This paper does not contain any details on this interesting problem but (025) does.

025 ERSHOV A P (editor)
The ALPHA Automatic Programming System
Academic Press London and New York (1971)

This book contains a collection of papers describing the ALPHA (an ALGOL-like language) compiler. The features of the compiler are summarized in (024). Details on the algorithms supporting these features can be found in this book. Four papers are of particular interest. A paper by Voloshin on *Programming operations over multiple arrays and complex variables in the ALPHA translator* discusses among other things loop jamming and reducing the nesting of loops of component-wise operations. A paper by Bezhanova and Pottosin on *Programming loops and index expressions in the ALPHA translator* discusses code motion, constant propagation, subscript calculation modifications, etc. A paper by Pottosin on *Economy of expressions in the ALPHA translator* discusses the elimination of redundant expressions. An interesting feature of this method is that multi-operand instructions are used rather than the usual two-operand instructions. Common subparts of such multi-instructions are found. A paper on *Economy and allocation of memory in the ALPHA translator* by Ershov, Zmiyevskaya, Mishkovitch, and Trokham is very interesting. The problem of minimizing the amount of storage space required at any time during the execution of the object program, a problem analogous to register allocation, is formulated as a graph colouring problem. Although this book describes work completed in a production compiler well over ten years ago, many of the techniques are more advanced than are currently found in most such compilers.

026 FONG A C and ULLMAN J D
Induction variables in very high-level languages
Conference Record of the Third ACM Symp on *Principles of Programming Languages* pp 104-112 Atlanta (Jan 1976)

In languages such as FORTRAN, an induction variable is a variable whose value assumes an arithmetic progression at a point in a program. A DO control variable is an example of an explicit induction variable. In theoretic languages such as SETL, the notion of an induction variable can be extended to include any variable for which successive values computed at a point in a loop differ by a small, easily computable amount. In a set forming operation such as $A=A \cup x$, the set A might be an explicit induction variable. Having identified an explicit induction variable, we would like to transform operations involving induction variables into explicit inductive computations. In this paper the notion of an induction variable in a set-theoretic language is explored. The conditions under which a transformation of an operation involving induction variables is profitable are considered. The work is in a quite preliminary stage and builds on work done by Earley (022) as well as earlier work on strength reduction (005,019) in lower-level languages. Its main interest is its attempt to establish a theoretical basis for the profitable identification of induction variables in a very general context.

027 GESCHKE C M
Global program optimizations
Doctoral Thesis Computer Science Dept Carnegie-Mellon University (1972)

The first part of this thesis proposes a collection of primitives for describing program optimizations. Code motion, redundant expression elimination, and strength reduction are then concisely described in terms of these primitives. This method of description is used in **(067)**. The second part of the thesis defines and examines 'similarity' functions which, along with the primitives, are used to describe an interesting set of new optimizations. Essentially the idea is to identify code sequences which are 'similar' and can be made parametrically identical. Having identified two or more similar code sequences, a subroutine can be created and the code sequences replaced by references to the subroutine. Applying this optimization to a 1000-word BLISS program resulted in a 28% savings in object code size as contrasted with 6% when only the classical optimizations were used. Subroutine call mechanisms are not always used for implementing such sequences. The thesis gives several other interesting transformations that can be made using similarity functions.

028 GRAHAM S L and WEGMAN M
A fast and usually linear algorithm for global flow analysis
Jour ACM vol 23 no 1 pp 172-202 (Jan 1976)

The global flow analysis algorithm for reducible flow graphs given in this paper treats a very general class of function spaces. By using an interesting variant on the graph transformations introduced by Hecht and Ullman in **(032)**, the speed of the algorithm can be shown to be proportional to the number of edges in the graph plus the number of exits from program loops. Thus the algorithm is linear for a program with one-entry and one-exit loops such as those written without **gotos** or similar constructs.

029 HANSEN G J
Adaptive systems for the dynamic run-time optimization of programs
Doctoral Thesis Carnegie-Mellon University (1974)

A novel approach to optimization is presented in this thesis. In **(041)** Knuth observed that a small part (5%) of the source code accounts for a large portion (50%) of the execution time. This observation, which is consistent with that of others, motivates the approach taken in this thesis. Programs are initially compiled to be interpretively executed. The interpretive form is augmented by a control flow graph and by counters which are monitored as the program is executed. Whenever the number of times a section of code has been executed (via interpretation) exceeds some threshold, then optimization is applied to that section. In fact the optimization may only be partial, for example initially only common sub-expressions may be eliminated, but if the section is executed frequently enough it may become completely optimized and be executable directly by the computer. The optimizations and the way they progress follows Allen **(004)**, which lets optimized inner loops be treated as 'black boxes' when optimizing their containing loop. The dissertation describes a prototype system built for the FORTRAN language. Performance of this system is compared with several existing FORTRAN compiler systems. Noting that the total time (compile time + execution time) is what is being optimized, this approach did better than any of the other compiler systems. We strongly recommend this paper to anyone considering designing a system in which the total time must be optimized.

030 HARRISON W
A class of register allocation algorithm
IBM Research Report RC5342 T J Watson Research Center Yorktown Heights (March 1975)

Global register allocation is considered in this paper. The approach incorporates several interesting new techniques. In order to decide which register to displace when a register is needed and none are free, the cost of the displacement (e g does the value in the register need to be stored) and the likelihood of the value being needed again soon must both be considered. This paper extends a well-known replacement algorithm for straight-line situations to flow graphs. A frequency weighted measure of distance to next use is established to aid in determining displacement. Following Beatty (013), allocation to symbolic registers is followed by assignment to absolute registers. In this paper, however, assignment is broken into two parts, symbolic assignment and absolute assignment. The symbolic assignment selects the actual code skeletons and can make the fine choices as to the instructions to be used. For a machine like the IBM 360 which provides alternatives such code selection can be very effective. Two examples from other papers are given and the code sequences produced by this approach are compared with them.

031 HARRISON W
Compiler analysis of the value range of variables
IBM Research Report RC5544 T J Watson Research Center Yorktown Heights (July 1975)

Many languages have the rule that subscripts must stay within range and, in general, any attempts to address outside the scope of the specified data objects are illegal. Such rules are generally not enforced because of the execution costs involved. This paper presents a method for determing at compile time the bounds on the range of values for variables. In some cases the bounds cannot be determined but for many of the interesting cases it seems likely precise and useful bounds can be found. In addition to its application in checking subscript ranges, unnecessary tests can be elided and it can be used as a sophisticated constant propagator. In fact the primary constraint on the usefulness of this analysis is the compile time cost of the algorithm. The approach taken in this paper recognizes that an optimizing compiler must use relatively fast algorithms and must necessarily compromise the completeness of the results.

032 HECHT M S and ULLMAN J D
Flow graph reducibility
SIAM Jour Comp vol 1 no 2 pp 188-202 (June 1972)

Two transformations (T1 and T2) on graphs are introduced and shown to be equivalent to intervals in terms of reducibility. The depth first spanning tree of a graph is defined and used in proving various graph characteristics.

033 HECHT M S and ULLMAN J D
A simple algorithm for global data flow analysis problems
SIAM Jour Comp vol 4 no 4 pp 519-532 (Dec 1975)

This paper has essentially two distinct parts. In the first part of the paper a node numbering algorithm is given for a graph. This algorithm uses the depth first spanning tree method of Tarjan to produce a reverse post order numbering of the nodes. Using this numbering, a back-dominator algorithm for reducible flow graphs is given. The discussion of both of these algorithms is interesting. The second part of the paper then gives two data flow propagation algorithms, one for available expressions and one for live analysis. However when these algorithms are compared to the interval-based algorithms in the conclusions their advantages are seen to be somewhat unclear since they may take up to 2.4 times as long as corresponding interval analysis algorithms.

034 HECHT M S and ULLMAN J D
Characterizations of reducible flow graphs
Jour ACM vol 21 no 3 pp 367-375 (July 1974)

The reducible flow graph was first defined in Allen (005) in terms of intervals. In (032) Hecht and Ullman introduced two transformations which were shown to reduce the same graphs as did intervals. This paper proves certain interesting properties about reducible graphs. Of particular interest are the properties of the depth first spanning tree of a graph.

035 HENDERSON P and MORRIS J H
A lazy evaluator
Conference Record of the Third ACM Symp on *Principles of Programming Languages* pp 95-103 Atlanta (Jan 1976)

The goals of the expression evaluation methods presented in this paper for pure LISP are to perform an evaluation step only when necessary and never to perform the same step twice. In particular the evaluation of parameters and list structures are delayed. The paper refers to Vuillemin (061) and others who have also considered this optimization.

036 HORWITZ L P, KARP R M, MILLER R E and WINOGRAD S
Index register allocation
Jour ACM vol 13 no 1 pp 43-61 (Jan 1966)

This early, fundamental paper gives a procedure which yields an optimal register allocation for straight-line programs. The problem is cast in terms of a computer with a limited number of registers where the object is to minimize the number of memory references. (No attempt is made to reorder the instructions.) When loading an index register its current value may contain information which must be stored in memory if it is subsequently needed and memory does not contain its current value. The problem can be viewed as finding the 'shortest' path through a weighted, directed graph of alternatives where the weight of a node is the cost (in terms of memory references) of the particular allocation alternative. Clearly a complete search of the graph for a 'shortest path' would be prohibitively expensive. Methods are given which sharply limit the amount of searching required but still find the shortest path and hence the optimal solution.

037 KAM J B and ULLMAN J D
Global data flow problems and iterative algorithms
Jour ACM vol 23 no 1 pp 158-171 (Jan 1976)

Kildall's (040) lattice-theoretic formulation of global data flow analysis established a means of detecting certain optimization possibilities not exposed by the bit vector methods introduced by Cocke (018). In this paper the Kildall approach is analysed in terms of the number of iterations through a graph with a depth-first ordering. A condition satisfied by the bit vector is defined and used to show that those methods converge to a solution after d+3 passes through the ordered graph, where d is the maximum depth of loop nesting. It is shown that Kildall's formulation does not satisfy the condition. The paper thus raises the question of whether or not the cost of the Kildall method is worth the extra information gathered.

038 KENNEDY K
A global flow analysis algorithm
Intl Jour Comp Math vol 3 pp 5-15 (Dec 1971)

For each point in a program it is sometimes interesting to know what variables are 'live', that is, are used on some path from this point before being redefined. This information is of particular interest when assigning index registers since it is desirable to try to retain a value in a register if that value is later used. An algorithm which does live analysis is given in this paper. It is based on an interval partition of the program flow graph and was the first paper to show that information (in this case exposed uses of variables) could be conveniently propagated backwards through an interval partition of the program flow graph.

039 KENNEDY K
Index register allocation in straight-line code and simple loops
In *Design and Optimization of Compilers* (editor R Rustin) pp 51-63 Prentice-Hall (1972)

A version of the algorithm given in (036) as well as in Hopgood's *Compiling Techniques* is discussed in this paper. Whenever a register is needed during the assignment, the choice of which register value to displace considers both the cost of the displacement (that is, does the value need to be stored) and the distance to next use. This latter can be easily precomputed by a backwards scan through the program. Possible heuristic extensions to an algorithm for which the initial and final configurations are given is discussed. In simple loops where these configurations should be consistent the problem of establishing such configurations is mentioned.

040 KILDALL G A
A unified approach to global program optimization
Record of ACM Symp on *Principles of Programming Languages* pp 194-206 Boston (Oct 1973)

In this excellent and fundamental paper, program analysis was first considered in generality. 'Structural partitions' are formed in which constants, variables, and expressions known to have the same value at a node are in the same partition. The usual bit vector methods of Cocke (018) and others cannot conveniently represent such information. Kildall then defines an analysis framework based on lattice theory. This allows him to prove that the algorithm he gives for propagating information through the graph does terminates and is correct. Examples show how the basic algorithm can be used in constant propagation, common sub-expression elimination, eliminating redundant register loads, and by going backwards through the graph, to live (see (038)) variable analysis.

041 KNUTH D E
An empirical study of FORTRAN programs
Software P & E vol 1 no 2 pp 105-133 (1971)

Fifty randomly selected FORTRAN programs were studied and the statistical results are summarized in this paper. The collection was analysed both statically and dynamically. A selected number were then analysed to determine the comparative effectiveness of degrees of optimization varying from none to anything except changing the algorithm or the data structure. The paper contains a wealth of interesting information. One of the most interesting results of the static analysis is that 68% of the assignment statements were of the form *A=B*. The dynamic analysis determined the number of times each statement was executed and the cost of the execution. Here it was found that less than 4% of a program accounts for more than half its running time. One of the conclusions of the optimization aspects of the study is that well done optimization leads to at least a four or five-fold increase in program speed. Among other things the paper recommends that such studies be made of other languages. We strongly agree even if they produced only a small fraction of the insights provided in this excellent paper.

042 LOMET D B
Data flow analysis in the presence of procedure calls
IBM Research Report RC5728 T J Watson Research Center Yorktown Heights (Nov 1975)

As a result of data flow analysis in the context of a system of procedures we would ideally like to know

1 the data flow effects at every instance of every procedure reference;

2 the aliasing relationships between parameters and globals so that a given procedure can be correctly analysed and optimized.

Allen (006) presents a method predicated on the constraint that each procedure be analysed only once. Different calling situations are not distinguished. Rosen (047) presents a method in which call instances are distinguished and very precise information obtained but a much more expensive computation is required. In this paper, Lomet presents a fast method which precisely computes both unaliased and pair-wise aliased information. Good approximations are obtained for higher-order aliasing.

043 LOVEMAN D B
Program improvement by source to source transformation
Conference Record of the Third ACM Symp on *Principles of Programming Languages* pp 140-152 Atlanta (Jan 1976)

The compilation model presented in this paper is one in which a parser produces a tree-structured internal form of the source program, optimizing transformations are made on this internal form, and an 'unparser' then recreates a source program. The author believes that the new, optimized source program can then be compiled using a quite naive code generation technique to produce very good code. The paper contains an interesting catalogue of transformations which is much more extensive than (008). It also contains a semi-formalism for expressing transformation rules which permits the expression of not only the rules but the predicates for applying a transformation and the optimizations to be subsequently tried.

044 LOW J R
Automatic coding: choice of data structures
Doctoral Thesis Stanford University (Aug 1974); also Technical Report No 1 Dept of Computer Science University of Rochester (1974)

Abstract data structures, such as sets, sequences, and relations, which exist in very high-level languages can be implemented by such low-level data structures as linked-lists, binary trees, and hash tables. Efficient execution of such languages as SETL, SAIL and QA4 depend critically on the intelligent choice of the concrete representations. This choice depends not only on the abstract structure but on the operations performed on it. This paper describes a system which automatically chooses representations from a fixed library. The representations are chosen by attempting to minimize the predicted space time integral of the program execution. An appendix contains an interesting set of execution time cost functions when each of seven possible concrete representations are used in operations on abstract structures.

045 LOWRY E and MEDLOCK C W
Object code optimization
Comm ACM vol 12 no 1 pp 13-22 (Jan 1969)

The optimization and code generation methods of the IBM/360 FORTRAN H compiler are described in this important paper. The context in which common subexpression elimination, code motion, induction variable optimization, subsumption, and register allocation is performed is a control flow graph. The usual control flow graph information has been augmented by identifying loops and by establishing back dominator chains. This latter is used to determine the possible back targets for code motion and in searching for possible redundant expressions. Before performing any of the optimizing transformations a data flow analysis is performed which establishes the variables which are 'busy-on-exit' from a block, that is the variables which have a subsequent use. The code generation phase uses the bit strip technique for selecting proper code sequences for each higher-level intermediate expression after registers have been assigned. In addition to the main optimizations listed above and whose implementation is described in detail in the paper, twelve others are mentioned. The paper states that for small loops of a few statements the compiler very often produces perfect code. Although many of the techniques used in this compiler are somewhat obsolete the paper is still very worth reading.

046 McKEEMAN W M
Peephole optimization
Comm ACM vol 8 no 7 pp 443-444 (July 1965)

Compilers, even optimizing compilers, often produce code which is locally far from optimal. By examining a few successive operations for certain common, sub-optimal sequences a large improvement in the object code can frequently be obtained. This short note discusses this and gives a few examples.

047 ROSEN B K
Data flow analysis for recursive PL/1 programs
IBM Research Report RC5211 T J Watson Research Center Yorktown Heights (Jan 1975)

In the process of establishing what is locally used, defined and modified in order to do global data flow analysis we would like to know the effects of a procedure reference on its arguments and on any other data item of mutual interest to the caller and callee. In (006) Allen gave a method for obtaining summary information about the possible effects of a procedure. While that method had the advantage of requiring only one analysis of a procedure, it did not distinguish between different call instances, could not handle recursion, and might produce quite pessimistic and imprecise, though correct, results. In this paper, Rosen presents a costlier method which produces precise results for each instance of a reference to a procedure. This is done by constructing Boolean expressions summarizing the effects of a procedure. For each instance of a call the expressions are solved for the particular relationships existing at the call.

048 RUSTIN R (editor)
Design and optimization of compilers
Courant Comp Science Symp vol 5
Prentice-Hall (1972)

The papers presented at a symposium on optimization are collected in this volume. *A catalogue of optimizing transformations* by Frances Allen and John Cocke is reviewed in (008). *A comparison of certain optimization techniques* by Patricia Goldberg discusses various approaches to global optimization and in particular contrasts transformations based on tree walks with those using the bit vectoring techniques. *Index register allocation in straight-line code and simple loops* by Ken Kennedy is discussed in (039). *A global register assignment algorithm* by J C Beatty is an earlier version of the approach given in (013). *Code optimization and finite church-rosser systems* by A V Aho, Ravi Sethi, and J D Ullman shows that certain transformations are finite church-rosser, that is, the application of the transformation until no longer possible yields a unique program and only finite sequences of application are possible. *The execution time profile as a programming tool* by Dan Ingalls discusses a system which monitors the execution of a program and states the results in terms of the source listing by giving the number of times each source statement and branch alternative was executed. The paper gives examples, discusses various applications for the information, and summarizes the use that was made of it in Knuth's study (041). *Monitoring execution time on the CDC 6000 Series machines* by Steve Jasik discusses an execution monitor on the CDC 6000.

049 SCHAEFER M
A mathematical theory of global program optimization
Prentice-Hall (1973)

This book is divided into two subsections: theoretical foundations and their applications to global program analysis. The section on theoretical foundations discusses relevant notions from graph theory, dominance relations, intervals, and reducible and irreducible graphs. A lattice algebra is defined and used in developing a very straightforward node splitting algorithm. The second section, on applications, discusses data flow analysis, constant subsumption, common subexpression elimination, code motion, strength reduction and other topics related to global program optimization.

and Loveman's (043) both contain good discussions of this.

050 SCHNECK P B and ANGEL E
A FORTRAN-to-FORTRAN optimizing compiler
Comp Jour vol 16 no 4 pp 322-330 (Nov 1973)

A system which transforms FORTRAN source programs into more efficient FORTRAN source programs is discussed in this paper. The system parses the program creating the usual text and dictionary tables, performs a flow analysis to identify basic blocks, extended basic blocks, back dominators, and intervals. Optimizations are then performed and a FORTRAN version of the transformed program is produced. The paper concentrates on a description of the flow analyser and optimizer. One of the interesting aspects of this paper is the extension of the value numbering technique given in Cocke and Schwartz (019) to much more general flow structures. As a result of tests made using this system the paper concludes that

> "such preprocessing followed by object code production without optimization could produce execution speeds almost as good as those produced using only the vendor-supplied optimizing compiler."

This seems quite surprising since the system does not expose hidden computations such as the code resulting from subscript expansions and from data conversions. For many FORTRAN programs, these computations are the most important targets for optimization. Also register allocation and code selection, two other very important optimization areas, cannot be done by a preprocessor system. Such a system does however have many advantages. This paper

051 SCHWARTZ J T
Automatic data structure choice in a language of very high level
Comm ACM vol 18 no 12 pp 722-728 (Dec 1975)

The structure of an optimizer for the SETL language is described in this paper. SETL is a very high-level, set-oriented language. The optimizer for this language uses techniques which determine data types (056), establishes relations of inclusion and membership, estimates the domains and ranges of mappings and proves the single valuedness of certain mappings. Once facts of this kind are established, the automatic choice of the concrete representations (e g for excerpt lists, bit vectors, hash tables) for the abstract data objects (for example, sets, tuples) can be done. Most of the paper is devoted to an interesting description of the optimizer and the interdependence of its various components.

052 SCHWARTZ J T
Optimization of very high-level languages – Part 1: value transmission and its corollaries
Comp Lang vol 1 no 2 pp 161-194 (June 1975)

This paper and its sequel (053), discuss some of the important optimizations which must be performed on very high-level languages if the use of such languages is to become economically feasible. It is our opinion that investigations of the type reported may, if they are successful, profoundly affect the entire programming process. It is likely that the gap which currently exists between the goals of automatic programming systems and the realities of a practical implementation will be significantly narrowed by investigations such as this. The context for this particular investigation is the SETL language, a very high-level, set oriented language. The first issue studied in this paper is copy optimization, that is the discovery of cases in which changes to a compound object can be made differentially without recopying the entire object. In order to accomplish this 'value flow analysis' is required. This analysis, a generalization of classical data flow analysis, can be used to support several other interesting optimizations such as detecting stackable objects and recognizing when an object in heap storage can be freed.

053 SCHWARTZ J T
Optimization of very high-level languages – Part II: deducing relationships of inclusion and membership
Comp Lang vol 1 no 8 pp 197-218 (Sept 1975)

The key problem which must be solved if very high-level languages, that is, languages having abstract data structures, are to be compiled into efficient programs is that of choosing the right concrete data structures to represent the abstract ones. In this paper, techniques are given for automatically finding relationships of inclusion and membership among the abstract objects of the very high-level program. The possible use of such relationships in automatic data structure choice procedures is then given.

054 SETHI R
Complete register allocation problems
SIAM Jour Comp vol 4 no 3 pp 226-248 (Sept 1975)

Given a straight-line sequence of assignment instructions of the form 'load a value into a register' or 'compute a value by applying a binary operator to values in registers', the problem considered in this paper is the complexity of assigning registers to such a sequence. If a result is never used more than once then linear time algorithms for assignment exist. Given a sequence in which sharing of results can occur and given an arbitrary number of registers, k, this paper shows that the problem if determining of the sequence can be computed using k registers is NP-complete.

055 SETHI R and ULLMAN J D
The generation of optimal code for arithmetic expressions
Jour ACM vol 17 no 4 pp 715-728 (Oct 1970)

Given a fixed number of registers, the problem of minimizing the number of program steps and/or the number of storage references in the evaluation of an expression is considered by this paper. An algorithm for the evaluation of expressions assuming no algebraic laws apply is given first. It is shown to produce a minimum cost program. An algorithm is then given for finding the shortest possible evaluation sequence when certain operators are commutative or both commutative and associative. It is then shown that the algorithms also minimize the number of storage references in the evaluation.

056 TENNENBAUM A
Compile time type determination in SETL
Proc ACM '74 pp 95-100 (Nov 1974)

If typeless languages, such as APL, SETL or SNOBOL, are to be compiled the types of the data objects must be at least partially determined. This paper presents two algorithms for such a determination within the context of the SETL language. One algorithm determines the types of an object at a given point from the way it is created. The second algorithm determines the type from the ways in which it is used. The methods are based on a type calculus which includes a set of rules for restricting the potentially combinatorial formation of complex types.

057 TENNENBAUM A
Type determination for very high-level languages
Doctoral Thesis Courant Computer Science Report No 3 Courant Institute of Mathematical Sciences New York University (1974)

The preceding paper (056) summarizes the results presented in this dissertation. This work contains some additional information including six interesting examples in which the types were deduced by the two methods mentioned in (056). The method of deducing types from usages gave better results than that which deduced types from definitions. Overall, 77% of the deduced types were exact.

058 ULLMAN J D
Fast algorithms for the elimination of common subexpressions
Acta Informatica vol 2 no 3 pp 191-213 (Jan 1974)

This excellent paper gives two algorithms for computing the set of expressions available at the entrance to the nodes of a control flow graph of a program. If n is the number of distinct expressions (formal identities) then the first algorithm takes on the order of $n \times e$ steps in a graph having the property that no node has more than two immediate successors. The second algorithm works only for reducible flow graphs and requires on the order of n log n extended steps.

059 ULLMAN J D
A survey of data flow analysis techniques
Proc 2nd USA-Japan Comp Conf AFIPS Press pp 335-342 (1975)

This paper is a must for anyone wanting a readable, current and non-superficial tutorial on data flow analysis techniques. After establishing the context in a compiler, three important analysis problems are given:

1 finding the expressions available at a node in a flow graph so that any redundancies in the node can be eliminated;

2 finding the relationships between definitions and their uses;

3 finding what variables are live at each node.

The bit vector methods for acquiring this information are discussed in terms of intervals and iterative methods. More general frameworks such as Kildall's (040) structured partitions are discussed.

060 URSCHLER G
Complete redundant expression elimination in flow diagrams
IBM Research Report RC4965 T J Watson Research Center Yorktown Heights (Aug 1974)

If a program flow graph could be transformed into a tree by replicating nodes it should be possible to eliminate most if not all of the computational redundancies. In this paper, a method, symbolic interpretation, is presented which makes optimization directed transformations to the control flow of the program. For example, loops are unrolled as long as redundancies can be removed. Clearly this approach needs practical constraints to avoid creating infinite or excessively large program sizes. The paper gives some heuristics for controlling the replication. The author makes no claim for the practicality of the transformation but its power is intriguing. In fact Loveman (043) mentions the use of a similar 'case splitting' transformation in an environment where optimization costs are of no concern. Wegman (065) also treats this transformation and gives conditions for assuring finiteness.

061 VUILLEMIN J
Correct and optimal implementations of recursion in a simple programming language
Jour Comp & Syst Sciences vol 9 no 3 pp 332-354 (Dec 1974)

This theoretical paper studies the mechanism of recursion in a simple LISP-like programming language. Using Scott's theory of computation, a general criterion for the 'correctness' of implementations of recursion is given. An implementation of recursion which is both correct and optimal in a general class of sequential computations is described. To do this, a computation mechanism called a delay rule ('Never do today what you can put off until tomorrow') is used to avoid duplicate evaluations. Henderson and Morris (035) use some of these ideas in their lazy evaluator.

062 WAGNER R A
Some techniques for algebraic optimization with application to matrix arithmetic expressions
Doctoral Thesis Carnegie-Mellon University (June 1968)

This dissertation considers the problem of generating optimal (in terms of both space and time) code for matrix expressions. The matrix operations + and * are the only operations considered but the expressions can be arbitrarily complex. Common sub-expressions are recognized but no attempt is made to apply the distributive or associative laws. Expansion alternatives are selected to satisfy the optimality goal and loop fusion used to coalesce the loops selected for operation sequences. One of the interesting results of the thesis is a set of sufficient conditions for fusing loops.

063 WEGBREIT B
The ECL programming system
Proc FJCC pp 253-262 (1971)

Most if not all of the papers included in this bibliography have been concerned with topics related to the analysis and optimization of programs by a compiling system. This fascinating paper gives an overview of a system, ECL, designed to optimize the total effort of program production.

064 WEGBREIT B
Mechanical program analysis
Comm ACM vol 18 no 9 pp 528-539 (Sept 1975)

The purpose of the program analysis described in this paper is to predict performance. This is done by deriving closed-form expressions of the running time of a program in terms of the sizes of its input. A system, METRIC, which is able to analyse simple LISP programs is described. In (066) Wegbreit discusses how the results of such an analysis can be used in goal-directed program transformations.

065 WEGBREIT B
Property extraction in well-founded property sets
IEEE Trans on *Software Engineering* vol 1 no 3 pp 270-285 (Sept 1975)

Much of the work in program analysis and optimization has been directed towards deducing the properties which are true at each program unit. The methods used guarantee that starting from local information and initial assumptions the properties form a partially ordered set with a minimum condition, that is they are well-founded. This paper establishes a set of conditions for this to be true. An algorithm is then given which computes such properties. The use of the algorithm is illustrated by two examples, one of which computes the range of values (see (081)) of variables. An algorithm is then given which replicates text at program joins (see (043) and (060)) when different properties exist on the different input paths. Techniques are given for property computation in both iterative and recursive programs. We found this a fascinating paper and while it is not clear how practical the techniques are their potential is intriguing.

066 WEGBREIT B
Goal-directed program transformation
Conference Record of the Third ACM Symp on *Principles of Programming Languages* pp 153-170 Atlanta (Jan 1976)

The thesis of this paper is that program transformations can be made goal-directed by a systematic process which first establishes performance goals by analysis and then uses the goals to direct the process of program transformation. The performance goals are established by first obtaining some idea of the minimum computation cost required to produce the input/output mappings being realized by the program. It then analyses the program to determine its computation cost. The discrepancies between these costs indicate the possibility of optimizing transformations on the program segments which have been identified during the analysis as targets for simplifications. The performance goals for identified segments are used to direct the transformations needed to approach the minimum for the segment. The paper contains a number of interesting transformations. LISP and APL examples of the ideas are given.

067 WULF, W A, JOHNSSON R K, WEINSTOCK C B, HOBBS S O and GESCHKE C M
The design of an optimizing compiler
American Elsevier New York (1975)

The design of an optimizing BLISS compiler for the PDP-11 is given in this book. Since BLISS does not contain **gotos** a tree representation of the program forms a convenient basis on which to perform the transformations. The two most interesting results are: a heuristic extension of an algorithm given in (055) which chooses the evaluation order of expressions in order to minimize the number of in-use registers and a strategy of assigning temporary names, measuring their lifetimes and importance and then packing them into storage. The main interest in this book is the overall structure of the compiler and how the different parts interact. Unfortunately neither the speed nor space of the compiler and its output are quantified, therefore its effectiveness is difficult to evaluate.

CONTRIBUTORS' REFERENCES

A number of references were supplied by the contributors of invited papers. These are given below in the sections headed by the contributors' names. The final section below, headed Analysis, *contains references, additional to those in the annotated bibliography, cited in the editorial of the Analysis part of this Report.*

ZELKOWITZ

100 IBM
The man behind FORTRAN
IBM Computing report II no 4
pp 7-10 (1966)

101 ALLEN F E
Program optimization, Annual Review
Automatic Programming vol 5 pp
239-307 (1969)

102 COCKE J and SCHWARTZ J T
Programming languages and their compilers
Courant Institute New York Univ
(1970)

103 LOWRY E S and MEDLOCK C W
Object code optimization
CACM no 12 pp 13-22 (1969)

104 MILLS H D
Mathematical foundations for structured programming
IBM Syst Div Report FSC72-6012
(1972)

105 BOHM C and JACOBINI G
Flow diagrams, Turing machines, and languages with only two formation rules
CACM no 9 pp 366-371 (1966)

106 KNUTH D
Structured programming with **goto** *statements*
Comp Surveys no 6 pp 261-302
(1974)

107 DAHL O J, DIJKSTRA E W and HOARE C A R
Structured programming
Academic Press New York (1972)

108 GRIES D
On structured programming
CACM vol 17 pp 655-657 (1974)

109 WIRTH N
Program development by stepwise refinement
CACM vol 14 pp 221-227 (1971)

110 PARNAS D L
On the criteria to be used in decomposing systems into modules
CACM vol 15 pp 1053-1058 (1972)

111 LISKOV B H and ZILLES S
Specification techniques for data abstraction
Intl Conf on *Reliable Software*
pp 72-87 Los Angeles (1975)

112 BAKER F T
Structured programming in a production programming environment
Proc ICRS pp 172-185 (1975)

113 ZELKOWITZ M V and BAIL W G
Optimization of structured programs
Software Practice and Experience vol 4 pp 51-57 (1974)

114 HAMLET R G and ZELKOWITZ M V
SIMPL systems programming on a minicomputer
IEEE Compcon pp 203-206 Washington (1974)

115 BASILI V R and TURNER A J
A transportable extendable compiler
Software Practice and Experience vol 5 pp 269-278 (1975)

116 KNUTH D
An empirical study of FORTRAN programs
Software Practice and Experience vol 1 pp 105-133 (1971)

117 McHUGH J and BASILI V R
SIMPL-R and its application to large sparse matrix problems
Univ Maryland Comp Sci Tech Report TR-310 (1974)

118 BASILI V R and TURNER A J
Iterative enhancement — a practical technique for software development
First Nat Conf on *Software Engineering* pp 56-62 Washington (1975)

119 GEAR C W
High speed compilation of efficient object code
CACM vol 8 pp 483-488 (1965)

120 GRIES D
Compiler construction
Wiley New York (1971)

121 HECHT M S and SHAFFER J B
Ideas on the design of a 'quad improver' for SIMPL-T
Univ Maryland Comp Sci Tech Report TR-405 (1975)

122 ROSEN B K
High level data flow analysis - Part 1
IBM Report RC5598 (1975)

NEWSTED

123 WIRTH N
On the composition of well-structured programs
Comp Surv vol 6 pp 247-259 (Dec 1974)

124 KRAFT P and WEINBERG G M
The professionalization of programming
Datamation vol 21 pp 169-172 (Oct 1975)

125 VAN DUYN J
Documentation Manual
Auerbach (1972)

126 WEINBERG G M
The psychology of computer programming
Van Nostrand Reinhold (1971)

127 BROWN P J
Programming and documenting software projects
Comp Surv vol 6 pp 213-219 (Dec 1974)

128 ROGO J T
How to prepare functional specifications
Datamation vol 20 pp 78-80 (May 1974)

129 LEDGARD H F
Programming proverbs
Hayden Book Co (1975)

130 LEDGARD H F
Programming proverbs for FORTRAN programmers
Hayden Book Co (1975)

131 VAN TASSEL D
Program style, design, efficiency, debugging, and testing
Prentice-Hall (1974)

132 KNUTH D E
Structured programming with **goto** *statements*
Comp Surv vol 6 pp 261-301 (Dec 1974)

133 SHNEIDERMAN B, MAYER R, McKAY D and HELLER P
Experimental investigations on the utility of flowcharts in programming
Tech report no 36 Comp Sci Dept Indiana Univ (1975)

134 ARON J D
The program development process: the individual programmer
Addison-Wesley (1974)

135 BROOKS F P
The mythical man-month
Addison-Wesley (1975)

136 SIME M E, GREEN T R G and GUEST D J
Psychological evaluation of two conditional constructions used in computer languages
Intl Jour of Man-Machine Studies vol 5 pp 105-113 (1973)

137 MILLER L A
Programming by non-programmers
Intl Jour of Man-Machine Studies vol 6 pp 237-260 (1974)

138 SHNEIDERMAN B and HO M
Two exploratory experiments in program comprehension
Tech report no 27 Comp Sci Dept Indiana Univ (1974)

139 NEWSTED P R
FORTRAN program comprehension as a function of documentation
Program Information Abstracts: Second Ann Comp Sci Conf p 25 Detroit Michigan (1974)

140 SACKMAN H
Man-computer problem solving
Auerbach (1970)

141 YOUNGS E A
Human errors in programming
Intl Jour of Man-Machine Studies
vol 6 pp 361-376 (1974)

142 GOULD J D and DRONGOWSKI P
An exploratory study of computer program debugging
Human Factors vol 16 pp 258-277 (1974)

143 BOIES S J and GOULD J D
Syntactic errors in computer programming
Human Factors vol 16 pp 253-257 (1974)

144 GOULD J D
Some psychological evidence on how people debug computer programs
Intl Jour of Man-Machine Studies
vol 7 pp 151-182 (1975)

145 NAGY G and PENNEBAKER M C
A step toward automatic analysis of student programming errors in a batch environment
Intl Jour of Man-Machine Studies
vol 6 pp 563-578 (1974)

146 McCRACKEN D
Personal communication
(Nov 5 1975)

147 NEWSTED P R
Grade and ability predictions in an introductory programming course
ACM SIGCSE Bulletin vol 7 pp 87-91 (June 1975)

SPIRN

148 BELADY L A
A study of replacement algorithms for virtual storage computers
IBM Systems Jour vol 5 no 2 pp 78-101 (1966)

149 BELADY L A, NELSON R A and SHEDLER G S
An anomaly in the space-time characteristics of certain programs running in paging machines
CACM vol 12 no 6 pp 349-353 (June 1969)

150 SPIRN J and DENNING P J
Experiments with program locality
Proc AFIPS FJCC vol 41 pp 611-621 (1972)

151 DENNING P J
The working set model for program behaviour
CACM vol 11 no 5 pp 323-333 (May 1968)

152 COFFMAN E G and DENNING P J
Operating system theory
Prentice-Hall Englewood Cliffs NJ USA (1973)

153 MATTSON R L, GECSEI J, SLUTZ D R and TRAIGER I L
Evaluation techniques for storage hierarchies
IBM Systs Jour vol 9 no 2 pp 78-117 (1970)

154 SPIRN J
Program behaviour: models and measurements
American-Elsevier New York (1976)

155 BELADY L A and KUEHNER C J
Dynamic space-sharing in computer systems
CACM vol 12 no 5 pp 282-288 (May 1969)

156 FELLER W
An introduction to probability theory and its applications
vol I (2nd ed.) Wiley New York (1957)

157 HATFIELD D J and GERALD J
Program restructuring for virtual memory
IBM Systs Jour vol 10 no 3 pp 168-192 (1971)

158 FERRARI D
Improving locality by critical working sets
CACM vol 17 no 11 pp 614-620 (Nov 1974)

159 McKELLAR A C and COFFMAN E G
The organization of matrices and matrix operations in a paged multiprogramming environment
CACM vol 12 no 3 pp 153-165 (March 1969)

160 BRAWN B S, GUSTAVSON F G and MANKIN E
Sorting in a paging environment
CACM vol 13 no 8 pp 483-494 (August 1970)

161 SHEDLER G S and TUNG C
Locality in page reference strings
SIAM J Computing vol 1 no 3 pp 218-241 (Sept 1972)

MANVILLE

162 MANVILLE W D
Microprogramming support for programming languages
PhD Thesis Univ of Cambridge Comp Laboratory (1973)

163 WILKES M V
The best way to design an automatic calculating machine
Manchester Univ Comp Inaugural Conf p 16 (1951)

164 BLEIWEISS L S *et al*
Conversational programming system
IBM Contributed Program Library 360D 03.4.016 (1967)

165 WEBER H
A microprogrammed implementation of EULER on IBM System/360 Model 30
CACM vol 10 p 549 (1967)

166 WIRTH N and WEBER H
EULER: a generalization of ALGOL, and its formal definition, Part II
CACM vol 9 p 89 (1966)

167 WILNER W T
Design of the Burroughs B1700
Proc AFIPS FJCC p 489 (1972)

168 RICHARDS M
BCPL: a tool for compiler writing and system programming
Proc AFIPS SJCC p 557 (1969)

169 RICHARDS M
The portability of the BCPL compiler
Software P & E vol 1 p 135 (1971)

170 WILKES M V and MANVILLE W D
The associative language AL-1
Intl Jour of Com and Inf Sci vol 1
p 327 (1972)

171 MELBOURNE A J and PUGMIRE J M
A small computer for the direct processing of FORTRAN statements
Comp Jour vol 8 p 24 (1965)

172 WILKES M V
The use of a writable control memory in a multiprogramming environment
5th Ann Workshop in *Microprogramming* Preprints p 62 (1972)

CAPON

173 KILBURN T, MORRIS D, ROHL J S and SUMNER F H
A system design proposal
Information Processing 68 North Holland

174 IBBETT R N
The MU5 instruction pipeline
Comp Jour vol 15 no 1

BURNS

175 BATES D (editor)
Structured Programming
Infotech State of the Art Report (1976)

PATEL

176 COFFMAN E G and VARIAN L C
Further experimental data on the behaviour of programs
CACM (July 1968)

177 BELADY L A and KUEHNER C J
Dynamic space sharing in computer systems
CACM (May 1969)

178 JOSEPH M
An analysis of paging and program behaviour
The Comp Jour (Feby 1970)

179 BRAWN B S and GUSTAVSON F S
Program behaviour in a paging environment
AFIPS vol 33 Part II (1968)

180 DENNING P J
On modelling program behaviour
AFIPS vol 40 (1972)

181 COFFMAN E G and RYAN T A
A study of storage partitioning using a mathematical model of locality
CACM (March 1972)

182 CHU W W and OPDERBECK H
Page fault frequency replacement algorithm
AFIPS vol 41 Part I (1972)

183 DENNING P J
Thrashing: its causes and prevention
AFIPS vol 33 Part I (1968)

184 GOTLIEB C C and MACEWAN G H
Performance of moveable-head disk storage devices
Jour of the ACM vol 20 no 4 (Oct 1973)

185 COFFMAN E G
Analysis of a drum input/output queue under scheduled operation in a paged computer system
Jour of the ACM vol 16 no 1
(Jan 1969)

BROWN P J

186 NAUR P
The design of the GIER ALGOL compiler
BIT vol 3 pp 122-140 145-166
(1963)

187 BOBROW D G and MURPHY D L
Structure of a LISP system using two level storage
CACM vol 10 no 3 pp 155-159
(March 1967)

188 COLIN A J T, McGREGOR D R and MITCHELL D
Paging STAB-1 code
Software P & E vol 5 no 3 pp 309-316 (1975)

189 BROWN P J
Throw-away compiling
Software P & E vol 6 no 3 pp 423-434 (July 1976)

190 BELL I R
Threaded code
CACM vol 16 no 6 pp 370-372
(June 1973)

191 DEWAR R B K
Indirect threaded code
CACM vol 18 no 6 pp 330-331
(June 1975)

192 DAKIN R J and POOLE P C
A mixed code approach
Comp Jour vol 16 no 3 pp 219-222
(1973)

193 DAWSON J L
Combining interpretive code with machine code
Comp Jour vol 16 no 3 pp 216-219
(1973)

194 NG T S and CANTONI A
Run-time interaction with FORTRAN using mixed code
Comp Jour vol 19 no 1 pp 91-92
(1976)

HANSEN AND WULF

195 KNUTH D E
An empirical study of FORTRAN programs
IBM report RC 3276 (1970)

196 DARDEN S C and HELLER S B
Streamline your software development
Comp Decisions vol 2 pp 29-33
(Oct 1970)

197 GRIES D
Compiler construction for digital computers
John Wiley & Sons Inc (1971)

198 ALLEN F E
Program optimizations
In Ann Review in *Automatic Programming* vol 5 pp 239-307 Pergammon New York
(1969)

199 ALLEN F E
Control flow analysis
In ACM Proc of Symp on *Compiler optimization*
SIGPLAN Notices vol 5 no 7 pp 1-19 (July 1970)

200 LOWRY E and MEDLOCK C W
Object code optimization
CACM vol 12 no 1 pp 13-22 (Jan 1969)

201 HARARY F
Graph theory
Addison-Wesley Co (1969)

202 COCKE J and SCHWARTZ J T
Programming languages and their compilers
Preliminary notes (2nd ed)
Courant Institute of Math Sci
New York Univ (April 1970)

203 *BLISS Reference Manual*
Comp Sci report Carnegie-Mellon Univ (Oct 1971)

204 CHARTRES B A
Algorithm 311 prime number generator 2
CACM vol 10 no 9 p 570 (Sept 1967)

205 FORSYTHE G E and MOLER C B
Computer solution of linear algebraic systems
Prentice-Hall Englewood Cliffs NJ (1967)

206 MOLER C B
Algorithm 423 linear equation solver
CACM vol 15 no 4 p 274 (April 1972)

207 GREGORY R T and KARNEY D L
A collection of matrices for testing computational algorithms
Wiley-Interscience New York (1968)

208 MOLER C B and STEWART G W
An algorithm for generalized matrix eigenvalue problems
SIAM J Numer Anal vol 19 no 2 pp 241-256 (April 1973)

209 *American standard FORTRAN*
American Standards Assocn Inc New York (March 1966)

210 HANSEN G J
Adaptive systems for the dynamic run-time optimization of programs
PhD Thesis Carnegie-Mellon Univ (March 1974)

PALME

211 PALME J
GNOSIS – a system for computer aided instruction
FOA P report C 8373 Rapportcentralen
FOA 1 104 50 Stockholm 80

212 KNUTH D E
An empirical study of FORTRAN programs
Software P & E vol 1 pp 105-133 (1971)

213 TAFVELIN, SVEN and WIKSTROM, AKE
Aspects of compact programs and directly executed languages
BIT vol 15 pp 203-214 (1975)

214 PALME J
Programming languages for the software engineer
Infotech State of the Art Report *Software Engineering* Infotech Maidenhead Berkshire England

215 PALME J
Protected program modules in Simula 67
FOA P report C 8372

216 PALME J
Security and programming languages
FOA P report C 8395 (A revised and improved version is to be published in Datamation under the title *Languages for reliable software*)

BURSTALL and DARLINGTON

217 BURSTALL R M and DARLINGTON J
Some transformations for developing recursive programs
Proc of Intl Conf on *Reliable software* pp 465-472 Los Angeles California (1975) Revised version to appear in Jour of Ass for Comp Mach

218 MANNA Z and WALDINGER R
Knowledge and reasoning in program synthesis
Artificial Intelligence Jour vol 5 no 2 pp 175-208 (1975)

219 DIJKSTRA E W
Guarded commands, non-determinacy and a calculus for the derivation of programs
Proc of Intl Conf on *Reliable software* Los Angeles California pp 2-2 13 (1975)

220 DARLINGTON J
Application of program transformation to program synthesis
Proc of Intl Symp on *Proving and improving programs* Arc-et-Senans France pp 133-144 (July 1-3 1975)

SCHNECK (1)

221 IBM
The IBM mathematical formula translating system, FORTRAN
IBM Corp (1954)

222 MILLER R C and OLDFIELD B J
Producing computer instructions for the PACT I compiler
Jour of the ACM vol 3 (1956)

223 SHERIDAN P B
The arithmetic translator – compiler of the IBM FORTRAN automatic coding system
CACM vol 2 (1959)

224 McKEEMAN W M
Peephole optimization
CACM vol 8 (1965)

225 BAGWELL J T Jr
Local optimizations
ACM SIGPLAN Notices vol 5 no 7 (1970)

226 ANDERSON J P
A note on some compiling algorithms
CACM vol 7 (1964)

227 NAKATA I
On compiling algorithms for arithmetic expressions
CACM vol 10 (1967)

228 REDZIEJOWSKI R R
On arithmetic expressions and trees
CACM vol 12 (1969)

229 SCHNEIDER V
On the number of registers needed to evaluate arithmetic expressions
BIT vol 11 (1971)

230 FINKELSTEIN M
A compiler optimization technique
The Comp Jour vol 11 (1968)

231 RANDELL B and RUSSELL L J
Single-scan techniques for the translation of arithmetic expressions in ALGOL 60
Jour of the ACM vol 11 (1964)

232 ALLARD R W, WOLF K A and ZEMLIN R A
Some effects of the 6600 computer on language structures
CACM vol 7 (1964)

233 THORLIN J F
Code generation for PIE (parallel instruction execution) computers
Proc SJCC (1967)

234 BLUM D, BROWN S K, CALAVANO A G, HEMPY H O and SUEZ J
Current technologies in FORTRAN object code optimization
TR 00 2240 IBM Corp (1971)

235 STONE H S
One-pass compilation of arithmetic expressions for a parallel processor
CACM vol 10 (1967)

236 HAN J C
Tree height reduction for parallel processing of blocks of FORTRAN assignment statements
Nat Tech Inf Service PB-207985 (1972)

237 RAMAMOORTHY C V and GONZALEZ M J
Subexpression ordering in the execution of arithmetic expressions
CACM vol 14 (1971)

238 BURKHARDT W H
Automation of program speed-up on parallel-processor computers
Computing vol 3 (1968)

239 MILSTEIN R E
Compiler design for the ILLIAC IV
Nat Tech Inf Service AD 719417 (1971)

240 LAMPORT L and PRESBERG D
Concurrent compiling
Nat Tech Inf Service AD 742279 (1972)

241 SCHNECK P B
Automatic recognition of parallel and vector operations in a higher level language
Proc ACM Nat Conf (1972)

242 KUCK D J, MURAOKA V and CHEN S-C
On the number of operations simultaneously executable in FORTRAN-like programs and their resulting speed-up
IEEE Trans on Computers vol C-21 (1972)

243 BACKUS J W *et al*
The FORTRAN automatic coding system
Proc WJCC (1957)

244 HORWITZ L P, KARP R M, MILLER R E and WINOGRAD S
Index reaister allocation
Jour of the ACM vol 13 (1966)

245 LUCCIO F
A comment on index register allocation
CACM vol 10 (1967)

246 DAY W H E
Compiler assignment of data items to registers
IBM Systs Jour vol 9 (1970)

247 PROSSER R T
Applications of Boolean matrices to the analysis of flow diagrams
Proc of EJCC (1959)

248 WARSHALL S
A theorem on Boolean matrices
Jour of the ACM vol 9 (1962)

249 RAMAMOORTHY C V
Analysis of graphs by connectivity considerations
Jour of the ACM vol 11 (1964)

250 ALLEN F E
Program optimization
Ann Review of *Automatic Programming*
Pergamon Press (1969)

251 KLEIR R L and RAMAMOORTHY C V
Optimization strategies for microprograms
IEEE Trans of Computers vol C-20 (1971)

252 GRIES D
Compiler construction for digital computers
John Wiley and Sons (1972)

253 RYAN J T
A direction-independent algorithm for determining the forward and backward compute point for a term or subscript during compilation
The Comp Jour vol 9 (1966)

254 MEDLOCK C W and LOWRY E S
Global program optimization
TR 00 1330 IBM Corp (1965)

255 LOWRY E S and MEDLOCK C W
Object code optimization
CACM vol 12 (1969)

256 BUSAM V A and ENGLUND D E
Optimization of expressions in FORTRAN
CACM vol 12 (1969)

257 YERSHOV A P
ALPHA — an automatic programming system of high efficiency
Jour of the ACM vol 13 (1966)

258 YERSHOV A P
The ALPHA automatic programming system
Academic Press (1971)

259 COCKE J and SCHWARTZ J T
Programming languages and their compilers
New York University (1969)

260 COCKE J and MILLER R E
Some analysis techniques for optimizing computer programs
Proc of the Second Hawaii Intl Conf of System Sciences (1969)

261 ALLEN F E
Control flow analysis
ACM SIGPLAN Notices vol 5 (1970)

262 COCKE J
Global common subexpression elimination
ACM SIGPLAN Notices vol 5 (1970)

263 ALLEN F E and COCKE J
Graph theoretic constructs for program control flow analysis
Unpublished paper

264 KENNEDY K
A global flow analysis algorithm
Intl Jour of Comp Maths vol 3 (1971)

265 SCHNECK P B and ANGEL E
A FORTRAN to FORTRAN optimizing compiler
The Comp Jour to be published (1973)

266 HECHT M S and ULLMAN J D
Flow graph reducibility
SIAM Jour of Comp vol 1 (1971)

267 COHAGAN W L
Vector optimization for the ASC
Presented at the Seventh Ann Princeton Conf on *Programming*

268 WEDEL D
FORTRAN for the Texas Instruments ASC system
Proc of Conf on *Programming languages and compilers for parallel and vector machines* SIGPLAN Notices vol 10 no 3 (1975)

269 ZWAKENBERG R G
Vector extensions to LRLTRAN
Proc of Conf on *Programming languages and compilers for parallel and vector machines* SIGPLAN Notices vol 10 no 3 (1975)

270 LOVEMAN D B and FANEUF R A
Program optimization: theory and practice
Proc of Conf on *Programming languages and compilers for parallel and vector machines* SIGPLAN Notices vol 10 no 3 (1975)

271 KNUTH D E
Semantics of context — free languages
Mathematical Systems Theory vol 2 no 2 (1968)

272 KNUTH D E
Examples of formal semantics
Symp on *Semantics of algorithmic languages*
Springer-Verlag (1971)

273 NEEL D and AMIRCHAHY M
Semantic attributes and improvement of generated code
Proc of Ann Conf of ACM (1974)

SCHNECK (2)

274 BACKUS J W *et al*
The FORTRAN Automatic Coding system
Proc WJCC (1957)

275 SCHNECK P B
A new class of program optimizations
To be published

276 SHERIDAN P B
The Arithmetic Translator-Compiler of the IBM FORTRAN Automatic Coding system
CACM vol 2 (1959)

277 SCHNECK P B and ANGEL E
A FORTRAN to FORTRAN optimizing compiler
The Comp Jour vol 16 no 4 (1973)

278 SCHNECK P B
Semantic preprocessing
Proc ACM Nat Conf (1974)

279 SCHWARTZ J T
On programming – an interim report on the SETL project
New York University (1973)

280 ASHCROFT E A
Program correctness methods and language definition
Proc of ACM Conf on *Proving assertions about programs* SIGPLAN Notices vol 7 no 1 (1972)

281 KNUTH D E
1974 ACM Turing Lecture CACM vol 17 no 12 (1974)

282 HOPKINS M E
Execution Time Optimizer
IBM Tech Disclosure Bulletin vol 14 no 10 (March 1972)

283 ALLEN F E
Interprocedural data flow analysis
Information Processing 74 North Holland Publishing Co (1974)

ANALYSIS

300 LEE J A N
Language processors
In *Encyclopedia of Computer Science* (editors A Ralston and C L Meek (1976)

301 DARDEN S C and HELLER S B
Streamline your software development
Comp Dec vol 2 no 10 pp 29-33 (Oct 1970)

302 BOON C (editor)
Microprogramming and systems architecture
Infotech State of the Art Report 23 (1975)

303 WULF W A
The influence of high-level languages on microprocessor design
In (302)

304 BATES D (editor)
Commercial language systems
Infotech State of the Art Report 19 (1974)

305 WHITE C H (editor)
Multiprocessor systems
Infotech State of the Art Report (1976)

306 LOVEMAN D B and FANEUF R A
Program optimization: theory and practice
SIGPLAN Notices vol 10 no 3 (March 1975)

307 KNUTH D E
The art of computer programming
Addison-Wesley

308 WIRTH N
On the composition of well-structured programs
Comp Surv vol 6 pp 247-259 (Dec 1974)

309 HOARE C A R
Hints on programming language design
Infotech State of the Art Report 20 *Computer Systems Reliability* pp 503-534 (1974); also Stanford Univ report STAN-CS-74-403 (1974)

310 KNUTH D E
Structured programming with goto *statements*
Comp Surv vol 6 pp 261-301 (Dec 1974)

311 BOON C (editor)
High-level languages
Infotech State of the Art Report 7 (1972)

312 SACKMAN H
Man-computer problem solving
Auerbach (1970)

313 BUNYAN C J (editor)
Computer systems reliability
Infotech State of the Art Report 20 (1974)

314 CHEATHAM T E and WEGBREIT B
A laboratory for study of automating programming
Proc AFIPS SJCC vol 40 pp 11-21 (1972)

315 TEITELMAN W
Towards a programming laboratory
In *Software Engineering Techniques* editors J Buxton and B Randell) (1970)

316 TEITELMAN W
INTERLISP reference manual
Xerox PARC (1974)

317 BUNYAN C J (editor)
Computer systems measurement
Infotech State of the Art Report 18 (1974)

318 WHITE C H (editor)
System tuning
Infotech State of the Art Report
(to be published 1977)

319 BUNYAN C J and BOON C (editors)
Virtual storage
Infotech State of the Art Report
(1976)

320 CHEATHAM T E
Research in program optimization techniques
Report ESD-TR-75-81 USAF Electronics Systems Division (1975)

INDEXES

CUMULATIVE SUBJECT INDEX

The entries in this index refer to all the published State of the Art Reports. The State of the Art Reports are listed below together with their reference numbers.

1	The Fourth Generation	17	Computer Design
2	Giant Computers	18	Computer Systems Measurement
3	Real Time	19	Commercial Language Systems
4	Computing Terminals	20	Computer Systems Reliability
5	The New Technologies	21	Management Information Systems
6	Computer Networks	22	Input/Output
7	High Level Languages	23	Microprogramming and Systems Architecture
8	Application Technique	24	Network Systems and Software
9	Incompatibility	25	Data Base Systems
10	Interactive Computing	26	Virtual Storage
11	Software Engineering	27	Structured Programming
12	Computing Economics	28	Real-time Software
13	Minicomputers	29	Multiprocessor Systems
14	Operating Systems	30	Program Optimization
15	Data Base Management	31	Distributed Systems
16	Computing Manpower		

Acceptance testing 18
Access control and protection 14,15,17,20,25,26,28
Access paths 25
Accounting routines 18
Adaptive redundancy 20
Adaptive routeing 6,24,31
Addressing 1,3,13,17,26
  associative 17,26
  Atlas 2,26
  B6500 2,26
  base-limit 17,26
  Basic Machine, the 2,26
  codewords (see *Descriptors*)
  descriptors 1,2,7,26
  GE 645 2
  lock-and-key 26
  MU5 2,26
  MULTICS 26
  paging 1,2,14,17,18,26
  segmentation 1,2,17,26
  System 360 26
  System 370 26
AED 7,10,13
AEVS 20,27,28
ALGOL 60 7,19,20
ALGOL 68 7,19,27
ALGOL W 7
Alternative routeing 24

AMTRAN 10,28
Analogue models 18
Analytical models 18,21
APL 7,10
Applications 2,8,9
  choice of 8,9,12
  data base 25
  efficiency 18
  giant computers 2
  graphics 10
  interactive computing 10
  minicomputers 13
  MIS 21
  networks 6
  real time 2,3,28
  terminals 4
Aptitude tests 16
Architecture 1,2,3,17,22,23,26,31
  approach 1
  for commercial languages 19
  for networks 1,6,24
  for real-time software 28
  influence of DBMS 15
  influence of interactive systems 10
  influence of language 7,17,19
  influence of microprogramming 23
  influence of operating systems 14
  influence of technology 5,17,23,26
  minicomputer 13
  variable 1,2,5,9,17,23
Arithmetic codes 20
ARPA network 6,24,31
Array referencing 26,30
Artificial intelligence 2
Assembly 9
Associative storage 1,15,17,23,25,26,29,31
Atlas 1,2,7,18,26
Auditing 18
Audit programs 20
Audit trails 20,25,28
Automatic Evaluation and Validation Systems
    (see *AEVS*)
Automatic programming 11,19
AUTOTAB 10
Availability 20,27,28,29,31

B1700 17,19,23,26
B5500 26
B6500 2,7,17
B6700 26,28
Back-end processors 28,31

BASIC	10,23
Basic Machine, the	2,7,26
BCL	1,7,9
BCPL	7,23,27,28
Benchmarks	11,18,25
Binding	25,26
Blocking	18,22,26
Blocking gate	20
Bottom-up design	27,28
Buddy system	26
Budgetary control	12
Buffer store	17,26
Buffering	18,22,25
Bulk core store	26
Bus schemes	13,20,22,29,31
Cache store	17,26,28
Cactus stack	28
CAD	5,15,17
CAMAC	13,22
Capabilities	17,20,24,26,28
CARE	20
Careers	16
CATV	2,4,6
Cellular machines	5,23
Central utility	1,2,8
Channels, data	13,22,23,26
Channel scheduling	18
Character recognition	4,5,8,9,22
Character sets	7
Chargeback	12,21
(see also *Job accounting*)	
Charge-coupled devices	28
Charging formulae	18
Checking circuits	20
Check-out compilers	20
Checkpoints	20,28
Checksums	20
Chief Programmer Teams	16,19,20,27,28
CICS	28
CIM	22
Circuit switching	6,24,31
C.mmp	17,31
COBOL	7,9,10,19,27,28
CODASYL	15,25,28
Codewords (see *Descriptors*)	
Colour displays	10
COM	5,8,22
COMET monitor	28
Command and control systems	28
Commercial programming languages	19
Communications in the DP industry	8,9,16

Communications processing 4,6,28
Compaction 26
Compatibility 1,2,9,13,14,22,23
Compiler compilers 1,7,9
Compilers 1,5,7,20,23,30
Complexity 27,28,30,31
Component reliability 20
Components, software 11,13
Computer Modules 31
Computer networks 4,6,9,24,28,31
(see also *Networks*)
Computer science 8,11,16,18
Concentrators 4,6,24
(see also *Multiplexing*)
Concurrency 13,28
Concurrent access 25
Conditional critical regions 28
Configuration 13,17,18,26
Conjoined computer systems 31
Connect time 6
Content-addressable storage 22,25,26,28
Continuous simulation models 18,21
Contracts 8,11
Control structures 27
Conversational systems 10
Conversion 9
Coordination of processes 14
CORAL 66 28
Correctness proofs 7,11,17,20,27,28,30
Cost 1,2,3,4,5,6,9,10,12
estimation 8,12,21
of input/output 22
of reliability 20,28
of training 16
Cost/benefit analysis 9,12,21
CP-67 18,26
CPU-peripheral overlap 18
CPU utilization 18,26,28
Critical regions 28
Cross assemblers 13
Cross compilers 13
Cryogenics 5
CS-4 28
Culler-Fried 10
Cut-over 8
CYCLADES network 24
Cycle times 18

Data administration 15,21,25
Data base design 15,21,24,25
Data base management 1,2,8,15,21,25,28
Data base management systems 25

design of 15,27
generalized v specialized 15
objectives 15
Data bases in real-time systems 28
Data channels 13,22,23,24
Data collection 22,25,31
DATACOM/DC monitor 28
Data communications 4,6,24,28
Data compression 15
Data description languages 15,25
Data dictionary 12,21,25
Data directory 25
Data duplication 15,21,25
Data/information distinction 21,25
Data independence 25,27
Data manipulation languages 15,25
Data preparation costs 22,25
Data preparation personnel 16
Data structure 2,6,8,9,15,21,25,27
DBTG proposals 15,21,25
Deadly embrace/deadlock 2,14,15,25,28,31
Debugging 1,3,7,8,11,19,20,23,25,27,28
Dedicated processors 17,25,31
Descriptors 1,2,7,19,26,28
Diagnostics 1,6,8,9,17
Dialogue, man-machine 4,10,12
Direct access devices
modelling 18
monitoring 18
Directed graphs 20,29,31
Direct memory access 13
Discrete event models 18
Disk transfer rates 18,28
Dispatching 18
Displays 4,8,10
colour 10
selection of 4
technologies 5,10,22
Distributed data bases 31
Distributed systems 1,2,3,4,8,13,14,15,17,20,21,22,23,25,28,31
control of 2,31
Distributed processing 5,6,8,17,21,24,28,31
Distribution of intelligence 4,17,28,31
Documentation 1,3,8,9,11,12,20,27
Domain tip propagation (DOT) 28
Drum storage 26
Dumping 20
Dynamic redundancy 20,28

Easy English 10
Economics 12

Editing
    of program 10
    of text 10
Education 16
Electroluminescent displays 10
Electron Beam Access Memory 28
Electronic disks 28
Electro-optic technology 5
Emulation 1,2,3,9,18,23,28
    of environment 2
Enhancement of operating systems 14,18,23
ENVIRON/1 monitor 28
Enquiry languages 15,21
Equipment selection 18
Error codes 20
Error containment 20,28
Error detection 17,20,25,28
ESS 20
Estimating 2,3,8,11,12
Expression evaluation 26

Facilities management 8,16
Factory, software 11,13
Fault-intolerant systems 20,28
Fault location 17,20,23
Fault-tolerant systems 17,20,28,29
FCPU 17,23
Feasibility studies 8
File management 1,2,8,9,14,15,25,28
File recovery 28
File residency 18
Financial control 12
Financing methods 12
Finite state machines 13,20,28
Firmware 10,17,23
FORTRAN 7,10,13,23,27,30
Fragmentation 26,28
Front-ending 4,9,13,14,17,28,31
Functional memories 17

Gantt charts 18
Garbage collection 26
General systems theory 21
GOTO statements 7,19,20,27,30
Graceful degradation 20,28
Graphics 10,15,22
Grosch's Law 2,11,18,31

Hamming codes 20

Hard copy 4,5,10,22
Hardware modules 13,23
Hardware monitors 18,22,28,30
    comparison with software monitors 18
Head contention 18
Heterogeneity 31
Hierarchical data structures 15,25
Hierarchical models 18
Hierarchical systems design 2,7,8,11,15,17,20,23,27
    of storage 2
High level languages 7,11,16,17,19,20,30
    and real-time software 28
    and software implementation 1,2,3,7,8,14,16
    and system design 2,7,23,28
    classification 7
    design 7,28
    extensible 7
    general purpose 7,9
    interactive 10
    special purpose 7,9
    specific (see language name)
    standardization 7,9,28
HIPO 27
HIVE 17,28
Holography 5,10
Homogeneity 31
Host language systems 15,25
Host-to-host protocol 6,24
HP 3000 23
Hybrid redundancy 20
Hybrid/simplex redundancy 20

Iconic models 18
IDMS 25,28
IDS 28
ILLIAC IV 2,17,20,23,31
Improved Programming Technology
    (see *IPT*)
IMS 25,28
Incompatibility **9**
    (see also *Compatibility*)
Industry
    growth of 16
    structure of 1,8,11,16,17
Influence, user/supplier 9
Informatics 8,11
Information specialist 21
Information system plan 21
Information utilities 2,**6**,**24**
Initialization 23
Input/output 1,3,11,13,**22**,23,26
    character recognition 4,5,8,9,22

COM 5,8,22
displays 4,5,8
electro-optic 5
hard copy 4,5
voice 10,22
technologies 5
Instruction mixes 18,30
Instruction sets 23
Instruction times 18
Instruction traces 18,30
Instrumentation of systems 18,28,30
Integration 21,25,28
Integrity 28
of data base systems 15,25
Intelligent terminals 4,31
Interative computing 10,12,18
Interactive systems 10
INTERCOMM monitor 28
Interconnection 13,31
Interfaces 1,9,13
man-machine 1,4,10,14,22
standardization 22,31
Intermediate languages 23
Interpreters 17,23
Inter-process communication 24,28,31
Interrupt handling 13,20,22,24,28,31
Inverted files 25
Investment 1,9,12,19
IPT 27,30
ISDOS 19

Job accounting 18
(see also *Chargeback*)
Job control language 10,14
Job description 16
Job mix 18
JOVIAL 28

Kernels 18
Key-to-tape/disk 22
Kiviat graphs 18

Languages 1,2,3,7,8,9,11,13,19,20,27,30
coding v programming 27
for structured programming 27
high level (see *High level languages*)
interactive 10
job control 10,14

macro 1,9
microprogramming 23
netword command 6
operating system 1,7,8,14
real time 3,28
standards 1,7,9
Large core storage 18
Latency 26
Legal protection of software 8,11
Library subroutines 18
Light emitting diode displays 5,10
Line loadings 18
LISP 7,23
List processing 26
Load control 26,31
Loading 13,25
Locality 26
Logic technology 5,17
Look-aside registers 26
Loose coupling 29,31
LP 70 14
LSI 5,13,17,28,31

Machine independence 1,9,19,28
(see also *Portability*)
MAC project 10
Macro languages 1,9
Macromodules 31
Magnetic bubble 28
Magnetic technologies 5
Maintenance
of programs 1,8,11,19,20,25
of systems 1,3,5,6,12,20,23,24,31
Man-machine interaction 4,10,12,18,22
Management 8
attributes of 16,21
categories 21
corporate 8,21
information requirements 21
of MIS 21
of software projects 1,2,3,8,11,12,16,19,27
of software writers 1,2,3,8
promotion into 16
remote 16
training 16,21
Management information systems 8,10,15,21
Manchester University Machine (see *MU5*)
Manpower 16
Manpower needs 16
Manpower planning 8,16
Market considerations 2,5,9,12,17
of data communications 4,6

MARY 28
Mathematics and computing 16
Measurement
- by monitor (see *Monitors*)
- by accounting routines 18
- of performance 1,2,3,4,6,8,10,11,12,14,15,17,18,22,23,24,26, 28,30,31
- of personnel 16
- of reliability 20,28
- overhead 18
- program self-measurement 18,30

MECRA 20
Memory partitioning 26
Message switching 6,24,31
MICR 8,9
Microdiagnostics 23
Microprocessors 23,31
Microprogramming 1,2,7,10,13,17,19,22,23,28,31
- and emulation 1,2,9,23

Middleware 28
Minicomputers 1,4,8,10,13,17,21,22,28,31
Modelling 8,10,12,18,24,31
- for software implementation 2,3,7

Models 18,21,28
- analytical 18
- of virtual storage systems 26
- simulation 18,24
- taxonomy 18
- workload 18

Modems 4,6
Modularity 1,7,8,11,13,14,51,20,23,27,28,30,31
Modularization 27,30
Monitor concept 28
Monitors
- hardware (see *Hardware monitors*)
- hybrid 18
- software (see *Software monitors*)
- taxonomy 18

Monoprogramming 22
Motivation 16
MU5 2,7,17,18,26
MULTICS 10,19,24,26
Multiplexing 4,6,24
Multiprocessor systems 1,2,3,13,14,17,20,23,28,29,31
Multiprogramming level 26
Multi-threading 28
Mutual exclusion 28

Natural language 10
Nested virtual machines 27,28
Network data structures 15,25
Networks 1,2,4,6,9,10,17,24,28,31

Network software 24
Non-procedural languages 19,25
Number crunching 2

OAO PPDS 20
Obsolescence 12
OCR 4,5,8,9,22
On-line data bases 28
On-line systems 10,21,25
Operand usage 18
Operating 1,2
Operating systems 1,5,14,22,25,28,29,30,31
  design 1,14,28
  efficiency 1,2,18
  for distributed systems 31
  implementation 1,7,8,14,28
  machine-independent 1
  management software 1
  microprogrammed support 23
  module residency 18,26
  overhead 18,22
  real time 1,3,14,28
  reliability 20,28
  scheduling 1,14,18
  tuning 18,26
  user interface 1,10,14
Operator performance 18
Operations management 8,26
Optics 5
Optimizing compilers 23
Order code 1,2,13,17,18,23
Overhead
  of data base systems 25
  of monitoring 18
  of operating system 18
  paging 18,26
  unproductive work 18
Overlaying 18,26

Packages 1,2,8,9,16,19
Packet switching 6,24
Page replacement algorithms 26
Pagination 26
Paging 1,2,17,18,26,28
PAL 7
Parallel processing 1,14,17,28,29,31
Parallel processors 1,2,17,23,29,31
Parameter passing 20,30
Parity checking 20
Part-compilation 20

Partitioning 20,**31**
PASCAL 7,28
Patents for software 8
PEPE system **29**,31
Performance
    and reliability 20
    definitions of 18,24,28
    measurement (see *Measurement of performance*)
    of data base systems 25
    of real-time software 28
    of structured programs 27
    of virtual storage systems 26
Peripherals (see *Input/output*)
Peripheral transfers 3,22
Personnel 1,2,3,16
    organization of 1,2,8,11,12,16
Petri nets **29**,**31**
Pipeline processors 2,17,18,23,29,31
PL/1 7,10,19,23,28,30
PL/1W 8
PL/360 20
Planning 12,21
Plasma displays 5,10,22
Plessey S-250 17,20,24
Plug-to-plug compatibility 9,22
Pluribus **29**,31
Pointer variables 20,25
Point-of-transaction devices 22
POP-2 7,10
Portability 2,7,**9**,11,15,19,23,28
POS 22,31
PRIME 20
Priority scheduling 18,26,28
Privacy 2,6,15,25
Problem definition 2,8
Problem statement languages 19
Procedure calls 7,20,27,30
Process control 3,13,20,28
Process dispatching 26,28
Process management 14,15,20
Process synchronization 28
Processors 1,**2**,13,17
    360/67 26
    360/195 2
    370/125 23
    7600 2
    array 5,17,29,31
    associative 29,31
    Atlas 1,2,7,18,26
    B6500 2
    B6700 28
    Basic Machine 2,7
    CDC STAR 2,29,31
    dedicated 17,31

ESS 20
HP 3000 23
ILLIAC IV 2,23,29,31
JPL STAR 20
M44/44X 26
MECRA 20
MLP-900 9,23
MU5 2,7,17,18
parallel 1,2,17,23,**29**,31
pipeline 2,17,23,29,31
Plessey S-250 17,20,24
real time 3
symbol 5
System/360 2,17,18,23
System/370 17,23
Procurement 12,18
Product codes 20
Production of microcode 23
Production of software 11,14,27
Professional bodies 8,9
Professionalism 11,16
Program design 7,8,20,26,**27**,**30**
(see also *Software design*)
Program development, on-line 4,10
Program maintenance (see *Maintenance of programs*)
Program measurement 18,**30**
Program structure **27**,30
Program tuning 18,26,**30**
Programmable logic arrays 23,31
Programmer productivity 1,2,3,4,8,11,16,19,25,27
Programming 7,8,11,16,28,30
and machine architecture 7,17,30
aptitude for 16
commercial **19**
simplification 16
standards 19
Programming aids 8,11,16,19,27
Project control (see *Management*)
Project SUE 22,24
PROM 31
Proofs, program correctness 7,11,17,20,27,28
Protection and access control 14,15,17,20,24,25,26,28
Protection rings 26
Protocol, host-to-host 6,24

Quadding 20
Query systems 25
Queueing theory 18,22,28
QUIKTRAN 10

RAM 31
Range checks 20
Read-only memory 13,17,23
Real-time languages 28
Real-time software 28
Real-time systems 2,3,17,28
 applications 2,3,21,28
 characteristics 2
 control programs 28
 operating systems 1,3,14,28
 required processing power 2,3
Reconfiguration 20,28,29,31
Recovery
 data base 25,28
 hardware 20
 software 20,28
Recruitment 16,19
 agencies 16
Redundancy 17,20,24,28
Re-entrant code 26
Registers 13
Relational data model 25
Relay-runner scheme 20
Reliability 1,2,3,4,5,6,10,15,17,18,20,24,27,28,29,31
 and correctness 27
 of data base systems 25
 of software 1,2,6,7,11,17,27,28,30
Relocation 26
Remote maintenance 23
Representation, theory of 9
Reprogramming, economics of 9
Residency of operating system modules 18
Residue codes 20
Resolution
 measurement interval 18
 simulation 18
Resource allocation 20,28,31
Resource utilization 18,26,28
Response time 3,6,10,14,15,18,21,24,26,28,31
Restart 28
Retraining 9
Retry 20
Roll-back 20,28
Routeing 6,24
RPG 8,19
RPS 22,28
RTL 3
RTL/2 28

Saturn V LVDC 20
Scheduling, operating system 1,14,18,28
Schema 15,25

Scrapbook system 27
Security 2,3,4,10,11,12,14,15,19,20,24,25,28
Segmentation 1,2,14,17,20,26
Segmentation with paging 26
Selection of personnel 16
Self-contained systems 15,25
Semaphores 13,20,24,28
Semiconductor technology 5,17,22,23
Sequencing discipline 20,27
SERF 20
Services industry 8
SHADOW II monitor 28
Sharing code and data 26
SIFT 20
Signalling 6
Simplicity 1,20,25,27,28
SIMSCRIPT 7
SIMULA 7,19,28
Simulation 3,9,11,13,14,15,18,20,21,24,28,30
  languages 7,18
  packages 18
SNA 28
SNOBOL 20,23
Soak-up program 18
Software components 11,13
Software contractors 8,16
Software, legal protection 8,11
Software design 1,3,7,8,11,13,20,27,30
Software engineering 1,2,3,11,13,16,27
Software factory 11,13
Software-first concepts 28
Software houses 8
Software implementation 1,3,11,13,14,27,30
  and languages 1,2,3,7,8,13,16,28
  general management 2,3,8,11,16
  problems of scale 1,2,8,11,16
  resource estimation 2,3,8,11,12,13
  technique 2,8,11
Software monitors 18,30
  comparison with hardware monitors 18
Software, networks 24
Software packages 1,2,8,9,16
Software, real-time 28
Software reliability (see *Reliability*)
Software testing 1,3,7,8,11,20,27,28,30
Sorting 26
Source data collection 22
Sparse addressing 26
Specification, of system 3,8,11,19,27
  standards 9
Speech recognition (see *Voice interaction*)
Spooling 18,22
Stacks 13,16,17,23,28
Standards 1,6,7,8,9,10,11,14,15,17,28,31

Standby sparing 20,28
STAR (CDC) 2,17,29,31
STAR (JPL) 20
STARAN **29**,31
Static redundancy 20,28
Step-wise refinement 27,28
Storage 1,2,13,17,**26**,28
  associative 1,15,17,25,26
  hierarchies 2,17,26
  management 1,2,3,13,14,15,17,18
  read-only 13,17,**23**,26,28
  structure 2,15,25
  technologies 2,5,17,26,28
  utilization 26,28,30
  virtual 2,14,15,17,**26**,28
String quotes 7
Structure, of data 2,6,8,9,15,21,25,27
Structured programming 11,17,19,20,23,**27**,28,30
Subroutine mechanism 7
Subschema 15,25
Supervisor state 18,20
Swapping 26
SWIFT monitor 28
Switching, in networks 3,6,24,28
Symbolic models 18
Syntax checking 20
Synthetic programs 18
System 2000 data base package 25,28
System configuration 1,2,13,17,18,31
System design 3,4,8,9,**17**,**23**,**31**
  (see also *Architecture and Processors*)
  human factors 2,4,8,21
  integrated 9,21
  languages for 7,14,19
  management for 2,11
  technological implications 5,17
System growth 20
System maintenance 1,3,5,6,12,20,23
System measurement (see *Measurement of performance*)
System operation 8,12
System profile 18
Systems analysis 1,8,9,16
Systems assurance 1
System specification 3,8,11,12,13,28
System tuning 18,26,28

Table-driven processing 27
Tagging 26
TASK/MASTER monitor 28
TDS 28
TEBOL 28
Technological change 5,12

constraints	1,5,9
Technology, hardware	4,5,13,17,23
TELCOMP	10
Telephone switching systems	20,24
Teleprocessing monitors	25,28
Terminals	1,4,6,10,22,28,31
ergonomics of	10
graphics	10,22,31
simplification of	10
technology	5
teletypewriters	10
VDUs (see *Displays*)	
Test beds	18
Test data generation	20,27
Testing of software	1,3,7,8,11,15,20,27,28,30
Text processing	10
Theory of operating systems	14,28
THIRST monitor	28
Thrashing	26
Throughput	18,24,26,28
Tight coupling	29,31
Top-down design	20,27,28,30
TOTAL data base package	25,28
Total systems	21
TPL2	28
Training	3,8,9,11,12,16,19
Transferability (see *Portability*)	
Transaction processing	28
Translation	2,9
Transmission	4,6,24
signalling	6
switching	6
Triple modular redundancy	20
Tuning	
data base	25
program	18,26,30
system	18
virtual storage	26
workload	18
Turnaround time	18,26
Turnover of staff	16
Type checking	20
Typesetting by computer	8
Unbundling	8,9,12
UNIX system	27
User interface	1,4,10,14,15,25
User microprogramming	23
Utilities	2,6,24
Utilization	18,26
CPU	18,26
I/O equipment	18,26

Validation
- of benchmarks 18
- of simulation models 18
- of software 20,27,28,30

Value-added network 24
Variable architecture 1,2,5,9,17,23
VDUs (see *Displays*)
Verification (see *Correctness proofs*)
Vested interests 9
Virtual machines 22,26,28
Virtual store management 2,14,17,26,28
Visible record computers 13,19
VM/370 22,23,26,28
Voice interaction 10,22
VTAM 28

WESTI monitor 28
Word length 13
Work
- definitions of 18
- (see also *Overhead*)

Work-files 26
Working set 26
Workload 18
- definition of 18
- modelling 18
- scheduling 18,26
- smoothing 18
- tuning 18

CONTRIBUTOR INDEX

There are three types of contribution:

1 *Extracts from the presentations and discussion sessions at the Infotech State of the Art Lecture Program Performance Optimization and from the invited papers. Page references for these are shown thus:* 4.

2 *Complete invited papers. Page references for these are shown thus:* **437.**

3 *Extracts from other sources. Page references for these are shown thus: 44. The source for each such extract is given in the Bibliography and References section.*

Contributor	*Page numbers of contributions*
BACHTIN O Ellemtel Utv AB	137
BROADBENT J K ICL	*75,77*
BROWN G G Brown's Operating Systems Services	*15,16*,120,122,123,**147**
BROWN P J University of Kent	76,77,80,81,82,83,**153**
BURNS D Software Sciences	49
BURSTALL R M University of Edinburgh	62,63,64,65,**161**
CAPON P C University of Manchester	10,121,129,130,131,**171**
CHEATHAM T E Jr University of Harvard	*115*
DARLINGTON J University of Edinburgh	62,63,64,65,**161**
FANEUF R A Massachusetts Computer Associates Inc	*92*
GUERTIN R L Stanford University	*144*
HANSEN Prof G J University of Florida	105,106,107,110,111,**185**

HOARE Prof C A R — *9,39,49*
Queen's University Belfast

JONES A — 209
Unilever Computer Services

KNUTH Prof D E — *38,50,51*,61
Stanford University

KOLENCE K — *125*
Institute for Software Engineering

LANKEY D — 123,126,217
Logica

LASKI J G — 36,40,41,54,99,100,101,103,110,235
University of Rennes

LOVEMAN D B — *92*
Massachusetts Computer Associates Inc

MANVILLE W D — 132,133,134,135,136,137,253
GEC Computers

McDOWELL J — 123
ICL

McMANUS P — 111
IBM (UK) Laboratories

MOREL E — 113
CII

MUNRO B — 15,16,17,124.141
SDI

NEWSTED Prof P R — 23,47,267
University of Wisconsin-Milwaukee

OUTRED C F J — *11,12*
Burroughs Machines Ltd

PALME J — 26,33,34,279
Swedish National Defence Research Institute

PATEL M — 20,121,291
ICL

RAMAGE I — 142,313
British Rail

ROSIN Prof R F — *78*
Iowa State University

SAMET Prof P A — 122,123
University College London

SCHNECK P B — 31,44,54,85,86,88,89,90,91,97,101,102,113,114,120,327,345
Goddard Institute of Space Studies

SPIRN Prof J R — 139,357
Pennsylvania State University

WHITE A — 136
Overseas Containers Ltd

WIRTH Prof N — *48*
Federal Institute of Technology Zurich

WULF Prof W A — *11*,*12*,105,106,107,110,111,185
Carnegie-Mellon University

ZELKOWITZ Prof M V — 13,52,55,57,58,59,369
The University of Maryland

SUBJECT INDEX

Abstraction 63
Adaptive optimization 105,160,187-208
Architecture-dependent optimization 87
Architecture-independent optimization 92
Array subscripts 93,176
ASC 91
Assembly language 31,33,285

BASIC 155
Binary search 141

Case studies 222-234
CDC STAR 91,129
Change vector 56
Clarity of programs 13,47,61,114
Code generation 72
Code motion 94,242,335
Coding techniques 12
  for virtual storage 140
Commercial programming 111
Common subexpression elimination 41,95,245,335
Compilation 69,72
  and interpretation 75,155
  in VS systems 308
  techniques 75
Compiler-programmer dialogue 38,102
Compiler structure 72
Complexity 49
Constant propagation 93,335
Constraints in program optimization 19,224
Correctness 65
Cost
  of hardware 10
  of optimizing compilers 11
  of programming 26,281

Dead code elimination 93,335
Diagnostics 76,82
Dynamic compiling 81,156
Dynamic optimization 105,160,187-208

Economics of optimization 19,126,347
Efficiency 7,33
Egoless programming 28
Error checking 157

Feedback 38,100
Flow analysis 36,54,241
Folding 63,94
FORTRAN 31
  DO-loops 37
  efficiency 52
  FREQUENCY statement 92,101
  Insecurity 34
  I/O 316
  optimizing compilers 39,85,99,105,187-208
FREQUENCY statement 92,101,336
Future developments in optimization 347-355

GOTO statement 47

Hand-optimization 13
Hardware costs 10
Hardware performance 9,49
High-level languages 235
History of optimization 85

ICL 2900 122
ILLIAC IV 91,129
Inefficiency of procedure calls 51
Input/output 147
Insecurity in FORTRAN 34
Instantiation 63
Instruction set enhancement 132,255-265
Interference of monitors 123
Interpretation 69
  and compilation 75
  benefits 77
Interval analysis 92

Language-dependency of optimization 110
Language design 33
Language processing 70
Lexical analysis 70
Locality 359
Loop constructs 242
Loop-invariant code 94

Machine code 238
Machine-dependent optimization 86
Machine efficiency 48
Microprogramming 79,132,255-265
Mixed code 160
Monitors 120
MU5 121,130,171
Multiple-accumulator machines 88

On-line systems 227
Optimizing compilers 20,85,187-208, 287,329-344

Paging 139
Parallel instructions 89
Parse tree 55
Peephole optimization 87
Pipeline 180
Pointers 250
Pragmats 43,101,243
Precompilers 286
Procedure calls 51,131,177
Program correctness 65
Program efficiency 7,33
Program monitoring 120
Program structure 248
Program transformation 61,163-169
  applications 64
  techniques 63
Program tuning 126
Programmer-compiler dialogue 38,102
Programming languages 27,31
  and efficient programs 33
  and optimizability 36
Programming methodology 12,27
Programming style 29
Psychology of programming 28,270

Recursion 163

Security in programming languages 26,34
Selective optimization 99
Semantic preprocessing 44,350
SETL 32
SIMPL 52,57
Sorting methods in VS 144
Source-expressible optimization 38
Stages of optimization 7
Strength reduction 94
String operations 183
Strongly connected region 191
Structured programming 27,47,115,272, 371-382
  and efficiency 51
  and optimizability 52
  control constructs 37
  flow analysis 54
  languages 52
Suboptimization 240-241
Subscript calculations 93
Syntax analysis 72
System degradation 20
System instrumentation 122
System tuning 320-326
System upgrade, avoidance of 15

Table look-up 141
Threaded code 160
Throw-away compiling 81,155
Trade-offs in optimization 7,20,25,281-289
Transformation 61,163
Translation techniques 69
Turnaround time 17

Unfolding 63
User microprogramming 136

Very high-level languages 32
Virtual storage 139,293-312,318,357

WATFIV 105
Workload tuning 15